Macpherson the Historian

To Seumas Bàn
May the odds be ever in your favour . . .

Macpherson the Historian

History Writing, Empire and Enlightenment in the Works of James Macpherson

Mairi MacPherson and Jim MacPherson

EDINBURGH
University Press

Edinburgh University Press is one of the leading university presses in the UK. We publish academic books and journals in our selected subject areas across the humanities and social sciences, combining cutting-edge scholarship with high editorial and production values to produce academic works of lasting importance. For more information visit our website: edinburghuniversitypress.com

© Mairi MacPherson and Jim MacPherson, 2023, 2024

Edinburgh University Press Ltd
13 Infirmary Street
Edinburgh EH1 1LT

First published in hardback by Edinburgh University Press 2023

Typeset in 10.5/13pt Sabon by
Manila Typesetting Company, and
printed and bound by CPI Group (UK) Ltd,
Croydon, CR0 4YY

A CIP record for this book is available from the British Library

ISBN 978 1 4744 1116 5 (hardback)
ISBN 978 1 3995 4111 4 (paperback)
ISBN 978 1 4744 1117 2 (webready PDF)
ISBN 978 1 4744 1118 9 (epub)

The right of Mairi MacPherson and Jim MacPherson to be identified as authors of this work has been asserted in accordance with the Copyright, Designs and Patents Act 1988 and the Copyright and Related Rights Regulations 2003 (SI No. 2498).

Contents

Acknowledgements vi

Introduction: James Macpherson, the Enlightenment and Eighteenth-century History Writing ... 1

1 Frameworks and Genealogies: Macpherson the Historian in Context ... 23

2 Poetry: James Macpherson's History Writing in *The Highlander* and Ossian ... 48

3 History: James Macpherson's Narrative Prose Histories ... 105

4 Politics and Empire: James Macpherson's Political Writings and the Crisis of Empire in the Late 1770s ... 171

Conclusion: James Macpherson – Enlightenment Historian and Imperial Gael ... 241

Bibliography 248
Index 283

Acknowledgements

This book has been a long time coming. It began life some fifteen years ago as the final chapter of a PhD thesis on James Macpherson, tacked on about three months before submission. In that odd way that academic work often develops, this 'afterthought' chapter became the focus of ongoing teaching and research, and the more we thought about James, the more we thought of him as, first and foremost, *an historian*. This argument developed over the years in a range of Highlands and Islands locations – from Kylesku to Durness, from Gedintailor to Kirkwall, on long drives to and from Newtonmore, and on many, many lovely dog walks across the region with Archie and Lulu.

Over the years, this book has benefited from the generosity of colleagues both near and far, in particular those of the Literature and History departments at the University of the Highlands and Islands and at Sabhal Mòr Ostaig, and that haphazard group of Ossian scholars brought together at various conferences, workshops and heritage festivals. Our particular thanks go to Domhnall Uilleam Stiùbhart and Ùisdean Cheape for their unfailing enthusiasm for rethinking James's work, and to Howard Gaskill and Paul deGategno, who provided such generous feedback and conversation over the years. The students on various undergraduate and postgraduate modules tackled Enlightenment history writing with thoughtful curiosity and, as is so often the case when research and teaching go hand in hand, made us think long and hard about our arguments and evidence, as did our research students, whose conversations about all things Ossian, eighteenth-century Badenoch, and the broader implications of Gaelic culture and British imperialism have been much valued. Particular thanks go to Tom Jones, who supervised the thesis that this book originated on, and whose understanding of eighteenth-century aesthetics and philosophical theory has shaped this whole project so much more than he knows.

But this book is one of community, too: of James's native Badenoch, where we were fortunate to be able to co-host the 2015 Kingussie Heritage Festival on 'Macpherson's Ossianic Legacy', which brought together scholars and a hugely enthusiastic public, and where subsequent heritage events have kept the memory of that fresh. Here, our thanks go to Mairi Brown, Ian Moffett and David Taylor for their willingness to embrace James and Ossian, and for their continued cheerful advocacy of the 'local boy done good', to use David's tongue-in-cheek phrase. Our thanks also go to Highlife Highland and, in particular, to the staff at Inverness Library, who loaned us two large boxes of first edition texts to share with the public at various events – including James's first published text *The Highlander*, of which there are only seven copies left. But it is also a book of another community, that of the Clan Macpherson and its Association and Museum. We were fortunate to have Sir William 'Cluny' Macpherson, the Chief at the time, and various members of the clan join us for that first heritage festival in 2015, and it is due to their enthusiasm, interest and trust that we have been able to place James at the centre of the new permanent exhibition at the Clan Macpherson Museum in Newtonmore, which we designed, wrote and built during 2021. Redesigning the Museum helped us to think about James's position as both Enlightenment historian and imperial Gael, and we are grateful to John MacKenzie and Stephen Foster for their inspiring insights into Macpherson entanglement in empire. Over the years the annual clan gathering in August has become an important part of our life, and the ongoing interest of clan members – in person, by video chat, in email conversations – has supported the completion of this book in no small way. To them we are very grateful, in particular to the trustees and members of the Museum Advisory Committee, to the officers at the Clan Macpherson Association, and to the myriad of clan members who have listened to our talks, come to our events and participated in our museum tours. The biggest thanks go to Ewen MacPherson, fellow historian and exhibition writer, who has kept us company these many years, and we also thank the Cluny family; Bruce, Helen, Sandy and Catherine; Angus and Valerie; John Barton and Mary Mackenzie. Our particular gratitude goes to Allan Macpherson-Fletcher, whose joyful exuberance, both in his own character and his championing of James, has made our times in Badenoch so enjoyable, and whose spirited hosting of the 2015 heritage festival group at James's house Balavil is a much-cherished memory.

We also thank the curators of the Clan Macpherson Museum that have accompanied our writing of this book, Ruis Alcorn and Aila Schaefer – you've been excellent company.

Finally, thanks are due to our friends and family, many of whom have lived with James for as long as we have. In particular, we'd like to thank Ian Blyth and Anna Frenkel, our fellow Oak Cottage humans (and all the Oak Cottage animals, especially Penny, Cedric, Archie, Lulu and Martha); Lesley Mickel, Tracy Kennedy, Ebby Ritchie, Lucy Dean, Iain 'James Macpherson' Robertson and David Worthington, our fellow travellers at UHI; Emma Major, Rhona Ramsay, Matthew Sangster, Daniel Cook, Justin Tonra, Rebecca Barr, David Fallon, Bill Zachs, Eileen Budd, Alice Sage, Chris and Jake Andrews, Christie Margrave, Lena Oetzel, Ros Powell, Rose Pimentel, Margaux Whiskin, Jeremy Davies and David Higgins, academic friends, collaborators and sources of reassurance and encouragement over the years.

This book was derailed by illness – chronic, as it turns out – and for a long time it was very unlikely that it would ever get finished. It became a joint effort, first out of necessity and then out of scholarly passion, and neither of us could have written this book without the other's ideas and thoughts. In the end, we both wrote about half of it, intermingled throughout, and we take joint responsibility for any mistakes that may have crept in.

Our greatest thanks, though, go to James himself. He brought us together and continues to make us think, and, with his 'hereditary good looks of the Macpherson's of Nuide' (Sinton's *Poetry of Badenoch*), brings us joy every day.

Introduction: James Macpherson, the Enlightenment and Eighteenth-century History Writing

Chuir e òr anns an talamh He put gold in the ground
Nach caraich fear feumach Which no needy man can move
'S nach urrainn fear rapach And which no greedy man is able
A sgapadh o chéile; To scatter asunder;

Tha e sgrìobht' aig MacMhuirich Macpherson's written it down
G'a chumail ri chéile – To keep it all together –
Chun na sìolaig a b' isle To the humblest of seedlings
Bha e dìleas d'a Eurla. He was loyal to his Earl.

Donnchadh MacAoidh, 'Cumha Sheumais Bhàin'
Duncan MacKay, 'James Macpherson's Lament' (1796)[1]

James Macpherson, renowned throughout the world for his collecting, translating and editing of the tales of Ossian, died in his Robert Adam-designed mansion in the heart of the central Highlands on a stormy February night in 1796.[2] Macpherson was mourned by many locals, including the poet and kirk elder in the local parish of Kingussie, Duncan MacKay. Composing the above 'Lament' to *Seumas Bàn* ('Fair James', on account of his good looks), MacKay commented on Macpherson's success, wealth, political career and 'fondness for women'.[3] Intriguingly, MacKay's only reference to his global literary fame occurs in the phrase '*Tha e sgrìobht' aig MacMhuirich / G'a chumail ri chéile* (Macpherson's written it down / To keep it all together)'. MacKay deliberately placed Macpherson's writing, and his quasi-bardic role preserving the region's memory through its stories, in the context of his concern for the welfare of his fellow Highlanders. Although glossing over some of Macpherson's more controversial methods of estate management, MacKay praised Macpherson's promotion of the region, his care for his tenants ('the humblest of seedlings') and his lengthy relationship with the Earl of Bute ('his Earl'), former Prime Minister and patron of many of Macpherson's publications during the 1760s and 1770s.[4] For MacKay, Macpherson's writing was inextricably linked with his cultural and commercial promotion of the *Gàidhealtachd*. Macpherson was highly skilled at supporting both his own interests and those of his fellow Gaels and was renowned for placing Highlanders in positions of power and influence across the British Empire, from India and the West Indies, to London.[5] It is to this context which MacKay's 'Lament' alludes and that, in turn, helps us to understand Macpherson as a writer – an historian – who wrote about the past in order to make sense of his own and the *Gàidhealtachd*'s place in the commercial modernity of the eighteenth-century British imperial state.[6]

This book argues that Macpherson was, first and foremost, an historian – that his published works, whether poetical, historical or political, were written as a form of history writing. From the poetry of *The Highlander* (1758) and the Ossianic Collections (1760–3) to his final political pamphlets in support of the British Empire against the rebellious American colonists, Macpherson wrote as an historian and in a self-consciously historiographical way.[7] In all of these publications, Macpherson was an Enlightenment historian, who used eighteenth-century ideas about historical narrative, erudition and philosophy to demonstrate that the Highlands and its people could make valuable contributions to the British imperial project. During the late 1750s, *The Highlander* and the Ossianic Collections arose in the context of the militia crisis during the Seven Years War, in which Macpherson's poetry was mobilised by the Scottish intelligentsia to make the case for a greater Scots' (and, therefore, Highland) presence in the war effort against the French.[8] Macpherson's later history writing, from *The History of Great Britain* and *Original Papers* (1775) to *The Rights of Great Britain Asserted Against the Claims of America* (1775/6) and *The History and Management of the East-India Company, from its Origin in 1600 to the Present Times* (1779), consistently defended the British imperial state, in both America and India, during the crisis of empire of the late 1770s.[9] In his early works, Macpherson wrote about the ancient Celtic past in order to demonstrate the culture and value of Highlanders in the present and how the region was militarily and commercially valuable to Britain in the aftermath of Culloden. Then, in his later history writing, Macpherson refined the techniques of Enlightenment history writing, which he used to rationalise both his and fellow Highlanders' increasing involvement in empire. Drawing upon and engaging with the ideas of Adam Smith,

David Hume, Hugh Blair, William Robertson and Edward Gibbon (all of whom Macpherson either worked with or knew well), Macpherson's history writing grappled with the major historiographical debates of the 1760s and 1770s. In particular, Macpherson was concerned with issues of truth, authenticity and sources, largely as a result of the controversy surrounding the publication of the Ossianic Collections.[10] However, writing about these concepts soon embroiled Macpherson in the contested world of eighteenth-century history writing. Here, Enlightenment historians, such as Hume and Robertson, were developing historiographical techniques that attempted to reconcile classical desires for a coherent historical narrative with emerging notions of 'philosophy' and 'erudition'.[11] How best to write a clear narrative, while providing philosophical explanations for past events that were rooted in the evidence of primary sources, became *the* historiographical concern of the age, and Macpherson's history writing demonstrates the influences of these debates. In applying these techniques to his history writing, Macpherson was also following the work of other Enlightenment historians who saw their writing about the past as important to understanding and justifying the project of the British Empire. From Adam Smith to Robertson and Gibbon, history writing was used both as a way to make sense of current crises of empire (especially during the 1770s) and to justify the actions of the British imperial state. As Priya Satia argues, 'the historical discipline helped make empire' during the second half of the eighteenth century, and Macpherson's history writing was integral to this imperial and colonial process.[12] Macpherson was part of this group of Enlightenment historians, and he wrote about the past in the service of the British imperial state.

As the first book-length study of Macpherson as an historian, we also consider how he writes about the past across different modes of writing. Macpherson wrote as an historian in three modes: in poetry, in historical prose, and in political propaganda. *Macpherson the Historian* is structured around these types of writing. While the ideological and identity functions of these texts are central to our argument, this book is concerned primarily with *how* Macpherson wrote about the past. Much critical ink has been spilt in attempting to ascertain Macpherson's political allegiance, ranging from his supposed latent Jacobitism to his support for a 'Celtic Whig' interpretation of British constitutional history.[13] This book eschews much of this debate by focusing on how Macpherson wrote about the past and, ultimately, placing this in the context of Macpherson's position as a Gael on the make and a Highland man of empire. From his first government appointment as secretary to

George Johnstone, Governor of the freshly-minted British colony of West Florida, in 1763, through to his work as agent to the Nawab of Arcot in the late 1770s with his great friend and collaborator (the later Governor-General of India), Sir John Macpherson, James was forever working and thinking about empire – and the past.[14] This imperial focus is reflected in his writing, both in terms of subject matter and Macpherson's historiographical techniques. Macpherson's history writing was a product of and response to both the Enlightenment and the crisis of the British imperial state. Macpherson makes a vital contribution to emerging discourses of British imperial power that were based in narratives of the past and used stadial theories (largely derived from his friend and fellow Highlander, Adam Ferguson) to legitimise the British imperial state in America and, to a lesser extent, in India. These ideas, however, were the product of Macpherson's self-consciously historiographical thinking – he didn't just write about the past, he also commented at length on *how* he wrote history. Macpherson was an Enlightenment historian who not only put history writing to work in the service of empire (like many of his more illustrious colleagues) but also sought to demonstrate, through history, that his homeland – the *Gàidhealtachd* – was intellectually, culturally, militarily and commercially a key part of the British imperial state.

Our focus in this book, therefore, is primarily on the form of Macpherson's writing rather than the content. It is a study of paratexts and practice, in which we measure how Macpherson writes as a self-conscious historian. We examine both the prefaces, dissertations and other accompanying materials where Macpherson discusses his historiographical methodology and how he puts this into practice in his historical narratives. In the main text of *The History of Great Britain* (1775) or *The History and Management of the East-India Company* (1779), Macpherson doesn't just explain the past – he also reflects on his historiographical approach in doing so. We analyse how Macpherson uses historical sources in versifying the past (as in *The Highlander*), how he uses the evidence of primary sources to make an argument about the past, and how this is all framed historiographically. Key sources are the paratextual and prefatory material that accompanied Macpherson's work, from the dissertations to the Ossianic Collections, to the prefaces of *The History of Great Britain* (1775) and the advertisements of *The Rights of Great Britain* (1775/6) and *A Short History of the Opposition* (1779).[15] In these writings, Macpherson justifies his approach and explains his methodology, situating himself in Enlightenment debates about truth and causation (echoing the likes of Hume and Blair), and writing about how he found, used and cited (through footnotes) the evidence of primary and secondary sources in his account of the past (much like we find in the history writing of Robertson and Gibbon in the 1770s). In our analysis of Macpherson's historical narratives, we are not concerned with whether his account of, for example, the ancient Celtic past in *An Introduction to the History of Great Britain and Ireland* (1771) or the Williamite revolution of the late 1680s in *The History of Great Britain* (1775) is 'correct' or 'truthful'. Instead, the book examines how and why Macpherson constructs these historical narratives and how Macpherson's method of history writing – his historiography – demonstrates a particular concern with the position of the Highlands in empire and the development of the British imperial state. In this approach, we have been inspired by Hayden White and his study of how nineteenth-century history writing grew out of late Enlightenment historiography. White explained his analysis of Michelet, Ranke, Hegel and others as an attempt to examine how these historians wrote about the past:

> I will not try to decide whether a given historian's work is a better, or more correct, account of a specific set of events or segment of the historical process than some other historian's account of them; rather, I will seek to identify the structural components of those accounts.[16]

For White, the form of an historical narrative was more important than the content, hence his focus on the tropes of 'Metaphor, Metonymy, Synecdoche, and Irony'.[17] While we do not follow his application of tropes in our analysis of Macpherson's history writing, we do proceed from White's basic premise of analysing the 'verbal structure' of history writing and its discursive effects.[18] As Carolyn Dean neatly summarised in her recent reappraisal of White's impact (or, rather, lack thereof) on the historical profession: 'White did not focus on whether such accounts get the facts right, but rather on how they tell stories; not on what historians say, but on how they say it; not on the intentions and biographies of historians, but on the deep linguistic structures of historiography.'[19] This book is about Macpherson's craft as an historian and how this develops over time. It is about how Macpherson used the techniques of Enlightenment history writing, learnt from and inspired by Hume, Blair and others, to make sense of his place in the world, as a Gaelic-speaking Highlander, immersed in the bardic world of the past but with an eye forever on the modernity of Enlightenment and empire.[20] In doing so, it demonstrates that Macpherson was, first and foremost, an historian. Thinking about his history writing in this way helps us to better understand Macpherson, moving beyond the impasse of Ossian, and places him in the context of a Scottish and British Enlightenment historiography that increasingly developed in the eighteenth century as a mode of imperial explanation and justification.

SCHOLARLY CONTEXTS: OSSIAN, THE ENLIGHTENMENT AND EIGHTEENTH-CENTURY HISTORY WRITING

> That a writer of the stamp of James Macpherson should have been destined to approach history at all was, I think, a remarkable freak of nature.[21]

Macpherson's lengthy literary and political career has long been dogged by his work as a young man in the 1760s, when he was only in his twenties. While his collecting, editing, translating and embellishing of the Ossianic tales brought Macpherson global fame, the controversy that arose became the lens through which almost everyone has since viewed his subsequent life and works. From the immediate hostile reaction of the likes of Samuel Johnson, to the critical response of scholars such as Arthur Parnell above and right up to the present day, any consideration of Macpherson is prefaced with caveats about Ossian and the 'authenticity' debate.[22] As Dafydd Moore has written in his own study of Macpherson, 'long before the death of the author it was received wisdom not to believe a word Macpherson said about anything, especially about his own literary efforts'.[23] This book moves beyond such Ossian-centricity and seeks to understand Macpherson's history writing in its own terms and in the context of eighteenth-century historiography. While it engages with existing scholarship on Macpherson and Ossian, it does so largely to highlight the absence of any sustained discussion of Macpherson's history writing. As such, this book also situates Macpherson's work in two other critical scholarly contexts: research that examines the development of Enlightenment historiography; and scholarship about the Highlands, the region's agency and its position within the British Empire.

Macpherson is best known for the group of poems referred to here as the 'Ossianic Collections'. Published in three instalments by Macpherson from 1760 to 1763, and in two collected editions in 1765 and 1773, the Ossianic Collections caused a stir and sparked a controversy that lasted well into the nineteenth century and haunts us to the present day.[24] The prose-poems, supposed translations of third-century Gaelic poetry, passed down largely orally in the Highlands of Scotland until Macpherson collected them in the 1750s and 1760s, are unusual not just in their genesis and form, but also in their blend of invention and imitation, of myth and tradition, of history and fiction.[25] The controversy surrounding their authenticity is well documented, both in the period and in contemporary criticism, to the detriment of research into not just the poems themselves (though this has somewhat been addressed in recent criticism), but also, more importantly, into Macpherson's non-Ossianic works.[26] This book seeks to redress this, by offering the first systematic study of Macpherson's writings that does not place the Ossianic Collections at the centre of its argument.

Instead, this book analyses Macpherson's principal writings through the lens of history. A handful of older scholars, such as his Victorian biographer T. Bailey Saunders, the above-mentioned Arthur Parnell, and D. B. Horn, did pay some attention to Macpherson's history writing.[27] However, it has only been in recent years that Macpherson's historical writings have begun to receive any kind of critical attention. Scholars have been increasingly willing to define Macpherson as an historian, labelling him 'a poet, historian, and controversialist' in the case of Dafydd Moore's recent description, or, as Colin Kidd argues, 'a self-consciously sceptical historian, deeply interested in the philosophy of history'. However, as Moore reminds us in his recent *International Companion to James Macpherson*, 'it is notable that the rest of Macpherson's career remains unconsidered in any serious way'.[28] This, then, is what this book is seeking to redress.

This book is the first in-depth study that explores Kidd's assessment of Macpherson's interest in historiography. In doing so, it builds upon the approaches taken by Paul deGategno, Robert W. Jones and Leith Davis in recent articles on *The Rights of Great Britain* (1775/6), *The History of Great Britain* (1775) and *A Short History of the Opposition* (1779), and *The History and Management of the East-India Company* (1779) respectively.[29] Developing his earlier brief overview of Macpherson's history writing, deGategno's article on *The Rights of Great Britain* analyses Macpherson's response to the rebellious American colonists.[30] It considers Macpherson as 'an historian' who builds an argument from the evidence of historical sources, yet there is little on exactly *how* Macpherson functions as a writer of history.[31] Likewise, Robert Jones examines Macpherson's *History of Great Britain* and *A Short History of the Opposition* as history writing, but with an emphasis on Macpherson's politics and his understanding of the concept of political 'opposition'. Jones rightly acknowledges the utility of reading Macpherson in the context of Enlightenment historiography. Outlining the recent reappraisals of the history writing of Hume, Robertson and Gibbon, Jones argues that Macpherson has been overlooked in these scholarly debates 'either because its author is still (erroneously) associated with "forged" histories or, more interestingly, because Macpherson is a rather awkward presence, neither fully committed to new developments in historiographic writing nor truly against them'.[32] Jones situates Macpherson in this literary context, but largely in commercial rather than intellectual terms.[33] He also calls out the focus of scholars on the 'accuracy of his writing' as the red herring it is, distracting us from Macpherson's texts and the contexts in which he wrote.[34] As we shall see below, Jones does briefly consider the way in which Macpherson wrote about the past but soon focuses instead on Macpherson's account of 'the twin problem of the royal prerogative and its opponents' during the second half of the seventeenth century.[35] This focus on the content rather than the form of Macpherson's history writing is followed by Leith Davis. *The History and Management of the East India Company* is analysed as evidence for Macpherson's status as an imperial Gael. However, Davis discusses Macpherson's representation of India rather than how he uses the techniques and methodologies of Enlightenment history writing to defend the British imperial state and his wealthy patron, the Nawab of Arcot.[36]

Macpherson's position in the Enlightenment intellectual community of Edinburgh, Glasgow and London has long been recognised by scholars. However, once again, this has largely been interpreted through the prism of Ossian. When the Ossian sensation broke in Edinburgh in late 1759, Macpherson was rapidly taken under the collective wing of the Scottish Enlightenment intelligentsia. As we shall see in Chapter 2, Adam Ferguson and Hugh Blair were Macpherson's way into this world. Ferguson, a fellow Gaelic-speaking Highlander, from Logierait in Perthshire, introduced Macpherson to John Home, the Scottish playwright who famously met Macpherson in Moffat in the autumn of 1759, sparking the whole Ossian episode.[37] Blair was a Church of Scotland Minister, one of the founding members of the Select Society (an important association of the Scottish Enlightenment) and the world's first chair of what we now know as 'English', when he was appointed Professor of Rhetoric and Belles Lettres at the University of Edinburgh in the early 1760s.[38] Blair became a mentor and friend to Macpherson, persuading him to publish the *Fragments* in 1760, writing scholarly frameworks for the Ossianic Collections and providing intellectual and practical assistance in their collecting, editing and publication. This friendship with Blair built upon the world of the Scottish Enlightenment that young James had experienced as a student at Aberdeen, and he soon became acquainted with most of the leading intellectual figures of the day, from David Hume to Adam Smith and William Robertson.[39] As Richard Sher argues, it was a 'coterie of Presbyterian clergymen affiliated with the Moderate wing of the Church of Scotland', such as Blair, Ferguson and

Robertson, who were at the heart of the 'Ossianic "cabal"' that supported Macpherson in his literary endeavours.[40] Beyond that, there were intellectuals such as Lord Kames, who provided financial support for Macpherson's Highland collecting tours of 1760 and 1761.[41] As Dafydd Moore rightly summarises, Macpherson operated 'within the discourse of accepted Enlightenment scholarship'.[42]

This established view of Macpherson as part of the Enlightenment world starts and stops, however, with Ossian. As we shall see in this book, Macpherson's later work needs also to be understood in this light, where Macpherson was an historian writing in the context of his fellow Enlightenment historians – and that his Gaelic homeland, Badenoch, was also a part of this world. Macpherson's relationship with this intellectual community continued throughout his life. In the late 1760s and early 1770s, Macpherson and his friend and fellow Highland historian, Alexander Dow, often visited David Hume for a night of drinking and philosophising at his London home.[43] Likewise, Macpherson's relationship with Adam Smith began in the early 1760s in connection with Ossian but continued throughout his career.[44] Perhaps unsurprising given their shared interest in empire, Smith and Macpherson corresponded about India during the 1770s. Smith was keen to promote the claims of a friend's son to a position in the East India Company and asked Macpherson for help. In his letter of recommendation sent to Madras in 1776, Macpherson described Smith as 'one of my best friends'.[45] Again, while some scholars have noted Macpherson's connection with this world, there has been little analysis of how this Enlightenment context shaped his history writing. Paul deGategno places Macpherson's work of the 1770s in the context of his relationship with Hume, Kames and Robertson, but he does not then analyse *how* Macpherson's history writing was similar to his more esteemed Enlightenment history colleagues.[46] Likewise, Robert Jones acknowledges the value of interpreting Macpherson in the context of Enlightenment historiography and its concerns with classical notions of narrative. However, Jones categorises Macpherson as 'a historian in the august classical tradition inaugurated by the Roman historian Tacitus', which misses the more subtle ways in which Macpherson engaged with the philosophy and erudition of eighteenth-century history writing.[47]

It is the scholarship of Enlightenment historiography that is key to interpreting Macpherson's history writing and moving debate beyond Ossian. This book uses the framework established by recent scholars of eighteenth-century historiography and applies it to the study of Macpherson. In particular, the approach taken by J. G. A. Pocock,

Mark Salber Phillips and Karen O'Brien in their studies of Gibbon, Hume, Robertson and others is useful in understanding the discourses of Enlightenment history writing that then informed Macpherson's work.[48] We place Macpherson in 'this company of historians', to borrow the phrase that Pocock attached to Edward Gibbon in his multi-volume study of *The History of the Decline and Fall of the Roman Empire* (1776–89).[49] Pocock applied Alfredo Momigliano's analysis of the three key parts of Enlightenment historiography – narrative, philosophy and erudition – to his study of Gibbon and how he brought together 'the erudite or antiquarian scholarship derived from the Renaissance and the philosophical historiography we think of as Enlightened'.[50] This is the same crucial framework that we use to understand Macpherson's history writing, and throughout this book we explore how Macpherson interweaved historical narratives that were rooted in erudite scholarship with the desire for philosophical reflection and generalisation on the value of history. Likewise, the work of Phillips and O'Brien provides a further scholarly context in which we can make sense of Macpherson's history writing. Phillips provides us with an insightful analysis of Hugh Blair's historiography, demonstrating how Blair's emphasis on the truthful and authentic qualities of an historian could be aligned with Enlightenment concerns to reconcile historical narrative with philosophical explanation.[51] O'Brien's analysis of Hume's writings and his notions of historical truth and causation also help us to understand how Macpherson wrote history during the 1760s and 1770s, as do her ideas about Robertson and stadial theories of history.[52] Summing up the historiographical universe in which Gibbon operated, Pocock declared that

> Hume was a philosopher who became a historian; Smith a philosopher who never converted conjectural history into full narrative civil history; Gibbon a historian who never intended to be anything else and employed philosophy as he had need of it.

To this list we can add Macpherson – a poet and translator who became an historian but then used the techniques and methodologies of Enlightenment historiography in his later works to robustly defend his own and the British state's imperial interests.

In seeking to fill the Macpherson-shaped hole in studies of eighteenth-century historiography, this book also contributes to our understanding of the people and place of Macpherson's world – the *Gàidhealtachd*. Establishing Macpherson as an Enlightenment historian who used history writing to make sense of his own and fellow Gaels' place in the British imperial state builds upon recent scholarship that has sought to emphasise the agency of the Highlands and the region's complex role in empire. There now exists a vibrant body of research that, at last, dispels the gloomy shadow cast over Highland historiography by Hugh Trevor-Roper, 'whose snooty critique of Scottish nationalism', Dan Hicks argues, 're-described the very notion of Highland and Island culture as nothing but a modern fabrication of bagpipe tartanry misrepresented as ancient custom'.[53] Such 'Tory po-mo' has been robustly challenged in the work of Matthew Dziennik, David Taylor and others, who stress the agency of the Highland elite and their enthusiastic participation in the opportunities of commercial modernity afforded by the late-eighteenth-century British Empire.[54] Much of Macpherson's history writing grapples with this, looking to use the past to make sense of the *Gàidhealtachd's* imperial present and future. Macpherson wrote during the 1760s and 1770s, a period of cautious optimism about the Highlands and its place in the world, in which, according to Fredrik Albritton Jonsson, 'the Highlands became the crucible for a new kind of conservatism intent on balancing the priorities of commerce and tradition'.[55] Macpherson applied stadial ideas to his writing about the past but developed this much further, using the Enlightenment strategies of narrative, philosophy and erudition to rationalise the place of the *Gàidhealtachd* in empire. Macpherson's later political works – *The Rights of Great Britain* (1775/6), *The History and Management of the East-India Company* (1779) and *A Short History of the Opposition* (1779) – were all about defining the boundaries of history, determining who belonged to the British imperial state by writing about the past. Highlanders, such as himself, belonged because their past could be reconciled and incorporated into a narrative of the British state; rebellious American colonists did not, because their past informed the revolutionary present and cast them as outwith history. Such a proto-Hegelian view of history and the state in Macpherson's history writing is discussed further in Chapter 4.[56] But, for now, it is important to note how Macpherson instrumentalised the past in the service of the British imperial state and that he did this as a Highlander, using the techniques of Scottish historical sociology to explain it all.[57] While his involvement in empire has been noted by some scholars, there has been little acknowledgement in work on Macpherson of the broader context in which Highlanders engaged with the project of empire.[58] We can see Macpherson as part of an eighteenth-century 'Gaelosphere', in which Gaelic-speaking Highlanders took full advantage of the opportunities afforded by the British imperial state.[59] Crucially, it was Macpherson's self-conscious historiographical modernity – using the techniques of Enlightenment history writing – which then demonstrated the modernity of the Highlands, shaping the British imperial state in ways comparable to the work of Robertson and Gibbon.

STRUCTURE

This book is structured to reflect our focus on *how* Macpherson wrote about the past. Moving chronologically through Macpherson's career, the book is organised by genre and by text. Following an overview of eighteenth-century historiography, each subsequent chapter examines a different genre of Macpherson's history writing: from his early poetry and the Ossianic Collections in the 1760s; to his prose history writing of the first half of the 1770s; and, finally, to his political writings in defence of the British imperial state during the second half of the 1770s that used the techniques and methodologies of Enlightenment historiography. Each chapter then has sections on his different texts, keeping our attention firmly on how Macpherson writes about the past and how this changes over time. We examine Macpherson's principal book publications, from *The Highlander* (1758) to *A Short History of the Opposition* (1779), with the exception of his translation of *The Iliad* (1773), which is only referred to briefly in Chapter 2. Macpherson's extensive magazine poetry and political journalism have been excluded, largely because most of these were published anonymously and were, therefore, a different kind of public performance of history writing.[60]

Chapter 1 situates Macpherson's history writing in the context of eighteenth-century historiography. It does this in two ways: first, through the scholarly frameworks outlined above that J. G. A. Pocock, Mark Salber Phillips and Karen O'Brien use in their studies of eighteenth- and early nineteenth-century history writing; and, second, through tracing the intellectual genealogies that inform Macpherson's work, from the early historiographical writings of Hume, Blair and Smith to the later Enlightenment history writing of Robertson and Gibbon. Pocock analyses the work of Gibbon through the 'Momiglianan triad' of narrative, philosophy and erudition, which this chapter demonstrates is a useful way of accounting for how Macpherson writes about the past and how this changes over the course of the 1760s and 1770s.[61] Equally, we see how Phillips and O'Brien's work on Hume, Blair and Robertson helps us to understand how Macpherson engaged with ideas about truth, cause and effect, historical narrative, and stadial theory. The second half of this chapter places Macpherson firmly in the historiographical universe of Enlightenment history writing. Through a close reading of Hume, Smith, Blair, Robertson and Gibbon, we explore the key intellectual influences on Macpherson's history writing. In his early work, especially the paratextual material to the Ossianic Collections, we see Macpherson drawing upon the ideas of Blair, Smith and Hume and applying them to his study of the ancient Celtic past. In his later writings, Blair's notions of historical authenticity are then married to the philosophical desire to explain the past which we find in Hume, Robertson and Gibbon. Macpherson's writings of the 1770s display an increasing concern with sources and how to footnote them, in a very clear display of erudition that places his historiographical practice in close proximity to that of Robertson and Gibbon.

Having established Macpherson's position in this world of Enlightenment historiography, Chapter 2 begins our detailed analysis of Macpherson's writings with his early poetry: *The Highlander* (1758), and the Ossianic Collections (1760–3). The first half of the chapter examines *The Highlander*, Macpherson's neoclassical epic poem about the tenth-century Viking invasion of Scotland. This section demonstrates how Macpherson used historical sources to versify the past, translating the fourteenth- and sixteenth-century history writing of John Fordun and George Buchanan into neoclassical verse. *The Highlander* also explores Macpherson's engagement with the British imperial state ('But o'er the trembling nations lift her arms'), which prepares us for our analysis of Macpherson and empire in the rest of the book.[62] This chapter builds on the work of Dafydd Moore and Mel Kersey in exploring Macpherson's 'Whig constitutionalism' and placing this in the context of Macpherson's imperialism. The second half of this chapter examines the paratextual material to the Ossianic Collections. In sections on the *Fragments* (1760), *Fingal* (1761/2) and *Temora* (1763), we analyse the advertisements, prefaces and dissertations that accompany these works, with a particular focus on Macpherson's methodology and historiographical practice. Macpherson draws upon the stadial theory of Adam Ferguson and others and connects this with a distinctly Enlightenment historiographical methodology, where sources and footnotes, authenticity and historical truth, historical causation, evaluating the evidence of sources, and the purpose of history are used to frame the Ossianic Collections. In the Preface and Dissertation to *Fingal*, we see Macpherson using the ancient past of the Highlands to make an argument about the role of Gaels in eighteenth-century commercial and imperial modernity. In the paratextual material to *Temora*, we see Macpherson engaging with Adam Smith's ideas about the purpose of history. In a critique of Smith's valorisation of ancient historians and their devotion to narrative, we see the emergence of a more philosophical approach to the past where

Macpherson demonstrates his engagement with the latest Enlightenment thinking.

Chapter 3 explores how Macpherson applied these Enlightenment ideas in his prose historical writings. It examines his three major works of history writing from the first half of the 1770s: *An Introduction to the History of Great Britain and Ireland* (1771); *The History of Great Britain from the Restoration to the Accession of the House of Hannover* (1775); and the *Original Papers, containing the Secret History of Great Britain from the Restoration to the Accession of the House of Hannover, with Memoirs of James II* (1775).[63] As in Chapter 2, we examine Macpherson's prefatory material to these works, where he engages in explicit historiographical discussion about how he writes history. Here, we see Macpherson applying Blair's ideas about truth and impartiality to his historical narratives of both the ancient Celtic past and the more recent history of Britain. In these works, Macpherson develops a particular concern with sources, evidence and footnotes, and while this is no doubt at least partially driven by criticism of the Ossianic Collections, this historiographical practice aligns closely with that of Robertson and Gibbon in their history writing of the 1770s. We then address how Macpherson comments historiographically throughout the main texts of his historical narratives. Like Hume (whose *History of England* series Macpherson continued in *The History of Great Britain*), we see Macpherson wrestling with the balance between narrative and philosophy. In particular, Macpherson uses stadial ideas to interpret the evolution of the British constitution. In *An Introduction*, Macpherson narrates the ancient Celtic past in such a way as to demonstrate the place of the Highlands in the evolution of the British state. Then, in *The History of Great Britain*, Macpherson accounts for the demise of the Restoration and the success of the Williamite revolution in terms that celebrate the triumph of 'Whig constitutionalism'. In his focus on warfare, Macpherson once again demonstrates his historiographical modernity, where the likes of Smith (in *The Wealth of Nations* (1776)) saw war as a driver of history and key to securing the future of the British Empire.

The crisis of the British Empire dominates Macpherson's later history writing. In Chapter 4, we examine Macpherson's three political book publications of the late 1770s, in which he defends the interests of the British state against the American colonists and the East India Company (EIC). While in terms of content all three (*The Rights of Great Britain Asserted Against the Claims of America* (1775/6); *The History and Management of the East-India Company, from its Origins in 1600 to the Present Times* (1779); and *A Short History of the Opposition During the Last Session* (1779)) are about contemporary politics, their approach and methodology is that of history writing. In particular, *The History and Management of the East India Company* is arguably Macpherson's most sophisticated historical work, where he combines a narrative of the Indian and imperial past with philosophical reflection, all underpinned with erudite and scholarly footnotes. The purpose of the *History and Management* is to defend the interests of the British state against the increasingly powerful (and corrupt) EIC, and to support his wealthy patron, the Nawab of Arcot. Yet, Macpherson does so using techniques of Enlightenment history writing that are closer in approach and methodology to Robertson's and Gibbon's works on empire.[64] The second half of the final chapter examines Macpherson's political writing about the American revolutionary war. Macpherson wrote both *The Rights of Great Britain* and *A Short History of the Opposition* in his role as political propagandist for Lord North's government. Both are fundamentally a defence of British imperial policy and an attack on the American colonists (and their British supporters). Yet each pamphlet is written as history, and in them – as in his other writings – Macpherson uses the past to make an argument about the present, creating historical narratives that seek to valorise the British imperial state and to cast its opponents as not just wrong, but as outwith history itself.

When Duncan MacKay wrote in 1796 about Macpherson's writing keeping 'it all together' he was thinking about both the global reach of Macpherson's political and commercial interests and the wide range of complex and multifaceted work that he had produced between 1758 and 1779. From Badenoch to Bombay, Macpherson's career was dedicated to the promotion of his own and his fellow Highlanders' engagement with empire. And, as this book demonstrates, much of Macpherson's writing aimed to rationalise and explain the position of the Highlands within the British imperial state. Macpherson did all this as an historian, writing about the past in order to make sense of the present. He did so across multiple genres, from epic neoclassical verse to translation of Gaelic oral tradition, to prose history writing and political propaganda. From *The Highlander* to *A Short History of the Opposition*, Macpherson wrote about the past as a way to think about the challenges of empire – from the Scottish militia crisis of the late 1750s, to the existential threat of revolution in America and corruption in India at the end of the 1770s. Macpherson thought about empire through the prism of history. And, as we shall see now in Chapter 1, Macpherson was at the heart of Enlightenment debate about how to write about the past. By placing him in the context of his more esteemed colleagues, such as Blair,

Hume and Robertson, we can understand how Macpherson was writing in the mode of Enlightenment historiography, and it is to this historiographical universe that we now turn.

Notes

1. Ronald Black, *An Lasair: Anthology of 18th Century Scottish Gaelic Verse* (Edinburgh: Birlinn, 2001), p. 331.
2. Anne Grant to Mrs MacIntosh, Glasgow, 20 February 1796, in Anne Grant, *Letters from the Mountains; Being the Correspondence with Her Friends, Between the Years 1773 and 1803, of Mrs Grant of Laggan. Vol. II*, edited by J. P. Grant (London: Longman, Brown, Green, and Longmans, 1845), p. 103.
3. 'S lìonmhor baintighearna ghasta / Mar shneachd na h-aon oidhche / Bhios ag ionndrainn a thlachda, / 'Aiteas 's a chainnte, / Bhios a deòiribh a' frasadh / 'S iad a' tachairt air 'adhlaic – / Ach se adhbhar an racaidh / Nach glac iad air làimh e.' ('There are many fine ladies / Like one night of snowfall / Who will miss his affection, / His gaiety and chatter, / Whose tears will be falling / As they come to his burial – / But the cause of their rending / Is not holding his hand.'). Black, *An Lasair*, p. 335.
4. Ronnie Black described MacKay's use of the phrase 'his Earl' as 'a reference to God', but it is more likely alluding to Macpherson's long-standing relationship with the Earl of Bute, politician and Prime Minister (1762–3). See Black, *An Lasair*, p. 516. On Macpherson's practice as a Highland laird, see David Taylor, *The Wild Black Region: Badenoch 1750–1800* (Edinburgh: Birlinn, 2016), pp. 200, 221–2, 251.
5. Taylor, *The Wild Black Region*, pp. 205–8; Stephen Foster, *A Private Empire* (London: Murdoch Books, 2010), pp. 69–72. For the broader context in which Highlanders contributed to the military and commercial activities of empire during the eighteenth century, see Andrew Mackillop, *Human Capital and Empire: Scotland, Ireland, Wales and British Imperialism in Asia, c.1690–c.1820* (Manchester: Manchester University Press, 2021).
6. For the purpose of this book, the *Gàidhealtachd* refers to the Gaelic-speaking Scottish Highlands and Islands. James Macpherson's homeland, Badenoch, was firmly part of this region during the eighteenth century. For an overview of definitions of the *Gàidhealtachd*, see Michael Newton, *Warriors of the Word: The World of the Scottish Highlanders* (Edinburgh: Birlinn, 2009), pp. 50–2. Our use of the term 'British imperial state' owes much to the analysis of Gurminder Bhambra. See, for example, Gurminder K. Bhambra, 'Brexit, Empire, and Decolonization', *History Workshop Online*, 19 December 2018, available at: https://www.historyworkshop.org.uk/brexit-empire-and-decolonization/ (accessed 17 March 2022); and Gurminder K. Bhambra, 'Relations of Extraction, Relations of Redistribution: Empire, Nation, and the Construction of the British Welfare State',

British Journal of Sociology, 73:1 (2022), pp. 4–15. For related, and useful, notions of Britain as an imperial state, see James Vernon, 'The History of Britain is Dead; Long Live a Global History of Britain', *History Australia*, 13:1 (2016), pp. 19–34.

7. James Macpherson, *The Highlander: A Poem in Six Cantos* (Edinburgh: W. Ruddiman Jr, 1758). The term 'Ossianic Collections' is used in this book to refer to the series of publications that dealt with the tales of Ossian: *Fragments of Ancient Poetry, Collected in the Highlands of Scotland, and Translated from the Gaelic or Erse Language by James Macpherson* (Edinburgh: G. Hamilton and J. Balfour, 1760); *Fingal, an Ancient Epic Poem, in Six Books: Together with Several Other Poems, Composed by Ossian the Son of Fingal* (London: T. Becket and A. de Hondt, 1762); *Temora, an Ancient Epic Poem, in Eight Books: Together with Several Other Poems, Composed by Ossian, the Son of Fingal* (London: T. Becket and P. A. de Hondt, 1763). See Kristin Lindfield-Ott, 'See SCOT and SAXON Coalesc'd in One: James Macpherson's *The Highlander* in Its Intellectual and Cultural Contexts, with an Annotated Text of the Poem', unpublished PhD thesis (University of St Andrews, 2011). Kristin Lindfield-Ott is Mairi MacPherson's former name.

8. Richard B. Sher, '"Those Scotch Imposters and Their Cabal": Ossian and the Scottish Enlightenment', *Man and Nature / L'Homme et La Nature*, 1 (1982), pp. 55–63; Fredrik Albritton Jonsson, *Enlightenment's Frontier: The Scottish Highlands and the Origins of Environmentalism* (New Haven, CT: Yale University Press, 2013), p. 13. For the broader context in which the expansion of military service in the Highlands during the eighteenth century was linked with the agricultural 'improvement' of the region, together with the subsequent creation of crofting, see Andrew Mackillop, *'More Fruitful Than the Soil': Army, Empire and the Scottish Highlands, 1715–1815* (East Linton: Tuckwell Press, 2000).

9. James Macpherson, *The History of Great Britain, from the Restoration, to the Accession of the House of Hannover*, 2 vols (London: W. Strahan and T. Cadell, 1775); James Macpherson, *Original Papers; Containing the Secret History of Great Britain, from the Restoration, to the Accession of the House of Hannover. To Which Are Prefixed, Extracts from the Life of James II, as Written by Himself*, 2 vols (London: W. Strahan and T. Cadell, 1775); *The Rights of Great Britain Asserted against the Claims of America: Being an Answer to the Declaration of the General Congress*, 2nd edition (London: T. Cadell, 1775/6); *The History and Management of the East-India Company, from Its Origin in 1600 to the Present Times* (London: T. Cadell, 1779).

10. For recent overviews of the Ossianic controversy, see Dafydd Moore, 'Introduction', in Dafydd Moore (ed.), *The International Companion of James Macpherson and* The Poems of Ossian (Glasgow: Scottish Literature International, 2017), pp. 2–10; James Mulholland, *Sounding Imperial: Poetic Voice and the Politics of Empire, 1730–1820* (Baltimore, MD: Johns

Hopkins University Press, 2012), pp. 93–8; and Leith Davis, 'Transnational Articulations in James Macpherson's *Poems of Ossian* and *The History and Management of the East-India Company*', *The Eighteenth Century*, 60:4 (2019), p. 443.
11. J. G. A. Pocock, *Barbarism and Religion. Vol. II. Narratives of Civil Government* (Cambridge: Cambridge University Press, 1999), pp. 4–6, 208; J. G. A. Pocock, 'The Re-description of Enlightenment', *Proceedings of the British Academy*, 125 (2004), p. 113.
12. Priya Satia, *Time's Monster: History, Conscience and Britain's Empire* (London: Allen Lane, 2020), pp. 6, 38–9.
13. For an overview of this debate, see Dafydd Moore, 'James Macpherson and "Celtic Whiggism"', *Eighteenth-Century Life*, 30:1 (2006), pp. 3–13; and Melvin Kersey, 'The Pre-Ossianic Politics of James Macpherson', *British Journal for Eighteenth-Century Studies*, 27 (2004), pp. 51–75.
14. For Macpherson's career in West Florida during the 1760s, see Emma Rothschild, *The Inner Life of Empires: An Eighteenth-Century History* (Princeton, NJ: Princeton University Press, 2011), pp. 39–45, 215–16; Douglas J. Hamilton, *Scotland, the Caribbean and the Atlantic World, 1750–1820* (Manchester: Manchester University Press, 2005), p. 170; Moore, 'Introduction', p. 4.
15. James Macpherson, *A Short History of the Opposition During the Last Session of Parliament* (London: T. Cadell, 1779).
16. Hayden White, *Metahistory: The Historical Imagination in Nineteenth-Century Europe* (Baltimore, MD: Johns Hopkins University Press, 1975), pp. 3–4.
17. Ibid., p. x.
18. Ibid., p. ix.
19. Carolyn J. Dean, '*Metahistory: The Historical Imagination in Nineteenth-Century Europe*, by Hayden White', *American Historical Review*, 124:4 (2019), p. 1339.
20. For the place of Macpherson and Ossian in Gaelic bardic culture, see Newton, *Warriors of the Word*, p. 105.
21. Arthur Parnell, 'James Macpherson and the Nairne Papers', *English Historical Review*, 12:46 (1897), p. 274.
22. For Samuel Johnson's response to Macpherson and Ossian, see Thomas M. Curley, *Samuel Johnson, The* Ossian *Fraud, and the Celtic Revival in Great Britain and Ireland* (Cambridge: Cambridge University Press, 2009). For a careful critique of Curley's Johnsonian analysis of Macpherson, see Matthew Wickman, 'Review of Thomas M. Curley, *Samuel Johnson, the Ossian Fraud, and the Celtic Revival in Great Britain and Ireland*', *Modern Philology*, 110:4 (2013), pp. 277–81.
23. Dafydd Moore, *Enlightenment and Romance in James Macpherson's* The Poems of Ossian: *Myth, Genre and Cultural Change* (Aldershot: Ashgate, 2003), p. 3.

24. In addition to *Fragments of Ancient Poetry* (1760), *Fingal* (1761/2), *Temora* (1763), Macpherson published several collected editions: *The Works of Ossian, the Son of Fingal: In Two Volumes. Translated from the Galic Language by James Macpherson* (London: T. Becket and P. A. de Hondt, 1765); *The Poems of Ossian. Translated by James Macpherson, Esq*, 2 vols (London: W. Strahan and T. Becket, 1773).
25. For an overview of earlier written versions of the Ossianic stories, see Newton, *Warriors of the Word*, p. 328.
26. For the late twentieth-century revival of critical interest in Macpherson's work and Ossian, see Fiona Stafford, *The Sublime Savage: James Macpherson and the Poems of Ossian* (Edinburgh: Edinburgh University Press, 1988); Howard Gaskill (ed.), *Ossian Revisited* (Edinburgh: Edinburgh University Press, 1991); Fiona Stafford and Howard Gaskill (eds), *From Gaelic to Romantic: Ossianic Translations* (Amsterdam: Rodopi, 1998); Moore, *Enlightenment and Romance in James Macpherson's* The Poems of Ossian; Howard Gaskill, *The Reception of Ossian in Europe* (London: Continuum, 2004). For more recent overviews, see Dafydd Moore, *The International Companion to James Macpherson and* The Poems of Ossian (Glasgow: Scottish Literature International, 2017); and Sebastian Mitchell (ed.), 'Special Issue: Forum on *Ossian in the Twenty First Century*', *Journal for Eighteenth-Century Studies*, 39:2 (2016), pp. 157–311. For the connection between Ossian and Gaelic tradition, see Derick S. Thomson, *The Gaelic Sources of Macpherson's 'Ossian'* (Edinburgh: Oliver & Boyd, 1951).
27. T. Bailey Saunders, *The Life and Letters of James Macpherson* (London: Swan Sonnenschein, 1894). For a response to Arthur Parnell's accusations of forgery, see G. Davis, 'Macpherson and the Nairne papers', *The English Historical Review*, 35:139 (1920), pp. 367–76. Horn described Macpherson's *History of Great Britain* (1775) as 'genuinely interested in the past'. See D. B. Horn, 'Some Scottish Writers of History in the Eighteenth Century', *The Scottish Historical Review*, 40:129 (1961), p. 14.
28. Moore, 'Introduction', p. 10; Dafydd Moore, 'James MacPherson' [sic], in *Oxford Bibliographies Online in British and Irish Literature* (Oxford: Oxford University Press, 2017), available at: https://www.oxfordbibliographies.com/view/document/obo-9780199846719/obo-9780199846719-0066.xml (accessed 11 January 2022); Colin Kidd, *Subverting Scotland's Past: Scottish Whig Historians and the Creation of an Anglo-British Identity, 1689–c.1830* (Cambridge: Cambridge University Press, 1993), p. 230. See also Moore's description of Macpherson as using 'the self-conscious historiographical methods of the Enlightenment' in Ossian and *An Introduction to the History of Great Britain and Ireland* (1771), in Moore, 'James Macpherson and "Celtic Whiggism"', p. 18.
29. Paul J. deGategno, 'Replying to a Crisis: James Macpherson's *The Rights of Great Britain Asserted against the Claims of America*', *Britain and the World*, 11:2 (2018), pp. 195–211; Robert W. Jones, 'Principles, Prejudices,

and the Politics of James Macpherson's Historical Writing', in Dafydd Moore (ed.), *The International Companion*, pp. 119–33; Davis, 'Transnational Articulations'.
30. Paul J. deGategno, *James Macpherson* (Boston, MA: Twayne, 1989), pp. 135–9.
31. deGategno, 'Replying to a Crisis', p. 211.
32. Jones, 'Principles, Prejudices, and the Politics of James Macpherson's Historical Writing', p. 119.
33. Ibid., p. 120.
34. Ibid., p. 121.
35. Ibid.
36. Davis, 'Transnational Articulations'.
37. Stafford, *The Sublime Savage*, p. 77. For the intellectual connections between Macpherson and Ferguson's thought, see Dafydd Moore, 'Adam Ferguson, *The Poems of Ossian* and the Imaginative Life of the Scottish Enlightenment', *History of European Ideas*, 31:2 (2005), pp. 277–88. For Ferguson's status as a Gaelic speaker, see Derick S. Thomson, 'Gaelic Poetry in the Eighteenth Century: The Breaking of the Mould', in Andrew Hook (ed.), *The History of Scottish Literature. Vol. II 1660–1800* (Aberdeen: Aberdeen University Press), p. 178. Thomson's view of Ferguson as a Gael stands in contrast to more recent studies of Ferguson's work (see Craig Smith, *Adam Ferguson and the Idea of Civil Society: Moral Science in the Scottish Enlightenment* (Edinburgh: Edinburgh University Press, 2019), pp. 14–16), which create a false dichotomy between his position as a Highlander and also a staunch supporter of the Hanoverian regime. As this book demonstrates in the case of James Macpherson, it was perfectly possible to be a Highland Hanoverian, and there was nothing unusual about that, especially by the 1750s and 1760s.
38. Richard B. Sher, 'Blair, Hugh (1718–1800)', *Oxford Dictionary of National Biography* (Oxford: Oxford University Press, 2004), available at: https://doi-org.eor.uhi.ac.uk/10.1093/ref:odnb/2563 (accessed 12 January 2022).
39. For Hume's initial enthusiasm for Ossian in the early 1760s, see Stafford, *The Sublime Savage*, p. 115.
40. Sher, '"Those Scotch Imposters and Their Cabal"', p. 55.
41. Jonsson, *Enlightenment's Frontier*, p. 30; Stafford, *The Sublime Savage*, pp. 116–17.
42. Dafydd Moore, '"As Flies the Unconstant Sun": Tradition, Memory and Cultural Transmission in The Poems of Ossian', *Eighteenth-Century Ireland*, 23:1 (2008), p. 78.
43. Jessica Patterson, 'Enlightenment and Empire, Mughals and Marathas: The Religious History of India in the work of East India Company servant, Alexander Dow', *History of European Ideas*, 45:7 (2019), p. 974.
44. JoEllen DeLuca, *A Feminine Enlightenment* (Edinburgh: Edinburgh University Press, 2015), p. 20.

45. Emma Rothschild, 'Adam Smith in the British Empire', in Sankar Muthu (ed.), *Empire and Modern Political Thought* (Cambridge: Cambridge University Press, 2012), p. 192.
46. deGategno, *James Macpherson*, p. 136.
47. Jones, 'Principles, Prejudices, and the Politics of James Macpherson's Historical Writing', p. 121.
48. Pocock, *Barbarism and Religion. Vol. II. Narratives of Civil Government*; J. G. A. Pocock, *Barbarism and Religion. Vol. IV. Barbarians, Savages and Empire* (Cambridge: Cambridge University Press, 2005); Mark Salber Phillips, *Society and Sentiment: Genres of Historical Writing in Britain, 1740–1820* (Princeton, NJ: Princeton University Press, 2000); Karen O'Brien, *Narratives of Enlightenment: Cosmopolitan History from Voltaire to Gibbon* (Cambridge: Cambridge University Press, 1997).
49. Pocock, *Barbarism and Religion. Vol. II. Narratives of Civil Government*, p. 1.
50. Ibid., p. 5.
51. Phillips, *Society and Sentiment*, pp. 40–5.
52. O'Brien, *Narratives of Enlightenment*, pp. 9, 59, 132–6. On Hume, see also, Claudia Schmidt, *David Hume: Reason in History* (University Park: Pennsylvania State University Press, 2003).
53. Dan Hicks, 'Event Density', in A. Boyd, J. Meades and D. Hicks, *Isle of Rust* (Edinburgh: Luath Press, 2019), p. 185.
54. Hicks, 'Event Density', p. 186; Matthew P. Dziennik, 'Whig Tartan: Material Culture and its Use in the Scottish Highlands, 1746–1815', *Past and Present*, 217 (2012), pp. 117–47; Taylor, *The Wild Black Region*. See also, David Worthington, 'The Settlements of the Beauly-Wick Coast and the Historiography of the Moray Firth', *Scottish Historical Review*, 95:2 (2016), pp. 139–63; Jim MacPherson, 'History Writing and Agency in the Scottish Highlands: Postcolonial Thought, the Work of James Macpherson (1736–1796) and Researching the Region's Past with Local Communities', *Northern Scotland*, 11:2 (2020), pp. 123–38. The historiography of Highland agency owes much to the pioneering work of Jim Hunter. See, for example, James Hunter, *The Making of the Crofting Community* (Edinburgh: John Donald, 1976) and *On the Other Side of Sorrow: Nature and People in the Scottish Highlands* (Edinburgh: Mainstream, 1995).
55. Jonsson, *Enlightenment's Frontier*, p. 15. This was before the more challenging period of the late eighteenth century and the acceleration of 'improvement' and clearance. As Jonsson argues, the 1780s were a particular hinge point that saw the loss of America interpreted by the British elite as an opportunity to accelerate the development of the Highlands as an 'internal colony'. See Jonsson, *Enlightenment's Frontier*, p. 2.
56. See also Ranajit Guha, *History at the Limit of World-History* (New York: Columbia University Press, 2002).
57. Kidd, *Subverting Scotland's Past*, p. 234.

58. See, for example, Leith Davis's analysis of Macpherson's work on India in Davis, 'Transnational Articulations'. For recent work on the Highlands and empire, see Mackillop, *Human Capital and Empire*; S. Karly Kehoe, 'Jacobites, Jamaica and the Establishment of a Highland Catholic Community in the Canadian Maritimes', *Scottish Historical Review*, 100:2 (2021), pp. 199–217; David Alston, *Slaves and Highlanders: Silenced Histories of Scotland and the Caribbean* (Edinburgh: Edinburgh University Press, 2021).
59. Domhnall Uilleam Stiùbhart, 'A Global Gàidhealtachd? Historical Gaelic Ethnoscapes', in Michel Byrne and Sheila Kidd (eds), *Lìontan Lìonmhor: Local, National and Global Gaelic Networks from the 18th to the 20th Century* (Glasgow: na Ceiltis & na Gàidhlig, Oilthigh Ghlaschu, 2019), pp. 1–19. See also, Allan I. Macinnes and Douglas J. Hamilton (eds), *Jacobitism, Enlightenment and Empire, 1680–1820* (London: Routledge, 2016); Domhnall Uilleam Stiùbhart, 'Traditionalising Empire: Imperial Commodities in Gaelic Popular Culture', British Studies and Centre for History Seminar, University of the Highlands and Islands, 26 October 2016, available at: https://youtu.be/vUEJmEt1sBI (accessed 28 January 2022).
60. For Macpherson's journalism, see James Noel Mackenzie Maclean of Glensada, 'The Early Political Careers of James "Fingal" Macpherson (1736–1796) and Sir John Macpherson, Bart. (1744–1821)', unpublished PhD thesis (University of Edinburgh, 1967). For Macpherson's early magazine poetry, see Stafford, *The Sublime Savage*, pp. 40–60.
61. Pocock, *Barbarism and Religion. Vol. II. Narratives of Civil Government*, p. 365.
62. Macpherson, *The Highlander*, p. 64.
63. James Macpherson, *An Introduction to the History of Great Britain and Ireland* (London: T. Becket and A. de Hondt, 1771); Macpherson, *The History of Great Britain, from the Restoration, to the Accession of the House of Hannover*; Macpherson, *Original Papers; Containing the Secret History of Great Britain, from the Restoration, to the Accession of the House of Hannover*.
64. Pocock, *Barbarism and Religion. Vol. IV. Barbarians, Savages and Empire*, p. 181.

1

Frameworks and Genealogies: Macpherson the Historian in Context

Macpherson can be understood as an historian in two related contexts: first, through recent scholarship on eighteenth-century history writing; and, second, by placing Macpherson in the emerging world of Enlightenment history writing during the 1760s and 1770s. This book interprets Macpherson using a framework about history writing derived from three key scholars: J. G. A. Pocock, Mark Salber Phillips, and Karen O'Brien. Through their work on David Hume, Hugh Blair, Adam Smith, William Robertson, Edward Gibbon, and others, these scholars have established the different ways in which these esteemed historians wrote about the past, placing them in the broader context of developing Enlightenment thought. While Pocock, Phillips and O'Brien examine broader changes in how history writing evolved across the eighteenth century and into the nineteenth, all have a focus on the period from the 1750s to 1780s, when their subjects were most active and when we see the development of a largely Scottish method of historical sociology.[1] Macpherson, as an historian, becomes a fascinating case study of how history writing was changing in this period. It is not that Macpherson is necessarily a better example of these changes – simply, that he is part of this intellectual community and that placing him in this context helps us to understand both this period and Macpherson. For those interested in Macpherson, it is a way of overcoming the Ossian impasse; for those who focus on Enlightenment historiography, this approach helps us to trace the pathways and effects of key ideas about history writing across non-canonical writers and texts.[2] In situating Macpherson within the genealogies of Enlightenment historiography, we can get a better understanding of how earlier ideas about historical narrative, truth and fidelity, and history's purpose as an instrument of amusement and instruction, developed into a broader mode of explanatory writing that combined narrative, philosophy and erudition. Macpherson's history writing was heavily influenced by historians from earlier in this period, such as Hume, Blair and Smith, especially when Macpherson lived in

Edinburgh during the 1760s and was in close contact with all three, particularly Blair. However, as history writing developed during the 1770s and became more concerned with the scholarly use of primary source evidence to account for historical change, Macpherson's work serves as a useful barometer of these historiographical innovations. In this context, Robertson and Gibbon became his history writing contemporaries. While Blair, Hume and Smith are theorists who bridge the gap between neoclassical and more modern ways of writing about the past, it is Robertson and Gibbon who emerge as the key practitioners of Enlightenment history writing in 1770s, and it is with them that Macpherson shares elements of history writing practice in his later works. Robertson and Gibbon's historiographical triangulation of narrative, philosophy and erudition also shaped Macpherson's *Introduction to the History of Great Britain and Ireland* (1771), *The History of Great Britain* and *Original Papers* (1775), and his political writings of the late 1770s. Macpherson shared their emphasis on sources and scholarly apparatus, such as footnotes, as mechanisms with which to establish truth, fidelity and impartiality in history writing. The key difference in Macpherson's history writing is how comprehensively he applied Enlightenment historiography to contemporary politics. Macpherson, Robertson and Gibbon all shared, to a greater or lesser extent, a commitment to a stadial view of history that saw the emergence of the Whig constitutionalism of the British state as a key evolutionary point in the development of civilisation. However, what makes Macpherson different is that he applied these ideas to a mode of history writing that explicitly focused on the defence of the British imperial state during the late 1770s crisis of empire.

This chapter is structured in two parts, examining the more recent scholarly debates about eighteenth-century history writing first before moving on to place Macpherson in the context of his Enlightenment historiographical contemporaries. It begins with an overview of scholarly debates about Enlightenment historiography. It focuses on Pocock's analysis of the emergence of more philosophical approaches to history writing during the eighteenth century and how we can understand the evolution of Macpherson's history writing in terms of these debates. Pocock's six-volume study of Gibbon's *History of the Decline and Fall of the Roman Empire* provides an exceptional account of the texts and contexts that shaped Gibbon's history writing, from Voltaire to Hume, Smith and Robertson. As such, our book adopts a similar approach when examining Macpherson's historiographical practice, while at the same time analysing his writing as part of the related set of ideas and discourses that also shaped and inspired Gibbon's work in the same decade – the

1770s.³ Likewise, the work of Phillips and O'Brien provides a framework within which to understand Macpherson as a product of the debates about history writing that were sparked by the ideas of Hume, Blair and Smith. The second half of the chapter then explores the historiographical notions and characteristics of these Enlightenment historians. It begins by analysing Macpherson's illustrious predecessors – Hume, Blair and Smith – and how their ideas about the purpose of history writing, its sources, and the nature of truth and evidence inspired Macpherson. Then, we address the two most significant historians who were practising at the same time as Macpherson's most productive period of history writing in the 1770s – William Robertson and Edward Gibbon. Here, we examine how Robertson and Gibbon reconciled the need to narrate the past with the growing demand to explain it and to justify that explanation with scholarly erudition. Comparing his historiographical practice with that of Robertson and Gibbon reveals how Macpherson was part of this broader debate about the nature and purpose of history writing – often in explicit ways, as revealed in Macpherson's prefaces, discussed in Chapter 3.

The scholarship on Enlightenment historiography is vast, but few have focused on *how* history is written in the sustained way that Pocock, Phillips and O'Brien do in their studies of eighteenth-century history writing.⁴ Recently, Robert Jones has noted the absence of Macpherson from such analyses of history writing during this period, and accounts for such silence because of the still rumbling Ossianic authenticity debate and Macpherson's equivocal position in relation to Enlightenment historiography.⁵ However, as this book demonstrates, Macpherson was immersed in such debates and we can better understand both his work and the history writing of the period if we view him through the frameworks outlined by Pocock, Phillips and O'Brien. As we argue throughout this book, it is important to analyse *how* Macpherson writes history, following Hayden White's injunction not to focus on the content of history writing during this period but, instead, to examine the 'structural components' of historiography.⁶

FRAMEWORK I: POCOCK ON NARRATIVE, PHILOSOPHY AND ERUDITION

The approach taken by J. G. A. Pocock in his monumental study of Edward Gibbon's *History of the Decline and Fall of the Roman Empire* offers a model of how to understand the evolution of history writing during the second half of the eighteenth century. Pocock's six-volume study of the first three volumes of *Decline and Fall* situates Gibbon at the junction between historiographical worlds.[7] In a recent reflection on his writing, Pocock argued that his turn to Gibbon in *Barbarism and Religion* marked his increased interest in 'the history of historiography, and focused on the "philosophical" histories which joined with the slightly older "philological" histories to transform, without replacing, the rhetorical narrative historiography had inherited from antiquity'.[8] In tracing the shift from neoclassical narratives of the past to the more complex philosophical history writing of the 1770s and 1780s, Pocock drew upon an intellectual framework pioneered in the 1950s by Arnaldo Momigliano in his work on the origins of Enlightenment historiography.[9] It was Momigliano who posited the centrality of Gibbon's history writing in the development of erudite 'scholarship derived from the Renaissance and the philosophical historiography we think of as Enlightened'.[10] Momigliano's hypothesis that this combination of philosophy and erudition was facilitated by a re-imagining of neoclassical historical narratives was then tested at length in Pocock's monumental study of Gibbon. Thus, we arrive at what Pocock termed 'the Momiglianan triad' – the ambition, emerging in Enlightenment historiography, to reconcile narrative, philosophy and erudition.[11] This is the framework in which Pocock sought to understand how Gibbon's history writing evolved through the navigation of these three concepts. Gibbon's historiography of the 1770s and 1780s was placed in the context of those historians before him who had begun to wrestle with these issues, from Voltaire and Giannone in Europe, to David Hume, William Robertson, Adam Smith and Adam Ferguson in Scotland. While Pocock's emphasis on the texts and contexts in which Gibbon writes has drawn some criticism, the value of examining 'this company of historians' can be extended to James Macpherson's history writing.[12] By analysing Macpherson's negotiation of narrative, philosophy and erudition, we can measure more clearly both where Macpherson can be situated in the development of Enlightenment historiography and the extent to which these ideas permeated broader debate about the nature of history writing during the 1770s and 1780s. So, just as Pocock used Momigliano's framework in his analysis of Gibbon, we can use Pocock's approach to understand Macpherson, tracing the genealogy of ideas that help to place both the texts of *Decline and Fall* in their intellectual context as well as Macpherson's history writing. For the purposes of this book, volumes two and four of Pocock's *Barbarism and Religion* are the most useful, where he explores the work of Hume, Robertson and Smith in ways which also help us to understand how Macpherson wrangled narrative, erudition and philosophy.[13] While part of Pocock's focus falls on 'the Enlightened narrative [as] a historiography of state and a historiography of society', using history writing to account for (and justify) the rise of the Western state and its attendant empires, only part of our analysis of Macpherson examines these elements of his history writing.[14] Instead, we pay closer attention to the mechanics of how Macpherson writes history, where engagement with sources, the use of scholarly footnotes, and the issues of historical truth, evidence and interpretation become more important.

The place of narrative in history writing had been a source of debate since antiquity. For Greek and Roman historians, 'the classical narrative of the exemplary actions of leading figures' was central to history writing.[15] Of course, ancient historians such as Thucydides and Tacitus were not content merely to narrate the past and had developed a more analytical historical narrative to account for human actions. Pocock identifies David Hume as a key eighteenth-century innovator in developing this narrative approach into something more systematically philosophical, becoming 'the first of British historians to master the writing of history in the double key of political narrative and sociological generalisation'.[16] As we shall see below, Hume's history writing had a significant influence on Macpherson, and comparing their related but distinct ways of both narrating the past and trying to explain it illuminates how these historiographical debates functioned during the 1770s.

The need for history writing to be rooted in erudition was also not an entirely new phenomenon in the eighteenth century. As Pocock notes, Renaissance historians sought to base their history writing in the scholarly collection of documents, often in the broader political service of establishing authority in early modern debates between church and state.[17] Partly in reaction to Voltaire's slap-dash approach to sources and references, historians such as Robertson and Gibbon began to pay greater attention to using primary sources as evidence in their interpretation of historical narratives and to take scholarly care in using footnotes to demonstrate this erudition.[18] Here, Macpherson's historiographical practice again demands our attention. While not quite as sophisticated as Gibbon or as thorough as Robertson in his use of footnotes, Macpherson's history writing is characterised by a consistent desire to demonstrate the provenance and authority of his evidence, underpinning his narrative of the past with the erudition of primary sources.

The emergence of philosophical reflection was perhaps the most significant innovation of eighteenth-century history writing. Here, we see historians such as Hume, Robertson and Gibbon developing the classical narrative of deeds of great men into 'the narrative of systematic changes in civilisation'.[19] In Hume's multi-volume *History of England* emerged a more philosophical way of narrating the past, accounting for change over time 'by constructing generalisations and noting conformities and exceptions to them'.[20] By the time Gibbon came to write the first volume of *Decline and Fall* in the mid-1770s, philosophical reflection had become focused on the historiography of the state and civilisation, in which the stadial ideas of Robertson, Ferguson, Smith and others shaped historiographical debate.[21] As we shall see, Macpherson's history writing was immersed in these philosophical notions. While much philosophical history writing of this period was intended to 'distance itself from controversy', Macpherson had no such qualms, using philosophy to think about both the place of the contemporary Scottish Highlands in the modern British world and, in his later political writing, to justify the actions of the British imperial state.[22]

FRAMEWORK II: PHILLIPS AND O'BRIEN ON NARRATIVE AND TRUTH IN THE WORKS OF HUME AND BLAIR

Karen O'Brien's *Narratives of Enlightenment* (1997) and Mark Salber Phillips's *Society and Sentiment* (2000) were published either side of Pocock's second volume of *Barbarism and Religion* (1999). Both O'Brien and Phillips shared Pocock's concern with key Enlightenment historians (Voltaire, Hume, Smith, Gibbon, Robertson) and his approach which saw them as part of an 'interpretative community' of writers and readers during this period.[23] While similar in subject matter and methodology to Pocock, both Phillips and O'Brien adopt crucial differences in their analysis of eighteenth-century historiography which, in turn, inform the approach taken in this book towards Macpherson. In making an argument about eighteenth-century developments in history writing and reading, Phillips explores historians' increasing concern with the social and sentimental innovations of commercial modernity. Phillips's range of historians is much broader than Pocock's, taking his argument into the late eighteenth and early nineteenth centuries through case studies of James Mackintosh, William Godwin and others. However, for the purpose of this book, it is Phillips's analysis of the earlier work of Hugh Blair that is particularly important for our study of Macpherson, especially the connection with Hume and his evolving historiographical practices in the 1760s. Karen O'Brien focuses on a narrower range of historians, closer to those examined by Pocock, in making her argument about the rise of 'cosmopolitan history' during the eighteenth century. For O'Brien, this 'cosmopolitan history' was a way of writing about the past in a more detached or philosophical way, rooted in 'an intellectual investment in the idea of a common European civilisation'.[24] Macpherson can be seen engaging with similar ideas in his work, but he then uses history writing to advance his personal and political ideas – not dissimilar, in some ways, to O'Brien's analysis of Voltaire, Robertson and the American historian David Ramsay.[25]

Phillips begins *Society and Sentiment* with a brief case study of Robert Henry's *History of Great Britain from the Invasion by the Romans under Julius Caesar* (1771–93). Henry's work of the 1770s aligned with Macpherson's key period of history writing and, indeed, drew upon James's and Rev. Dr John Macpherson's books on the Celtic past.[26] Phillips argues that Henry's extraordinary efforts to write about the past using seven simultaneous narratives (ranging from civil and military history to manners, virtues and vices) captured a moment when history writing, as a genre, was publicly and visibly wrangling with itself, attempting to reconcile the classical demands for narrative with the emerging Enlightened focus on explanation.[27] These tensions were not novel to Henry's work, but their ubiquity helps to explain the 'literary and philosophical culture' of the period.[28] The same could be said of Macpherson's history writing, where similar tensions abounded, especially when his application of Enlightenment methodologies of impartiality and source analysis were put to use defending the politics of the British imperial state in the late 1770s. Throughout *Society and Sentiment*, Phillips focuses on the development of different and more sophisticated ways of writing historical narratives. Here, the historiographies of Hume and Blair are given particular attention as ways of exploring the relationship between classical and post-classical modes of history writing. Phillips examines the interaction of the mimetic and didactic purposes of history, identifying the work of Hume, Blair and others as examples of eighteenth-century history writing that created new narrative forms in order to reconcile the desire to both represent the past and to learn from it. The instructive didacticism of the past became increasingly emphasised in eighteenth-century history writing, encapsulated by Bolingbroke's argument that history was 'philosophy teaching by example'.[29] However, both Hume and Blair persisted in efforts to reconcile the instructional aspects of history writing with its ability to represent the past and, as Phillips argues, developed new narrative strategies along the way. In particular, this book uses Phillips's analysis of Blair as a framework in which to understand Macpherson's history writing. As we shall see, Blair was a significant influence on Macpherson, and not just as the early inspiration and facilitator of the Ossianic Collections, examined in

Chapter 2.[30] Indeed, it is Blair's *Lectures on Rhetoric and Belles Lettres* that had a continuing and profound influence on Macpherson's historiographical practice during the 1760s and 1770s. Blair first delivered these lectures in Edinburgh during the autumn of 1759, just as he and Macpherson were beginning to get to know each other. Phillips focuses on Blair's Lecture XXXV on 'Comparative Method of the Ancients and the Moderns – Historical Writing' and on Blair's definition of history as recording 'Truth' in order to uphold principles of 'Impartiality, Fidelity, and Accuracy'.[31] Blair's emphasis on both imitation and instruction is seen by Phillips as signalling the emergence of a more philosophical approach to history writing, where 'history must instruct us through the medium of narrative itself'.[32] This analysis of Blair's historiography helps us to understand how Macpherson writes history during the 1770s, building on this approach to both representing the past through the careful analysis of source material and using that analysis to instruct – in Macpherson's case, to provide a defence of the British imperial state.

The interplay of narrative and philosophy also lies at the heart of Karen O'Brien's analysis of Enlightenment historiography. Here, O'Brien's treatment of Hume's impartiality and Robertson's stadial theories are of particular interest in helping us understand the context in which Macpherson was writing history. For O'Brien, Hume developed a 'regard to truth' in his history writing as a way to avoid accusations of party bias. In his *History of England* (1754–62), Hume sought to overcome the 'Whig or Tory partialities' that had characterised previous accounts of English history, especially of the revolutionary period of the seventeenth century.[33] As we shall see in Chapter 3, Macpherson adopted a similar approach in his *History of Great Britain* (1775) and *Original Papers* (1775), where he combined the Blairite faithfulness to source material outlined above with Hume's concern to write history without regard to faction. Whether Macpherson (or, indeed, Hume) succeeded or not is immaterial, but what is important is that both historians shared a commitment to a particular methodology which was intended to be impartial. Similarly, O'Brien's analysis of William Robertson's stadial history provides a context in which to examine how Macpherson applied such ideas about the development of society in his own history writing. While Robertson defined different stages of history according to 'their mode of subsistence', Macpherson's account of stadial history (examined in Chapters 2 and 3) is closer to Adam Ferguson and his emphasis on property.[34] However, as O'Brien argues, Robertson used stadial ideas in his *History of America* (1777) to formulate an indirect critique of the American colonists' revolution against British rule. Macpherson has no such subtlety and applies stadial thought to an outright denunciation of the Americans, in *The Rights of Great Britain* (1775/6).[35] In their related yet different ways, the work of Pocock, Phillips and O'Brien provides a scholarly framework within which to analyse Macpherson's history writing, demonstrating how Macpherson triangulated narrative, philosophy and erudition, together with contextualising his approach in the mimetic and didactic elements of history writing, issues of truth and impartiality, and the stadial nature of the past. In the next section, we trace the intellectual genealogies that inspired and influenced Macpherson's history writing, from Hume, Blair and Smith in the 1760s to Robertson and Gibbon in the 1770s.

HUME, BLAIR AND SMITH: AMUSEMENT AND INSTRUCTION, NARRATIVE AND TRUTH

David Hume, Adam Smith and Hugh Blair were not only three giants of the Scottish Enlightenment – they were also friends and acquaintances of James Macpherson. As we have seen, Blair worked most closely with Macpherson, especially around the time of the *Fragments* and when Macpherson was compiling *Fingal* and *Temora*. While not as close, both Hume and Smith crossed paths with Macpherson extensively during the 1760s and 1770s. Hume was consistently on the fringes of the Ossianic controversies, evolving from sceptical supporter in the early 1760s to privately hostile towards Macpherson and his writing in the mid-1770s.[36] Likewise, Smith was part of the broad group of intellectuals connected with the Select Society of Edinburgh who supported Macpherson's collecting and editing of Gaelic poetry in the early 1760s.[37] Smith later maintained correspondence with Macpherson regarding matters of empire, as we shall see in Chapter 4.[38] It is not surprising, then, that the ideas of Hume, Smith and Blair had a significant impact on Macpherson's history writing. Here, in this section, we sketch out some of the lines of intellectual connection between Macpherson and his Enlightenment colleagues, tracing a genealogy of ideas that helps to explain why Macpherson wrote history in the way that he did. We can see the influence of Hume and Smith in how Macpherson conceptualised history writing, especially in terms of the purpose of history and how Macpherson dealt with historical causation. Macpherson's approach to history writing was often similar to Hume's, but with the crucial difference that Macpherson placed a greater emphasis on source material, the analysis of evidence, and footnotes. Macpherson stressed the importance of erudition in history writing which, when combined with Hume's narrative and philosophical approach, demonstrates Macpherson's historiographical modernity, especially in his later writings. Smith's approach to history was more starkly classical, especially in his analysis of poetry and the narrative style of ancient historians. While we do see him following Smith's line of thinking (especially in the dissertation to *Temora*, examined in Chapter 2), Macpherson used this understanding of ancient sources as a way to distinguish his own account of the Celtic past. Finally, we examine how Blair's concepts of truth and impartiality in history writing were crucial to Macpherson's history writing. From *Fingal* onwards, Blair's ideas underpin Macpherson's use of source material in constructing historical narratives that seek to explain the past. This interpretation of Blair's historiography leads to Macpherson's more philosophical history writing of the 1770s, where we can see Blair's ideas functioning as a bridge towards a more sophisticated historiography and in which the influence of Robertson and Gibbon are clearer.

David Hume is most famous as an historian for his six-volume *History of England* (1754–62), which ends where Macpherson's *History of Great Britain* begins. Unlike the other eighteenth-century historians in this section, and unlike Macpherson, Hume was very much a professional historian: he was able to live off history writing.[39] 'For over sixty years', Trevor-Roper noted, 'Hume dominated the interpretation of English history. He was the first of the "philosophical historians"', concerned foremost with causes and effects.[40] The *History* itself is, of course, an actual history, and not a historiographical treatise; instead, Hume's earlier *Essays: Moral, Political, and Literary* (first published 1741) contain numerous references to the practice of history writing. The lighthearted 'Of the Study of History', which was included in editions of the *Essays* from 1741 to 1760, is perhaps the most directly historiographical. It is a short essay that ostensibly encourages 'female readers' to take up the study of history, but its ideas are central to our understanding of Hume's theory of history.[41] In the essay Hume advocates history writing because it is entertaining and instructive, in addition to making the reader more virtuous. While his remarks are, particularly in the early part of the essay, flippant advice for ladies, the essay does, in fact, address the virtues of history writing in a more serious manner. The study of history, Hume argues, is useful because it instructs and delights: 'history is a most improving part of knowledge, as well as an agreeable amusement'.[42] In fact, 'what more agreeable entertainment to the mind' is there, Hume asks, 'than to be transported into the remotest ages of the world, and to observe human society, in its infancy, making the first faint essays towards the arts and sciences'? For Hume, here, the purpose of the study of history was threefold: 'The advantages found in history seem to be of three kinds, as it amuses the fancy, as it improves the understanding, and as it strengthens virtue.'[43] Hume was following long-standing, classical notions of the didactic qualities of history. What was different in Hume's approach was how he married this older view of history with more modern and philosophical ways of writing about the past. For Hume, history not only was 'a most improving part of knowledge, as well as an agreeable amusement', it was also 'part of what we commonly call *Erudition* . . . an acquaintance with historical facts'.[44] As Pocock argues, 'Narrative which entertains, and philosophy which instructs, are once more combined to render history the *magistra vitae*; and erudition . . . appears in a somewhat ambiguous light.'[45] Indeed, Hume's equivocal relationship with erudition, sources and footnotes is in contrast to Macpherson's enthusiastic embrace of these more modern scholarly conventions.[46] As we shall see in Chapters 3 and 4, Macpherson, in the 1770s, used sources and footnoted them far more thoroughly than Hume, which indicates how Macpherson's historiographical practice was closer to the likes of Robertson and Gibbon during that decade.

Hume's belief in the didactic qualities of history was echoed by Adam Smith. Several of Smith's *Lectures on Rhetoric and Belles Lettres* (particularly Lectures XVII, XVIII, XIX of January 1763) focus on history writing.[47] In Lecture XVII, Smith discusses the narratology of historical writing and draws a distinction between narrative and didactic history writing: 'When we narrate transactions as they happened', he says, 'without being inclined to any party, we then write in the narrative Stile'.[48] This objective writing, also advocated by Hume, becomes didactic writing when the historian not only lays down the facts, but instead 'sets himself to compare the evidence that is brought for the proof of any fact and weighs the arguments on both Sides'.[49] For Smith, effective history writing relates facts, depicts causes and events and, above all, lets us learn from the past. Echoing some of the didactic qualities of Hume's historiography, Smith argues:

> The design of historicall writing is not merely to entertain; (this perhaps is the intention of an epic poem) besides that it has in view the instruction of the reader. It sets before us the more interesting and important events of human life, points out causes by which these events were brought about and by this means points out to us by what manner and method we may produce similar good effects or avoid Similar bad ones.[50]

Smith is thus an uneasy philosophical historian: while his focus is on objectivity and causes and effects, the allure of narrative and the didactic qualities of history writing are hard to resist. As Phillips argues, Smith's commitment to classical historical narrative was tempered by developing 'notions of sympathy and spectatorship'.[51] This insight into the affecting nature of history writing counters some of Smith's more conservative views of the value of narrative above all else. In Lecture XVIII, Smith praises the ancient historians and condemns more modern ones:

> It is not his [the historian's] business to bring proofs for propositions but to narrate facts. The only thing he can be under any necessity of proving is the events he relates. The best way in this case is not to set a labourd and formall demonstration but barely mentioning the authorities on both sides, to shew for what reason he had chosen to be of the one opinion rather than of the other. Long demonstrations as they are no part of the historians province are seldom made use of by the ancients. The modern authors had often brought them in.[52]

While valuing the authenticity of more modern history writing, Smith also recognised the mimetic qualities of ancient ways of writing about the past. In contrasting history with 'a Romance' and 'A well contrived Story', Smith emphasises the importance of authenticity: 'the facts must be real, otherwise they will not assist us in our future conduct, by pointing out the means to avoid or produce any event'.[53] However, Smith once again returns to classical ways of representing the past. 'In the ancient times', Smith explains in Lecture XIX, poetry and history overlapped: 'the Poets were the first Historians of any'.[54] Smith's understanding of early-poetry-as-history is familiar: bards, mythological history, exploits of the gods, military heroes all feature in his description. Unlike later eighteenth-century historians, however, Smith does not question the authenticity of early history writing. Authenticity only becomes important when poets and historians diverged, that is when verse and prose become distinctly associated with the two genres.[55] This is, of course, important for our study of Macpherson: as this book argues, the purpose of his writing, rather than the mode in which he writes, marks him as an historian and, as we see in Chapter 2, Macpherson critiques the reliance on ancient classical sources in his dissertation to *Temora*.

Macpherson's history writing was also influenced by Hume's and Smith's emphasis on the importance of cause and effect in composing historical narratives. As with his reflection on the purpose of history, Hume's clearest thought on historical causation may be found outwith his formal history writing. In the third section of *An Enquiry Concerning Human Understanding* (1748), Hume argues that historical narratives are created by the historian's analysis of cause and effect. Describing this narrative as 'that great chain of events', it is the historian's task to then explain 'each link in this chain'. As Claudia Schmidt argues, 'In other words, the historian seeks to describe a sequence of actions, to explain these as products of human motives within a particular context, and to describe the effects of these actions on a subsequent series of events.'[56] In his Lecture XVIII, Adam Smith also stresses the importance of causation in formulating historical narratives. As always, Smith's conservatism hides a more radical, philosophical approach to history writing. Smith begins Lecture XVIII by stating the value of narrating events in the order that they occurred:

> The next thing in order that comes to be considered with regard to historicall composition is the arrangement in which the several parts of the narration are to be placed. In general the narration is to be carried on in the same order as that in which the events themselves happened. The mind naturally conceives that the facts happened in the order they are related, and when they are by this means suited to our natural conceptions the notion we form of them is by that means rendered more distinct. This rule is quite evident and accordingly few Historians have trespassed against it.[57]

Smith pre-empts later, more postmodern historiography that stress the narratological basis of reality and, therefore, of how it can be represented in history writing through narrative.[58] However, Smith takes this further and, like Hume, gives the historian agency in explaining the connections between events in an historical narrative:

> But tho the connection of time and place are very strong, yet they are not to be so invariably observed as to supercede the observance of all others. There is another connection still more striking than any of the former, I mean that of cause and Effect. There is no connection with which we are so much interested as this of cause and effect; we are not satisfied when we have a fact told us which we are at a loss to conceive what it was that brought it about.[59]

When we examine Macpherson's account of his own historiographical practice, we can see the influence of both Hume and Smith in how Macpherson constructs historical narratives in a way that pays close attention to cause and effect.

Throughout the *Essays* Hume returns to history writing and its broader uses for understanding the human condition, whose influence we can again trace in Macpherson's historiography.[60] Hume praises objective history, and the writers thereof; that is how sources are authenticated.[61] Objective historians write civil history, which, along with civil liberty, is the focal point of many of Hume's essays. Civil history is the history of human interactions; it allows us to compare the present to the past and learn from it.[62] Biographical historians are necessarily most interested in civil history, but unlike philosophical historians (such as Hume and, by extension, Macpherson) are less concerned with causes and effects. Here, again, we can see Hume's influence on Macpherson's history writing, especially in terms of his Whig constitutionalist reading of British history in *The History of Great Britain* and the *Original Papers* (1775). As Pocock wrote of Hume, Robertson and Gibbon, these historians 'display a peculiar concern with ascertaining the general laws under which modern government, commercial and polite, can exist and the actions of statesmen and statecraft intersect with them' and we can see a similar historiographical approach in Macpherson's work.

Perhaps the greatest influence on Macpherson's history writing, however, was Hugh Blair. Like Hume in his *Essays* and Smith in his *Lectures*, Hugh Blair devotes a number of his own *Lectures on Rhetoric and Belles Lettres* (published 1783) to history writing. Blair first worked on these lectures in the autumn of 1759, during the same period in which he met Macpherson and began working with him on the *Fragments*.[63] While their close relationship in the production and publication of the Ossianic Collections is important, it is Blair's ideas about history writing that are key to understanding Macpherson's own historiographical practice. Like Smith, we find Blair paying due deference to the qualities of classical history writing. Initially, he groups poets and historians together (Lecture XXXV), and discusses the differences between ancients and moderns: 'Among the Antients, we find higher conceptions, greater simplicity, more original fancy. Among the Moderns, sometimes more art and correctness, but feebler exertions of genius.'[64] This analysis of the advantages of ancient historians echoes Smith's discussion of the modern historian's penchant for dissertations that 'render them less interesting than those wrote by the Antients'.[65]

Like other writers, Blair also emphasises authenticity and objectivity when it comes to historical writing. Blair's definition of history writing, though, is crystal clear about the historian's imperative to be impartial:

> As it is the office of an Orator to persuade, it is that of an Historian to record truth for the instruction of mankind. This is the proper object and end of history, from which may be deduced many of the laws relating to it . . . As the primary end of History is to record Truth, Impartiality, Fidelity, and Accuracy, are the fundamental qualities of an Historian. He must neither be a Panegyrist, nor a Satyrist. He must not enter into faction, not give scope to affection; but, contemplating past events and characters with a cool

and dispassionate eye, must present to his Readers a faithful copy of human nature.[66]

For Blair, an historian *must* be impartial, and this position was defined by a faithfulness to the evidence of source material. Blair is thus, like Robertson (as we shall see below), focused on truth and impartiality and on instruction through causes and effects. Indeed, as Phillips argues, Blair's position here takes the classical view of the mimetic and didactic qualities of history and interprets them through the philosophical concerns of the mid-eighteenth century: 'the emphasis rests in truthful imitation, but in the course of further discussion, the balance shifts from imitation to instruction'.[67] Like Smith, Blair was cautious about 'excessive didacticism', but argued that the historical narrative itself should explain and instruct.[68]

Like Hume, Blair also emphasises the importance of cause and effect for the cohesiveness of historical narratives. Here, Blair again indicates the philosophical potential of history writing in seeking broad explanations and generalisations for historical change:

> in the conduct and management of his subject, the first attention requisite in an Historian, is to give it as much unity as possible; that is, his History should not consist of separate unconnected parts merely, but should be bound together by some connecting principle, which shall make the impression on the mind of something that is one, whole and entire [. . .] Whether pleasure or instruction be the end sought by the study of History, either of them is enjoyed to much greater advantage, when the mind has always before it the progress of some one great plan or system of actions; when there is some point or centre, to which we can refer the various facts related by the Historian.[69]

The unity of Blair's historical narrative is not tied to examples but instead is dependent on structure: a skilled writer 'trace[s] all the secret links of the chain, which binds together remote, and seemingly unconnected events'.[70] On the part of the historian, this requires 'a thorough acquaintance with human nature' and 'political knowledge, or acquaintance with government'; the first to understand (and write about) individuals, and the latter for societies.[71] Blair's philosophical intent emphasised the historian's commitment to truth, achieved through faithfulness to source material and the creation of an historical narrative that sought to explain cause and effect and to offer an overview of 'political narrative and sociological generalisation'.[72] It was these historiographical principles that we can see influencing the kind of history that Macpherson went on to write in the 1770s, where Macpherson's work can be understood in comparison to the historiographical practice of two of his most illustrious historian counterparts – William Robertson and Edward Gibbon.

ROBERTSON AND GIBBON: NARRATIVE, PHILOSOPHY AND ERUDITION

Macpherson's history writing matured in the 1770s, during a decade of exceptional wider historiographical achievement, exemplified in the writings of William Robertson and Edward Gibbon. From Robertson's *History of America* (1777) to the first volume of Gibbon's *History of the Decline and Fall of the Roman Empire* (1776), Macpherson was writing in a historiographical context where the Enlightenment triad of narrative, philosophy and erudition was being refined to a high degree. Especially in his later works, from *The History of Great Britain* (1775) to *The History and Management of the East-India Company* (1779), Macpherson can be seen engaging in these debates about historical narrative, the role of historians' explanations and digressions, and how to use primary source evidence and scholarly footnotes. In particular, it is these issues of erudition that Macpherson commented on most clearly, echoing the self-consciously historiographical practice of both Robertson and Gibbon.

In two of the texts that are most closely related to the topics of Macpherson's history writings, *The History of Scotland* (1759) and *The History of America* (1777), Robertson outlined his approach and method in clear and precise prefaces. William Robertson furnished his *History of Scotland, During the Reigns of Queen Mary and King James VI. Till the Accession to the Crown of England* (1759) with both a Preface and a 'Review of the Scotch History previous to that Period'. He assures us that his history is different from earlier histories: 'I have departed, in many instances, from former Historians' because he has 'placed facts in a different light' and has 'drawn characters with new colours'.[73] In other words, Robertson's work is different because he is selective in choosing his evidence, his interpretation differs to other historians and he thinks historiographically as a philosophical historian.[74] As Nicholas Hargreaves has argued, Robertson's historical narrative interweaved with broader reflection in innovative ways, using 'narrative history as an instrument for advocating his concept of modern Scottish society'.[75]

Like Hume and Blair, Robertson was also concerned with authenticity but with a greater emphasis on how this came from the evidence of primary sources. Robertson stressed that as his *History* was published with the papers that it is taken from, he has the 'evidence, on which, at the distance of two centuries, I presume to contradict the testimony of contemporary, or of less remote Historians'.[76] For Robertson evidence was necessarily written; he is not a conjectural historian, in the sense that he did not speculatively attempt to account for the broad conditions of society.[77] Indeed, Robertson emphasises that 'every thing beyond that short period, to which well attested annals reach, is obscure', which leaves room for 'invention' and 'events, calculated to display [a nation's] own antiquity, and lustre'.[78] History is clearly the realm of truth; invention, therefore, must belong in the land of fiction. Robertson here echoes Bolingbroke's (and Aristotle's) distinction between fiction and history. However, Robertson admits that while all good history is a 'record of truth', used to 'teach wisdom', it 'often sets out with retailing fictions and absurdities'. And the Scots are particularly prone to that: they 'rely[. . .] upon uncertain legends, and the traditions of their bards, still more uncertain', an intriguing comment on the eve of the publication of *The Fragments*.[79]

In the Preface to the *History of America*, Robertson also emphasises the importance of sources and footnotes to his historiographical methodology. Robertson is thorough in listing the archives and sources that have underpinned his account of the process of Spanish colonisation. He argues that the novelty of his evidence then leads to an interpretation of the past that is different to previous historians:

> I have departed in many instances from the accounts of preceding historians, and often related facts which seem to have been unknown to them. It is a duty I owe the Public, to mention the sources from which I have derived such intelligence, as justifies me either in placing transactions in a new light, or in forming any new opinion with respect to causes and effects.[80]

Much like Macpherson, Robertson emphasises the need to support the use of primary sources with detailed footnotes – the 'minute references' which authenticate his historical narrative. Here, Robertson acknowledges the influence of Gibbon and how this led him to publish a separate 'catalogue of the Spanish books I have consulted', rather than 'encumbering the page with an insertion of their full titles', recognising Enlightenment concerns to avoid interrupting the narrative flow of history writing.[81] Macpherson resembles Robertson in this search for authenticity through primary sources, which we will see in Chapter 3.

While Robertson was in close communication with Gibbon, Macpherson's relationship with Gibbon was less clear. As we shall see in Chapter 3, Gibbon referred to Macpherson's *Introduction to the History of Great Britain and Ireland* (1771) in the fourth volume of *The Decline and Fall of the Roman Empire*, published in 1788, and they would have known each other in the 1770s through their shared political support for Lord North's administration.[82] Though they were not close colleagues, they were part of a shared historiographical universe, and we can see echoes of Macpherson's approach to history writing in Gibbon's better-known work. Gibbon's account of his historiographical methodology was not as fulsome as either Robertson's or Macpherson's. It was only in the fourth volume of *The Decline and Fall of the Roman Empire* (1788) that Gibbon included a preface, explaining his approach. Here, Gibbon uses evidence in a similar way to Macpherson and Robertson, but in less forthright tones than the two Scottish historians:

> For the present I shall content myself with renewing my serious protestation, that I have always endeavoured to draw from the fountain-head; that my curiosity, as well as a sense of duty, has always urged me to study the originals, and that, if they sometimes eluded by search, I have carefully marked the secondary evidence, on whose faith a passage or a fact were reduced to depend.[83]

Gibbon's faithfulness to the source material was clear, but his methodology is not outlined in the same detail as Robertson and Macpherson, with their greater focus on sources, evidence, footnotes and the all-important concepts of historical truth and authenticity.

As Pocock and others have argued, both Robertson and Gibbon were key historians in reconciling classical imperatives for a clear historical narrative with Enlightenment concerns for a more philosophical explanation and reflection on the past. In their emphasis on sources, Gibbon and especially Robertson were adding an older concept of erudition into this historiographical mix: 'Erudition must in a certain sense be placed first.'[84] In his practice as an historian, Macpherson followed suit and we can better understand the nature of his history writing if we situate him in the context of his contemporaries, especially the work of Robertson and Gibbon during the 1770s. Moreover, as we shall see in Chapter 3, Robertson and Gibbon were both concerned with the issue of empire. The late 1770s crisis of empire, and especially the existential threat of the American Revolution, shaped in varying ways the kind of history written by both Robertson and Gibbon. While Gibbon was somewhat equivocal about contemporary politics in his history writing and Robertson deliberately cut short his *History of America* before having to tackle the more contentious issues of the present, Macpherson had no such qualms.[85] Especially in his final, more political works, Macpherson applied philosophical, erudite historiography to writing a historical narrative that justified the present policy of the British imperial state.

CONCLUSION

Writing to his London publisher, William Strahan, in 1770, David Hume argued that 'I believe this is the historical Age and this the historical Nation.'[86] This statement that the 1770s would be a particularly fertile era for history writing in both British and Scottish literary culture was prompted by Hume's identification of 'no less than eight Histories' that were about to be published, including 'Dr Robertson's American History' which appeared in 1777.[87] Hume's letter, however, was primarily concerned with promoting the forthcoming work of Robert Henry, whom we encountered at the beginning of this chapter. Hume's letter was all about positioning Henry's work as part of 'the historical Age' of 'this the historical nation'. Describing Henry's *History of Great Britain* (1771) as containing 'a great deal of Good Sense and Learning', Hume's letter was essentially one of recommendation, wishing that 'you and Mr Cadel [sic] may usher it in to the Public'.[88] Hume did likewise for Macpherson, placing him in an Enlightenment historiographical universe. Writing to Strahan in 1773, Hume pondered which historian should continue his *History of England* series and weighed up the merits of several candidates. Macpherson was described as having 'Style and Spirit, but is hot-headed, and consequently without Judgement'.[89] Hume's equivocal assessment of Macpherson's qualities as an historian is not the point – what matters is that Hume situated Macpherson in the world of credible historians at the beginning of the 1770s. This chapter has followed in Hume's footsteps, analysing Macpherson's history writing through the historiographical frameworks of recent scholarship and tracing the genealogy of ideas that connect Macpherson with his better-known Enlightenment historian counterparts. J. G. A. Pocock's application of the 'Momiglianan triad' to the work of Hume, Robertson and Gibbon may also fruitfully be used to interpret the history writing of James Macpherson. The desire to follow classical notions of historical narrative that were challenged by emerging philosophical explanations of the past was one shared by both these Enlightenment historians and by Macpherson. In the work of Mark Salber Phillips and Karen O'Brien, we see particularly in their analysis of Blair and Hume useful ideas that help situate Macpherson's history writing, especially in terms of notions of narrative, truth and fidelity to sources. Having established this scholarly framework, we can then more accurately trace the genealogy of historiographical ideas that emerged in the mid-eighteenth century and help us to understand the kinds of history that Macpherson wrote. The influence of Hume, Smith and Blair on Macpherson's history writing was profound. From Hume's and Smith's ideas on the mimetic and didactic purposes of history to Blair's emphasis on truth and fidelity to sources, we can see Macpherson incorporating these historiographical reflections into his own writing. Then, as Macpherson moved from poetry to the prose of history in his works of the 1770s, we increasingly see the historiographical practice of the likes of Robertson and Gibbon being followed by Macpherson. In *The History of Great Britain* and his later political writing, Macpherson pays particular attention to sources, footnotes and their epistemological function – these were historiographical tools that helped Macpherson manifest Blair's requirement for 'Impartiality, Fidelity, and Accuracy'. The following chapter, however, focuses our attention on the beginning of Macpherson's writing career. Here, we see Macpherson consistently engaging with the past, either in terms of using historical source material or thinking historiographically. But, unlike in the bulk of his later writing, in *The Highlander* and in the Ossianic Collections, Macpherson does this first as a poet. At the end of the 1750s, Macpherson versifies the past in *The Highlander*, an account of medieval Scottish conflict against the Vikings. The poem's historical narrative not only explains the past, but also demonstrates Macpherson's interest in a Whig constitutional reading of the recent British past which he uses to articulate his developing loyalty to the British imperial state, rendering Enlightenment and empire in epic neoclassical form. Then, at the beginning of the 1760s, Macpherson's collecting, translating and editing of the Ossianic Collections marks the start of his history writing in prose and his explicit theoretical engagement with the process and practice of historiography. Here, in the paratextual material to *Fingal* and *Temora*, Macpherson writes historiographically about the Ossianic tales and engages with the ideas of Blair, Smith and Hume. These Enlightenment historians (along with the stadial theories of Adam Ferguson) were then wrangled and woven by Macpherson into his account of an ancient Celtic past that would take Europe and the world by storm.

Notes

1 Kidd, *Subverting Scotland's Past*, p. 234.
2 For a similar approach to a contemporary of Macpherson (and fellow historian), see William Zachs, *Without Regard to Good Manners: A Biography of Gilbert Stuart 1743–1786* (Edinburgh: Edinburgh University Press, 1992), p. xiii.
3 Richard Wolin, 'Symposium on J. G. A. Pocock's *Barbarism and Religion*', *Journal of the History of Ideas*, 77:1 (2016), p. 105.

4 For an overview of scholarship on Enlightenment historiography, see David Allan, 'Scottish Historical Writing of the Enlightenment', in José Rabasa, Masayuki Sato, Edoardo Tortarolo and Daniel Woolf (eds), *The Oxford History of Historical Writing: Volume 3: 1400–1800* (Oxford: Oxford University Press, 2012), pp. 497–517; Karen O'Brien, 'English Enlightenment Histories, 1750–c.1815', in Rabasa et al. (eds), *The Oxford History of Historical Writing: Volume 3: 1400–1800* (Oxford: Oxford University Press, 2012), pp. 518–35; Karen O'Brien, 'The Return of the Enlightenment', *American Historical Review*, 115:5 (2010), pp. 1426–35; Karen O'Brien and Susan Manning, 'Historiography, Biography and Identity', in Susan Manning (ed.), *The Edinburgh History of Scottish Literature. Vol. II: Enlightenment, Britain and Empire (1707–1918)* (Edinburgh: Edinburgh University Press, 2007), pp. 143–53; Alexander Broadie, *The Scottish Enlightenment: The Historical Age of the Historical Nation* (Edinburgh: Birlinn, 2001).
5 Jones, 'Principles, Prejudices, and the Politics of James Macpherson's Historical Writing', p. 119.
6 White, *Metahistory*, pp. 3–4.
7 For an overview of Pocock's writing of *Barbarism and Religion* and how the later volumes of Gibbon's work would require a different approach, see J. G. A. Pocock, 'Gibbon's Second Trilogy: An Introductory Survey', *History of European Ideas*, 43:7 (2017), pp. 701–31.
8 J. G. A. Pocock, 'From *The Ancient Constitution* to *Barbarism and Religion*; *The Machiavellian Moment*, the History of Political Thought and the History of Historiography', *History of European Ideas*, 43:2 (2017), p. 140.
9 Arnaldo Momigliano, *Contributo all Storia degli Studi Classici* (Rome: Edizioni di Storia e Letteratura, 1955); Arnaldo Momigliano, *The Classical Foundations of Modern Historiography* (Berkeley: University of California Press, 1990).
10 Pocock, *Barbarism and Religion. Vol. II. Narratives of Civil Government*, p. 5.
11 Ibid., p. 365.
12 Ibid., p. 1. For a critique of Pocock's application of 'Cambridge methodology' to his study of Gibbon, see Helen Rosenblatt, 'On Context and Meaning in Pocock's *Barbarism and Religion*, and on Gibbon's "Protestantism" in His Chapters on Religion', *Journal of the History of Ideas*, 77:1 (2016), pp. 147–55. For Pocock's robust response, see J. G. A. Pocock, 'Response and Commentary', *Journal of the History of Ideas*, 77:1 (2016), pp. 157–71.
13 Pocock, *Barbarism and Religion. Vol. IV. Barbarians, Savages and Empire*.
14 Pocock, *Barbarism and Religion. Vol. II. Narratives of Civil Government*, p. 2.
15 Ibid., p. 5.
16 Ibid., pp. 207–8.
17 Ibid., pp. 5, 70. For a recent study of the older historiographical roots of erudition used by Renaissance humanist historians, see Anton M. Matytsin,

'Enlightenment and Erudition: Writing Cultural History at the Académie des Inscriptions', *Modern Intellectual History* (2021), pp. 1–26.
18. Pocock, *Barbarism and Religion. Vol. II. Narratives of Civil Government*, pp. 158, 278; Pocock, *Barbarism and Religion. Vol. IV. Barbarians, Savages and Empire*, pp. 183–6. For a recent reappraisal of Voltaire's approach to erudition and sources, see Pierre Force, 'The "Exasperating Predecessor": Pocock on Gibbon and Voltaire', *Journal of the History of Ideas*, 77:1 (2016), pp. 129–45; and Pierre Force, 'Voltaire and the Necessity of Modern History', *Modern Intellectual History*, 6:3 (2009), pp. 457–84.
19. Pocock, *Barbarism and Religion. Vol. II. Narratives of Civil Government*, p. 10.
20. Ibid., p. 208. For a recent analysis of Hume's philosophical history and the relationship between causes and historical facts, see Pedro Faria, 'David Hume, the Académie des Inscriptions and the Nature of Historical Evidence in the Early Eighteenth Century', *Modern Intellectual History*, 18:2 (2021), pp. 299–322.
21. Pocock, *Barbarism and Religion. Vol. II. Narratives of Civil Government*, p. 370.
22. Ibid., p. 5.
23. O'Brien, *Narratives of Enlightenment*, p. 5.
24. Ibid., p. 2.
25. Ibid., p. 8.
26. Kidd, *Subverting Scotland's Past*, p. 238.
27. Phillips, *Society and Sentiment*, p. 3.
28. Ibid., p. 8.
29. Ibid., p. 22.
30. Stafford, *Sublime Savage*, pp. 78–9, 115–16, 128.
31. Phillips, *Society and Sentiment*, p. 41.
32. Ibid., p. 43.
33. O'Brien, *Narratives of Enlightenment*, p. 59.
34. Ibid., pp. 133–4.
35. Ibid., p. 154.
36. Schmidt, *David Hume*, pp. 390–1.
37. deGategno, *James Macpherson*, p. 4; Jonsson, *Enlightenment's Frontier*, p. 16; Saunders, *Life and Letters of James Macpherson*, p. 73; Sher, '"Those Scotch Imposters and their Cabal"'; Pocock, *Barbarism and Religion. Vol II. Narratives of Civil Government*, p. 269.
38. Emma Rothschild, 'Values, Classical Political Economy and the Portuguese Empire', *Journal of Economic Methodology*, 19:2 (2012), p. 111; Rothschild, *The Inner Life of Empires*, pp. 215–16. See also Smith's correspondence with Sir John Macpherson, James's great friend and collaborator, in F. P. Lock, 'An Unpublished Letter from Adam Smith to Sir John Macpherson', *Scottish Historical Review*, 85:1 (2006), pp. 135–7.

39 Indeed, 'Hume's writings testify abundantly to his deep, wide-ranging, and lifelong interest in history' – an interest that was, unlike Macpherson's, professional. See Schmidt, *David Hume*, p. 377.
40 Hugh Trevor-Roper, *History and the Enlightenment* (New Haven, CT: Yale University Press, 2010), p. 120. Trevor-Roper observes that 'the Scots may boast of having produced the Scottish Enlightenment, but the fact remains that all of its great figures took pains to dissociate themselves from their own literature and associate themselves with England'. See Trevor-Roper, *History and the Enlightenment*, p. 123. Macpherson, of course, did not: his *History* is a *History of Britain* (as was Hume's originally).
41 David Hume, 'Of the Study of History', in *Essays: Moral, Political, and Literary* (Indianapolis, IN: Liberty Fund, 1987), p. 566.
42 Ibid.
43 Ibid., p. 565.
44 Ibid., p. 566.
45 Pocock, *Barbarism and Religion. Vol. II. Narratives of Civil Government*, p. 182.
46 Schmidt, *David Hume*, pp. 394–5.
47 Smith first gave these lectures in 1748 and the record we have of them is from notes taken in 1762–3. Smith, *Lectures on Rhetoric and Belles Lettres*, p. 12.
48 Ibid., p. 89.
49 Ibid., p. 90.
50 Ibid.
51 Phillips, *Society and Sentiment*, p. 85.
52 Smith, *Lectures on Rhetoric and Belles Lettres*, 'Lecture XVIII', p. 102.
53 Smith, *Lectures on Rhetoric and Belles Lettres*, 'Lecture XVII', p. 91.
54 Smith, *Lectures on Rhetoric and Belles Lettres*, 'Lecture XIX', p. 104.
55 In this Smith of course echoes Aristotle: 'the difference between the historian and the poet is not that the one writes in prose and the other in verse [. . .] The difference is that one tells of what has happened, the other of the kinds of things that might happen.' See Aristotle, 'Poetics', *Classical Literary Criticism*, edited by T. S. Dorsch and Penelope Murray (London: Penguin, 2000), pp. 57–97.
56 Schmidt, *David Hume*, p. 385.
57 Smith, *Lectures on Rhetoric and Belles Lettres*, 'Lecture XVIII', p. 98.
58 David Carr, 'Narrative Explanation and its Malcontents', *History and Theory*, 47:1 (2008), pp. 19–30.
59 Smith, *Lectures on Rhetoric and Belles Lettres*, 'Lecture XVIII', p. 98.
60 Schmidt, *David Hume*, p. 393.
61 'Those who employ their pens on a political subject, free from party-rage, and party-prejudice, cultivate a science, which, of all others, contributes most to public utility, and even to the private satisfaction of those who

addict themselves to the study of it.' See Hume, 'Of Civil Liberty', in *Essays: Moral, Political, and Literary*, p. 87. Of course, it could be argued that memoirists allow the historian to compile histories that can be authenticated on the basis of primary evidence.

62 'In *civil* history, there is found a much greater uniformity than in the history of learning and science, and that the wars, negociations, and politics of one age resemble more those of another, than the taste, wit and speculative principles.' See Hume, 'Of Eloquence', in *Essays: Moral, Political, and Literary*, p. 97.

63 Robert M. Schmitz, *Hugh Blair* (New York: King's Crown Press, 1948), pp. 44–5.

64 Hugh Blair, 'Lecture XXXV', in *Lectures on Rhetoric and Belles Lettres* (Carbondale: Southern Illinois University Press, 2005), p. 394.

65 Smith, *Lectures on Rhetoric and Belles Lettres*, p. 102.

66 Blair, 'Lecture XXXV', p. 397.

67 Phillips, *Society and Sentiment*, p. 41.

68 Ibid., p. 43.

69 Blair, 'Lecture XXXV', pp. 397–8.

70 Ibid., p. 398.

71 Blair, 'Lecture XXXVI', p. 402.

72 Pocock, *Barbarism and Religion. Vol. II. Narratives of Civil Government*, p. 208.

73 William Robertson, *The History of Scotland, During the Reigns of Queen Mary and King James VI. Till the Accession to the Crown of England. With a Review of the Scotch History Previous to that Period; And an Appendix containing Original Papers*, 2 vols (London: A. Millar, 1759), I, p. iii.

74 See Gilbert Stuart, for example, who notes that Robertson 'selects those portions of the Scottish History which he can adorn, but does not place the whole before the eye'. See Gilbert Stuart, *Critical Observations Concerning the Scottish Historians Hume, Stuart, and Robertson* (London: T. Evans, 1782), p. 37. Stuart was also influenced by Macpherson's work in his writing. See Kidd, *Subverting Scotland's Past*, p. 239.

75 Neil K. Hargreaves, 'National History and "Philosophical" History: Character and Narrative in William Robertson's *History of Scotland*', *History of European Ideas*, 26:1 (2000), p. 20.

76 Robertson, *History of Scotland*, p. iii.

77 Neil Hargreaves, 'The "Progress of Ambition": Character, Narrative, and Philosophy in the Works of William Robertson', *Journal of the History of Ideas*, 63:2 (2002), p. 263.

78 Robertson, *History of Scotland*, p. iii.

79 Ibid., p. ii.

80 Robertson, *The History of America*, pp. vi–vii.

81 Ibid., pp. xv–xvi; Phillips, *Society and Sentiment*, p. 43.

82 O'Brien, *Narratives of Enlightenment*, p. 170.

83 Gibbon, *The History of the Decline and Fall of the Roman Empire. Vol. IV*, p. iii.
84 Pocock, *Barbarism and Religion. Vol. II. Narratives of Civil Government*, p. 399.
85 Pocock, *Barbarism and Religion. Vol. IV. Barbarians, Savages and Empire*, pp. 5–6, 181; O'Brien, *Narratives of Enlightenment*, p. 183.
86 David Hume to William Strahan, August 1770, in *The Letters of David Hume, Vol. II*, edited by J. Y. T. Grieg (Oxford: Clarendon Press, 1932), p. 230.
87 For an assessment of the complex meaning of Hume's statement, see Allan, 'Scottish Historical Writing of the Enlightenment', in Rabasa et al., *The Oxford History of Historical Writing: Vol. III*, p. 497. See also Mark G. Spencer, 'Introduction: Hume as Historian', in Spencer (ed.), *David Hume: Historical Thinker, Historical Writer* (University Park: Pennsylvania State University Press), p. 1.
88 Hume to Strahan, August 1770, in *The Letters of David Hume, Vol. II*, p. 231. Henry's *History of Great Britain from the Invasion of it by the Romans under Julius Caesar* was eventually published in 1771 by Thomas Cadell, one of Strahan's friends and business partners. For the role of publishers like Strahan and Cadell in promoting Enlightenment texts, see Richard B. Sher, *The Enlightenment and the Book: Scottish Authors and Their Publishers in Eighteenth-Century Britain, Ireland, and America* (Chicago: Chicago University Press, 2007).
89 Hume to Strahan, 30 January 1773, in *The Letters of David Hume, Vol. II*, p. 269.

2

Poetry: James Macpherson's History Writing in *The Highlander* and Ossian

> The extent of his design has been, to give Homer as he really is: And to endeavour, as much as possible, to make him speak English, with his own dignified simplicity and energy. How far he has succeeded, he leaves to the candour and judgement of the impartial Public: Who, he hopes, will not attribute either to self-sufficiency or vanity, what he only meant for explanation.[1]

Writing in the Preface to his 1773 translation of *The Iliad*, James Macpherson captured many of his ideas about the past, the use of sources, issues of authenticity, causation, poetry and translation.[2] This is a snapshot of his thinking in the early 1770s, but echoes more clearly his practice as a poet, translator, editor, compiler and historian during the previous decade or so. In *The Highlander* (1758) and the Ossianic Collections (1760–73), Macpherson grapples in these texts with historical source material, translation and authenticity, revealing a tension between his emerging appreciation of the principles of Enlightenment historiography and the proto-Romantic sentimental emphasis on feeling inspired across the world by Ossian in the second half of the eighteenth century.[3] In *The Highlander* and the Ossianic Collections, Macpherson's writing career begins seemingly as a poet. However, a close examination of the poetry of *The Highlander* and the paratextual material – the advertisements, prefaces and dissertations – of the Ossianic Collections, reveals that while he wrote in the mode of poetry and its translation, he did so from the perspective of an historian. The key Enlightenment historiographical issues that we identified in the previous chapter – how to reconcile historical narrative with philosophical explanation, while developing an erudite engagement with sources – feature to varying degrees in Macpherson's writings of the late 1750s and early 1760s. In *The Highlander*, he creates a narrative in verse that was based on historical source material, demonstrating an element of Macpherson's erudition, which he then used to make a Whig constitutional argument about Scotland's place in the British Empire. In the Ossianic Collections, Macpherson adds philosophy to this mix. The prose paratexts to the *Fragments of Ancient Poetry*, *Fingal* and *Temora* are self-consciously historiographical, where Macpherson comments on sources, their relationship to concepts of truth and authenticity, causation, the purpose of history and the stadial nature of the past. Through this approach, Macpherson creates a narrative of ancient Celtic history that seeks to reconcile the Gaelic world with the commercial modernity of the British imperial state.

The texts examined in this chapter demonstrate two quite distinct ways in which Macpherson functioned as an historian. In *The Highlander*, Macpherson versified historical sources – that is to say, he took historical source texts by John Fordun and George Buchanan and turned them into epic poetry. In the Ossianic Collections, Macpherson compiled, translated, edited and embellished texts and the oral tradition of the *Gàidhealtachd* – but he also contextualised them historiographically, using prefaces, dissertations and other paratextual apparatus to demonstrate his engagement with the latest thinking in Enlightenment history writing.[4] Macpherson's 'A Dissertation Concerning the Antiquity, &c. of the Poems of Ossian the Son of Fingal' functions as the crux between these two approaches. As a framing text for *Fingal* (1761/2), this dissertation reveals the tension between Macpherson's poetic impulse to be a storyteller (in terms of both his contemporary literary urges and from his understanding of the Gaelic oral tradition) and his desire to be an Enlightenment historian, following the methodological and theoretical approaches of his friends and mentors in Edinburgh, Hugh Blair and Adam Ferguson.

This chapter focuses on *The Highlander* and the Ossianic Collections, but with an emphasis in this second set of works on how Macpherson uses paratextual prefaces and dissertations, rather than an analysis of the Ossianic tales themselves. Of course, most scholarship on Macpherson focuses on these stories. While some attention in this field has been paid to how history functions in the Ossianic Collections, most scholars have dwelt on how Macpherson's versions of the Ossianic stories can be interpreted as commentary on Scottish and British political thought of the late 1750s and early 1760s.[5] Likewise, critical responses to *The Highlander* have, understandably, focused on how Macpherson's account of medieval Scottish history was a reflection of Whig constitutionalism.[6] However, little is said about how Macpherson engages with the past through historical sources in this epic verse poem. *The Highlander* is a form of historical narrative, in which Macpherson's fidelity to these historical sources demonstrates his Enlightenment credentials. In neoclassical verse about medieval Scotland, Macpherson promotes a vision of the eighteenth-century British imperial state that 'o'er the trembling nations lift her arms' and in which Scots and Highlanders could help fight the French in the great late 1750s crisis of empire – the Seven Years War.[7]

The chapter is divided into two parts, organised into sections on each of the texts (*The Highlander*; *The Fragments*; *Fingal*; *Temora*; *Poems of Ossian*). First, we focus on how Macpherson presents history in verse in *The Highlander*. Fordun's fourteenth-century *Chronicle* (*c*.1360) and Buchanan's sixteenth-century *Rerum Scoticarum Historia* (1582) are used by Macpherson as source material for his poetry, partly as a translation of these narratives into verse and partly as an adaptation where he adds an element of sentimental romance to these historical accounts. Crucially, with both approaches, Macpherson demonstrates his fidelity to the original Fordun and Buchanan texts, injecting an element of Enlightenment historiographical thinking into his creative process. In *The Highlander*, Macpherson also makes use of the past in his poetic verse. In evoking both the past and the interplay between past and present, Macpherson brings figures from history to life as actors in the tenth-century present of the poem and establishes Scotland as firmly part of British history in an early stadial version of 'Celtic Whiggism'. Macpherson's poem concentrates on both a Highland and Scottish identity, emphasising the civilised conduct of Highlanders in warfare (echoing elements of stadial theory) and also laying the foundation of Macpherson's argument that the Highlands and Scotland were both integral to the British imperial state. Second, we examine the Ossianic Collections, but with a focus on the prefaces and dissertations, instead of the poetry itself. In the Ossianic Collections, Macpherson was beginning to think in more explicit ways as an Enlightenment historian, using the ideas of Ferguson, Blair, Smith and (to a lesser extent) Hume to write about the Celtic past. In the paratextual advertisements, prefaces and dissertations, we focus on analysing Macpherson's methodology and historiographical practice. Here, Macpherson applies a type of stadial theory, akin to Adam Ferguson's stages of history, to a distinctly Enlightenment historiographical methodology, where sources and footnotes, authenticity and historical truth, historical causation, evaluating the evidence of sources, and the duty of history to amuse the reader are used to frame the Ossianic Collections. However, Macpherson's attempt to apply Enlightenment principles in the Ossianic Collections is constrained by the nature of the source material. Macpherson's Gaelic sources were taken from the oral tradition of the *Gàidhealtachd* and assembled using the collection practices of ethnography, rather than history.[8] Instead of consulting books and manuscripts in archives across Europe as he did in his later history writing, Macpherson collected material by travelling across the Highlands and Islands with a number of fellow Gaels, interviewing people and recording their Ossianic stories, and only occasionally consulting the odd manuscript where these stories had been written down.[9] This emphasises the liminal nature of both Macpherson and his practice as poet, collector, editor, translator and historian, certainly at this early point in this career. As a Gaelic-speaking Highlander, Macpherson was simultaneously immersed in both a culture of oral tradition and an education system that was sophisticated enough to regularly send ambitious boys (like Macpherson) to university.[10] He stood on the cusp of what Ranajit Guha has described as the wonder of poetry and the 'prose of history'. Guha reflects on how the 'ancient Indian concept of wonder' in oral tradition as a mode of representing the past was replaced by Hegel's conception of world-history and its focus on the state in the late eighteenth and early nineteenth centuries.[11] Here we see Macpherson grappling with these two different approaches to writing history, especially in the dissertation to *Fingal*. Macpherson's argument that the oral tradition of the ancient Highlands gave value to the region's history and culture was at odds with his claims to be writing in the mode of an Enlightenment historian. Furthermore, in *Temora*, Macpherson engages with Smith's use of classical historians as source material about the Celtic past, especially their emphasis on the importance of historical narrative. Yet, for Macpherson, Greek and Roman writing lacked the qualities of modern history, with its reliance on written evidence and source analysis. This tension between being a storyteller in the tradition of Gaelic oral poetry and using the theories and methodologies of Enlightenment historiography to contextualise these stories lies at the heart of this chapter, and it reveals much about the changing position of both Macpherson and the Gaelic world from which he came during this period. It reflects the liminal position of the *Gàidhealtachd* during the eighteenth century, in which the region could be said to have undergone a process of 'internal colonisation' at the hands of the British imperial state, while at the same time Highlanders from all social strata participated enthusiastically in the project of empire.[12] Macpherson was no exception to this, as we shall see in later chapters, from the early patronage of Lord Bute, through to his colonial service in West Florida, and his role as government propagandist in Lord North's administration. This world was opened to Macpherson through his contacts with the Edinburgh literati, from Ferguson to Blair and Hume – all enthusiastic Unionists and imperialists, whose Enlightenment ideas then had increasing influence on Macpherson's history writing.[13] Writing about Alexander Pope, Tom Jones has argued that Pope's engagement with Clarendon's *History of the Rebellion* demonstrates how his 'poems work as history writing' and how 'Pope's historiographic self-conception changes over the course of his career'.[14] Such an approach can also be applied to Macpherson's writing, especially when considering the historiographical tensions in the dissertation to *Fingal*, where the foundation is laid for the emergence of Macpherson the Enlightenment historian in his works of prose history examined in Chapters 3 and 4.

THE HIGHLANDER (1758)

Our analysis of Macpherson's history writing begins with *The Highlander*, his first book-length publication. Often overlooked by critics as an early work that bears little relation to his later writing, *The Highlander* does, in fact, establish Macpherson's approach to the past which then runs through the rest of his literary career. There are two key historiographical strands at work in *The Highlander*: a fidelity to historical sources in constructing this narrative about tenth-century Scotland; and an application of this writing about the past to the contemporary present, especially in the poem's emphasis on the unity and sovereignty of the British imperial state in the concluding Hermit's prophecy in Canto V.

It is likely that Macpherson wrote *The Highlander* while in Edinburgh during 1757 and 1758, after a stint as a schoolteacher at Ruthven in his native Badenoch.[15] He lived with Donald Macpherson and possibly attended lectures at the University of Edinburgh, and it was during that time that Macpherson began writing in earnest while working for Balfour the publisher.[16] Macpherson wrote for the monthly magazines from the mid-1750s, but this later period in Edinburgh saw him undertaking a much larger and more sustained poetical effort: *The Highlander*. Published anonymously in April 1758 by Walter Ruddiman Jr, only seven known copies of it now exist.[17] An advertisement in the 'New Books, Edinburgh' section of the *Scots Magazine* confirms this date.[18] The print run is unknown, and the only two recorded purchasers are Colin Campbell, customs officer at Fort William (whose copy Malcolm Laing obtained) and Isaac Reed, the editor and book collector (who inscribed the National Library of Scotland's copy).[19] The poem has been included in two editions of Macpherson's works: the *Poetical Works of James Macpherson* (1802) and Laing's *Poems of Ossian* (1805).[20] It is available in facsimile in two modern collections (as well as on *Eighteenth-Century Collections Online*): John MacQueen's 1971 reprint of Laing's edition, and Dafydd Moore's 2004 *Ossian and Ossianism*, also a reprint of Laing's edition.[21]

According to the 'Literary Anecdotes' in Ruddiman's *Weekly Magazine*, the poem 'had a very rapid sale', but we have no other evidence for this.[22] It has been claimed that Macpherson tried to suppress *The Highlander* after its publication, but this is likewise hearsay.[23] The 'Literary Anecdotes' mention is the only notice of the poem until Donald Macpherson's letter of 1797 regarding the Highland Society of London's enquiry into the origins of Macpherson's Ossian.[24] Laing insists that 'the Highlander fell still-born from the press', which, for him, is the reason why Macpherson 'transferred his pen from poetry, professedly original, to the more profitable task of translation from the Erse'.[25] He elaborates a little on the commercial failure of *The Highlander*: 'the miscarriage of his first Epic, the Highlander, was secretly ascribed to the envy and meanness which affect to despise contemporary genius', but unfortunately he gives no indication as to who regarded the poem in this way.[26]

The Highlander is, essentially, a reworking of historical events. It is set in the tenth century and tells of the battle between Scots and Vikings near Cullen on the Moray Firth in 962. Its main character is Alpin, a simple Highlander, who single-handedly defeats the Vikings. He falls in love with Princess Culena, the daughter of the Scottish king Indulph. Eventually it turns out that Alpin is, in fact, Duffus – Indulph's nephew, and the rightful heir to the throne. He marries Culena, Indulph dies, and Duffus is crowned King of Scotland.

Although presented as fiction – its full title is *The Highlander: A Poem* – the poem is more than a mere reworking of history. It is a translation of sources into a different genre and is historical in two ways: more obviously through its tenth-century setting, but also because the past is tangibly present throughout the poem. As such, its faithful adherence to facts accepted as historical and accurate by his contemporary audience raises questions of historicity, authenticity and the role of fiction. While Macpherson's emphasis on the title page that *The Highlander* was a mere 'poem' (not 'historical poem', or 'history') – together with his magazine publications – speaks to his ambitions to be a poet (thwarted by the Ossianic adventure, perhaps), we should not rely on his classification. As this chapter demonstrates, *The Highlander* is a verse history, with clearly traceable sources and a sustained historical framework that surrounds the action. Although Macpherson takes one important liberty – he adds a romance element to the plot – to appeal to contemporary tastes for sentimental fiction, this is far outweighed by his otherwise faithful translation of Fordun and Buchanan, and his sustained engagement with history throughout the poem.

The Highlander is an under-researched work, and the critics that have engaged with it have largely seen it as a predecessor of the Ossianic Collections, as evidence of either Macpherson's latent Jacobitism or his nascent British or Celtic Whiggism.[27] As such, scholars have traced it to the Fingal legends and the Magnus ballad and have only given cursory attention to its historical sources. This brings the poem closer to the Ossianic Collections and allows scholars to establish a connection that sees *The Highlander* mostly as a precursor to the Ossianic Collections. What makes the poem unusual, though, is not its shared Gaelic references, but instead its insistence on historical accuracy. Seen on its own – outwith the overbearing context of the Ossianic Collections – Macpherson's translation of actual history into neoclassic verse is singularly important. The poem is based almost entirely on clearly traceable material: with the exception of the love story involving Duffus and Culena the basic plot of *The Highlander* is taken from John Fordun's fourteenth-century *Chronicle* (of about 1360; it is, of course, the groundwork for Walter Bower's *Scotichronicon* (from the 1440s)) and from George Buchanan's sixteenth-century *Rerum Scoticarum Historia* (published in 1582). *The Highlander* is unusual amongst Scottish poetic works of the 1750s in that it is based on clearly traceable historic events, and not principally, like John Home's play *Douglas*, on a Gaelic ballad, or, like William Wilkie's poem *Epigoniad*, on the *Iliad* and other classical epic poems. It is, of course, also influenced by epic poetry and shares some traits with Gaelic ballads – indeed, it has been argued that it is inspired by the same ballad that *Douglas* is based on, if not based on *Douglas* itself.[28] But it is Macpherson's historic awareness and fidelity to historical source material that singles it out from other, more commercially successful, works. It thus provides a clear link to Macpherson's broader interests and preoccupations: using history writing to reframe Scotland's heroic past in British imperial terms.

The poem's plot centres around the Danish invasion of Scotland and Northern England, which had begun almost a century before the events of *The Highlander*.[29] It is the story of King Ildulb, a son of Constantín son of Áed, who was probably killed in 962 in the North East after reigning for eight years.[30] Macpherson borrows this story and makes the next king, Dub, the son of Mal Coluim, its hero. Macpherson here conflates events somewhat: Dub is not actually mentioned in the chronicles as having taken part in the episode that forms the plot of *The Highlander*. While this could be read as essentially a deviation from history, with Macpherson taking great liberties with facts in a way that anticipates his amalgamation of existent Gaelic material with his own composition in the Ossianic Collections, this interpretation oversimplifies Macpherson's engagement with the past in *The Highlander*.[31] Like his embellishing of the plot with episodes from epic poetry and romance, such as the games in Canto IV and the hero rescuing the 'damsel in distress' in the same Canto, or the convenient transformation of Cuilén, Ildulb's son, into Culena, Indulph's daughter, the integration of Ildulb's story with Dub's shows Macpherson working as an historian, but with an eye on plot, tension and a keen understanding of epic poetry. Indeed, he manipulates facts to stay firmly grounded in history. Duffus's obscure upbringing as Alpin, Rynold's son, might come from the Fiann legends, but the complex system of succession explains why – historically as well as in the poem – Duffus had to succeed as the next king.[32] Similarly, Culena is a suitable partner for Duffus but no threat to the historically accurate line of succession.

The decision to use established historical narratives as source material for *The Highlander* demonstrates Macpherson's emerging credentials as an historian. Macpherson uses two key texts: John Fordun's *Chronica Gentis Scotorum* (c.1360), the precursor of Bower's *Scotichronicon* (1440s) and George Buchanan's *Rerum Scoticarum Historia* (1582), available to Macpherson when he was a student at King's College and Marischal College in Aberdeen between 1753 and 1756, and also in Edinburgh. Both were reprinted in the eighteenth century: an edition of the *Scotichronicon* was published in Oxford in 1722 and in Edinburgh in 1749, and Buchanan's *History of Scotland* was reprinted in English in London in 1734 and in Edinburgh in 1751, and in Latin in Edinburgh in 1727. The *Chronicle of the Kings of Alba* on the other hand, was not in print until W. F. Skene's edition in 1867, so we can safely disregard it as a possible source for *The Highlander*.[33]

John Fordun's *Chronicle* is generally credited as the first attempt to write a continuous history of Scotland. Macpherson himself mentions that he is familiar with Fordun's *Chronicle* in the Preface to *Temora* (1763). Fordun's 'fragments of Scottish history ... deserved credit', in Macpherson's estimation, although he describes him as being overly reliant on Irish sources, leading to 'those improbable fictions, which form the first part of his history'.[34] Despite his later reservations, Macpherson draws heavily upon Fordun in *The Highlander*, both in terms of historical narrative and more specific language and ideas. Fordun's entry for Ildulb's reign (in Skene's 1872 translation) details the following:

> At length, while they happened, one day, to be scattered by companies, laying the country waste near a place called Collyn, the king stationed an ambuscade under cover, not far from the coast; for he happened, by mere chance, to be there at that time, with a few followers — but would that he had not been!

So while the spoilers were roving about, scattered by companies throughout the fields and towns, he rushed impetuously upon them with shouts, slew a great number, and forced the rest to have recourse to flight. Finally he, high-spirited as he was, having unfortunately thrown away his weapons, so that he might pursue the runaways more swiftly, was struck in the head by a dart out of one of the ships, and died that same night.[35]

Some of the basic plot details are there: the Viking invasion, the Scots' response to it, and Indulph's death by arrow. But, more importantly, Macpherson also takes specific phrases and adapts them into *The Highlander*. For example, 'the king stationed an ambuscade under cover, not far from the coast' becomes

> The full form'd columns, in the midnight hour,
> Begin their silent journey tow'rds the shore (I, 147–8)
> Within the womb of night,
> Confirm the troops, and arm the youth for fight (I, 166–7)[36]

Similarly, 'he rushed impetuously upon them with shouts, slew a great number, and forced the rest to have recourse to flight' turns into

> Onward they rush, and in a shout engage.
> Two swords thro' air their gleaming journeys fly,
> Crash on the helms and tremble in the sky.
> Groan follows groan, and wound succeeds on wound,
> While dying bodies quiver on the ground (II, 104–8)

> The Danes beholding their commander die,
> Start from their ranks, and in confusion fly (II, 254–5)

Finally, 'was struck in the head by a dart out of one of the ships, and died that same night' is adapted into

> Thus godlike Harold brought his floating aid
> [...]
> An arrow tore thro' air its murm'ring path,
> Fell on the king and weigh'd him down to death (VI, 165; 175–6)

As we can see, Macpherson directly translates Fordun's description into eighteenth-century neoclassic verse. As such, not only does *The Highlander* preserve most of the historical 'plot' that Fordun notes, but Macpherson is careful to retain Fordun's detailed observations in the poem.

Buchanan's account is far more comprehensive than Fordun's and Macpherson is careful to include these details in *The Highlander*.

POETRY: *THE HIGHLANDER* AND OSSIAN

He mentions a number of aspects of the historical narrative that Fordun lacks, but that Macpherson evidently included in the poem. Buchanan's entry (in Bond's 1722 translation) records:

> When Indulfus heard of their landing, he marched towards them, before they could well have any Notice of his coming; and first he set upon the straggling Plunderers, and drove them to the rest of their Army, but made no great Slaughter of them, because the Camp of the Danes was near, to which they might make their Retreat. When the Armies came in sight of each other, they both drew up in Battel array, and fell to it with equal Force and Courage: Whilst they were thus fiercely fighting, Grame and Dumbar, with some Troops of Lothian-Men, appeared on the Rear of the Danes; which put them in such a Pannick, that they all run away, some to their Ships, others to unknown Places, whithersoever the Fear of the Enemy drove them: But the greater part of them drew up in the Form of a Circle, in a woody Vale, and there waited an occasion in acting with Valour or dying with the last Resolution. Indulfus, as if his Enemies had been wholly overcome, rode up and down with a few Attendants, and casually lighting into their Hands, was slain, at the beginning of the tenth Year of his Reign. Some say he was kill'd by an Arrow, shot out of a Ship, having disarmed himself, that he might be more nimble in the Pursuit, and press the more eagerly upon them, as they were going a Shipboard.[37]

In *The Highlander* there are also battles before the main battle, stragglers faced away from the group, a Danish camp nearby, and an emphasis on the equality of the Scots and Danes. In the poem Indulph is also slain when he least expects it. No mention is made of Alpin or Duffus in the description of the battle, but he is, of course, listed as the next king after Indulph: 'after his Death, Duffus, the Son of Malcolm, got the Kingdom'.[38]

Like the examples above, Macpherson directly versifies extracts from Buchanan's account. For example, 'When the Armies came in sight of each other, they both drew up in Battel array, and fell to it with equal Force and Courage' becomes

> On either side, thus stretch'd the manly line,
> With darting gleam the steel-clad ridges shine:
> On either side the gloomy lines incede,
> Foot rose with foot, and head advanc'd with head.
> [...]
> Thus march the Danes with spreading wings afar,
> Thus moves the horror of the Scottish war;
> [...]
> On either side, devour'd the narrow ground
> The moving troops.

> [...]
> As yet the battle hung in doubtful scales;
> Each bravely fought, in death or only fails.
> [...]
> The Scots, a Stream, wou'd sweep the Danes away,
> The Danes, a Rock, repell'd the Scots' array.
> They fight alternate, and alternate fly.
> Both wound, both conquer, both with glory die (II, 77–80; 87–8; 99–100; 119–20; 127–30)

Buchanan's precise description of the climax of the battle, when 'the greater part of them drew up in the Form of a Circle, in a woody Vale, and there waited an occasion in acting with Valour or dying with the last Resolution', also appears in *The Highlander*:

> [Haco] winds his hasty march along the coast,
> Fights as he flies, and shields his little host.
> At length, within a wood o'ershades the sea,
> With new fell'd oaks he walls his thin array:
> Bent on his fate, and obstinately brave,
> There mark'd at once his battle-field and grave (II, 312–17)
>
> All, all are bent on death or victory,
> Resolv'd to conquer, or with glory die (II, 121–2)

Macpherson also includes the warriors that Buchanan mentions: 'Grame and Dumbar, with some Troops of Lothian-Men, appeared on the Rear of the Danes' turns into

> Brave Grahame thro' mighty Canute urg'd the spear,
> Where, 'twixt the helm and mail, the neck was bar (II, 272–3)
>
> The great Dumbar upon the right repell'd
> Young Haco's force, and swept him off the field (II, 310–11)

Hago – together with Helricus one of the two 'Admirals of the Fleet' in Buchanan's account – becomes the main Danish character in the poem:

> At length the Hero's dusky journey ends,
> Where Haco feasted with his Danish friends;
> Haco, by more than Sueno's blood was great;
> The promis'd monarch to the triple state (I, 201–4)

As we can see, Macpherson again translates his source directly into the poem. However, Macpherson necessarily conjectures the detail with which he populates his verse. *The Highlander* is composed in six cantos, totalling 1,798 lines, while its sources are fairly short. The poem, then, is part direct translation, and part adaptation of traditional histories into a different genre; an adaptation that necessarily changes some of the 'plot' details for dramatic reasons and adds a sentimental layer to the factual chronicling of the historical accounts.

The most noticeable change Macpherson makes is the choice of Duffus as the hero of the poem. In the chronicles Dub was not involved in Ildulb's campaign against the Danes, and he was not present at his death. Neither was he brought up in obscurity; during Ildulb's reign Dub was Lord of Cumbria (or the Kingdom of Strathclyde). Neither was he Ildulb's nephew, nor the direct heir to the throne.

Duffus is not the only character with which Macpherson takes poetic liberties in the adaptation from historical source to poem. Culena, Indulf's daughter and Duffus's bride, is based on Cuilén, Ildulb's son. Not much is known about the historical Cuilén, other than that he became King of Alba after Dub's death. He was, according to Fordun, 'useless and slack in the government of the Kingdom; and nothing kingly or worthy of remembrance was done in his days' (I.161). Macpherson

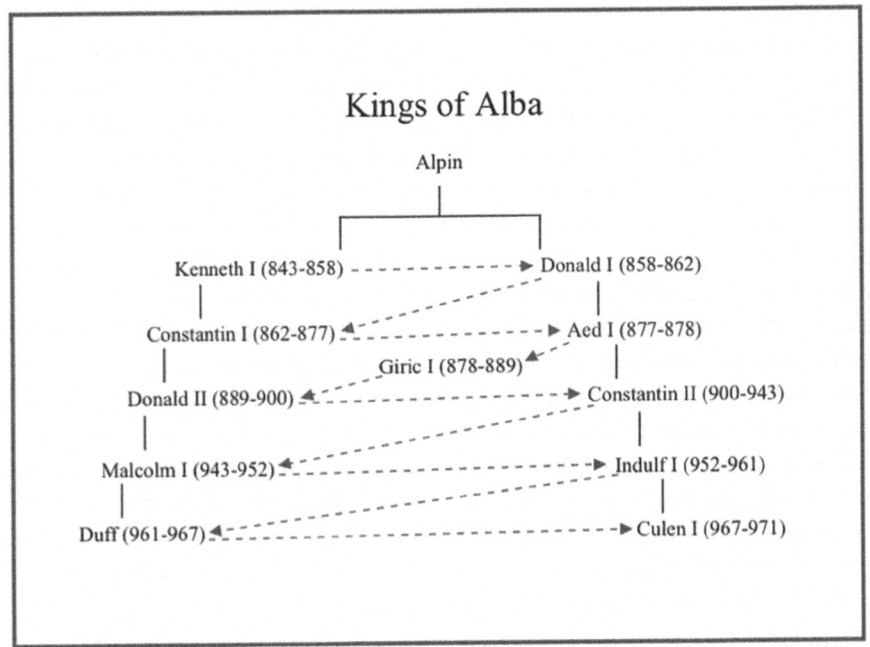

Figure 2.1 Diagram showing the line of succession in ninth- and tenth-century Scotland. © Kristin Lindfield-Ott, 2011.

took just the name, not the character traits of Cuilén, when he created Culena; she is graceful, virtuous, modest and, above all, fair. Through her royal birth Culena is, of course, a suitable match for Duffus, and by joining her with Duffus Macpherson not only ensures the fulfilment of the hermit's prophecy from an earlier canto, but also manages to retain the historically accurate line of royal succession without compromising either plausibility or the poem's happy end. While Cuilén, the historical figure, and Culena, the character in the poem, have no more in common than their name and parentage, the use of Cuilén in *The Highlander* is significant as a further indicator of Macpherson's engagement with history and sources. He could have easily invented a female character to suit his love interest, but instead chose to adapt Cuilén, whose authenticity is warranted by the chronicles. Macpherson does not *alter* the events depicted in the chronicles. He adapts the characters; occasionally, as in Culena's case, retaining no more than a common name, but he is faithful to the episodes depicted in the chronicles. Here, Macpherson reflects both Hugh Blair's concern with fidelity to sources and David Hume's interest in sentimental history writing, demonstrating that even when he was writing as a poet, he was thinking about Enlightenment historiography.[39]

Macpherson's adaptation and versification of the historical narratives of Fordun and Buchanan in *The Highlander* demonstrate his desire to be a poet historian, shaped by the aesthetic and philosophical considerations of the mid-eighteenth century. David Hall Radcliffe has observed that 'if his poems lack the consistency expected from historical documents [...] Macpherson achieves the coherent design expected from probable romantic fiction'.[40] Unlike the Ossianic Collections, *The Highlander* is foremost a history in verse, with only a few sentimental elements. Its very genre – epic – is symptomatic of this: while both the Ossianic Collections and *The Highlander* have been interpreted as an attempt to formulate, or recover, *the* Scottish epic, the Ossianic Collections have been successfully reinterpreted as romance. *The Highlander*, though, is an epic that was more historical than antiquarian: its sentimental concessions, as Gerard Carruthers observes about the Ossianic Collections, are due to the period's need for 'antique subject-matter collid[ing] with the predilections of the age of sensibility'.[41] Dafydd Moore has pointed out the treatment of vanquished foes in the Ossianic Collections as a symptom of this sensibility – something that can easily be extended to the earlier *Highlander*, as Duffus also refuses to take advantage of his enemy, Haco, throughout the poem.[42] Of course, *The Highlander*, with its neoclassic form and emotional hero, is far removed from the grandeur and sublimity of the Ossianic Collections. Yet, like the Ossianic Collections (and, Carruthers would argue, like most Scottish literature of the age), *The Highlander* adapts older material and presents an idea of Scotland both ancient and contemporary.

History is also very tangible in *The Highlander*: the past is constantly evoked. This allows Macpherson to establish contemporary Scotland as steeped in British history: the Scottishness of the poem is not a threat to Union, but a celebration of it that demonstrates the role of Scotland and the Highlands in the British imperial state during the militia crisis of the late 1750s. *The Highlander* is very much a Scottish work: set in ancient 'Caledonia', and of course written by a Scottish author. Unlike other works of the period, however, the poem is Scottish through and through: plaids, bagpipes and Scottish steel are more than simple colouring here. Unlike Home's *Douglas*, for example, which is set mainly in and near a castle – and not a particularly Scottish one at that – and which only mentions rugged mountains and violent streams in passing, the action of *The Highlander* takes place, identifiably, both in the Highlands and in the Lowlands, as well as in the 'dome of state' (I. 34) – a Scottish hall of fame, a decidedly Scottish 'senate' (I. 27). The senate, we are told, meets in a 'city' which the Scandinavians 'prepar'd, at once [...] to invade' (I. 21), in order to 'conquer Caledonia in [its] head' (I. 22). The implication here is twofold: that the city, home of the senate and King Indulph, is naturally the prime target for the invading Danes, but also that the city, merely by virtue of being a city, is the head of the country. The phrasing 'in her head' encourages the latter reading: to conquer Scotland in its head implies the elevation of city over country, Lowlands over Highlands, Enlightenment over primitivism, in a Whig and stadial reading of the Scottish past.

History is deeply ingrained in the poem. Not only is it a historical poem – datable, due to its historic characters and sources, to the later tenth century – but within the poem history is ever-present. When Duffus and his men reach King Indulph's 'dome of state' in Canto I, Macpherson treats us to a 'best-of' Scottish history:

On either side the gate, in order stand
The antient kings of Caledonia's land.
The marble lives, they breathe within the stone,
And still, as once, the royal warriors frown.
　　The Fergus's are seen above the gate;
This first created, that restor'd the state.
In warlike pomp, the awful forms appear,
And, bending, threaten from the stone the spear;
While to their side young Albion seems to rise,
And on her fathers turns her smiling eyes.

> And next appears Gregorius' awful name,
> Hibernia's conqu'ror for a gen'rous fame.
> Incass'd in arms, the royal hero stands,
> And gives his captive all his conquer'd lands.
> The filial heart of hapless Alpin's son,
> In marble melts and beats within the stone.
> Revenge still sparkles in the hero's eye;
> Around the Picts, a nameless slaughter, lye. (I. 39–56)

Macpherson presents these statues as active characters – they 'stand' (l. 39), welcoming the warriors to the senate. Indeed, they are only identified as inanimate in the next couplet, when the narrator emphasises that they are, in fact, statues, and not additional characters: 'the marble lives, they breathe within the stone, / And still, as once, the royal warriors frown' (I. 41–2). Importantly, however, the statues take on an active role here, too – like actual characters they live, breathe and frown. In addition, the named individuals, 'seen above the gate' (I. 43), the two Ferguses and Gregorius, are also living history, 'threaten[ing] from the stone the spear' (I. 46), as is Kenneth MacAlpin: 'the filial heart of hapless Alpin's son, / In marble melts and beats within the stone' (I. 53–4). Finally, 'young Albion', the spirit of Caledonia and also one of the statues, 'seems to rise, / And on her fathers turns her smiling eyes' (I. 47–8). This passage illustrates Macpherson's engagement with history through more than just the setting. *The Highlander* is a historical poem – not only because it is set in the past, like later historical novels, but because there is a constant interplay between past and present even within the tenth-century present of the poem.

There are other instances in the poem when our heroes' ancestors are figuratively brought to life. In Canto III, for example, Indulph rallies his troops with a rousing speech, in which he references the connection between present warrior and the past: 'in vain Death wrapt our fathers in his gloom, / We raise them, in our actions, from the tomb' (III. 31–2). Similarly, in Canto IV Indulph distributes the weapons of the 'fathers' as prizes during the games episode. The ancient heroes thus survive in the present of the poem; much like the statues in Canto I the warriors of the past continue to interact with those of the present. The implication here is, of course, that the present warriors also have this sort of impact on the future – down to Macpherson's contemporary present. Here we see Macpherson framing his Enlightenment historical narrative, rooted in his fidelity to historical sources, with older, Gaelic-world notions of genealogy and ancestry. For Macpherson and his fellow Gaels, the ancestors were always with them, using their ghostly influence in shaping the present.[43]

Throughout the poem history is thus tangibly present: the Scotland presented here is steeped in it, with its historically authenticated characters affecting not just the poem but, ultimately, the Scotland of the 1750s.

Apart from the historicalness of the poem, *The Highlander* also demonstrates Macpherson's attitude towards the British imperial state. While it is first and foremost a Scottish poem – set in Scotland, with a Scottish author, Scottish heroes and based on Scottish sources – the poem is, in fact, an exploration of a British identity that, instead of negating the legitimacy of its constituent part at the expense of English colonialism, celebrates Scottishness *as* British, thereby making a claim for Highland involvement in the project of empire.

There is no intimation in *The Highlander* that Scotland is seen as either superior or inferior to England. Indeed, while there is an early reference that 'England's subdu'd, the Saxons are o'ercome, / and meanly own a Danish lord at home. / Scarce now a blast from Scandinavia roars, / But wafts a hostile squadron to our shores' (I. 119–22), this merely contextualises the setting of the poem, both in terms of time and space. Moreover, instead of developing this contrast between defeated 'Saxons' and free Scots further, Macpherson draws attention to the inevitability of war, in the close of Indulph's speech a few lines later: 'thus war returns in an eternal round, / Battles on battles press, and wound on wound' (I. 125–6). Ultimately, thus, the focus here is on similarities, and not on differences; war is inexorable. Indeed, throughout the poem Macpherson carefully avoids comparisons between England and Scotland, and focuses instead on Romans and Danes. When we first meet Indulph he reminds his warriors that their 'sire brought oft the Roman Eagles down', while they themselves 'have caus'd the haughty Dane, / To curse the land, he try'd so oft in vain' (I. 94–6). The Danes, of course, are the enemy in the poem (as they are in the Ossianic Collections), and Indulph demands that 'whoe'er would raise his house in Albion, shou'd / Lay the foundation in her en'mies blood' (I. 91–2). His followers are eager to comply: Duffus, representative of the nation's youth

> ... 'midst rocks afar,
> heard of Denmark, and of Sueno's war.
> My country's safety in my bosom rose;
> For Caledonia's sons should meet her foes.
> We ought not meanly wait the storm at home,
> But rush afar, and break it 'ere it come. (I. 79–84)

Although this passage could be read as a reference to Macpherson's latent Jacobitism, with the recent uprising and the Jacobite army's march to Derby in November and December 1745 as another instance of the Scots eagerly meeting their foes afar, Macpherson here, as elsewhere, emphasises the Scots' justification for fighting: their country's safety. This is echoed in the rousing finish of Duffus's speech: 'we come to serve our country, fame, and you!' (I. 86). Every Scot is 'at once his country's soldier and her son', with 'the patriot kindling in each gen'rous breast'. (I.106, 108).[44] The Scottish militia crisis of the late 1750s provides the resonant context for Macpherson's verse here and echoes the demands of Adam Ferguson and other leading Enlightenment figures for a citizens' army that would stabilise the British imperial state and contribute to the defence of the nation against the threat of France.[45] Towards the end of this section the focus returns to the enemy at hand, again emphasising the conscious absence of England, and English foes: 'in thought each Hero sweeps the bloody plain, / And deals, in fancy, death upon the Dane' (I. 111–12). *The Highlander*, then, focuses on common enemies, rather than internal division and on the prospect of 'Caledonia's sons' contributing militarily to the work of empire and colonisation abroad.

Similarly, Canto II presents the Scots' attention divided between sport and battle: 'now fought for food, and now for liberty: / Now met the sport of hills, now of the main, / Here pierc'd a stag, and there transfix'd a Dane' (II. 34–6). Although they prefer the play (and humble peasant life) of peacetime, they unequivocally come to their country's aid when needed: 'tho' nature's walls their homely huts inclose, / To guard their homely huts tho' mountains rose; / Yet feeling Albion in their breasts, they dare / From rocks to rush and meet the distant war' (II. 37–40). It is important to note the use of 'dare' here; the Scots do not want or need to rush to war, but instead courageously venture forth for the sake of liberty and national honour. The Danes, on the other hand, relish the challenge: 'haughty, he [Magnus] moves, and catching flame from far, / Looks tow'rds the Scots, anticipates the war; / Feels cruel joys in all his fibres rise, / And gathers all his fury to his eyes' (II. 65–8). These 'cruel joys' are noticeably absent from the Scottish side. In fact, the preference for homely pursuits extends to battle: 'not infamous their aim, o'er lands afar / To spread destruction and the plague of war; / To meet the sons of battle as they roam, / Content to ward them from their native home' (III. 33–6). Indeed, Macpherson later refers to the sport of the hills as 'mountain-war' (VI. 4). Paul deGategno reads the poem differently: he argues that in *The Highlander* Macpherson 'paints an entire nation as war-mad'.[46] However, while primarily engaged in war during the poem, the Scots are nonetheless portrayed as peaceful and honourable. In *The Highlander* war is a defensive act; there is no room for Jacobite antics in the contemporary world of the Seven Years War against the French. Moreover, Macpherson's emphasis on the noble conduct of the Scots in war reflected his friend Adam Ferguson's views about the civilising properties of military service. Fiona Stafford has argued that Ferguson's influence on Macpherson's poetry was at its height during the period in 1760–1 when Macpherson was composing *Fingal*. This connects the Ossianic Collections with Ferguson's campaign for a Scottish militia later during the Seven Years War.[47] However, as Fredrik Albritton Jonsson indicates, Ferguson had been promoting the need for a Scottish militia from the outset of the conflict in 1756, the same year that he published his pamphlet *Reflections Previous to the Establishment of a Militia*.[48] Here, in *The Highlander*, we see Macpherson framing historical Scots of the tenth century in such a way that they would have appeared to contemporaries as noble, civilised military men who should be allowed to contribute to the war effort against the French.

Macpherson's promotion of a civilised Scottish martial spirit is echoed throughout *The Highlander*. In Canto IV, for example, the senate discusses future defence tactics:

> No high-flown zeal the patriot hurl'd along,
> No secret gold engag'd the speaker's tongue.
> No jarring seeds are by a tyrant sown,
> Nor cunning senate undermines the throne.
> To public good their public thoughts repair,
> And Caledonia is the gen'ral care. (IV. 132–7)

This is followed by the symbolic presentation of Dumbar's sword to Duffus. The 'great Dumbar', who had once fought on Duffus's father's side, when 'beneath the royal banner, Scots afar / Had urg'd on Humber's banks the foreign war' (IV. 150–1), ceremoniously bestows his sword on Duffus, thus emphasising the turning-away from the old, belligerent ways to Duffus's modern peaceful ways. And, on a more prosaic level, this scene is followed by games, not battle, to reinforce this idea. As mentioned above, the ancient Caledonian heroes are recalled during the games, urging the reader into a similar comparison to that between Dumbar's deeds of old and Duffus's modern Caledonia: the 'antique bow' won by 'great Fergus' when fighting the Romans goes to the most skilful archer, and 'mighty Kenneth's' buckler to the best spear-thrower.

This reluctance to precipitate war is mirrored in the odd friendship that develops between Duffus and Haco, and is emblematic of the aforementioned sentimentalism of the poem. Duffus in particular is singled out as compassionate: throughout the poem he displays unexpected sympathy towards Haco; twice he has the opportunity to kill him in nocturnal duels, and both times he is overcome by sentiments. The first time he 'scorn'd to take advantage of the foe' (I. 238), he is rewarded by Haco's respect and, more materially, Haco's shield so that they can evade one another in the coming battle. The second time, in Canto III, Duffus is moved by Haco's feelings for his bride, Aurelia, who followed Haco to the battle. When Duffus realises that the lovers are torn between love for one another and love for their country he immediately ceases the attack: 'it touch'd his feeling breast, / He stopt the war' (III. 295–6). This is the second time in the poem that Duffus had the chance to kill Haco but chooses not to, and it emphasises his gentle nobility and thoughtful sentimentality. Kenneth Simpson has identified 'the voice of feeling' as the only one in Macpherson's writings; unlike other Scottish authors Macpherson's poetry 'reveals no [...] diversity'.[49] However, in this instance it is more than sentimentality; this time, Duffus's decision does not just concern Haco and himself, but also the other warriors on either side. As for the Scots, Duffus explains, 'our Caledonia, now reliev'd of fear, / Feels pity rising in the place of care' (III. 297–8). Once again, the Scots are here shown to be peace-loving rather than belligerent, defending their country rather than attacking. Because the sentimentality is extended to all Scots, Macpherson is able to translate the valour and courage of the Scots suggested by Buchanan into this, an eighteenth-century version of those terms.

Duffus himself provides yet another example of the poem's emphasis on peace. When Duffus relates his early life at the end of Canto IV he apologises to the senate that he was but 'brought up in mountains, and from councils far, / I am a novice in the art of war' (I. 165–6). Highlanders, it seems, are not traditionally belligerent in the world of *The Highlander*; their patriotic sentiment carries them through when their experience is limited to sport and farming. Indeed, at the end of Canto IV Indulph assures Duffus and the other warriors that their deeds matter more than their reputation: 'nobler the youth, who, tho' before unknown, / From merit mounts to virtue and renown, / Than he, set up by an illustrious race, / Totters aloft, and scarce can keep his place' (IV. 300–3). Success in battle is more important than experience; family lines are negligible. Indeed, here we can see a clear example of how a Jacobite reading of Macpherson is problematic; instead of nourishing latent Jacobite tendencies, as has been claimed by some critics, Macpherson here supports quite the opposite, and a Jacobite reading of *The Highlander* is, at best, awkward. This is especially compelling when we compare it to the following lines from the beginning of Canto V that echo the aftermath of the 1745 rising. Duffus relates a previous battle, where the warriors were faced with fighting while their homes and families were destroyed or forced to flee: 'this breathes his life thro' the impurpled wound, / While his proud villa smokes along the ground. / That with the foe maintains unequal strife, / While his dear offspring fly, and dearer wife' (V. 25–8). The repeated use of distinct landmarks in this section, such as the River Tay, emphasises this: the Scots are defending themselves, and not attacking on foreign soil; Duffus, and the new Scotland, still choose peace over war.

The single most important part of the poem is the Hermit's prophecy in Canto V. It brings together the poem's historicity with a confirmation of its British and imperial outlook, and it is also the most pronounced argument for peace. Indeed, unlike the rest of the poem, Canto V represents a sustained 'political vision' in which 'the task of seeing the future is allotted to an unnamed hermit' reminiscent of Thomson and Mallet's hermit in their masque *Alfred* (1740).[50] While Kersey reads this section of *The Highlander* as an example of Macpherson's belief in a Bolingbrokean ancient Whig constitutionalism, it also reveals much about Macpherson's understanding of British identities. Here, Duffus tells Indulph about the time just before the beginning of the poem, when his father Rynold died in battle and sent him to the hermit to learn about his destiny:

> They long escape, but yet the wicked die.
> With distant time, O youth! my soul's imprest;
> Futurity is lab'ring in my breast:
> Thy blood, which rolling down from Fergus came,
> Passes thro' time, a pure untainted stream.
> Albion shall in her pristine glory shine,
> And, blest herself, bless the Fergusian line.
>   'But ah! I see grim treason rear its head,
> Pale Albion trembling, and her monarch dead;
> The tyrant wields his scepter 'smear'd with blood;
> O base return! but still great heav'n is good:
> He falls, he falls: see how the tyrant lies!
> And Scotland brightens up her weeping eyes:
> The banish'd race, again, resume their own;
> Nor Syria boasts her royal saint alone.
> Its gloomy front the low'ring season clears,
> And gently rolls a happy round of years.
>   'Again I see contending chiefs come on,
> And, as they strive to mount, they tear the throne;
> To civil arms the horrid trumpet calls,
> And Caledonia by her children falls.
> The storm subsides to the calm flood of peace;

> The throne returns to Fergus' antient race.
> Glad Caledonia owns their lawful sway;
> Happy in them, in her unhappy they!
> See each inwrapt untimely in his shroud,
> For ever sleeping in his gen'rous blood!
> Who on thy mournful tomb refrains the tear?
> O regal charms, unfortunately fair!
> Dark Faction grasps her in his sable arms,
> And crushes down to death her struggling charms:
> The rose, in all its gaudy liv'ry drest,
> Thus faintly struggles with the blust'ring west. (V. 139–74)

The hermit instantaneously creates a bond between past, present and future: he addresses Duffus (in the present of the poem) as 'thy blood, which rolling down from Fergus came, / Passes thro' time, a pure untainted stream. / Albion shall in her pristine glory shine, / And, bless herself, bless the Fergusian line' (V. 145–8). The reference to Fergus provides the past context, while the prediction for Albion points to the future.

As Kersey has argued, 'the Hermit's vision picks up the narrative of Scotland's mythical history where Buchanan's *Rerum Scoticarum Historia* (1582) had stopped'.[51] He proceeds to outline that narrative, linking the hermit's predictions to historic events. Yet *The Highlander* is far from mythical. Buchanan's ancient history might well be speculation but compared to the ancient 'history' presented in the Ossianic Collections it is very much steeped in tangible historical facts. This is emphasised by the fact that the hermit's predictions are all true. The hermit alludes to Charles I's execution ('pale Albion trembling, and her monarch dead' (V. 150)); Charles was, after all, the first 'British' monarch in the sense that he ruled over both kingdoms (though not over a United one) from the beginning of his reign. He was also, of course, a Stuart – and thus a Scottish – king. Indeed, 'Albion', which throughout the earlier parts of the poem was used as synonymous with 'Caledonia' and 'Scotland', takes on a wider British meaning here. The 'tyrant' who 'wields his scepter 'smear'd with blood' (V. 151) is Cromwell, and 'the banish'd race' that 'again, resume their own' (V. 155) is the Stuarts, through Charles II, who reigns, it seems, for 'a happy round of years' (V. 158). Syria's royal saint (V. 156) is Andrew of Crete (*c.* 650–74), a saint in the Eastern Orthodox – that is, Syriac – Church, who of course shares his name with Andrew the Disciple, the patron saint of Scotland. Then, as Kersey points out, the hermit alludes to the 'Glorious Revolution' (1688–9), when the hermit 'see[s] contending chiefs come on, / And, as they strive to mount, they tear the throne; / To civil arms the horrid trumpet calls, / And [most importantly] Caledonia by her children falls' (V. 159–62).⁵² Macpherson is a little vague about William and Mary: 'the storm subsides to the calm flood of peace; / The throne returns to Fergus' antient race' (V. 163–4). This likely refers to them, but the next section is less clear: 'Glad Caledonia owns their lawful sway; / Happy in them, in her unhappy they! / See each inwrapt untimely in his shroud, / For ever sleeping in his gen'rous blood! / Who on thy mournful tomb refrains the tear?' This could be interpreted in different ways: it might – as in Kersey's reading – refer to William and Mary, in which case 'they' are the rulers, and 'her' is Caledonia.⁵³ Or it could refer to the Jacobites – they, the exiled Stuarts; her, Caledonia. But a third reading, hinted at by Kersey but not fully explored, seems more probable: these lines suit Queen Anne much better – monarch of the Union of 1707. Indeed, 'glad Caledonia owns their [that is, the Stuarts'] lawful sway; / Happy in them, in **her** [that is, Anne] unhappy they!' (V. 165–6). They are unhappy because, as the next line says, 'See each inwrapt untimely in his shroud' (V. 167) – all her children died young, and she was the last Stuart monarch.⁵⁴ The detail in this passage combines to add authenticity to the poem: the historical accuracy – from the future to the present of the poem; and from (recent) past to Macpherson's contemporary readership – emphasises, yet again, Macpherson's engagement with history, whatever genre he is writing in.

The close of the hermit's vision celebrates a British imperial identity. It also negates the possibility of Jacobitism in Macpherson's United, and unified, Kingdom. The prophecy runs as follows:

> Why mention him in whom th'eternal fates
> Shall bind in peace the long-discording states?
> See Scot and Saxon coalesc'd in one,
> Support the glory of the common crown.
> Britain no more shall shake with native storms,
> But o'er the trembling nations lift her arms. (V. 175–80)

Despite the obvious importance of these lines for our understanding of Macpherson's politics, critics have been reluctant to engage with *The Highlander*. Kersey, one of the few scholars to do so, rightly reads these lines as 'complicat[ing] any reading of Macpherson as a Jacobite' because Jacobitism has 'no future in Macpherson's vision of a unified 'Britain".⁵⁵ However, Kersey reads the rhetorical question as separate from the rest of the passage. The narrator's reluctance to mention 'him' by more than this cryptic couplet is, for Kersey, a clear allusion to Charles Edward Stuart: 'the Pretender is finished: "Why mention him" in a nation in which "Scot and Saxon" are happily mixed, or "coalesced in one"?'⁵⁶ However, this is too simplistic: the use of 'shall' here implies a more future-oriented meaning: 'him in whom th'eternal fates shall bind in peace the long-discording states' – in other words, he who brings peace to a united Britain – is George II, and not Charles Edward Stuart. It is under George II's 'common crown' that 'Scot and Saxon' are finally – after the '45 rising – 'coalesc'd in one', and under his rule that 'Britain no more shall shake with native storms, but o'er the trembling nations lift her arms'.[57] Indeed, this imperial vision is echoed later, when Indulph predicts that 'posterity for Albion's crown may fight, / And couch ambition in the name of right; / With specious titles urge the civil war / And to a crown their guilty journey tear' (VI. 133–6). Similar to the prophecy, Macpherson here again unambiguously takes the government's side: the '45 rising is seen as nothing but ambition 'couch[ed] in the name of right'. The 'specious titles' are those of Charles and his father James, styled, respectively, Charles III and James IX by their followers. The Pretender – and Jacobitism – has no part in Macpherson's contemporary Scotland where loyalty to the British imperial state is all.

As we have seen, *The Highlander* is a stringent adaption of history into verse. From directly translated details to the wider sustained inclusion of history, in the form of the statues, characters and the continuation of ancestral lineage, the poem shows Macpherson as an historian who uses clearly traceable sources and only rarely takes poetic licence. Macpherson creates an historical narrative based on a fidelity to source material, a technique of Enlightenment historiography which he used throughout his literary career, where a focus on narrative and erudition were never far from his mind. Furthermore, the poem is a case study that exemplifies Macpherson's politics. In *The Highlander*, Macpherson uses the past to comment on contemporary political ideas and identities – an approach which he returns to with gusto in his later history writing. As this analysis of *The Highlander* has shown, Macpherson promotes an inclusive Britishness that upholds Scottish identity while making an argument about the Scottish and Highland role in empire. At this particular point of imperial crisis, during the Seven Years War, the poem demonstrates Macpherson's persistent engagement with history, historical sources and British imperial politics.

FRAGMENTS OF ANCIENT POETRY (1760)

The first of Macpherson's Ossianic Collections, the *Fragments of Ancient Poetry, Collected in the Highlands of Scotland, and Translated from the Galic or Erse Language* was published in Edinburgh in June 1760.[58]

Accompanied by a 'Preface' written by Hugh Blair (but unsigned), and published anonymously (though attributed to Macpherson almost immediately), the *Fragments* were initially taken as just that by contemporary readers: fragments. This section examines the *Fragments* in the context of Macpherson's other works, and as an example of the same overarching historiographical mindset; it evaluates both Blair's 'Preface' and the poems themselves in light of the broader argument of this book, that Macpherson wrote as an historian across a range of genres. Here, the focus of this chapter begins to shift from the poetry itself to the framing paratextual material. *The Fragments*, as the first of the Ossianic Collections, does render elements of the Celtic past in poetry – but in a very different kind of poetry, lacking the verse, rhyme, rhythm and structure of *The Highlander*. As Fiona Stafford argued, *The Fragments* are 'fifteen pieces of strange prose ... [but] in many ways a more successful collection of poetry than the rambling epics which followed'.[59] From the outset, the Ossianic Collections present a narrative of the past – albeit, a rather vague and sometimes confusing one – but derived from different source material: the oral tradition of Gaelic poetry. In the eighth fragment, we encounter 'old Oscian ... the last of the race of Fingal' who sings about the past 'and lamented the dead'.[60] Ossian relates historical narratives, and the past is consistently applied by the bard in interpreting the world of his present – 'Ossian *is* history', as James Mulholland suggests.[61] In this section, however, we focus on how *The Fragments* are framed in historiographical terms in the preface. Here, we examine the profound influence of Hugh Blair, the author of the preface and Macpherson's close friend and collaborator. As one of the key figures in Scottish Enlightenment historiography, Blair provides the conceptual framework which then goes on to inspire Macpherson's own historiographical practice. Blair's short preface to *The Fragments* briefly introduces ideas of authenticity, sources and stadial history, all concepts that inform Macpherson's work, both in the paratexts to the later parts of the Ossianic Collections and in his history writing of the 1770s.

Hugh Blair met James Macpherson in the autumn of 1759, just as word of Macpherson's access to ancient Gaelic poetry was starting to gain traction in the world of the Edinburgh literati.[62] Blair was a Church of Scotland minister and emerging literary scholar, who was to become the first professorial chair of English when appointed to the University of Edinburgh in 1760.[63] When he met Macpherson in 1759, Blair was at a pivotal point in his career and preparing to deliver his *Lectures on Rhetoric and Belles Lettres*.[64] From this point on, Macpherson and Blair worked in close proximity, both physically and intellectually.

Macpherson lodged 'in rooms below his mentor's on Blackfriar's Wynd in Edinburgh's Old Town' and 'Macpherson's stuff was meat for Blair's theories, and Blair's theories were ... the food on which Macpherson's poetical efforts throve and fattened'.[65] Scholarly accounts of the relationship between Macpherson and Blair have tended to focus either on this poetic relationship, or on broader philosophical connections in their work. Stafford and Moore concentrate on Blair's admiration for this kind of 'primitive literature' and how such epic poetry as the Ossianic Collections could emerge from 'the earliest states of society'.[66] Such an emphasis on Enlightenment stadial theory is echoed by Kidd, who argues that Blair's preface 'deals with aesthetics and conjectural sociology, but without any mention of Ossianic poetry's historiographical significance, the most prominent feature of Macpherson's own glosses'.[67] While this section builds upon Kidd's argument it also takes this much further, both in terms of a close reading of Macpherson's prefaces and dissertations to the Ossianic Collections and in examining the historiographical impact of Blair on Macpherson. This section develops the argument outlined in Chapter 1 – that Hugh Blair's 1759 *Lectures* should be read historiographically, alongside their literary and philosophical impact, as Mark Salber Phillips has suggested.[68] As we argue above, placing Blair and Macpherson together in this way helps us to understand both the context in which the Ossianic Collections emerged in the early 1760s and how Macpherson's career as an historian developed in the 1770s.

Hugh Blair's 'Preface' to *The Fragments* opens with a strong statement about the authenticity of Macpherson's collection of Gaelic poetry: 'The public may depend on the following fragments as genuine remains of ancient Scottish poetry.'[69] This opening reassures the reader: they can 'depend' on the fact that the *Fragments* are the 'genuine remains of ancient Scottish poetry'; that they are, in fact, incomplete examples of a particularly Scottish kind of poetry that has survived from an indeterminate past. Here, the preface does not identify the poems' form as anything other than incomplete poems – 'fragments'; this is significant as the monologues and dialogues in the Ossianic Collections resemble prose compositions in how they are set out on the page. Next, the preface expands on the notion that they are 'remains of ancient Scottish poetry' by telling us that 'the date of their composition cannot be exactly ascertained', but that 'tradition, in the country where they were written, refers them to an æra of the most remote antiquity'.[70] This is where the authenticity debate starts: because the preface explicitly says that the poems were 'written', readers and scholars have determined that the poems must be modern productions as very little written Gaelic literature survives. However, this might be due to a cultural misunderstanding on the part of Hugh Blair, who conflates 'composition' and 'writing'.

The preface is informed by Enlightenment historiographical thinking: Blair notes that the poems 'belong to the most early state of society', which echoes Adam Smith's theory of four stages of history but more closely foreshadows the development of Adam Ferguson's stadial theories.[71] However, as we shall see below, Macpherson develops his own particular version of stadial history that privileged the earlier 'state of nature'.[72] Similarly, Blair's opening sentence that introduces the poems as 'genuine remains of ancient Scottish poetry' uses the language of historiography: 'genuine', here, is part of the rhetoric of truth and authenticity that is so prevalent among Enlightenment historians, not least in the work of Blair and Smith, in whose intellectual circles Macpherson also moved.[73] Whether or not this claim is justified is another matter, but the fact that it uses this language places the *Fragments* in the realm of historiography. Blair also demonstrates conjectural thinking in the preface: while his argument that the absence of clanship in the poems points to their composition before 'the establishment of clanship in the northern part of Scotland' is not taken seriously by today's scholars, the *way he argues* here is conjectural, and thus another example of Enlightenment historiography at work.[74] Later in the preface Blair discusses the role of the bard who, he states, composed the poems in the collection. The bard's function, Blair argues, is 'to record in verse, the illustrious actions of that family'; the bard, that is, is a verse chronicler who hands down their chronicle 'from race to race; some in manuscript, but more by oral tradition'.[75] While 'verse' signifies poetry or fiction to the modern reader, to an Enlightenment audience this is merely the form that the chronicle is recorded in; our modern distinction between history as truth and fiction as made up is not an eighteenth-century one, expressed, for example, in Smith's admiration for poets 'as the first historians of any'.[76] In the Enlightenment, the difference in these modes of writing rested largely on the content of texts rather than their form, but even those distinctions were blurred: William Godwin, political philosopher and novelist, argued later in the eighteenth century that novels were a better form of writing about the past than non-fiction history writing because they allow the reader to see what could happen, rather than what did happen, focusing on generalities rather than specifics.[77] While this is not the argument that Blair posits here, it is part of the same eighteenth-century discussion of verse and prose, and fiction and history. Blair's (and Macpherson's) bards are verse historians; it is their purpose as recorders of actions, rather than the form in which they do so, that makes them that.

The final section of the preface concerns the character of Fingal and is generally viewed as an advertisement for the next project in the Ossianic Collections – *Fingal*, published 1761/2 – in an attempt to raise subscriptions, and with the promise of a complete epic poem; a promise that did much to advance the authenticity debate. While attracting subscribers is undoubtedly its purpose, its methodology is yet again historiographical. Fingal, the hero of the poem, is first mentioned earlier in the preface when Blair floats the idea that the fragments might be 'episodes of a greater work' that relate 'to the wars of Fingal'. Here, Fingal, is presented as a historical figure about whose wars 'innumerable traditions remain, to this day, in the Highlands of Scotland'.[78] This is echoed towards the end of the preface: after the summary of the subject matter of the poem Blair notes that recovery of the whole poem 'might serve to throw considerable light upon the Scottish and Irish antiquities'.[79] The ultimate aim, then, of producing *Fingal*, and of Macpherson's field trips to the Highlands later in 1760 and 1761, was to illuminate Scotland's Celtic past – its history. The stated aim, here, is explicitly to recover antiquities, not to collect poetry. This places the undertaking safely in the realm of historiography and is another example of the historiographical framework that is key to all of Macpherson's published works.

FINGAL (1761/2)

Like the *Fragments*, the second Ossianic volume *Fingal* (Edinburgh 1761, London 1762) was supplied with a range of paraphernalia: an 'Advertisement', a 'Preface', and a 'Dissertation'. In addition, the poems themselves are accompanied by long editorial footnotes. This section will examine these in turn to see how *Fingal* fits into Macpherson's historiography. The focus, then, will be on this paraphernalia, rather than on the poems themselves; on Macpherson's theory, rather than his poetic practice. In the advertisement, preface and dissertation, we find Macpherson framing *Fingal* in ways which are increasingly redolent of the Enlightenment debates about history writing that were occurring in Edinburgh during the early 1760s. Macpherson is overtly historiographical in these paratexts, placing a greater emphasis on his sources, their authenticity, the scholarly apparatus of footnotes, and using his evidence to engage with and critique other historians. However, the nature of Macpherson's sources for *Fingal* – the oral tradition of the *Gàidhealtachd* – problematises his emerging historiographical practice. Macpherson struggles to reconcile the superiority of the written record with the power of oral tradition's storytelling, indicating both the liminal status of Macpherson's position as an imperial Gael and how he oscillated between being a poet and being an historian at this early stage in his career.

Macpherson's historiographical intent is evident from the very first page of *Fingal*. The one-page advertisement is the first thing the reader sees after the title page. It appears before the table of contents, and while such documents are often dismissed as peripheral to the main work, the advertisement can help us understand Macpherson's historiographical approach in the Ossianic Collections. The first paragraph of the advertisement is concerned with the 'Originals' of *Fingal*, and the second paragraph is about the subscribers and patrons of the volume. This is not unusual; such paraphernalia is common in eighteenth-century works. However, as so often in our book it is not *what* the text is about, but *how* it is written that sheds light on Macpherson's historiography. The first paragraph consists of a discussion about the availability of the 'Originals'. Here, Macpherson notes the two options for making these available to the public: by publishing them through subscription, or by depositing them in a public library to be viewed. Neither of these have happened, he argues; no subscribers came forth, which 'he takes it for the judgment of the public that neither the one [publishing by subscription] or the other [depositing in public library] is necessary'.[80] This approach is historiographical in its concern for sources, as it is elsewhere in his works. In the case of the Ossianic Collections this is, of course, complicated by the authenticity debate, and ongoing discussion about oral culture and the provenance of his material. The fact, however, that Macpherson deliberates about how to make his source material available to the public is part of the wider historiographical debate about sources, footnotes and citation, and anticipates the publication of the *Original Papers* in the 1770s. Indeed, the proposed subscription volume of 'Originals' would be that sort of work: an anthology of sources. This would necessarily be a different kind of publication than the *Original Papers*, which are composed of written material; the difficulty of publishing oral Gaelic material for an English-speaking reading audience places Macpherson in the role of not just anthologist and editor, but of quasi-bardic *cultural transmitter*.[81] Seeing his concern with sources in the broader sense – outwith the Ossianic Collections – is key here; Macpherson does not only discuss the availability of his source material *because* the authenticity of his translations had been questioned, but because he is, at heart, an Enlightenment historian who demonstrates an understanding of the importance of sources and interpretation. Macpherson, then, at this point functions as both Gael (concerned with his role as tradition bearer) and Enlightenment historian.[82] Authenticity works in several ways here: the authenticity of Macpherson's Ossianic Collections as 'genuine' translations of Ossian's works; the authenticity of the sources as part of an ongoing Gaelic oral tradition, as well as manuscript material; and historiographical authenticity, to do with Macpherson's process. The first two of these form the core of the authenticity debate: what are the poems (translations or inventions; fact or fiction; genuine or fake) and to what extent can we translate or edit something that is part of an ongoing oral tradition. The last one, however, is different: authenticity is not just a matter of the sources or the final product, but also of the writer's process, and that is how it is of historiographical interest. Examining what Macpherson says about his process – such as the discussion about making sources available here in the advertisement – is a different kind of authenticity debate: it is to do with his method. Instead of looking at his sources or the final product, this approach is concerned with how Macpherson presents the Ossianic Collections, using paratextual material to address the same issues and ideas as in his later historical writing. This is why the advertisement is a useful source: as in his histories of the 1770s, Macpherson is concerned with sources, and while this has traditionally been seen in connection with the authenticity debate, it is also an example of his ongoing, and sustained, practice of historiography that we can see throughout his writings.

In the 'Preface' to *Fingal*, Macpherson is overtly historiographical, dealing with sources, authenticity, scholarly debate, conjectural history, and the purpose of history writing. Much of it is concerned with anticipating criticism and responding to objections he had to face as a result of the *Fragments*. However, the language of the historian litters this work. Transmission history, for example, occupies a paragraph:

> It is now two years since the first translations from the Galic language were handed about among people of taste in Scotland. They became at last so much corrupted, through the carelessness of transcribers, that, for my own sake, I was obliged to print the genuine copies.[83]

This genesis of the *Fragments* sets Macpherson up as an historian: he is the editor of a body of work, concerned with collating primary sources. These sources, he claims, are 'genuine'; more genuine than alternative versions of the poems that have been circulated, such as those by Jerome Stone and others.[84] We can disagree with him on that – 'genuine', particularly with regards to oral poetry, is difficult to assess – but his methodology here as elsewhere is that of an historian: to assess sources, and present those judged most appropriate by the trained historian. He links this to *Fingal*: presented as an epic poem, he discusses collecting sources through fieldwork, and leaves judgement on the poems' literary merit to 'criticism'.[85] Macpherson, that is, does not assume the role of literary critic: he presents himself clearly as scholarly editor.

A large portion of the preface is taken up with a plot summary. This, Macpherson argues, is to 'prevent that obscurity which the introduction of characters utterly unknown might occasion'.[86] We can read this summary as a piece of Macpherson's historiographical apparatus: as anticipating, in some small way, the joint publications of his *History of Great Britain* and the *Original Papers* in 1775. The poems of *Fingal* become the *Original Papers* in this scenario – the anthology of primary sources – while the plot summary becomes the *History* derived from these sources. As such, the plot summary becomes a form of historiographical practice, where Macpherson the historian puts his historiographical skills to good use. The purpose of this – 'to be well understood' – chimes neatly with Enlightenment historiographical theory: the role of the historian is to elucidate and clarify in 'explanatory narratives'.[87]

The final section of the preface, after the plot summary, is perhaps the most historiographical part of *Fingal*. Here, Macpherson explicitly discusses the notion of *Fingal* as history: 'The story of this poem is so little interlaced with fable, that one cannot help thinking it the genuine history of Fingal's expedition, embellished by poetry.'[88] Here, Macpherson's argument deals with the relationship between history and fiction. However, this was far less clear-cut in the eighteenth century than it is now. As Adam Smith argued in outlining his neoclassicial historiography, poetry can be history in verse; what matters is not its form but its approach to content.[89] This eighteenth-century understanding of poetry, and particularly of *oral* poetry, is the reason why Macpherson can argue that 'the compositions of Ossian are not less valuable for the light they throw on the ancient state of Scotland and Ireland than they are for their poetical merits'.[90] Here, he presents the materials contained in *Fingal* as primary sources to be interpreted by the modern historian and that help the modern reader understand the past better.

The preface also contains a section relevant to our thinking about Britishness, Scottishness and the place of the Gael within the British imperial state. Here, Macpherson explores contemporary bias against Gaelic culture; 'the prejudices of the present age against the ancient inhabitants of Britain' are, he argues, the chief cause of the objections that he had to face in the eighteen months since the *Fragments*' publication.[91] The reasons for these prejudices lie in his contemporaries' disbelief that the poems in the *Fragments* are full of 'generous sentiments', which, he argues, is not something they think Ossian and his world capable of.[92] For them, sentiment belongs to a more modern age. It is interesting that Macpherson does not draw a distinction between Scots, Gaels and others; Ossian and the other characters are Britons. This foreshadows the framing of the later Celtic History as *An Introduction to the History of Great Britain* – not the History of Scotland, or the History of the Gaels but, instead, a narrative of the past that seeks to place the Highlands at the heart of the British imperial project. His audience, Macpherson knows, is broader than that. In setting up Ossian as a Briton, rather than a Gael, while at the same time responding to those of his contemporaries who objected to the *Fragments* because of their issues with the poems' sentimentality, Macpherson constructs an argument about *present* differences, not past ones. In the past, Britons came in all shapes and sizes – including Gaels – and, because of the absence of other early documents or poetry available to Macpherson's, the *Fragments*, and their sentimentality, are indicative of wider early British life. Ossian's poems are *not* solely about the *Gàidhealtachd*; they are about early Britain and the British Isles more broadly. Ossian and his contemporaries are 'our forefathers' – not just the Scots' forefathers, but the ancestors of *all* Britons.[93] This is a subtle argument: we're all British, but some of you think some of us are less British than you are. Critics of the *Fragments*, then, become less British in Macpherson's eyes: in an argument that reflects Colin Kidd's analysis of 'North British' articulations of Scottish patriotism, by not accepting Ossian as their British ancestor, this throws doubt on their contemporary faith in the British state.[94] And, in contrast, emphasises the loyalty of Highlanders to British imperialism.

The 'Dissertation' published in the *Fingal* volume (1761/2) is Macpherson's earliest piece of writing that can be comfortably classified as prose historical writing. It anticipates the book-length *An Introduction to the History of Great Britain and Ireland* (1771) both in form and content and provides us with an insight into Macpherson's historiographical principles and practice. As its title informs us, the dissertation concerns 'the Antiquity, &c. of the Poems of Ossian the Son of Fingal'; it investigates the material circumstances of the alleged third-century composition of the poems. This is important: in this title Macpherson is sending out a historiographical bat signal to his readers and critics. The dissertation is not about the authenticity of the poems (as other contemporary dissertations were, such as Hugh Blair's from 1763), but about the period of antiquity when they were composed.[95] In other words, the dissertation is about history – both the past and how to write about it. That alone shows Macpherson's historiographical mind: instead of refuting claims of inauthenticity with a direct response, he turns to history writing.

In addition to giving us a taste of Macpherson's history writing practice, however, the dissertation also sheds light on his historiographical thought – his understanding of history, historians and the process of history writing. Again, this speaks to the influence of Hugh Blair and how that intellectual relationship places Macpherson at the heart of Scottish Enlightenment historiography.

The dissertation opens with a statement that is directly linked to Enlightenment historiography: 'Inquiries into the antiquities of nations afford more pleasure than any real advantage to mankind.'[96] That is, they sit on the side of *delectare* (amusement), not *prodesse* (instruction); they are skewed towards enjoyment.[97] Macpherson explains the reason for this: 'the ingenious may form systems of history on probabilities and a few facts; but at a great distance of time, their accounts must be vague and uncertain'.[98] What he describes here is a form of conjectural history, and shows an awareness of current historiographical thinking as well as an understanding of classical historiography. There is no mention of morality here, which for Hume, and others, was one of the three purposes of history writing – to amuse, instruct and to 'strengthen ... virtue'.[99] Macpherson plays down the usefulness of conjectural history: because the facts are scarce, we cannot really learn from the past, and that is why it 'affords more pleasure than [...] advantage'.[100] This comes, he explains, from the simple state of affairs in antiquity. Pre-empting Adam Ferguson's stadial theory, Macpherson explains that it is 'the arts of polished life, by which alone facts can be preserved with certainty', and these are 'the production of a well formed community'. Only then, in this advanced state, 'historians begin to write'.[101] This shows an awareness not only of current theory, but also a certainty about who is (and is not) an historian. Before the advent of written history 'the actions of former times are left in obscurity, or magnified by uncertain traditions' – but they are not recorded historians. This is the first inkling of Macpherson's ambiguous and equivocal relationship with oral tradition and its connection with history writing. Macpherson argues that the unrecorded nature of the past means that 'we find so much of the marvellous in the origin of every nation', echoing Smith's comments in 1763 about 'the Language of wonder' in the poetry of the 'first historians'.[102] Tantalisingly Macpherson tells us that there were 'good historians' among the Greeks and Romans, but not what made them good. The only clue is that these 'good historians' do not share the 'weakness' for 'the most absurd fables concerning the high antiquities of their respective nations'.[103] They are not, it seems, conjectural historians. This, as Ranajit Guha has argued, also lay at the heart of Hegel's distinction between the Western world and their possession of a history and those places outwith history because they had no history of the state: 'A people or a nation lacked history, [Hegel] argued, not because it knew no writing but because lacking as it did in statehood it had nothing to write about.'[104] Macpherson's geographical focus on both the Highlands and Ireland in *Fingal* creates a tension here, between the desire to narrate the oral tradition of this past and the emerging principles of Enlightenment history writing that not only privileged written sources as evidence but also saw the business of history to narrate the rise of the state. This, in turn, reveals Macpherson's ambivalence about stadial history as an explanation for the development of 'commercial civilisation'. Macpherson's ideas about societal development were a more equivocal version of Adam Ferguson's 'model of civic virtue', trying to reconcile the 'metropolitan provinces' of the ancient Celtic world with the modernity of the British imperial state.[105]

Following on from this initial discussion of historians, history and tradition, Macpherson shifts his focus to Celtic history. Unlike the Greeks and Romans, he argues, the Celts 'trusted their fame to tradition and the songs of their bards, which, by the vicissitude of human affairs, are long since lost'.[106] They did not, in other words, *write* their history. The history that follows this introduction to the 'Dissertation' is based on 'the testimony of the best authors', whose proximity to Britain 'makes the opinion probable'.[107] In telling us this, Macpherson displays another trait of modern historians: an evaluation of sources. The history that follows, he argues, is derived from *primary sources* as close to the events and conditions he relates both in time and place. This is another example of how Macpherson places himself in the context of emerging Enlightenment historiography that consciously evaluated – and engaged with – their sources and shared this evaluation with their readership. Macpherson's practice here builds upon the rather minimal approach to sources and their evaluation developed by Hume and foreshadows the more precise work of William Robertson, discussed in Chapter 3.[108] This attitude is confirmed by his ongoing foot-/side-noting in the parts of the dissertation that are not focused on Ossian. Sources such as Pliny, Caesar, Tacitus and Strabo are only some of the classical authors referenced thus by Macpherson.[109] There are some instances where Macpherson directly engages with his sources in his text, such as this example:

> Diodorus Siculus mentions it as a thing well known in his time, that the inhabitants of Ireland were originally Britons; and his testimony is unquestionable, when we consider that, for many ages, the language and customs of both nations were the same.[110]

In doing so, Macpherson contextualises and evaluates his source, reassuring his readership that what he writes is trustworthy; he shares his reasons for accepting Diodorus Siculus's account. In another section he builds a sustained argument disagreeing with Tacitus, who, Macpherson says, 'was of the opinion that the ancient Caledonians were of German extract'.[111] Macpherson counters this assessment, arguing instead that the Caledonians were different from the Germans because of the dissimilarity of their languages.

After quickly setting the scene thus, Macpherson moves on to a discussion of the Caledonians, but this time his evidence comes from the poems contained in *Fingal*. While this leaves him open to criticism – he does, after all, contextualise his history with what he had earlier dismissed as tradition – he nonetheless operates as an historian in this section of the dissertation. Instead of giving written evidence from external sources, he refers, variously, to contemporary Gaelic poetic practice (on the absence of religion in the Ossianic poems), or to oral tradition (on what Ossian is 'said to have' discussed with the Culdees) and how this then establishes the poems as ancient, bearing 'the genuine marks of antiquity'.[112]

While building his argument *from* the content of the Ossianic poems is, as many critics point out, problematic for resolving the authenticity debate, we can explore this in a more constructive way in the context of this book.[113] Here, we are not concerned with whether or not Macpherson's sources are *true*, but with *how* he uses, categorises and evaluates them. Let us, then, step past the criticism of using his 'own' poetry to contextualise the Ossianic poems, and instead focus on his method. In his engagement with the Ossian corpus as a source (albeit a non-written one), Macpherson consistently uses the poetry much like he uses classical historians in the earlier parts of the dissertation, or, indeed, the letters, journals and other primary sources in his later history writing, explored in Chapter 4: he examines, analyses and evaluates the poems. While this does not make his argument sound, his methodology is valid; his premises might be false, but he employs them in such a way as to necessitate his conclusions. The dissertation is a good case study to illustrate this point: discussion about when Ossian lived is argued constructively both from evidence within the poems (such as the absence of Christian thought in them) and from contextual primary sources and well-established facts (such as the death of Emperor Severus as recorded by his contemporary, historian Cassius Dio).[114] In other words, his method of combining contextual evidence with scholarly sources demonstrates Macpherson's fidelity to Enlightenment notions of history writing.

In the final section of the dissertation, when Macpherson turns to the question of authenticity, his argument is weakest. Here, he does not present any evidence to back up his assertions, but instead presents his narrative as facts accepted by those who are 'acquainted with the ancient state of northern Britain'.[115] This is not a terribly effective argument and leaves Macpherson open to criticism from his opponents. In this section he falls back on labelling those that object to his narrative as 'men unacquainted with the ancient state of the northern parts of Britain'; those, by extension, that are unfamiliar with Gaelic oral tradition (which he, of course, is).[116] Towards the end of this section Macpherson explicitly places himself in the role of witness when he argues that

> By the succession of these bards, the poems concerning the ancestors of the family were handed down from generation to generation; they were repeated to the whole clan on solemn occasions, and always alluded to in the new compositions of the bards. This custom came down near to our own times; and after the bards were discontinued, a great number in a clan retained by memory, or committed to writing, their compositions, and founded the antiquity of their families on the authority of their poems.[117]

This is the role Macpherson fulfils here: recording oral tradition through a partially new written composition. Historiographically, this is a fundamental flaw in how Macpherson approaches the authenticity debate: he stops arguing as a modern historian, but instead places himself as an expert witness, an approach which Matthew Wickman has eloquently discussed in *The Ruins of Experience*.[118] In doing so, Macpherson shifts from historian to storyteller; from the rationalism of the Enlightenment to the myths of Romanticism. But as a member of the *Gàidhealtachd* – of the living Gaelic oral tradition – he acts as one of those bards he describes in the passage quoted above. This, then, is where we might see the distinction between history and fiction in eighteenth-century terms: it is not to do with form, but with methodology and approach.

Macpherson's urge to implement the Enlightenment historiographical practices of Blair, Hume and others clashed with his desire to represent the agency and value of Highland culture in *Fingal*. An intriguing passage at the very end of the dissertation illuminates what Dafydd Moore describes as 'the delicate balancing act ... between the notion of confident cultural transmission and the idea of cultural decay and forgetting [which] is another expression of the tension within him between Celtic mythologiser and sceptical whig historiographer'.[119] However, Moore's analysis focuses largely on the poetry itself rather than the paratexts examined in this chapter, which, instead, demonstrate both Macpherson's ambitions to be an historian (fulfilled, as we shall see, in Chapters 3 and 4) and his vision of a Highland modernity that could reinvigorate the Gaelic world through commerce and empire. Macpherson concludes the dissertation with a reflection on the challenging modernity of the eighteenth-century Highlands:

> The genius of the highlanders has suffered a great change within these few years. The communication with the rest of the island is open, and the introduction of trade and manufactures has destroyed that leisure which was formerly dedicated to hearing and repeating the poems of ancient times. Many have now learned to leave their mountains, and seek their fortunes in a milder climate; and though a certain *amor patriae* may sometimes bring them back, they have, during their absence, imbibed enough of foreign manners to despise the customs of their ancestors. Bards have been long disused, and the spirit of genealogy has greatly subsided. Men begin to be less devoted to their chiefs, and consanguinity is not so much regarded. When property is established, the human mind confines its views to the pleasure of progress. It does not go back to antiquity, or look forward to succeeding ages. The cares of life increase, and the actions of other times no longer amuse. Hence it is, that the taste for poetry is at a low ebb among the highlanders. They have, however, thrown off the good qualities of their ancestors. Hospitality still subsists, and an uncommon civility to strangers. Friendship is inviolable, and revenge less blindly followed than formerly.[120]

Scholars have read this paragraph as confirmation of Macpherson's vision of 'defeat and despair' for the Gaelic world of his youth and that 'his own collection of Gaelic poetry [was] a hopeless gesture towards the preservation of Celtic Scotland'.[121] Others have noted the 'covert resistance and ... fugitive power' of such rhetorical 'elusiveness', yet Macpherson's vision of Highland modernity, riding the coat-tails of his Enlightenment modernity, remains under explored.[122] Macpherson's account of the recent Highland past emphasises the change wrought to the region by commercialisation, 'improvement', militarisation and empire.[123] In the dissertation to *Fingal*, Macpherson argues that the contemporary Highlands had abandoned poetry. But Macpherson chose to revive the region by making this poetry part of the desirable modernity of commerce and empire. Macpherson's translations and adaptations of Gaelic poetry then make these stories of Gaelic culture fashionable literary objects – for those in the Highlands as much as anywhere else. So, by revisiting their own culture through Macpherson's interpretation of the region's past, Highlanders can embrace the modernity of the present. The poems were not relics, as Ian Duncan argues, of 'a phantom cultural past realized in the present of its extinction', in which the

Gaelic language was 'obliterat[ed] in order to recreate it as a dead poetic language embalmed in English prose, also effectually obliterat[ing] a modern tradition of Gaelic poetry'.[124] Indeed, as Gaelic scholars have demonstrated, the Ossianic Collections inspired a tremendous creative response from the *Gàidhealtachd*, offering 'a new sense of literary, spiritual and cultural aspiration'.[125] In countering James Hunter's argument that Macpherson's Ossianic Collections marked the beginning of a ruinously romantic Highland 'Celtic Twilight', Alastair McIntosh suggests a rather more positive assessment of Ossian:

> There's a quality here that the Greeks call *parrhesia* – a fearless speech from a place of truth you'd die for. A sense of *Wha's like us? Damn few, and they're a' deid!* And yet, that very utterance reveals its own contradiction. *Because we're still here!*[126]

It is important to remember that in the early 1760s, when Macpherson composed the Ossianic Collections, the broader process of economic, social and cultural decline in the *Gàidhealtachd* was by no means inevitable. Despite the existential crisis of the last failed Jacobite uprising and the British state's efforts to crush the Highlands in a process of internal colonisation, there was a resilience and resistance to the people of the region that saw them adapt rapidly to the new realities of their thorough incorporation into the British imperial state. The social elite of the Highlands (of which Macpherson, of course, was one) proved themselves adept at turning this situation to their advantage, reviving and retaining clan networks and loyalties in order to survive the harshness of life post-Culloden. As Matthew Dziennik argues, the British state's efforts 'were co-opted and used to enhance chiefly legal authority at the very time that traditional sources of chiefly legal rights were breaking down under the strain of socioeconomic change'.[127] Macpherson himself was no stranger to this process, functioning as de facto Chief of Clan Macpherson during the 1770s and 1780s – a period when the actual Chief, Duncan was away fighting for the British Army or imprisoned in America – and using his considerable political clout to ensure that the annexed Cluny estate was returned to Duncan in 1784. As David Taylor argues about James, 'Chief he could never rightly be, but the power behind the throne was a destiny for which he was more than adequately prepared'.[128] Macpherson was equally adept at using the tools of British literary culture to make a case, as he does in this passage above from the dissertation to *Fingal*, for valuing Highland culture and embracing its modernity. The Ossianic Collections demonstrated how Highland culture and history was just as valid and important in shaping the modern world as the cultures of others. The poetry of Ossian, for Macpherson, is not the poetry of a dead or dying race – it is a story of the Gaelic past, which continues to have value and importance in the present.[129]

TEMORA (1763)

In the 'Dissertation' to *Temora* (1763), Macpherson continues to prevaricate about the place of oral culture in recording the past and how this fits into his emerging Enlightenment historiography. However, in framing the final part of the Ossianic Collections, Macpherson's Gaelic bardic orality takes a back seat to more pressing concerns regarding stadial history, engaging with other historians, and evaluating the truth and authenticity of evidence. As such, the dissertation to *Temora* foreshadows Macpherson's first foray into book-length history writing – *An Introduction to the History of Great Britain and Ireland*, published in 1771 and examined in Chapter 3. In the dissertation, Macpherson narrates the ancient Celtic past in ways which pre-empt his account in *An Introduction*. Moreover, Macpherson's desire to follow the principles of Enlightenment historiography in this dissertation are then explored more fully in his later history writing. As such, then, the dissertation to *Temora* can be seen as a hinge point between the Ossianic Collections and Macpherson's explicit prose narrative history writing.

Macpherson writes historiographically from the outset of the dissertation to *Temora*, discussing ancient historians' focus on 'fable' rather than facts. The very beginning of the dissertation frames this through stadial history: 'Nations, small in their beginnings and slow in their progress to maturity, cannot, with any degree of certainty, be traced to their source.'[130] These are familiar concepts: the idea of progress towards maturity, and the search for sources or origins, which Macpherson picks up with 'Fergusonian' gusto towards the end of the dissertation.[131] But Macpherson focuses here at the beginning on a discussion of the role of historians. 'The first historians', he argues, 'in every country, are [...] obscure and unsatisfactory' because of the difficulties in tracing the progress of nations back to the source, and because they are 'swayed by a national partiality' which means that they 'adopted uncertain legends and ill-fancied fictions' as history, rather than impartial, truthful or authentic accounts.[132] This is another example of how Macpherson is attuned to Enlightenment historiographic theory, and how he values the same qualities in an historian as Blair had outlined in his recent *Lectures on Rhetoric and Belles Lettres*.[133] The key quality of a good historian, according to Macpherson, is to be able to distinguish fact and fiction, and this is something that the ancient historians lacked: 'without judgment or discernment to separate the probable and more antient traditions, from ill-digested tales of late invention, they jumbled the whole together, in one mass of anachronisms and inconsistencies'.[134] The ancient historians, in other words, were unable to judge their sources, and this made their history unreliable. Macpherson also invokes the readers of these ancient histories and compares them to modern ones, who prefer to 'trust their national fame to late and well-attested transactions' instead of 'ages, dark and involved in fable'.[135] Modern readers, that is, want facts, and they want their historians to evaluate sources effectively. Macpherson's analysis of the difference between ancient and modern historians echoed similar arguments being made by Adam Smith in 1763. Giving one of his lectures on rhetoric in early January that year, Smith accounted for the development of contemporary 'historicall Composition' by comparing emerging Enlightenment historiography to the practice of ancient historians, such as Tacitus and Pliny. For Smith, the latest innovations in history writing were not necessarily an improvement, and much of his historiographical reflection defends the purity of classical historical narratives.[136] It was the historian's job, according to Smith, 'to narrate facts':

> The best way in this case is not to set a labourd and formall demonstration but barely mentioning the authorities on both sides, to shew for what reason he had chosen to be the one opinion rather than of the other. Long demonstrations as they are no part of the historians province are seldom made use of by the ancients. The modern authors have often brought them in.[137]

Smith goes on to argue that 'Historicall truths are now in much greater request than they ever were in the ancient times' – a position that Macpherson agrees with in the dissertation to *Temora*.[138] However, the crucial difference between Smith and Macpherson is that Macpherson sees this historiographical concentration on facts, evidence and sources as desirable – these are the qualities that make a good historian, according to Macpherson but not to Smith. Writing at roughly the same moment in early 1763, it is Macpherson who is the more historiographically progressive.[139] It is Macpherson who embraces the modernity of the new history writing, fulfilled in his history books of the 1770s where his historiographical practice is closer to leading Enlightenment historians such as Robertson and Gibbon (examined in Chapter 3).

Macpherson's enthusiasm for emerging Enlightenment methodologies can be seen in the section of the dissertation concerning the evaluation of primary sources. Macpherson first discusses Roman historians as 'the only authentic accounts of the northern nations'.[140] 'Authentic' is key here: Macpherson evaluates Roman history as primary texts; the accounts are authentic because they are compiled 'live', rather than accounts that discuss the distant past. Although outsiders to their field of study, the Roman historians are the best historians of the northern nations for this early period, because these countries were 'destitute of the use of letters' and thus 'had no means of transmitting their history to posterity'.[141] The Romans here act as credible witnesses. When their accounts match those tales preserved by oral tradition, then these traditions, too, can become part of history: 'Traditions, however, concerning remote periods, are only to be regarded, in so far as they co-incide with cotemporary writers of undoubted credit and veracity.'[142] For Macpherson, the Roman historians are those contemporary writers who lend credibility and authenticity to tales and traditions. Whether or not this is true, or a sound argument, has been the focus of other studies; what we are concerned with here is Macpherson's approach to this. Like a modern cultural historian who uses a variety of sources in their history writing, Macpherson's historiography allows for a mixture of written and oral sources – provided they do not contradict each other. Macpherson's emphasis on the 'credit and veracity' of the historian reiterates this; they achieve these qualities through their careful evaluation of sources. He picks up this line of argument later in the dissertation, when he depicts Ossian as one of those storytellers of tradition whose tales 'agree so well with what the antients have delivered'.[143] Indeed, Ossian is framed as an historian in the dissertation, and the poems in *Temora* are examples of how Ossian 'preserved [...] history' and that 'history [was] preserved by Ossian'.[144] Similarly, Ossian's poems are contextualised as genuine: 'That part of the poems, which concerned the hero who was regarded as ancestor, was preserved, as an authentic record of antiquity of the family, and was delivered down, from race to race, with wonderful exactness.'[145] We can disagree with Macpherson here, but – as ever in this book – this is not our line of enquiry. His description of orally transmitted tales as 'an authentic record', however, is important, demonstrating, as we saw in the paratexts to *Fingal*, a view of orality that lies outwith some of the more modern Enlightenment historiographical ideas about sources that Macpherson also embraced. Macpherson's defence of Gaelic oral tradition is, once more, at odds with his desire to embrace historiographical modernity. The way in which Macpherson describes oral transmission also demonstrates his need to present the Gaelic world in a way that makes sense to modern eighteenth-century non-Gael English speakers. As in *Fingal*, we see Macpherson caught between the wonder of poetry and the prose of history. In *Temora*, Macpherson describes 'Ossian's poems' as preserving the genealogy of Highland families with 'wonderful exactness'. This emphasis on the unchanging (and therefore verifiable) nature of oral transmission sits uneasily with our understanding of the practice of orality.[146] As Guha argues about Indian oral poetry, 'the once-told and once-heard is never the same when repeated next time. The once-again is separated from each previous instance by an irreducible hiatus, which would continue to generate variations, and with them wonder, at every retelling.'[147] For Macpherson, the 'wonderful exactness' of Ossian presents the oral tradition rather differently, trying to shoehorn it into Enlightenment modes of fixed understanding.

Macpherson's Enlightenment perspective continues in the dissertation to *Temora* through his criticism of early Scottish historians as chroniclers who, as Lowlanders who spoke no Gaelic, 'contented themselves with copying from one another, and retailing the same fictions, in a new colours and dress'.[148] This argument resides in two historiographical tenets: the distinctions between chronicler and historian, and the chronicler's inability to speak Gaelic. The first is symptomatic of wider Enlightenment critique of early history: Macpherson, like his contemporaries such as Smith and Hume, sees history writing as that which explores causes and effects, and that which is concerned with more than royal lineage.[149] The second point can be linked to the Enlightenment emphasis on primary sources: if the history of the Highlands and Islands is told in a medium other than that in which its sources are composed (either oral or written), then this history is inevitably going to be based on secondary knowledge and sources. Macpherson explores this notion further through a discussion of John Fordun's history, which, of course, was one of the source texts for Macpherson's earlier epic poem, *The Highlander*. One of Macpherson's points concerns Fordun's conflation of Irish and Scottish history, which he uses as an example to support his argument about the importance of knowing Gaelic if one is an historian focused on this period. Macpherson criticises Fordun's approach as an example of what happens when historians do not – or are not able to – evaluate their sources properly. As Macpherson explains, Fordun looked to Irish bards and 'it was from them he took those improbable fictions, which form the first part of his history', and later historians, in turn, 'followed his system' without questioning his sources or methodology.[150] This, he argues, is why much early Scottish history is unreliable when judged against emerging modern, Enlightenment standards of history writing. This is another example of Macpherson's explicit engagement with historiographical methodology; he notes that the later historians 'followed [Fordun's] system' but differed in their interpretation by changing details or chronology.[151] In other words, they shared his approach, if not his conclusions. Here, Macpherson is overtly interested in methodology, not content. One of those successors is George Buchanan (again, used in *The Highlander*), whom Macpherson takes care to praise for the 'elegance and vigour of his stile' – that is, for *how* he writes, not for *what* he writes. In doing so, Macpherson once more focuses on historiography in his analysis of his historian predecessors. Buchanan's flaw as an historian, according to Macpherson, is his lack of impartiality, one of the historian values praised by the Enlightenment: 'blinded with political prejudices, he seemed more anxious to turn the fictions of his predecessors to his own purposes, than to detect their misrepresentations, or investigate truth amidst the darkness which they had thrown around it.'[152] Buchanan is here judged by Macpherson against Enlightenment historiographical theory that insists on impartiality, truth and authenticity. Macpherson shows us the importance of historiographical theory to his thinking: it is through this lens that he compiles the dissertation, and it shapes his thinking here and elsewhere. Indeed, his deconstruction of Buchanan's approach to history writing in *Temora* demonstrates how Macpherson's engagement with historiography was evolving in the early 1760s, from his endorsement of Buchanan's *Rerum Scoticarum Historia* as a valid historical source in *The Highlander* (and which underpinned Macpherson's emerging 'Whig historiography'), to criticising Buchanan's impartiality in the dissertation.[153]

There are other instances in the dissertation where Macpherson shows that he constructs his arguments with theory in mind. For example, when discussing the origins of 'Caledonians' he not only shows evidence for why he thinks it is related to 'Celts', but he explicitly states that this evidence 'is sufficient to demonstrate' his ideas.[154] We can disagree with him or prove him wrong, but unlike earlier historians who presented their ideas as facts, Macpherson explains the connection between evidence and idea; he inserts overtly historiographical statements like the one above into his argument to show his readership why his analysis is trustworthy. He does not just tell the reader facts, he shows why and how these facts prove his points. Later in the dissertation he notes that the way he constructs his argument – through giving evidence – leads to a certain conclusion: 'the establishing of this fact, lays, at once, aside the pretended antiquities ...'[155] He also uses words and phrases such as 'evidently', 'consequently', 'it is certain', 'authentic', 'highly probable', which are all used to justify his conclusions.[156] Indeed, 'probability' is used as a concept by Macpherson to explain his historiographical triangulation between different sets of sources: 'By comparing the history preserved by Ossian with the legends of the Scotch and Irish writers, and, by afterwards examining both by the test of the Roman authors, it is easy to discover which is the most probable.'[157]

Macpherson's engagement with Enlightenment ideas about the past is further demonstrated in a section of the dissertation to *Temora* which explores the notion of stadial history, and identifies three stages of societal development.[158] Most of the works usually cited from this period that explore the notion of stadial history post-date Macpherson, including William Robertson's often-quoted explanation of stadial social analysis in *The History of America* (1777): 'In every inquiry concerning the operations of men when united together in society, the first object of attention should be their mode of subsistence. Accordingly as that varies, their laws and policy must differ.'[159] However, as we saw earlier in Blair's 'Preface' to the *Fragments*, stadial ideas about progress and civilisation were already emerging as part of Enlightenment historiography, largely through the influence of Montesquieu's *Esprit des Lois*, published in 1748.[160] Smith had begun to experiment with stadial ideas in his *Lectures on Jurisprudence* and the first draft of *The Wealth of Nations*, both written in 1763, the same year as the publication of *Temora*.[161] While Smith and others saw stadial theory as a way of explaining how the civilisation of modernity developed through commercialism, Adam Ferguson's account emphasised the martial spirit of 'politically active and armed citizens' as essential to a patriotic civil society.[162] Ferguson was a fellow Highlander, and became a friend and mentor of Macpherson in a similar vein as Blair. Born in Logierait in Highland Perthshire, Ferguson was probably already friends with Macpherson before he had arranged the famous meeting with the Scottish playwright, John Home, that sparked the broader cultural craze for Ossian and Gaelic poetry.[163] As we have seen, at the moment when they met in 1759, Ferguson was leading the campaign for the creation of a Scottish militia that would contribute to the war effort against the French.[164] Building on Smith's stadial thought and his account of the rise of civilisation as the rise of commercial modernity, Ferguson added 'martial spirit' as a vital ingredient in ensuring the maintenance of civil virtue. Ferguson's *Essay on the History of Civil Society* (1767) outlined this 'progressive history of the human species' in a similar fashion, as Fiona Stafford argues, to Macpherson in *Temora*.[165] Unlike some of his contemporaries, Macpherson identifies three distinct stages of society, not four:

> The first is the result of consanguinity, and the natural affection of the members of a family to one another. The second begins when property is established, and men enter into associations for mutual defence, against the invasions and injustice of neighbours. Mankind submit, in the third,

to certain laws and subordinations of government, to which they trust the safety of their persons and property.[166]

He places Ossian and the Ossianic tales in the first of those stages, which is 'formed on nature' and 'is the most disinterested and noble'.[167] In this section we can see Macpherson explicitly engaging with Enlightenment notions of progress and civilisation as a man of letters outwith the university environment, but within the same intellectual circle as the leading literati of the day. Macpherson's ambivalence about the progress of modernity was matched in Ferguson's later work. Macpherson's account of stadial history, however, is not as 'profoundly pessimistic' as Fiona Stafford appears to suggest, especially in this section from the dissertation to *Temora*. Here, the Fergusonian 'poetic representation of martial valour' that Moore identifies in the poetry of *Temora* is reconciled with the emergence of modern society in an Enlightenment narrative of civil government.[168] This kind of 'hybrid modernity' arose in the proposals for Highland 'improvement' being developed in the 1760s by the likes of Lord Kames and Rev. John Walker in their efforts to 'preserve a spirit associated with primitive agriculture in the midst of a new commercial order'. Kames was one of the sponsors of Macpherson's Highland collecting tour in the early 1760s (when Kames had just become a commissioner on the Board for Annexed Estates), and the dissertation to *Temora* reflects this broader intellectual community which nurtured and sustained Macpherson's poetry and ideas.[169]

Macpherson saw himself as an historian, operating in the context of Enlightenment debates about history writing that were raging around him during this period when he was living in Edinburgh and working closely with Blair and Ferguson. In the dissertation to *Temora*, we see most clearly the influence of Adam Smith, especially in Macpherson's approach to evidence and in characterising the work of ancient historians. However, while Smith saw classical historians as a model to follow in the present, Macpherson was far more eager to embrace the modern historiography of source analysis, evidence and explanation of cause and effect. Likewise, in his application of stadial theory to the history of the Highlands, Macpherson adopts a cautious modernity, providing a template for combining military service and commercialism which underpinned the British state's notions of 'internal colonisation' in the Highlands during the 1760s.[170] Just as we saw in *Fingal*, Macpherson attempts to reconcile the ancient Celtic past and the Highland culture of the present with the modern world in *Temora*. But such a juxtaposition appears less strange and not as contradictory when we situate Macpherson in the broader intellectual context of the 1760s and the efforts of his friends and colleagues – including Adam Ferguson and Lord Kames – to make sense of the place of the Highlands within the commercial imperatives of the British imperial state.

THE POEMS OF OSSIAN (1773)

The final work considered in this chapter, *The Poems of Ossian*, was Macpherson's last publication about the Ossianic tales. Macpherson had already brought together the Ossianic Collections in a two-volume edition, the *Works of Ossian*, in 1765, but the paratextual materials were gathered from the earlier publications and also included Blair's *Critical Dissertation*.[171] The second collected edition of *Ossian* was published as *The Poems of Ossian* in 1773 and may well have been the proximate inspiration for Johnson and Boswell's tour of the Highlands and Islands.[172] *The Poems of Ossian* contains a new 'Preface' dated 15 August 1773, in which Macpherson yet again frames Ossian in historiographical terms. In this final Ossian paratextual publication, Macpherson pays particular attention to issues of translation, truth, and the chronological order of historical narratives.

Macpherson begins his new preface with commentary on the improvements to the poems since the first publication of *Fingal*, in particular concerning issues of diction and imagery. These changes are framed in terms of 'correctness': 'he hopes, he has brought the work to a state of correctness, which will preclude all future improvements'.[173] This is part of Macpherson's ongoing project to present himself as the translator of *Ossian*: unlike newly composed poems, translations can be corrected; there is an element of right or wrong to translation that cannot be attached to new compositions. However, 'correctness' also harkens back to Macpherson's overarching historiographical framework and speaks to the Enlightenment notion of 'truth' as expressed by Hume, Blair and others. A translator, like an historian, renders sources comprehensible to their readership, and they work in the same framework of objectivity and authenticity that Blair identified in his *Lectures on Rhetoric and Belles Lettres*. Macpherson, then, posits himself as an historian-translator at the beginning of this preface; both history and translation are overarching frameworks in which he then operates in the 1770s, when he produces *An Introduction to the History of Great Britain and Ireland* (1771), the translation of *The Iliad* (1773) and *The History of Great Britain* (1775).

The other key historiographical point made by Macpherson in this preface is to justify his reordering of the sequence of the Ossian poems.

Macpherson uses Enlightenment notions of chronology and historical narrative to explain why he presents *The Poems of Ossian* in a different order: 'one of the chief improvements, on this edition, is the care taken, in arranging the poems in the order of time; so as to form a kind of regular history of the age to which they relate'.[174] That is, their chronology has been altered so that the poetry becomes more explicitly historical: their purpose, here, is to become source material to illuminate the period when they are set. Whether they achieve this or not is another matter; they might not be a reliable or trustworthy source, but this is not our focus. Our book is about Macpherson's approach – how he presents his works – and we can clearly see that here, as elsewhere, he frames his works historiographically. He might call himself a translator, but he is thinking and working as an historian. Although this preface is not tremendously long or ground-breaking, it is yet another example of how Macpherson's thinking is shaped, affected and surrounded by history. In particular, Macpherson's justification for presenting the poems as a chronological narrative indicates the continued effect of Enlightenment thinking from the 1750s and 1760s as his work evolved into the 1770s. Here, we see the ongoing influence of Adam Smith's *Lectures on Rhetoric and Belles Lettres*. In Lecture XVIII, Smith argues that historical narratives should be ordered chronologically and that this helps to establish the philosophical logic of cause and effect:

> The next thing in order that comes to be considered with regard to historicall composition is the arangement in which the severall parts of the narration are to be placed. In general the narration is to be carried on in the same order as that in which the events themselves happened. The mind naturally conceives that the facts happened in the order they are related, and when they are by this means suited to our natural conceptions the notion we form of them is by that means rendered more distinct. This rule is quite evident and accordingly few Historians have trespassed against it.[175]

This belief in the necessity of chronological narrative was linked by Smith to the idea of causation: 'There is no connection with which we are so much interested as this of cause and effect; we are not satisfied when we have a fact told us which we are at a loss to conceive what it was that brought it about.'[176] It is this kind of reasoning which underpins Macpherson's reordering of the *Poems of Ossian* as a 'regular history of the age to which they relate' and demonstrates that he thinks of poetry through the eyes of an historian – and an Enlightenment one at that, well versed in the thought of Smith and others.

CONCLUSION

Writing to the bluestocking Elizabeth Montagu in May 1771, Lord Kames was eager to defend the reputation of Macpherson against the rising chorus of critics who doubted the authenticity of Ossian. In claiming that 'the manners described by Ossian were the genuine manners of his country', Kames argued that Macpherson was a 'poet as a true historian'.[177] In this chapter, we have explored two different modes of poetic expression – *The Highlander* and the Ossianic Collections – that demonstrate Kames's assessment of Macpherson and how in verse and in collecting, editing and translating Gaelic poetry Macpherson thought both historically and historiographically. Macpherson not only thought and wrote about the past – he also thought about *how* to write about the past in these earlier poetic forms and their accompanying paratexts.

In *The Highlander* we saw how Macpherson used historical sources to create his narrative of medieval Scottish history. Fordun and Buchanan provided Macpherson with his source material and their historical narratives are then rendered as verse in *The Highlander*. This versification of historical sources demonstrated Macpherson's adherence to emerging Enlightenment ideas about history writing that stressed fidelity to sources. In *The Highlander*, Macpherson also used a representation of the medieval Scottish past to comment on contemporary politics, creating a Whig constitutional narrative that valorised the British imperial state. In his first major work, Macpherson creates an instrumental view of the past that he returns to with gusto in his later political history writing, examined in Chapter 4. Then, in the Ossianic Collections, the paratextual advertisements, prefaces and dissertations demonstrate Macpherson's engagement with the historiographical community of Enlightenment historians and philosophers in Edinburgh and Glasgow in the early 1760s. In these writings that frame the poetry of Ossian, we see Macpherson beginning to function as an historian in prose. We see the influence of Hume and Blair in Macpherson's concern with notions of truth and fidelity to source material. Given their physical proximity to each other in the early 1760s, living in the same building, it is no surprise that Hugh Blair's impact on Macpherson's ideas about history and history writing was profound, and continued to shape his developing historiography of the 1770s. The dissertation to *Temora* reveals Macpherson's close engagement with the work of Adam Smith. In particular, Smith's and Macpherson's characterisation of the narrative abilities of the ancient historians was similar, but Macpherson used this as a point of departure. Unlike Smith, Macpherson saw ancient historians as lacking the desirable qualities of modern historians, with their emerging focus on issues of source material, evidence and explanation. This was a hinge-point in Macpherson's historiographical thinking, which he was to develop more fully in his history writing of the 1770s where he sought to combine historical narrative with philosophical reflection and explanation, all supported by scholarly erudition.

In the Ossianic Collections, Macpherson also thought as an historian in his consideration of stadial history. In key sections of the dissertations to both *Fingal* and *Temora*, we can see the influence of both Adam Smith and Adam Ferguson in Macpherson's positioning of the ancient Celtic world and the contemporary *Gàidhealtachd* in relation to the emergence of ideas of commercial modernity and military virtue in the eighteenth century. There is undoubted tension in Macpherson's defence of Gaelic oral culture, where he struggles to rationalise the 'poetry of wonder' of the Gaelic world with the 'prose of history' of the Enlightenment that he was so eager to embrace. However, situating the dissertations to both *Fingal* and *Temora* in the context of early 1760s debates about the place of the Highlands in British modernity helps us to understand that Macpherson was not as pessimistic as some might think – and that Macpherson's writing, in *Temora* especially, reveals the influence of Ferguson and Kames and their ideas about how to reconcile commercial modernity with the traditional oral culture of the Gaelic world. In the *Poems of Ossian*, Macpherson's preface from 1773 is one last blast of established Enlightenment thinking – in echoing Adam Smith's ideas about chronological historical narratives – before his history writing of the 1770s begins to engage with more novel notions of source criticism and scholarly erudition. It is then, in the next chapter, that we see Macpherson grappling more thoroughly with the balance between narrative, philosophy and erudition that places him in the same historiographical universe as Robertson and Gibbon.[178]

Notes

1 James Macpherson, 'Preface', *The Iliad of Homer. Vol. I* (London: T. Becket and P. A. de Hondt, 1773), p. xx.

2 For the recent scholarship on Macpherson's translation of *The Iliad*, see Kristin Lindfield-Ott, 'Epic Scotland: Wilkie, Macpherson, and Other Homeric Efforts', in Roberts Simms (ed.), *Brill's Companion to Prequels, Sequels, and Retellings of Classical Epic* (Leiden: Brill, 2018), pp. 357–74; Sebastian Mitchell, 'Macpherson, Ossian, and Homer's *Iliad*', in Gerard Bär and Howard Gaskill (eds), *Ossian and National Epic* (Frankfurt: Peter Lang, 2012), pp. 55–72.

3 For the Romanticism of Macpherson's Ossian and its influence on global Romanticism, see Fiona Stafford, 'Romantic Macpherson', in Murray Pittock (ed.), *The Edinburgh Companion to Scottish Romanticism* (Edinburgh: Edinburgh University Press, 2011), pp. 27–38; Dafydd Moore, 'The Critical Response to Ossian's Romantic Bequest', in Gerard Carruthers and Alan Rawes (eds), *English Romanticism and the Celtic World* (Cambridge: Cambridge University Press, 2003), pp. 38–53; Gaskill, *The Reception of Ossian in Europe*.

4 For a recent overview of Macpherson's relationship with Gaelic folklore and literature, see Lesa Ní Mhunghaile, 'Ossian and the Gaelic World', in Moore, *The International Companion to James Macpherson*, pp. 26–38; Thomson, *The Gaelic Sources of Macpherson's 'Ossian'*.

5 See, for example, Moore, 'James Macpherson and "Celtic Whiggism"'.

6 Kersey, 'The Pre-Ossianic Politics of James Macpherson'.

7 Macpherson, *The Highlander*, p. 64; Richard B. Sher, *Church and University in the Scottish Enlightenment: The Moderate Literati of Edinburgh* (Edinburgh: Edinburgh University Press, 1985), pp. 243–4.

8 See Thomas A. McKean, 'The Fieldwork Legacy of James Macpherson', *The Journal of American Folklore*, 114:454 (2001), pp. 447–63; James Porter, '"Bring Me the Head of James Macpherson": The Execution of Ossian and the Wellsprings of Folkloristic Discourse', *The Journal of American Folklore*, 114:454 (2001), pp. 396–435; Victoria Henshaw, 'James Macpherson and His Contemporaries: The Methods and Networks of Collectors of Gaelic Poetry in Late Eighteenth-Century Scotland', *Journal for Eighteenth-Century Studies*, 39:2 (2016), pp. 197–209.

9 Stafford, *Sublime Savage*, pp. 113–28.

10 Taylor, *The Wild Black Region*, pp. 188–9.

11 Guha, *History at the Limit of World-History*, p. 65.

12 Jonsson, *Enlightenment's Frontier*, pp. 28–34. For a recent analysis of Highlanders as both victims and perpetrators of colonialism, see Kehoe, 'Jacobites, Jamaica and the Establishment of a Highland Catholic Community in the Canadian Maritimes'.

13 Kersey, 'The Pre-Ossianic Politics of James Macpherson', p. 70.

14 Tom Jones, 'Pope and the Ends of History: Faction, Atterbury, and Clarendon's *History of the Rebellion*', *Studies in Philology*, 110:4 (2013), p. 882. For Pope's influence on Macpherson, see Kersey, 'The Pre-Ossianic Politics of James Macpherson', pp. 63–4.

15 deGategno places this in spring 1757. See deGategno, *James Macpherson*, p. 3.

16 Saunders, *The Life and Letters of James Macpherson*, p. 63; deGategno, *James Macpherson*, p. 3.

17 The English Short Title Catalogue lists copies in Aberdeen University Library, the British Library, Inverness Public Library, the National Library of Scotland, Columbia University Library, the New York Public Library,

University of Michigan Library. For the role of Thomas and Walter Ruddiman in transmitting 'a tradition of Scottish humanist scholarship' to an eighteenth-century readership, see Zachs, *Without Regard to Good Manners*, pp. 1–2.

18 'The Highlander; a poem, in six Cantos. 1s. *Crawfurd, Gordon, &c.*'. See *Scots Magazine*, April 1758, p. 224.

19 The inscription is by Isaac Reed and reads 'This Poem is a Curiosity being the first production of James Macpherson Esq Author of Ossian, Historian, & Translator of Homer. I am told this Poem was suppressed by the Author. See Dissertation at the end of 'The History of Scotland from the accession of James VI to the Union' by Malcolm Laing Esq., 2 vols, 8^{uo} 1800, where the Author without hesitation attributes and proves the poems of Ossian to be productions of Macpherson. Among other proofs the strong resemblance discoverable between this Poem *The Highlander* & Fingal both in sentiment and expression is adduced. June 1764 James Macpherson Esq was appointed Secretary General to the province of West Florida and immediately embarked with Governor Johnstone.'

20 *The Poetical Works of James Macpherson* (Edinburgh: P. Hill, 1802); *The Poems of Ossian &c. Containing the Poetical Works of James Macpherson, Esq. in Prose and Rhyme*, edited by Malcolm Laing (Edinburgh: T. Cadell Jr and W. Davies, 1805).

21 John MacQueen (ed.), *Poems of Ossian. Vol. II* (Edinburgh: Mercat Press, 1971), pp. 527–83; Dafydd Moore (ed.), *Ossian and Ossianism. Vol. I Beginnings* (London, Routledge, 2004).

22 Anon., 'Literary Anecdotes of James Macpherson, Esq', *The Weekly Magazine, or Edinburgh Amusement*, 18 January 1776, p. 97.

23 Saunders writes that 'it is also said that he was conscious himself of the defects of the poem, and tried to suppress it'. See Saunders, *Life and Letters of James Macpherson*, p. 47; deGategno argues that 'he soon recognized the poem as a failure, and asked the publisher to destroy any remaining copies'. See deGategno, *James Macpherson*, p. 3.

24 National Library of Scotland, MS 73.2.13 f 23, Donald Macpherson to Rev. J. Anderson, October 1797. Donald Macpherson was Macpherson's friend, and the two lived together in Edinburgh when *The Highlander* was written. Donald's letter to the Highland Society of Scotland includes some details of Macpherson's early life, but these are recollections made half a century later.

25 Malcolm Laing, *The History of Scotland, from the Union of the Crowns on the Accession of James VI to the Throne of England, to the Union of the Kingdoms in the Reign of Queen Anne*, with 'An Historical and Critical Dissertation on the Supposed Authenticity of Ossian's Poems, 4 vols (London: T. Cadell Jr and W. Davies, 1800), Vol. II, p. 406.

26 Ibid., p. 448.

27 In her book, *The Sublime Savage*, Fiona Stafford concludes her chapter on *The Highlander* by arguing that the 'The step from here to *The Poems of*

Ossian was not very large.' See Stafford, *The Sublime Savage*, p. 75. For a critique of Jacobite characterisations of Macpherson and *The Highlander*, see Moore, 'James Macpherson and "Celtic Whiggism"', pp. 3–5; and Kersey, 'The Pre-Ossianic Politics of James Macpherson', pp. 61–2.
28 Sher, *Church and University in the Scottish Enlightenment*, pp. 243–4.
29 Alex Woolf, *From Pictland to Alba 789–1070* (Edinburgh: Edinburgh University Press, 2007), p. 41.
30 Ibid., pp. 193–5.
31 See Stafford, *The Sublime Savage*, p. 70.
32 During the rule of the Mac Alpin dynasty, direct patrilineal succession was not practised. Instead, the line repeatedly branched off into two separate lines, which in the case of Indulf and Duffus led to the the line passing from Constantine II to Malcolm I, his cousin, then to Indulf, Constantin II's son, then to Duff I, Malcolm I's son, then to Culenus, Indulf's son. See Michael Lynch, *Scotland: A New History* (London: Pimlico, 1992), p. 42.
33 The manuscript is MS. COLB. BIB. IMP. PARIS, 4126.
34 Macpherson, 'A Dissertation', *Temora*, p. iii.
35 John Fordun, *Chronicle of the Scottish Nation*, edited by William F. Skene, translated by Felix J. H. Skene, 2 vols (Edinburgh: Edmonston & Douglas, 1872), Vol. I, p. 160.
36 All subsequent references in this chapter to the text of *The Highlander* are taken from the edited edition of the poem in Lindfield-Ott, 'See SCOT and SAXON Coalesc'd in One', pp. 44–113.
37 George Buchanan, *Buchanan's History of Scotland. In Twenty Books. The Second Edition, Revised and Corrected from the Latin Original, by Mr. Bond* (London: J. Bettenham, 1722), pp. 243–4.
38 Ibid., p. 244.
39 For a discussion of Hume's 'sentimental historiography', see O'Brien, *Narratives of Enlightenment*, pp. 60–7.
40 David H. Radcliffe, 'Ancient Poetry and British Pastoral', in Gaskill and Stafford, *From Gaelic to Romantic*, p. 35.
41 Gerard C. Carruthers, 'The Invention of Scottish Literature During the Long Eighteenth Century', unpublished PhD (University of Glasgow, 2001), p. 187.
42 Moore, *Enlightenment and Romance in James Macpherson's* The Poems of Ossian, p. 94.
43 For the role of ancestors in present-day Gaelic Scotland, see Iain MacKinnon, 'Recognising and Reconstituting *Gàidheil* Ethnicity', *Scottish Affairs*, 30:2 (2021), pp. 212–30.
44 This sentiment is repeated throughout the poem, for example 'carrying all their country in their breast' (II. 32).
45 Smith, *Adam Ferguson and the Idea of Civil Society*, p. 214.
46 deGategno, *James Macpherson*, p. 16.
47 Stafford, *The Sublime Savage*, pp. 157–8.

48 Jonsson, *Enlightenment's Frontier*, pp. 19–20. See also Smith, *Adam Ferguson and the Idea of Civil Society*.
49 Kenneth Simpson, *The Protean Scot: The Crisis of Identity in Eighteenth-Century Scottish Literature* (Aberdeen: Aberdeen University Press, 1988), p. 41.
50 Kersey, 'The Pre-Ossianic Politics of James Macpherson', pp. 66, 68.
51 Ibid., p. 67.
52 Ibid., p. 67.
53 This is unlikely to refer to Mary, as Macpherson took a particularly dim view of her involvement in British politics. See Macpherson, *The History of Great Britain*, pp. 575–6.
54 Kersey, 'The Pre-Ossianic Politics of James Macpherson', p. 67.
55 Ibid., p. 68.
56 Ibid.
57 Howard Weinbrot also reads these lines as pro-Union. See Howard Weinbrot, *Britannia's Issue: The Rise of British Literature from Dryden to Ossian* (Cambridge: Cambridge University Press, 1993), p. 540. Furthermore, Colin Kidd notes that 'a British allegiance coexists with a conventional Scottish identity' here. See Colin Kidd, 'Macpherson, Burns and the Politics of Sentiment', *Scotlands*, 4:1 (1997), p. 29.
58 *The Scots Magazine*, 22 (1760), p. 335.
59 Stafford, *The Sublime Savage*, p. 96. See also Dafydd Moore, 'James Macpherson, *Fingal* and Other Poems', in David Wormsley (ed.), *A Companion to Literature from Milton to Blake* (Oxford: Blackwell, 2001), p. 381.
60 Macpherson, *Fragments of Ancient Poetry*, p. 37.
61 Mulholland, *Sounding Imperial*, p. 98.
62 Stafford, *The Sublime Savage*, pp. 77–9.
63 Sher, 'Blair, Hugh (1718–1800)', in *Oxford Dictionary of National Biography*.
64 Schmitz, *Hugh Blair*, p. 45.
65 Moore, *Enlightenment and Romance in James Macpherson's* The Poems of Ossian, p. 25; Schmitz, *Hugh Blair*, p. 45, quoted in Stafford, *The Sublime Savage*, p. 97.
66 Stafford, *The Sublime Savage*, p. 99; Moore, 'James Macpherson, *Fingal* and Other Poems', p. 382.
67 Kidd, *Subverting Scotland's Past*, p. 228. For the historiography (and historicity) of the poetry itself in the Ossianic Collections, see Eric Gidal, *Ossianic Unconformities: Bardic Poetry in the Industrial Age* (Charlottesville: University of Virginia Press, 2015), p. 7; Mulholland, *Sounding Imperial*, p. 98.
68 Phillips, *Society and Sentiment*, pp. 14–15, 40–5.
69 Macpherson, *Fragments of Ancient Poetry*, p. iii.
70 Ibid.

71 '1st, the Age of Hunters; 2dly, the Age of Shepherds; 3dly, the Age of Agriculture; and 4thly, the Age of Commerce'. See Adam Smith, *Lectures on Jurisprudence*, edited by R. Meek, D. Raphael and P. Stein (Oxford: Clarendon Press, 1978), p. 27. Adam Smith gave both the Lectures on Jurisprudence and Rhetoric and Belles-Lettres in 1762, but these were not first published until 1896. See Pocock, *Barbarism and Religion. Vol. II. Narratives of Civil Government*, pp. 319–25.
72 Stafford, *The Sublime Savage*, p. 159.
73 Macpherson, *Fragments of Ancient Poetry*, p. iii; Phillips, *Society and Sentiment*, pp. 40–1; Pocock, *Barbarism and Religion. Vol. II. Narratives of Civil Government*, pp. 325–6.
74 Macpherson, *Fragments of Ancient Poetry*, pp. iii–iv.
75 Ibid., p. vi.
76 Adam Smith, *Lectures on Rhetoric and Belles Lettres*, edited by J. G. Bryce (Indianapolis, IN: Liberty Fund, 1985), p. 104; Richard Bourke, 'J. G. A. Pocock and the Presuppositions of the New British History', *Historical Journal*, 53:3 (2010), pp. 765–7.
77 William Godwin, 'Of History and Romance', *Caleb Williams*, edited by Maurice Hindle (London: Penguin, 2005), pp. 359–74. For an overview of Godwin's distinction between history and fiction, see Phillips, *Society and Sentiment*, pp. 118–21.
78 Macpherson, *Fragments of Ancient Poetry*, p. v.
79 Ibid., p. viii.
80 Macpherson, *Fingal*, n.p.
81 For bardic cultural transmission in the Gaelic world see Robert Dunbar, 'Vernacular Gaelic Tradition', in Sarah Dunnigan and Susan Gilbert (eds), *The Edinburgh Companion to Scottish Traditional Literatures* (Edinburgh: Edinburgh University Press, 2013), pp. 51–62.
82 McKean, 'The Fieldwork Legacy of James Macpherson', p. 448. For an account of how the role of poet and historian is often conflated in the Gaelic world, see Hugh Cheape's recent analysis of Sorley MacLean. Hugh Cheape, '"A Mind Restless Seeking": Sorley MacLean's Historical Research and the Poet as Historian', in Ronald W. Renton and Ian MacDonald (eds), *Ainmeil thar Cheudan: Presentations to the 2011 Sorley MacLean Conference* (Sabhal Mòr Ostaig, An t-Eilean Sgitheanach: Clò Ostaig, 2016), pp. 121–34.
83 Macpherson, *Fingal*, p. iii.
84 For an overview of these, see Ní Mhunghaile, 'Ossian and the Gaelic World', pp. 26–7.
85 Macpherson, *Fingal*, p. iv.
86 Ibid.
87 Ibid. Pocock, *Barbarism and Religion. Vol. II. Narratives of Civil Government*, p. 258.

88 Macpherson, *Fingal*, p. ix.
89 Smith, *Lectures on Rhetoric and Belles Lettres*, p. 104.
90 Macpherson, *Fingal*, p. ix.
91 Ibid., p. ii.
92 Ibid.
93 Ibid.
94 Colin Kidd, 'North Britishness and the Nature of Eighteenth-Century British Patriotisms', *Historical Journal*, 39:2 (1996), pp. 361–82.
95 Hugh Blair, *A Critical Dissertation on the Poems of Ossian, the Son of Fingal* (London: T. Becket and P. A. De Hondt, 1763).
96 Macpherson, 'A Dissertation Concerning the Antiquity, &c. of the Poems of Ossian the Son of Fingal', *Fingal*, p. i.
97 'Aut prodesse volunt aut delectare poetae'. See Horace, 'Ars Poetica', in Niall Rudd (ed.), *Horace: Epistles Book II and Epistle to the Pisones ('Ars Poetica')* (Cambridge: Cambridge University Press, 1989), line 333, p. 69.
98 Macpherson, *Fingal*, p. i.
99 Hume, 'Of the Study of History', in *Essays: Moral, Political, and Literary*, p. 565.
100 Macpherson, *Fingal*, p. i.
101 Ibid.
102 Ibid. Smith, *Lectures on Rhetoric and Belles Lettres*, p. 104.
103 Macpherson, *Fingal*, p. i.
104 Guha, *History at the Limit of World-History*, p. 9.
105 Moore, 'Adam Ferguson, *The Poems of Ossian* and the Imaginative Life of the Scottish Enlightenment', p. 287; Pocock, *Barbarism and Religion. Vol. II. Narratives of Civil Government*, p. 331; Eugene Heath and Vincenzo Merolle, 'Introduction', in E. Heath and V. Merolle (eds), *Adam Ferguson: History, Progress and Human Nature* (London: Pickering & Chatto, 2007); Mackillop, *Human Capital and Empire*, p. 3.
106 Macpherson, *Fingal*, p. ii.
107 Ibid.
108 Schmidt, *David Hume*, pp. 394–5.
109 For example, see the footnotes on Homer and Strabo in Macpherson, *Fingal*, pp. 4, 5.
110 Ibid., pp. ii–iii.
111 Ibid., p. iii.
112 Ibid., p. vii. 'Culdees' were 'proto-presbyterian monks' said to have been prevalent in the ancient Celtic past. See Kidd, *Subverting Scotland's Past*, p. xii, 189–91.
113 See, for example, Moore, *Enlightenment and Romance in James Macpherson's The Poems of Ossian*, p. 37.
114 Macpherson, *Fingal*, p. viii.
115 Ibid., p. x.

116 Ibid.
117 Ibid., pp. xi–xii.
118 Matthew Wickman, *The Ruins of Experience: Scotland's 'Romantic' Highlands and the Birth of the Modern Witness* (Philadelphia: University of Pennsylvania Press, 2007).
119 Moore, *Enlightenment and Romance in James Macpherson's* The Poems of Ossian, p. 170.
120 Macpherson, *Fingal*, p. xv.
121 Moore, *Enlightenment and Romance in James Macpherson's* The Poems of Ossian, p. 163; Stafford, *The Sublime Savage*, p. 160.
122 Fiona Stafford and Howard Gaskill, 'Editors' Preface', in Stafford and Gaskill, *From Gaelic to Romantic*, pp. xiii–xiv.
123 For an overview of these changes to Highland society during the eighteenth century, see Jonsson, *Enlightenment's Frontier*, p. 2; and Allan I. Macinnes, *Clanship, Commerce, and the House of Stuart, 1603–1788* (East Linton: Tuckwell Press, 1996).
124 Ian Duncan, 'The Pathos of Abstraction: Adam Smith, Ossian, and Samuel Johnson', in Leith Davis, Ian Duncan and Janey Sorenson (eds), *Scotland and the Borders of Romanticism* (Cambridge: Cambridge University Press, 2004), p. 49.
125 Donald Meek, 'The Sublime Gael: The Impact of Macpherson's *Ossian* on Literary Creativity and Cultural Perception in Gaelic Scotland', in Gaskill, *The Reception of Ossian in Europe*, p. 66.
126 Alastair McIntosh, 'Foreword', in James Hunter, *On the Other Side of Sorrow: Nature and People in the Scottish Highlands* (Edinburgh: Birlinn, 2014), pp. xxvi, xxx.
127 Matthew Dziennik, '"Under ye Lash of ye Law": The State and the Law in the Post-Culloden Scottish Highlands', *Journal of British Studies*, 60:3 (2021), p. 611.
128 Taylor, *The Wild Black Region*, pp. 196–7; Maclean, 'The Early Political Careers', pp. 235, 305, 23.
129 Jim MacPherson, 'History Writing and Agency in the Scottish Highlands, pp. 123–38.
130 Macpherson, *Temora*, p. i.
131 Moore, 'Adam Ferguson, *The Poems of Ossian* and the Imaginative Life of the Scottish Enlightenment', p. 287.
132 Macpherson, *Temora*, p. i.
133 Phillips, *Society and Sentiment*, pp. 40–1.
134 Macpherson, *Temora*, p. i.
135 Ibid., p. i.
136 Phillips, *Society and Sentiment*, pp. 55–6.
137 Smith, *Lectures on Rhetoric and Belles Lettres*, pp. 101–2.
138 Ibid., p. 102; Pocock, *Barbarism and Religion. Vol. II. Narratives of Civil Government*, pp. 325–6.

139 Smith gave Lecture XVIII at Glasgow on Friday, 7 January 1763, and *Temora* was published on 27 January 1763. Smith, *Lectures on Rhetoric and Belles Lettres*, p. 98; *St. James's Chronicle*, 27 January 1763, p. 2.
140 Macpherson, *Temora*, p. ii.
141 Ibid.
142 Ibid.
143 Ibid., p. vii.
144 Ibid., p. ix, xi.
145 Ibid., p. xvi.
146 For discussion of this in the context of Macpherson and Ossian, see Porter, '"Bring Me the Head of James Macpherson"', pp. 411, 417–19; and James Mulholland, 'James Macpherson's Ossian Poems, Oral Traditions, and the Invention of Voice ', *Oral Tradition*, 24:2 (2009), pp. 393–414.
147 Guha, *History at the Limit of World-History*, p. 68.
148 Macpherson, *Temora*, p. iii.
149 Smith, *Lectures on Rhetoric and Belles Lettres*, p. 98; Schmidt, *David Hume*, p. 385.
150 Macpherson, *Temora*, p. iii.
151 Ibid.
152 Ibid., p. iv.
153 Kersey, 'The Pre-Ossianic Politics of James Macpherson', p. 72.
154 Macpherson, *Temora*, p. iv.
155 Ibid., p. x.
156 Ibid., pp. v–vii.
157 Ibid., p. xi.
158 Ibid., p. xii. For an overview of stadial history, see O'Brien, *Narratives of Enlightenment*, p. 133; and, more recently, see Silvia Sebastiani, *The Scottish Enlightenment: Race, Gender, and the Limits of Progress* (New York: Palgrave Macmillan, 2013); and Bruce Buchan and Silvia Sebastiani, '"No Distinction of Black or Fair": The Natural History of Race in Adam Ferguson's Lectures on Moral Philosophy', *Journal of the History of Ideas*, 82:2 (2021), pp. 207–29.
159 Robertson, *The History of America. Vol. I*, p. 324. See Henry Kames, *Sketches of the History of Man* (1774), Ferguson, *Essay on Civil Society* (1767), Adam Smith, *Wealth of Nations* (1776), John Millar, *Observations Concerning the Distinction of Ranks in Society* (1771).
160 Buchan and Sebastiani, '"No Distinction of Black or Fair"', p. 210; Pocock, *Barbarism and Religion. Vol. II. Narratives of Civil Government*, p. 331.
161 Pocock, *Barbarism and Religion Vol. II Narratives of Civil Government*, pp. 322–4; Sebastiani, *The Scottish Enlightenment*, p. 150.
162 Sebastiani, *The Scottish Enlightenment*, p. 146; Pocock, *Barbarism and Religion. Vol II. Narratives of Civil Government*, p. 331; Smith, *Adam Ferguson and the Idea of Civil Society*, p. 193.

163 Saunders, *The Life and Letters of James Macpherson*, pp. 64–6; Stafford, *The Sublime Savage*, p. 77; Fania Oz-Salzberger, 'Ferguson, Adam (1723–1816)', *Oxford Dictionary of National Biography* (Oxford: Oxford University Press, 2004), available at: https://doi-org.eor.uhi.ac.uk/10.1093/ref:odnb/9315 (accessed 23 December 2021).
164 Jonsson, *Enlightenment's Frontier*, p. 19.
165 Buchan and Sebastiani, '"No Distinction of Black or Fair"', p. 211; Stafford, *The Sublime Savage*, p. 158.
166 Macpherson, *Temora*, p. xii.
167 Ibid.
168 Pocock, *Barbarism and Religion. Vol. II. Narratives of Civil Government*, p. 370.
169 Jonsson, *Enlightenment's Frontier*, pp. 28–30, 34–8.
170 Ibid., p. 28.
171 Macpherson, *The Works of Ossian*.
172 deGategno, *James Macpherson*, p. 103.
173 Macpherson, *The Works of Ossian*, p. v.
174 Ibid., p. xiii.
175 Smith, *Lectures on Rhetoric and Belles Lettres*, p. 98.
176 Ibid.
177 Quoted in Jonsson, *Enlightenment's Frontier*, p. 30.
178 Pocock, 'The Re-description of Enlightenment', p. 113.

3

History: James Macpherson's Narrative Prose Histories

Macpherson's interest in the past had been firmly established in his poetry of the late 1750s and early 1760s. In *The Highlander* (1758) and the Ossianic Collections of the *Fragments* (1760), *Fingal* (1761/2) and *Temora* (1763), Macpherson did more than simply use the past as a source for his stories. Instead, primary sources from the past (both written and from the oral tradition) were used by Macpherson to create his historical narratives that demonstrated his engagement with the past in ways that were thoroughly modern and influenced by the Enlightenment intellectual circles in which he moved. While rooting these poetic forms in primary source evidence was key, Macpherson also used these narratives of the past to articulate his own version of stadial history – the notion that history could be delineated into distinct stages, determined by mode of subsistence, that led human societies from the 'savagery' of ancient times to the 'civilisation' of the modern era.[1] In his poetry, Macpherson made the argument that the early history of the Highlands laid the foundation for later developments in the region, while also demonstrating how Highlanders were part of a broader civilisation across the British Isles from which contemporary understandings of Britishness were beginning to emerge in the mid-eighteenth century. Using poetry in this way, to create a narrative understanding of the past, demonstrated the essential mimetic qualities of poetic form and echoed the recent claims of Adam Smith regarding poetry as the ideal form of history writing.[2]

These concerns with the past then translated into Macpherson's formal prose historical writing of the early 1770s. Building on his Enlightenment roots in Edinburgh (especially the lectures of Hugh Blair) and the intellectual circles he moved in following his move to London in 1766 (including historians Alexander Dow and the great David Hume), Macpherson wrote about a distant Celtic past and a recent British one using similar historiographical strategies. In his history writing, Macpherson developed his use of source material, explicitly engaging with extensive primary sources from the past and framing them with the scholarly scaffolding of footnotes. Macpherson echoed Hume's injunction that history writing should both amuse and instruct, placing an emphasis on history's didactic qualities in his later writings. To this, Macpherson gave additional weight to concepts of truth and impartiality, reflecting both his closeness to Blair's philosophy of history writing and the revived Ossian authenticity debate, stoked by the publication of Samuel Johnson's *Journey to the Western Islands of Scotland* in 1775.[3] Building on these philosophical ideas, Macpherson's history writing of the 1770s develops an approach that combines narrative and explanation, supported by the erudition of sources and footnotes. In *The History of Great Britain* (1775), we see perhaps Macpherson's clearest engagement with Enlightenment ideas to date, and this chapter helps to place Macpherson in this context and to understand him as an Enlightenment historian. In his formal history writing, Macpherson further develops stadial ideas as a key part of *An Introduction to the History of Great Britain and Ireland* (1771). While these ideas of progress are less central to *The History of Great Britain* (given that the book deals with a later period), they do inform Macpherson's interpretation of the evolution of the British constitution during the seventeenth century – which then underpins Macpherson's use of history writing to interpret the late-1770s crisis of empire, explored in the next chapter. Through this formal history writing, Macpherson further articulates a sense of British identity, one that encompasses both the 'Celtic Whiggism' of *An Introduction to the History of Great Britain and Ireland* and the outright Whig constitutionalism of *The History of Great Britain*. It is this historiographical foundation which then forms the basis for Macpherson's political vision of the British imperial state in his later works.

This chapter explores Macpherson's approach to writing about the past in his formal prose histories: *An Introduction to the History of Great Britain and Ireland* (1771), *The History of Great Britain* (1775) and the *Original Papers* (1775). Here, we explore Macpherson's sources, methodologies and philosophies of history writing through detailed close readings of each of these texts in turn. As well as discussing Macpherson's historiographical method, we explore how Macpherson uses the past in his works, and to what purpose. The chapter also examines Macpherson's understanding of Britain and Britishness. As such, we again address the old argument that Ossian is some kind of pro-Jacobite Highland fantasy by showing that Macpherson's wider corpus of works contains a set of distinctively British pieces, which form the focus of this chapter. Identity is complicated, and the British focus of these works does not negate any Celtic, Scottish or empire identities in his other works. They do show, however, that labelling Macpherson as a Jacobite, insular Highlander, Scot-who-loathed the English or Scottish instead of British is problematic.[4] As elsewhere in this book, discussion is based on his *writings*: this study is interested in what Macpherson presents to the world through his texts and how he uses the 'tools of sceptical Enlightenment historiography' in his later prose history writing.[5]

Macpherson's engagement with this Enlightenment historiography is at the heart of this chapter, exploring how Macpherson wrangles these issues of narrative, philosophy and erudition that so preoccupied the likes of Hume, Blair and Robertson and how this kind of history writing could function as a tool of identity formation. Both *An Introduction* and *The History of Great Britain* are 'authentic', in that they are based on clearly traceable sources. Both celebrate a British and imperial (though strongly Scottish-influenced) past and future. In addition, this chapter also engages with the companion volume to *The History of Great Britain*, the *Original Papers*, an anthology of sources for the 'Secret History' made public in his *History of Great Britain*. As such, this chapter is central to the argument of this book: it combines a sustained discussion of Macpherson's historiographical principles with his reflections on identity and restores his largely overlooked prose histories to the principal position they deserve. This connects the past with the present and develops the argument of our book from examples of conjectural approaches in *An Introduction to the History of Great Britain and Ireland* to rigorous source-based analysis in *The History of Great Britain* in a significant way, both in terms of the works explored in this chapter, and to set up our final chapter – on Macpherson's writings on the politics of empire during the late 1770s.

This chapter examines Macpherson's engagement with Enlightenment approaches to prose history writing across two distinct time periods, from the distant Celtic past to more recent British history. *An Introduction to the History of Great Britain and Ireland*, Macpherson's first booklength foray into prose history writing explores early 'Celtic' history. Macpherson narrates the preceding 100 years or so in *The History of Great Britain* and its accompanying volume of sources, the *Original Papers*, which cover the period from the 'Glorious Revolution' to the death of Queen Anne. Together they exemplify a sustained engagement with history writing that bears comparison with more illustrious and celebrated Enlightenment historians. In prefaces to works such as

The History of Scotland (1759), *The History of America* (1777) and *The History of the Decline and Fall of the Roman Empire* (1776–88), William Robertson and Edward Gibbon outlined their historiographical method, focusing especially on the erudition of their sources and footnotes. In Macpherson's prefaces of the 1770s, we find him echoing, and in some instances pre-empting, these concerns and functioning as a self-consciously historiographical Enlightenment historian. These texts demonstrate how Macpherson functioned as a formal historian in prose, where he explores how ideas of truth, impartiality, narrative, erudition and philosophy function in his version of Enlightenment history writing at the beginning of the 1770s. Moreover, Macpherson used this history writing of the early 1770s to consolidate a persistent British and imperial identity, especially in his focus on warfare as both driver of history and key to the success of empire.

AN INTRODUCTION TO THE HISTORY TO GREAT BRITAIN AND IRELAND (1771)

An Introduction to the History of Great Britain and Ireland, published in April 1771, is Macpherson's earliest book-length work explicitly published as a work of prose narrative history writing. As its advertisement in the *Scots Magazine* of that month tells us, its purpose is to 'dispel the shade which covers the antiquities of the British nations, to investigate their origin, and carry down some account of their character, manners, and government, into the time of records and domestic writers'.[6] It is, therefore, set out as a history that connects the oral tradition of Ossian with foreign records and written sources. The title of this work is, perhaps, misleading for today's reader; it is not the introduction to the later *History of Great Britain* (1775), but a history of Celtic Britain. Here, Macpherson is self-consciously historiographical: *An Introduction* is the earliest work of his that is directly sold and marketed as a history and where he puts 'forth claims as an historian'.[7] Of course, as we have seen already, Macpherson's methodology and mindset is that of an historian from his earliest publications, but *An Introduction* is a clear public statement of this, especially his engagement with a range of eighteenth-century ideas about history writing that builds on the Ossianic Collection's paratexts and points towards his later prose history writing of the 1770s. This section is structured around the different approaches to history writing that Macpherson takes in *An Introduction* that mark him out as an Enlightenment historian. Macpherson uses the 'Preface' to *An Introduction* as a way to outline his methodological approach, exploring the purpose of his history writing, its engagement with other scholars, his philosophical method and his use of primary sources. We then consider how Macpherson's methodology outlined in the preface is echoed by self-conscious historiographical reflection in the main body of *An Introduction*. Macpherson frames this account of the early Celts with a key Enlightenment belief about history writing: that its purpose, as Hume argued, was to both amuse and instruct. *An Introduction* also contains much discussion about the genre of history writing and how, in its unstable mid-eighteenth-century form, it could contain elements of fiction, romance and genealogy. Macpherson, though, distinguished his history writing from these other ways of writing about the past through his use of primary source materials, largely based on classical writers from the period such as Diodorus of Sicily and Tacitus, but also using the evidence of language. Here, Macpherson uses the emerging scholarly convention of footnoting to demonstrate a longer-standing historiographical practice: his erudition. Yet this older attention to sources Macpherson places in a thoroughly modern context by combining it with a way of writing about the past that is both narrative and philosophical, echoing the practice of other Enlightenment historians. The final part of this section demonstrates Macpherson's use of one of the key Enlightenment ideas – the stadial development of society from one stage to another. Here, we see Macpherson making an argument about the Celtic contribution to the evolution of Western civilisation, one that marks him out as a proponent of Whig constitutional ideas that he had already developed in *The Highlander* that come to fruition in his later works of history writing and political propaganda.

That Macpherson 'embarked in the character of an historian' in writing *An Introduction* was recognised by his Enlightenment contemporaries.[8] *An Introduction* was written at a time when Macpherson was keeping company in London with the likes of David Hume and Alexander Dow. Hume expressed his admiration for *An Introduction* in a letter to Dow (who, as discussed in the next chapter, was Macpherson's flatmate):

> My compliments to Ossian. He has given us a work last winter, which contains a great deal of genius and good writing; but I cannot assent to his system. I must still adhere to the common opinion regarding our origin, or rather your origin; for we are all plainly Danes or Saxons in the low countries.[9]

While Hume disagreed here with Macpherson's arguments about the Celtic origins of modern Britain, he approved of his method and writing and recognised him as a fellow Enlightenment historian. Likewise, while Macpherson's insistence on the primacy of the Celts over Anglo-Saxon origin myths of Europe began to attract sustained criticism during the last decades of the eighteenth century, Edward Gibbon was complimentary about Macpherson's work and used it in the fourth volume of *The Decline and Fall of the Roman Empire*, published in 1788:

> In the dark and doubtful paths of Caledonian antiquity, I have chosen for my guides two learned and ingenious Highlanders, whom their birth and education had peculiarly qualified for that office. See, Critical Dissertations on the Origin and Antiquities, &c., of the Caledonians, by Dr. John Macpherson, London, 1768, in 4to.; and Introduction to the History of Great Britain and Ireland, by James Macpherson, Esq., London, 1773, in 4to. third edit.[10]

As we shall see below, it was no accident that Gibbon bracketed together James and Rev. Dr John Macpherson, as James was heavily influenced by the work of John, who was a crucial point of historiographical argument in *An Introduction*.

The more recent scholarly reception of Macpherson's *Introduction* has moved beyond older readings of the text as simply a response to the Ossian authenticity debate. Rather than being just 'a logical extension of his interest in the Ossianic material', as Paul deGategno argues, *An Introduction* has been characterised by Colin Kidd and Dafydd Moore as a work of history that engages seriously with conjectural and stadial history writing.[11] Kidd argues that Macpherson was a 'sceptical historian of Scottish liberty', using the framework of stadial history to argue that the 'Whig values' of freedom and liberty could be found 'in the Celtic past'.[12] This 'Celtic Whiggism' was then examined further by Dafydd Moore, who argues that *An Introduction* was Macpherson's 'major work of conjectural history'.[13] Moore describes Macpherson's use of 'English Whiggism' to analyse the Celtic past as 'a more subversive activity than has hitherto been appreciated', because of Macpherson's emphasis on 'appropriating those values for the Celt at the explicit expense of the Anglo-Saxon'.[14] While these issues are discussed further below, our focus, as ever, is on Macpherson's approach to history and his methodology, not on interpreting the content of the book – this section examines the techniques of history writing that Macpherson employs in *An Introduction* and analyses how Macpherson's use of such stadial approaches led to an understanding of British constitutional history which then underpinned his later political writings.

Macpherson's historiographical approach in *An Introduction* is outlined in the 'Preface'. As in his other prefatory and supplementary material, this is where he is at his most historiographical as he explicitly discusses his methods and approach. The first section of the preface is focused on Macpherson's motives for writing *An Introduction*. He argues that because ancient history – and ancient Celtic history in particular – is not very popular, there is no hope to use such a publication to gain literary fame and thus, he assures us, 'he was induced to proceed by the sole motive of private amusement'.[15] Macpherson's distinction between fame and his own enjoyment is significant. With his political career comfortably underway, financed by secure income from at least one government pension as a result of his time in Florida during the 1760s, Macpherson no longer needed to try as hard to be taken seriously as a literary writer as he had in the 1750s, with his magazine poetry and *The Highlander*. As a government writer (but not yet a politician in his own right), his identity was that of 'man of letters'. Writing a history for 'private amusement' fits in well with this attitude and with broader Enlightenment thought, where Hume's notion that history 'amuses the fancy' was still important in framing how the past was written about.[16] In this same section of the preface Macpherson raises another important point: his contemporaries were not only not interested in Britain's ancient past – 'inquiries into antiquity are so little the taste of the present age' – but are, in fact 'prejudiced against the subject', most likely a reflection of the still-rumbling Ossian controversy. This prejudice, he argues, stems from a long-held belief that assigns this ancient history to 'fiction and romance'. While later eighteenth-century thinkers, such as William Godwin, explore the interconnection between history and romance, Macpherson here uses 'fiction and romance' as the antithesis of Enlightenment history writing, with its concern for truth, authenticity and faithfulness to sources, causation and similar issues. However, as Macpherson points out there is nothing inherent about ancient history that makes it 'fiction and romance'; indeed, he notes, this is something 'which we have been taught'. Here, then, Macpherson demonstrates an awareness of Enlightenment historiographical theory: by situating his history of ancient Britain in opposition to 'fiction and romance', he positions himself as a modern historian who, like Hume, writes for his own amusement.

Macpherson further explores these notions in the next section of the preface, where he discusses his methodology explicitly. He says that he 'has studied to be clear in disquisition, concise in observation, just in inference'. This is reminiscent of Hugh Blair's emphasis on the need for 'impartiality, fidelity, gravity and dignity' in an historian.[17] Macpherson's first two points – clarity and conciseness – are stylistic ones, similar to Blair's about the gravity and dignity with which the historian should treat their subject, explored in Chapter 1. The third – 'just in inference' – concerns Blair's first two ideas about the historian's treatment of sources. To approach sources impartially and faithfully requires the historian to infer appropriately and reflects Blair's 'new rules of historical composition'.[18] Furthermore, in the same section of the preface Macpherson notes the following:

> An enemy to fiction himself, he imposes none upon the world. He advances nothing as fact without authorities; and his conjectures arise not so much from his own ingenuity, as from the proofs which the ancients have laid before him.

In doing so, Macpherson positions himself as an Enlightenment historian. He addresses the distinction between 'history' and 'fiction' that he alluded to in the opening section of the preface, in a move designed to forestall criticism from those who questioned the authenticity of the Ossian poems. When he says that he is 'an enemy to fiction', Macpherson is making a claim to be taken seriously as an historian, at the forefront of historiographical thinking. Indeed, Macpherson's insistence on 'authorities' speaks to his method of writing history from primary sources; in the case of *An Introduction* these 'authorities' are records written as near to the period in question as he has access to. As Pocock argues in the context of Hume's *History of England*, 'The central obligation of the neo-classical historian was to follow the ancient historians, or those contemporary with the event, in reporting what they had told him.'[19] This was the approach promoted by Enlightenment historiography, and Macpherson's link between 'conjectures' (that is, his interpretation of the sources, or the connections he draws between them) and the 'proofs' given by his primary source echoed the concerns of the likes of Blair to narrate the past with 'some connecting principle'.[20] *An Introduction* is, then, not merely a companion piece to Ossian, but – seen in its own right, as a history of ancient Britain – an example of modern Enlightenment history writing in which Macpherson follows the historiographical example of Hugh Blair and places greater emphasis on sources, evidence and proof than he had in the paratexts to the Ossianic Collections.

This is a point that Macpherson picks up in the next section of the preface to *An Introduction*, where he discusses his attention to the detail of his evidence:

> The darkness, with which the prejudice and vanity of the Scots and Irish have covered their origin has forced the Author to examine that point with a minuteness, which a dispute so unimportant seems not to deserve. But the

disquisitions of many learned men had given a kind of consequence to the subject, when they rendered it perplexed and obscure. To extricate truth from the polemical rubbish of former antiquaries was a task of labour.

Here, Macpherson makes a distinction between antiquarians and historians, and places himself firmly on the side of the latter. Unlike previous antiquarian writing on Britain's ancient past, Macpherson claims that he is paying close attention to every detail by consulting primary sources wherever possible, rather than relying on later histories. This is a fundamental historiographical point: Macpherson's primary-source-led research is a stark change from the kind of history writing that was popular before the Enlightenment, and which relied on the stories of great men.[21] Moreover, Macpherson analysed primary sources in order to 'extricate truth', demonstrating a more philosophical approach to erudition than the 'former antiquaries', such as Father Thomas Innes (1662–1744), Jacobite antiquarian and the author of *A Critical Essay on the Ancient Inhabitants of the Northern Parts of Britain or Scotland* (1729), against whom Macpherson positioned his Celtic history. This philosophical use of sources, rather than the historian's narrative or 'truffle-hound' accumulation of material, distinguished Macpherson's more modern approach from antiquarians such as Innes and, indeed, marked a development from Macpherson's own practice in the paratexts to the Ossianic Collections.[22]

Macpherson also alludes to the Enlightenment concerns with objectivity in the preface to *An Introduction*: his search for 'truth' stands in marked contrast to the 'polemical rubbish' he identifies in the work of antiquarians. In considering how the evidence of primary sources establishes the 'truth' of the past, Macpherson was moving beyond the position of the likes of Hume, who argued that truth was determined by 'impartiality more than exhaustive research'.[23] Indeed, here Macpherson was closer to the rigorous use of sources proposed by William Robertson in his history writing in the second half of the eighteenth century.[24] In doing so, Macpherson emphasised yet again his perception of himself as a modern historian, rather than a hobbyist antiquarian.

The final section of the preface focuses on a discussion of sources, both primary ones and recent secondary Celtic scholarship. Macpherson singles out his acquaintance and collaborator Rev. Dr John Macpherson's manuscript notes as a modern source that he has used. These notes formed the basis of John Macpherson's *Critical Dissertations on the Origin, Antiquities, Language, Government, Manners, Religion of the Ancient Caledonians, their Posterity, the Picts, and the British and Irish*

Scots (published posthumously in 1768).[25] The Rev. Dr John's approach was similar to James's, where they both rejected elements of Innes's methodology and analysis in framing their erudite scholarship about the Celtic past with modern stadial theories that emphasised the commercial modernity of the Highlands.[26] While James Macpherson acknowledges the use of 'some modern writers' in the preface to *An Introduction*, he is also careful to point out that 'he neither borrows their sentiments nor relies upon their judgment'. In other words, Macpherson uses these sources for their facts rather than their interpretation or narrative. Other than that, however, his focus is largely on classical primary sources, following the approach outlined in the dissertation to *Temora*:

> He looks upon antiquity through the medium of the ancients, and thinks he sees it in its genuine state. His work is formed on the general result of the information which the writers of Greece and Rome have transmitted from every quarter; and if his system is not satisfactory, it, at least, is new.

This is a significant statement: Macpherson argues that consulting primary sources that date from as close to the period under study as possible is different to other historians' approach to the past, in particular for a period lacking in written evidence. This makes the preface to *An Introduction* a key source for examining Macpherson as historian: it shows how he views his approach to history writing as different from other historians, and it also demonstrates his familiarity with Enlightenment historiographical theory that was increasingly concerned with reconciling historical narrative with scholarly erudition in explaining and analysing the past.

While the preface is the most historiographical part of *An Introduction*, Macpherson engages with theoretical notions about the nature of history throughout the work. At key points in the main body of *An Introduction*, Macpherson deals with issues regarding the purpose of history writing, the range of sources available to historians (from ancient classical texts to the evidence of language and genealogy), and the balance between historical narrative, the erudition of footnotes, and philosophical reflection on broader societal change and stadial history. Macpherson is also self-consciously historiographical, not just in his explicit reflection on his own methodology and approach, but in his criticism of other historians – especially eighteenth-century ones, such as Fr Thomas Innes.

Throughout the main text of *An Introduction*, Macpherson reflects on the purpose served by writing about the past, echoing his discussion in the preface about amusement and the perils of fiction. In the chapter on 'Irish Extraction of the Scots Examined', Macpherson explicitly discusses why he wrote *An Introduction*: he 'has taken up arms against fiction and romance, and he will not lay them down till the whole are subdued'.[27] In doing so, he says, he is 'destroying the fantastic fables, which deform the obscurity of our ancient history'. While he admits debunking conceived notions about certain periods might lead to more gaps in our collective knowledge of the past, he argues that 'oblivion itself is better than inauthentic fame'.[28] In other words, challenging myths is preferable to believing in unauthorised fiction. Here, we can see Macpherson thinking in a self-consciously historiographical way, following the principles he had established in the preface to *An Introduction*. Macpherson is also familiar with the historiographical concept outlined by David Hume in 'Of the Study of History', that history – of all the genres – is best placed to instruct and amuse the reader. This is not a new idea – indeed, it is generally traced to Horace's statement that poets should both instruct and entertain.[29] It is, however, something emphasised by Enlightenment historians and theorists; Hume is not alone in giving the two concepts equal weighting in his discussion of history writing, and Macpherson's great historian mentor, Hugh Blair, also emphasised both the mimetic and the didactic elements of history writing.[30] In *An Introduction*, Macpherson concludes his discussion of the Gaëls, Cimbri, and Belgæ with reference to this: 'to descend into a minute detail of the various petty tribes into which the three British nations were subdivided, would neither furnish instruction nor amusement', and this is enough reason for him to curtail his discussion.[31] At another point in *An Introduction*, he dismisses etymology as 'always unentertaining and dry'; while etymology might well be instructive, it falls short on the *delectare* side.[32] He returns to this notion later on in *An Introduction*, when he argues that 'it is only when history descends into the cultivated periods of a well formed community, that it becomes an object of pleasure, and the means of improvement'.[33] Here, his concern with the agreeable purpose of history writing demonstrates that, like Hume and others, Macpherson is an Enlightenment historian, who writes in a self-consciously historiographical way.

Macpherson's historiographical engagement with the concepts of 'fiction and romance' can also be seen in his discussion of sources in the main text of *An Introduction*. In this context, Macpherson comments on the increase in genealogical documents in the Middle Ages and links this to a new approach in land management: 'lands and honours becoming hereditary, gave birth to a pride of family among the great barons; and they endeavoured to add lustre to the distinctions which they had acquired by tracing their ancestors through the same path of eminence to a remote antiquity'.[34] Indeed, he presents genealogy as a form of history writing: tracing back one's lineage to antiquity is a similar approach to linking events through causation and demonstrates how Macpherson fuses older forms of genealogical thinking about the past taken from the Gaelic world with Enlightenment ideas.[35] This is related to the ancients' dearth of written sources: their failure to record deeds for posterity leads to an eventual blank. In this genealogical history writing, Macpherson points out, 'romance' was a key part: 'men possessed of the little literature of the times, and a talent for fable, either through ignorance or vanity, indulged the romantic passions of an ignorant race of men, by deducing the origin of their respective nations from very distant æras'. Genealogy thus becomes fiction; when there are no written records, tracing family connections necessarily sits in the realm of 'legends'.[36] As such, we see here, again, the tension between an understanding of the past based on the Gaelic genealogical world and an Enlightenment emphasis on the importance of written records as evidence in history writing. In this discussion Macpherson shows awareness of contemporary thinking regarding the distinction between history and fiction; in the Enlightenment there is a clear separation between the two, though the Romantics bring the two together and admit the central role of narrative to both fiction and history. This point is picked up when he discusses the state of history writing in early Britain in particular, where – due to the absence of written records – fiction reigns much longer than on the continent: 'The British nations', he argues, 'till of late years, were much more remarkable for the performance of great actions in the field, than for recording them with dignity and precision in the closet'. That is, history writing and record keeping is not seen by Macpherson as a British trait, and 'the early part of our annals still remains in the possession of fiction and romance'.[37] This is what his *An Introduction* aims to address: 'to dispel the shades which cover the antiquities of the British nations, to investigate their origin, to carry down some account of their character, manners, and government, into the times of records and domestic writers, is the design of this Introduction'.[38] Here, Macpherson identifies a number of functions that Enlightenment history writing needed to fulfil: to tell the truth about the past through careful research and interrogation of sources, and to focus on the customs of the society it investigates, rather than on chronicling their deeds. This mirrors Hume's emphasis on social history and is another example of how Macpherson self-consciously reflects on Enlightenment historiographical theory in his own histories.[39]

Macpherson's key sources in *An Introduction*, though, are ancient classical texts, reflecting the Enlightenment preoccupation of the likes of Adam Smith with the work of Greek and Roman historians. Building on his argument in the dissertation to *Temora*, Macpherson examines the ancients' 'aversion to the study of letters', which, he argues, is noticeable in the absence of 'any authentic monuments' from the Celts of northern Britain: 'The Caledonians were not more destitute of the means of preserving their history in the intermediate century between Agricola and Severus, than their posterity were for a considerable time after the Romans had relinquished the dominion of Britain.'[40] He draws an interesting comparison in relating this: that the ancients' lack of interest in preserving their history through written records is the opposite of their desire to distinguish themselves in battle: 'they thought every pursuit not immediately subservient to the profession of arms mean and dishonourable' without considering 'that this prejudice was a fatal enemy to the fame which they sought after with so much eagerness in the field'. Indeed, without written records 'in vain were exploits worthy of memory performed, when the only certain means of transmitting them to posterity were discouraged and despised'.[41] This speaks to Macpherson's historiographical understanding of ancient times: the way he approaches this discussion is through the looking glass of history. As an Enlightenment historian the process of written memorialisation is vitally important to his understanding of the past: without records the past becomes blurry. In pointing out the discrepancy between the ancients' desire for fame in battle and their lack of commemoration through written accounts, Macpherson draws on one of the fundamental roles of history: to record the past for posterity. Macpherson is careful to point out that this absence of written records is not unique to the Celts, but indeed a pan-European phenomenon; nations without contemporary written records are 'covered with that impenetrable cloud which invariably involves illiterate nations who lie beyond the information of foreign writers'.[42] In doing so, he discusses the purpose of early history writing: 'to record temporal events'.[43] This, he explains, marks out the Romans stationed in Britain, such as Agricola: 'who, for the first time, displayed the Roman eagles beyond the friths, was not more successful in the field than he was happy in an historian to transmit his actions with lustre to posterity'.[44] Agricola, Macpherson tells us, has equal desire for renown in battle and for his actions to be recorded; his historian was, of course, his son-in-law, Tacitus. This approach of recording events is markedly different, though, from the purpose of Enlightenment history writing, which seeks to make the connections between events obvious in its focus on causality.

In *An Introduction*, Macpherson is faithful to the Enlightenment practice of using ancient historians as a source of evidence. But, unlike Adam Smith, Macpherson uses footnotes to demonstrate his classical erudition, which are then balanced with philosophical reflection in the historical narrative of the text. Because there are no direct primary sources from the place and period he is writing about, the Greek and Roman authors take the place of primary sources; while they are not Celtic primary sources, they are mostly contemporary with the period Macpherson discusses. These ancient historians' accounts are the closest thing to primary sources to which he has access, helping Macpherson tell the stories of the Celts: 'The Greeks threw the first feeble light on the Barbarians of the North and West.'[45] It is through the lens of the Greeks and Romans that Macpherson narrates British history in *An Introduction*. In doing so, he makes use of footnotes to contextualise his works, citing a variety of classical writers and supplying quotations from their work in Greek and Latin in his footnotes. This shows a modern approach to history writing both through an emphasis on the evidence of primary sources, and through sharing this evidence with the reader in footnotes. During the mid-eighteenth century, historians were beginning to make greater use of footnotes and, here in *An Introduction*, Macpherson was following the practice that Hume and others were starting to embrace. While omitting footnotes in his first two volumes of *The History of England* that he had published in the 1750s, Hume made sure to include them in the last four books in the series and to insert 'the Quotations and Authorities for the reigns of James I and Charles I'.[46] Macpherson showed no such reluctance in *An Introduction*, happily grappling with this key feature of emerging historiographical modernity. This echoed Robertson's 'philosophical history' in the recently published *History of Charles V* (1769), combining 'philosophical generalisation' with 'marshalling and evaluating the antiquarian evidence on which the history rests'.[47] While Macpherson's text consists largely of paraphrasing, the footnotes – prominently placed on the same page – allow the reader to examine Macpherson's sources for themselves. In doing so, Macpherson's history writing focuses on narrative; he constructs a story in fluent prose uninterrupted by quotations and reflecting Blair's injunction 'against allowing excessive didacticism to interrupt the flow of narrative'.[48] However, narrative here does not come at the expense of truth or erudition, evident from his careful footnoting. Macpherson does not paraphrase other non-contemporary accounts of ancient Britain but pieces together his historical narrative from primary sources. The balance between philosophical reflection, erudition and narrative was, as Pocock has argued, the central issue of Enlightenment history writing and here, once more, we see Macpherson wrangling these ideas in ways similar to the 'giants of the new historiography' – Hume, Robertson and Gibbon.[49]

Macpherson also connects his use of contemporary and near-contemporary classical sources to a more overtly philosophical historiographical methodology: 'From these revolutions of the Celtæ on the continent we shall, in a subsequent section, deduce the origin of the British nation.'[50] Trained in Logic at Marischal and King's College, Aberdeen, Macpherson was comfortable with the idea of deductive reasoning – the process of deriving conclusions that, if the premises are true, are themselves necessarily true. Here, again, we see the influence of Hume's ideas about 'causal reasoning' in history writing, where 'we judge the probability that an event has occurred in the past by reasoning from evidence that we encounter in the present'.[51] That is, Macpherson employs his academic training to justify his process; as his evidence from what he considers primary sources is 'true', then his conclusions about the Celts will necessarily also be true. While we can disagree with this value-judgement – his premises may be flawed – his methodology is sound and demonstrates his academic knowledge. Macpherson reminds the reader of this process in his discussion of the 'secret springs' that connect his discussion of 'Ancient Europe' with modern manners and arts. In doing so, he notes again the absence of written records by 'those Barbarians, whose want of the means of transmitting their history to posterity has perhaps contributed to their fame'.[52] Macpherson is keenly aware of his contemporaries' and predecessors' lack of interest in ancient British history: 'satisfied with the renown of latter transactions, they are as indifferent concerning their remote annals and origins as they who profit by the inundations of the Nile are about the distant fountain from which it takes its rise'.[53] In other words, because the origins of Britain are obscure – that is, not recorded in writing – modern historians do not venture there. Macpherson, however, is different, and although he admits that 'Britain, before the arrival of Cæsar, was rather heard of than known', he uses deductive reasoning to turn a variety of evidence into his account of early Britain.[54] This is directly related to the Enlightenment methodology of conjectural history, that was also applied to the ancient British past by contemporaries such as Gilbert Stuart.[55] In *An Introduction*, too, Macpherson uses this concept explicitly, describing his deductive reasoning as 'conjecture'. This is needed because of the lack of written records: 'whether Britain was inhabited, or rather perambulated, by a race of Barbarians before the Gaël of the continent extended their name with their arms into all the regions of Europe, is a circumstance which lies buried in impenetrable darkness'. Deductive conjectural reasoning is how Macpherson counters this darkness. Indeed, the antiquity of the period 'has left only room for conjecture'.[56]

Macpherson's use of conjecture is tied closely to his use of contemporary primary sources from elsewhere: 'We must judge of the æra [...] from its effect on those nations who had the means of transmitting their own history, as well as some account of their enemies, to after ages.'[57] In other words, Macpherson's *Introduction* is written using contemporary written sources from abroad, from those peoples who kept written records. It is worth noting that his approach to this is not one-sided: in discussing sources from both 'those nations' and 'their enemies' he demonstrates the same approach as in *The History of Great Britain*, where he uses both Hanoverian and Jacobite primary sources to construct his narrative. In doing so, he is attempting to alleviate allegations of bias and partisanship. Whether Macpherson is successful in that is a matter for debate outwith the scope of this book, but his stated methodology is clearly that of an historian who uses a range of sources to construct a narrative of the past that is framed by philosophical reflection.

The section on 'The Ancient Irish' demonstrates how Macpherson develops a comparative approach in dealing with this variety of primary sources. Here, he argues for 'the British extraction of the old Irish', that is, that the 'inhabitants of [Ireland] transmigrated, in an early period, from [northern Britain]'.[58] As elsewhere, the truth of this assertion does not concern us here; Macpherson can argue that the Gaels settled on the moon for all we care. What does concern us is his approach: *how* he constructs his argument. In this section, Macpherson again uses evidence from ancient classical sources that, as we have seen in other parts of *An Introduction*, are as near contemporary to the period he is investigating as he can find. His argument is explained in the following section, which is supported with four footnotes:

> The ancients with one voice agreed to give Ireland the appellation of a British Island. Ptolemy calls it the lesser Britain, and Strabo in his Epitome gives the name of Britons to its inhabitants. Diodorus Siculus mentions it as a fact well known in his time, that the Irish were of British extract, as well as that the Britons themselves derived their blood from the Gauls. Cornelius Tacitus affirms that the nature and manners of the Irish did not, in the days of Domitian, differ much from the Britons; and many foreign writers of great authority give their testimony to the British descent of the old inhabitants of Ireland.[59]

Here, Macpherson's argument stems from his examination of primary sources, supported by erudite footnotes. A companion piece to this passage is his argument a few pages later about the state of learning in early Ireland. Like in the passage quoted above, here Macpherson constructs his argument from primary sources, including the Irish Psalter Cashel as well as continental ones.[60] Macpherson also evaluates these different sources and compares how they discuss similar ideas. In doing so, he explicitly engages with the historiographical concept of arguing from evidence; for example, as he says, 'the authority of Diodorus not only destroys the fiction of the early knowledge of letters in Ireland, but also ruins that system of antiquities, to support which, the fiction itself was first framed'.[61] This is echoed in his criticism of Irish historians that they 'conceal[ed] from the public those monuments of their ancient history from which they pretend to derive their information'.[62] The central section of *An Introduction* exemplifies Macpherson's source-driven approach. Here, over the course of fifty pages, he explores arguments for and against the Irish extraction of the Scots. In doing so, he engages in detail with the arguments put forward by other writers, examining their evidence and disproving it when it does not support his own position. These sources, in other words, provide the evidence on which Macpherson builds his argument.

Furthermore, Macpherson deliberately evaluates this material in order to determine their usefulness as sources. In a footnote to his discussion of Strabo's account of ancient Ireland, Macpherson connects his own extrapolations with an awareness of what Strabo does and does not say explicitly: 'It is but justice to observe that Strabo does not vouch for the authenticity of the above account; but it is impossible to suppose that even the report of such barbarity could exist, had the Irish been more humanized than their Celtic brethren in Britain.'[63] Macpherson's evaluative activities continue throughout *An Introduction*. One aspect of this is Macpherson's reviewing of sources of Irish history, and his identification of their authors as 'Bards, annalists, and antiquaries' – not historians.[64] What they lack is a theoretical framework, which makes them different from historians. Macpherson notes this in his evaluation of Fr Thomas Innes in the same section, where he argues that Innes has achieved what the non-historians have not: he has 'reduced the origin of the Scots into a regular system'.[65] Innes, that is, has set up a theoretical system in his history that hints at a more philosophical approach to the past. However, 'the ingenious father' was flawed in his evidence and argument, where the 'proofs from the ancients' were against Innes's 'Hibernian revolution'.[66] Macpherson demonstrates his historiographical credentials here not simply by dismissing Innes as an antiquarian (as he does elsewhere in *An Introduction*) but by evaluating his use of sources.

As well as discussing contemporary sources and methodology, Macpherson also criticises more recent history writing in the main text of *An Introduction*, with a focus once again on Ireland and Irish historians.⁶⁷ Macpherson begins by discussing the approach taken prior to the eighteenth century:

> The first domestic writers of the history of North Britain were too ignorant, as well as too modern, to form any probable system concerning the origin of their nation. Destitute of records at home, they found themselves obliged to fill up the void in their antiquities with tales which had been growing in Ireland, for some ages before, on the hands of the succession of ignorant Bards and Fileas. After the study of critical learning was prosecuted with success among other nations, what part of it extended to Scotland was only employed to remove some of the absurdities of the old fables, and not levelled in a manly manner against the whole of that fabric of fiction which had so long dishonoured the antiquities of that country.⁶⁸

That is, Macpherson criticises earlier historians for being antiquarians who relied on Irish tales as their evidence. Macpherson continues this same argument later in *An Introduction*, when comparing and contrasting the approach taken by historians of Ireland. Here, as before, his argument rests on the connection between 'letters' (that is, the written transmission of culture), 'history' and civilisation:

> The antiquaries of that country [Ireland], in proportion as the general history of the world became more known to them, reformed, new-modelled, and retrenched the extravagancies of the first rude bards of Hibernian antiquities formed by the Bards and Fileas. Had letters been cultivated in Ireland in so early a period as is pretended, systems of the history of that country would have been so anciently formed, and so well established by the sanction of their antiquity, that neither Keating nor O'Flaherty durst, in the seventeenth age, give a compleat turn to the Irish antiquities. But that no such system was formed, is demonstrable from the silence concerning the times of Heathenism, in the most ancient annals of Ireland, of the existence of which we have any satisfactory proof.⁶⁹

In his analysis of the seventeenth-century Irish antiquarians Geoffrey Keating and Roderic O'Flaherty, Macpherson's argument rests on their assertion regarding the 'systems of history' formed in Ireland.⁷⁰ Indeed, his criticism of Irish historians continues throughout this section of *An Introduction*. For example, in his 'Preliminary Observations' to the chapter on 'Antiquities of the British and Irish Scots', Macpherson argues that 'to the common gloom, which covers the origin of other nations, the Bards of Ireland have added clouds of their own', which makes their 'ancient history' a 'desart'. The link between oral tradition, antiquity and history is clear but, as Macpherson argues, early Irish history is full of 'absurdities' in the 'annals of their remote ages'.[71] Here, Macpherson discredits established historical narratives through the same argument about the unreliability of oral tradition when it is not backed up by contemporary written sources:

> Whatever dreamers in remote antiquities may be pleased to say, it is an undisputable fact, that the transactions of a nation, illiterate in itself, and too distant or obscure to be distinctly seen by foreign writers, must for ever lie buried in oblivion. The Irish, we have already seen, were so far from having the advantage of the Greeks and Romans in an earlier knowledge of letters, that, on the contrary, they remained much longer in ignorance than the inhabitants of the regions of the West and North, whom the latter of those illustrious nations subdued and humanized.[72]

Macpherson's argument hinges, yet again, on the connection between recording and preserving facts through written sources. In particular, the absence of contemporary written sources from elsewhere to confirm the oral tradition means that, for Macpherson, Irish accounts of early events are not trustworthy.

Macpherson explicitly engages with the notion of oral tradition as separate from history in the chapter on 'Antiquities of the British and Irish Scots'. Here, he identifies oral tradition as a way to 'preserve the memory of [...] actions', recorded through 'the rhimes of the Bards'. Macpherson argues that bards are a common feature of 'all the illiterate nations descended from the great Celtic stock'; they were a pan-Celtic institution.[73] But, here, Macpherson creates a hierarchy of evidence to distinguish between Irish and Scottish accounts of the Celtic past. In Ireland, the oral tradition of the bards was 'the only means the old Irish had to preserve the memory of their actions'. Macpherson remarks on the 'known uncertainty of history in rhime', once more demonstrating the paradox between his desire to ground his historiographical approach in the analysis of written sources and the Gaelic oral tradition – which, of course, was the foundation of the Ossianic Collections and, at the very least, frames his understanding of the Celtic past in *An Introduction*. Here, Macpherson questions the extent to which bardic tradition can transmit an accurate record of historical events: 'we may affirm that a dull narrative of facts in verse could never take hold of the human mind in a degree sufficient to transmit knowledge of events, by oral tradition, through any considerable length of time'. He places the boundary for successful oral transmission 'in the middle of the fifth age'.

Here, Macpherson's argument rests on the arrival or Christianity and, with it, letters:

> but as it is not, in any degree, probable that the first converts in Ireland would employ their time in collecting and recording historical poems, which were tinctured, perhaps, with the ancient superstition, we may naturally place the commencement of the fabulous, as well as of the true history of that Ireland, posterior to the introduction of Christianity.[74]

Macpherson draws a distinction between 'true history' and 'the fabulous', between veracity and fiction. He expands this point later in *An Introduction*, arguing that after 'letters' were introduced in the fifth century, they were 'not employed in recording historical transactions for some centuries posterior to that period'.[75] Macpherson's dismissal of Irish bardic tradition rests in contemporary historiographical theory concerning the need for truth and veracity in historical narratives – and that this can be measured through an analysis of written sources.

Macpherson matches his criticism of Keating, O'Flaherty and others with equal scepticism about early Scottish historians. A particularly interesting example of this is Macpherson's discussion of how historians have upheld the Irish-origin story of the Scots that he is trying to disprove:

> It was convenient for the divine, that the bard should propagate a belief of the connexion between the Scots of both the Isles; and the authority of the former could establish any doctrine in the minds of an ignorant, credulous, and superstitious people. The senachies were impudent, the bards formidable, and both were eloquent. If any scepticism remained against their well-told tales, the missionaries destroyed it altogether by the weight of their sanctified character. This system, once established, was propagated, and became the traditional belief of after ages. The little progress that learning made in Scotland when its first histories were written, could not enable the zealous abettors of its antiquities to overturn that system of the origin of the nation, which had been so long obtruded upon the world; and the Scottish writers who, in a much later period, distinguished themselves in critical inquiries into the history of their ancestors, were at more pains to adorn the fictions of their predecessors, than to expose their absurdities.[76]

Macpherson explicitly engages with historiographical notions, where older historians' method is scrutinised. Unlike the more modern historiographical practice of critically questioning sources and assumed wisdom, the historians described by Macpherson build on earlier histories and perpetuate received notions, rather than investigate their claims.

Having dismissed the efforts of ancient and early modern antiquarians and historians, Macpherson turns his attention to the eighteenth-century historian Fr Thomas Innes. Macpherson had already addressed Innes in the preface, but in the main body of *An Introduction* he focuses on Innes's lack of critical source analysis and his poor knowledge of the Gaelic language. Innes attempted to discredit the notion that Scotland's history was simply the result of Irish colonisation as he 'wrested the sceptre of Scotland from the first Fergus, and thirty-nine of the ideal successors of that pretended monarch, and passing over into Ireland discomfited that motley army of Bards, Fileas and Senachies, which had been so long fortifying itself in rhimes, traditions, and fabulous records'.[77] However, Macpherson is also quick to identify the flaws in Innes's approach: 'setting out upon wrong principles, and being an utter stranger to the Galic language, he fell into unavoidable mistakes; and endeavoured to obtrude upon the world opinions, concerning the origins of the Scots, no less improbable than those tales which he had exploded with so much success'.[78] Here, he criticises Innes's methodology; according to Macpherson, Innes is a flawed historian because the 'principles' with which he composes his history are wrong, and his limited knowledge of Gaelic is problematic. Innes lacked the Enlightenment approach championed by Macpherson's contemporaries: he is an antiquarian who did not match his erudition with the kind of philosophical reflection being demanded by the likes of Robertson and Gibbon. This critique extends to other modern historians: 'though Scotland has of late years produced men distinguished for their talent in historical disquisition, none of them has thought proper to search for the genuine origin and history of his ancestors among those fables which obscure the antiquities of the nation'.[79] That is, other historians have neglected to use oral tradition as a source for their history writing or abstained from more ancient history altogether. Indeed, Macpherson has little respect for antiquarians who do not have the Gaelic:

> those who treated of the antiquities of North Britain were utter strangers to that only name by which the Scots distinguished the corner of Britain which their ancestors possessed from the remotest antiquity. From an ignorance, so unpardonable in antiquaries, proceeded that erroneous system of the origin of the Scots, which, for many ages, has been, with so much confidence, obtruded on the world.[80]

His argument here hinges on etymology; Macpherson proposes a link between 'Gaeltachd' and 'Caledonia' that, as he explains in a footnote, 'first occurred to the Author of this Essay, and he communicated it to Dr. Macpherson, who adopted it from a conviction of its justness'.[81]

Macpherson places himself in the modern scholarly context of his namesake John Macpherson, in order to further distinguish his history writing from earlier antiquarians and historians.[82] James Macpherson follows John's linguistic approach in *An Introduction* through his emphasis on language, which 'next to authentic records, is the best evidence of the extract of a people' and helps James to justify his complex relationship with oral tradition.[83] Macpherson's use of language pre-dates the mostly German research into Indo-European languages in the nineteenth century but aligns with eighteenth-century efforts to delineate the competing claims of Celtic and Anglo-Saxon languages as the foundation of modern European culture.[84] While his conclusion that 'wherever any of these three languages [that he identifies as the 'three original tongues'] is spoken with most purity, there the blood of the great nation, from which it takes its names, most prevails' is dubious, his *method* is what concerns us here.[85] For Macpherson, language was a link between the period he was writing about and his eighteenth-century present; it forms another layer of evidence, alongside primary sources, in his methodology. He uses this argument to counteract the lack of direct evidence from ancient British sources: 'though it is impossible to fix with precision on the æra of the invasion of Britain by the Gaël, no doubt can remain concerning the existence of the fact itself. The Gaël of Britain and Ireland retain a proof of their origin in their indigenous name.'[86] His comments here are also evidence – if such evidence is needed – to counteract the old argument that Macpherson knew only little Gaelic.[87] Moreover, Macpherson self-consciously explains how his ideas build upon those of Rev. John. In the chapter on the 'Ancient Scots', Macpherson outlines how his work differs from that of scholarly colleagues like John; while John Macpherson, he argues, has 'reduced lately into form and precision the antiquities which Innes had left in confusion and disorder', his analysis does not go far enough. This is where Macpherson's own work in *An Introduction* comes in, following the footsteps of John Macpherson's 'remarks'.[88] Because John Macpherson had not 'extended his remarks as far as he might have been enabled to do by his erudition and great knowledge of all the branches of the Celtic language' there is 'occasion for this Essay [Macpherson's *Introduction*]'.[89] This is an overtly historiographical statement by Macpherson; he discusses the place of his own work – and the merit of it – in connection with that of other historians and demonstrates how *An Introduction* develops John Macpherson's approach.[90]

As well as demonstrating the historiographical modernity of his approach by building upon the work of other historians and scholars, Macpherson's narrative of the ancient Celtic past is ultimately framed by modern stadial theory that connects with his belief in the supremacy of the British imperial state. Macpherson links this with ideas about the oral transmission of knowledge, and the relationship between orality and letters, in a short section called 'Reflections' in his chapter on the 'Ancient Irish'. Echoing his ideas from *Fingal* and *Temora*, he discusses the role of oral transmission in the composition of history, and as the way that the history of early societies is preserved. Macpherson analyses oral history through the idea of civilisation in a stadial argument reminiscent of Adam Ferguson, as we also saw in Chapter 2.[91] Macpherson's focus, however, is not on the stadial nature of society itself, but the role that an awareness of one's own history, and an attempt to record it, plays in that: 'The art of perpetuating ideas, and of transmitting the wisdom of one age to another, is the first means of civilizing mankind out of their natural ferocity and barbarity.' For Macpherson, history transmission is a marker of civilisation: 'when some certain marks are found to send down the memory of inventions and transactions through a series of generations, a nation becomes polished in proportion to the length of time it has been in possession of that art'. Indeed, it is specifically the arrival of 'letters' – of ways of preserving and transmitting their history – that turns nations from 'Barbarians' into those that make a 'figure [...] in history'.[92] He uses this argument to deconstruct the notion that Ireland was 'a seat of polite literature many ages before Greece itself rose out of ignorance and barbarity'.[93] Again: what is important here is not what Macpherson says, but *how* he goes about it. In his argument about the development of civilisation he uses history – the transmission of knowledge about one's culture – as his marker. Similarly, Macpherson highlights the distinction between history and fiction in a slightly later section: 'every other polished people, who, in the times of ignorance, had set up high schemes of antiquity, have now extricated their history from the fables of their dark ages'. Here, history is again seen as a marker of civilisation. In turn, this is linked to truth, as Macpherson identifies this kind of history – freed from fable – as 'a true history of their ancestors'.[94] Civilisation, then, sheds light on the dark, fabled past of Ireland.

Macpherson used this particular idea of history as rooted in the recording of the past to define his view of civilisation. In creating a stadial view of the Celtic past, in which civilisation can be found in the ancient Highlands but not in Ireland, Macpherson makes an argument that knowing your history gives you and your culture power and agency in the present – and that history writing is crucial to this process. Increasingly, Macpherson uses a framework of the rise of the state to adjudicate whether a culture or people have a history. Those outwith this historical (and often stadial) process are then outwith history itself.

This rhetorical device then frames Macpherson's understanding of the crisis of empire later in the 1770s. Here, at the beginning of the decade, Macpherson uses such a formulation to ascribe a history to Highlanders, but not to the Irish. We saw in Chapter 1 that such an approach places the rise of the state at the heart of history writing.[95] This, in turn, helps us to understand how Macpherson conceptualises the early history of the Celtic peoples as part of a stadial framework that portrays them as the progenitors of elements of Whig constitutionalism.

It is this genealogy of ideas which marks out Macpherson's approach to stadial history, where the Celts become a vehicle for Whig ideas of freedom, liberty and the ancient constitution that define his later understanding of the British imperial state. Dafydd Moore has made a persuasive argument about Macpherson's identification of the Celts as the early proponents of these political ideas and how he used 'the tools of skeptical Enlightenment historiography in order to deflect charges of barbarity and superstition away from the Celt and onto other lesser primitives', i.e. the Anglo-Saxons.[96] While Moore pinpoints Macpherson's emphasis on concepts of freedom in the Celtic world, it is important to understand how Macpherson develops this idea in the context of the 1770s. In a section subtitled 'Form of the Ancient British Government', Macpherson is clear in describing these Celts as 'The Ancient British Nations' – it is they who 'were extremely fond and very tenacious of their political freedom'.[97] Macpherson goes on to outline this system of government in terms that mark out his late eighteenth-century Whig constitutionalism:

> Though, from a conviction that civil society cannot maintain itself without subordination, they had their judges, their princes, and kings, the power of those dignified persons was very much circumscribed. In the midst of barbarity they formed as just notions of liberty as other free nations have done in the most cultivated times. They were convinced, that they not only had a right to elect their magistrates, but also to prescribe those laws by which they chose to be governed.[98]

In this passage, Macpherson defines a system of government where the power of the state is limited by the freedom and liberty of the people – an argument similar to that made by his contemporary, Gilbert Stuart.[99] Here, Macpherson locates the origins of the late seventeenth-century Williamite revolution in the distant Celtic past, making the claim that the Highlanders of the past are crucial to the political evolution of the current British state and that the region's people were a key military resource that would maintain its imperial power.[100] Macpherson's argument that there were 'whig values residing in the Celtic past' extended to throwing shade on the achievements of the Anglo-Saxons.[101] As Moore points out, Anglo-Saxon 'barbarity' was highlighted in Macpherson's *Introduction* as 'the rude elements which time has improved into the present constitution of English government'.[102] Such a characterisation of the Anglo-Saxons was, in itself, an affirmation of a particular type of Whig constitutionalism from this period, one that railed against the 'Saxon yoke' – a political trope that found vogue during the Seven Years War.[103]

An Introduction marks a hinge point in Macpherson's journey as an historian. The book is about an ancient Celtic past that is similar to the setting of the Ossianic Collections and Macpherson's account of the Gaelic world in all these texts is shaped by the tension between oral tradition and emerging Enlightenment historiographical conventions and how that may be accommodated within stadial views of history. Macpherson's approach to writing about the past is a little different, though, in *An Introduction*, especially in the preface. By the early 1770s, Macpherson had absorbed much current Enlightenment historiography, including the ideas of Hume, Blair and Smith regarding the use of classical primary sources as evidence, history writing's purpose to amuse and instruct, explicit debate with other historians about their interpretation of the past, and ideas about the impartiality of the historian and their commitment to truth. Macpherson was able to take these ideas that had been expounded in the 1750s and 1760s and combine them with some of the cutting-edge ideas about the philosophical nature of history writing beginning to emerge in the work of Blair, Hume and Robertson. Macpherson's control of narrative, analytical reflection and erudition became more assured in *An Introduction*. Together with harnessing stadial history to developing notions of Whig constitutionalism, Macpherson's voice as an historian was beginning to emerge. In the next section, we explore how Macpherson established a sophisticated and thoroughly modern way of history writing in his next works – the *Original Papers* and *The History of Great Britain* – that firmly establish his credentials, in the mid-1770s, as an Enlightenment historian.

THE ORIGINAL PAPERS (1775) AND THE HISTORY OF GREAT BRITAIN (1775)

By 1769 Hume had decided – and informed his London publisher, William Strahan – that he did not wish to extend his *History of England* beyond 1688.[104] Strahan was determined to continue publishing the series, and four years later had two candidates in mind: Macpherson and

John Dalrymple.[105] Hume responded, 'wish[ing] my continuators good Success', praising Macpherson's 'Style and Spirit', though lamenting his hot-headedness and lack of judgement.[106] Macpherson was chosen, and delivered *The History of Great Britain, from the Restoration, to the Accession of the House of Hannover* in 1775. The title itself is a sign of his loyalty to the British imperial state, still going strong almost twenty years after the publication of *The Highlander* – Hume's history was, after all, a History of England. Eager to continue the strain of authenticity that he had set up in *An Introduction to the History of Great Britain and Ireland*, Macpherson published, on the same day, most of the documents he used as the basis for his *History of Great Britain* as the *Original Papers; Containing the Secret History of Great Britain, from the Restoration, to the Accession of the House of Hannover. To which are Prefixed Extracts from the Life of James II, As Written by Himself*.[107] This section first examines the *Original Papers*, where Macpherson establishes his research methodology and discusses the kind of sources that he uses for *The History of Great Britain*, where he found them, and how he has applied concepts of impartiality to the selection and analysis of this source material. We then turn our attention to *The History of Great Britain* itself, perhaps the clearest and most important expression of Macpherson's credentials as an Enlightenment historian, certainly at this stage in his career. As in the Ossianic Collections and *An Introduction*, Macpherson's 'Preface' to *The History of Great Britain* functions as a statement of his methodology and historiographical approach – arguably, his most fulsome account of how he sees himself thinking and writing as an historian. Then, as we have with Macpherson's work in both Chapters 2 and 4, we compare the methodology of the preface to his historiographical practice in the main body of *The History of Great Britain*. Here, we see the emphasis of Macpherson's history writing shift: while issues of instruction and amusement in writing about the past remain, Macpherson pays greater attention to the use of primary sources, their referencing in erudite footnotes, and how these provide the evidence that establishes the truth of his account. Alongside these features, Macpherson also develops some of the more philosophical elements of his history writing, not just combining a narrative of the past with sociological generalisation and explanation, but also evaluating the nature of knowledge upon which his analysis rested. Finally, we examine how Macpherson's account of the development of the British state during the late seventeenth and early eighteenth centuries lays the foundation for his later use of the past to make political claims during the imperial crisis of the second half of the 1770s. This we do through two case studies, focusing on Macpherson's narrative of the Restoration of the monarchy in 1660 and his engagement with notions of British identity. Here, we directly compare Macpherson's accounts with Hume, where Macpherson's book overlaps with the last two volumes of Hume's *History of England*. What emerges is a more thorough engagement with ideas of Whig constitutionalism in Macpherson's work, together with a markedly different style of narration, where Macpherson brings the flair of writing about Ossianic battles to his descriptions of seventeenth-century warfare against the Dutch and others.

This direct comparison with Hume is a useful way in which to contextualise the reception of Macpherson's work in the 1770s and to explore how scholars have subsequently dealt with *The History of Great Britain* and the *Original Papers*. Hume had, of course, been the writer of the famous *History of England* series, published in the 1750s and 1760s. Hume wrote his history backwards, beginning with *The History of Great Britain, vol I, Containing the Reigns of James I and Charles I* in 1754, followed by a second volume on the seventeenth-century Stuart monarchy in 1756. The series was then reconceptualised as the *History of England*, where Hume moved from the Tudors right back to the Romans, with a complete set of all six volumes appearing in 1762.[108] Strahan was unable to persuade Hume to continue writing the series and, by 1773, had decided to ask Macpherson to complete the project.[109] As Pocock argues, Hume's age, ill-health and growing unease with 'the increasingly violent language of ancient constitutionalism during the 1760s and 1770s' made him indisposed to continue writing this history, leading to his rather equivocal assessment of Macpherson's talents as his successor.[110] Hume's earlier approval of Macpherson's 'style and spirit' changed to outright opposition following publication of the *History* in 1775, writing to Strahan that the book was 'one of the most wretched Productions that ever came from your press'.[111] This hostile reaction was echoed by others, with Horace Walpole famously describing the book as 'a heap of insignificant trash and lies' and framing his criticism in the context of the Ossian controversy.[112] Such a connection by Walpole was understandable, given the revival of the authenticity debate following the publication of Samuel Johnson's *Journey to the Western Isles* in January 1775, just a couple of months before Macpherson's *History* and *Original Papers*.[113] More recent scholarly responses to Macpherson's history writing have continued to be shaped by the debate surrounding publication in 1775. Dafydd Moore introduces these later histories by highlighting that 'Hume disapproved of both the choice of author and the finished product', emphasising only the negative elements of Hume's assessment of Macpherson the historian.[114] Robert Jones's analysis of the relationship between Hume's and Macpherson's history writing is more generous, recognising that Macpherson's book needs to be understood in the context of other popular histories of the time, by the likes of Smollett and Robertson, that sought to continue Hume's work.[115] Indeed, while Jones and others have recognised the modernity of publishing both a work of history and a collection of primary sources upon which that history is based, allowing readers to 'become active students of the past', little attention has been given to the historiographical methodology and techniques Macpherson actually used in his history writing.[116] In the *Original Papers* and *The History of Great Britain*, we find Macpherson combining historical narrative with scholarly erudition and philosophical reflection in ways that, as we shall see, can be usefully compared to the Enlightenment historiographical practice of William Robertson and Edward Gibbon.

THE *ORIGINAL PAPERS* (1775)

Macpherson framed his *Original Papers* with an explanation of his practices as an historian. The *Original Papers* contain an advertisement and an introduction, both aimed at accounting for the sources of the work. The Stuart section of the *Papers*, Macpherson explains, is taken from the diary and correspondence of Sir David Nairne, courtier to James II and III, which had come into the hands of Thomas Carte, the English historian.[117] The Hanoverian section is taken from 'the correspondence and secret negotiations of the house of Hannover, their agents and their friends in Britain, throughout the reign of Queen Anne', with the 'Extracts from the *Life of James II*' derived from both Carte and papers at the Scots College in Paris, which Macpherson had visited in 1774, just as Hume had in compiling his earlier history of the Stuarts.[118] He also exhibited the 'Originals' at Strahan's shop in the Strand.[119] These meticulously recorded sources make Macpherson's work stand out: though hardly recognised as such by neither more general critics nor Macpherson scholars, Horn noted in the 1960s that 'Macpherson's main importance as a collector of new material was in the papers which he obtained', and that he and Dalrymple 'between them added more new information to the store of historical knowledge than the rest of their contemporaries put together'.[120] It is notable that Macpherson's *Original Papers* are still consulted by historians today, such as in Alastair J. Mann's recent work on James VII and II.[121] Moreover, Macpherson's credentials as an historian whose methodology was rooted in the meticulous examination of primary sources, such as the *Original Papers*, was recognised by none other than Leopold van Ranke – the nineteenth-century German historian so often characterised as the founder of the modern methods and techniques of history writing.[122] In his own multi-volume *A History of England*, Ranke narrates the reign of James II and uses Macpherson's *Original Papers* as a source, commenting on the provenance of the Carte papers:

> James Macpherson (he to whom the world is indebted for Ossian) bought them of Carte's widow and then went himself to Paris, in order to complete them. He made use of them in an historical work; but this time, with more prudence than in the publication of the Gaelic poems, he had his authorities printed at the same time. No one has ever doubted their authenticity.[123]

Ranke's assessment is intriguing. Here, he views Macpherson through the prism of Ossian, as was so often the case, but in order to frame his history writing as different. Ranke, as an historian still profoundly influenced by Greek and Roman historians in his practice, uses the classical term 'authorities' to describe his source material and it is these, through their authenticity, that demonstrate the value of history writing.[124] Indeed, Macpherson's careful attention to sources emphasises his desire to be an authentic historian, and the nature of the sources – a diary and an autobiography – underlines his biographical approach that, like much of Hume's *History of England*, focused on a history of monarchs and their political actions.[125]

Macpherson furnished the *Original Papers* with a ten-page introduction to explain how he acquired the material contained therein. His motive in gathering (and publishing) the papers is objectivity:

> to ascertain [...] the genuine circumstances of former transactions; to redeem history from the misrepresentations of the designing, the errors of the ignorant, and the weakness of the prejudiced; to give to characters their genuine colour; to shew mankind, without either fear of favour, as they were.[126]

Macpherson's language pre-empts Ranke's famous phrase that the task of the historian was to show the past 'how it essentially was', and he applied this approach to the faction-riven world of 1770s politics. Though working for the government under Lord North at the time, Macpherson – like Hume – sought to rise above party politics, finding fault with both sides and declaring his disapproval of 'rest[ing] the justice of their respective claims on the authority of former ages'.[127] Indeed, Macpherson protests that 'nothing [...] is more ridiculous, than to suppose that freedom can be received as a legacy; or that abject progenitors have any right to entail slavery on their posterity'.[128] Macpherson designed his work to suit both factions, and in that, in an administration such as North's, which, though often labelled 'Tory' was comprised of a number of ex- and almost-Whigs, he was trying not to offend. Of course, in so doing, Macpherson ended up incurring the wrath of almost everyone, and the impression that Macpherson was a closet Jacobite-Tory cohered then and persists to this day.[129] However, as Colin Kidd argues, much as the *Original Papers* 'subvert[ed] English whig shibboleths', Macpherson should be 'viewed as a sophisticated and latitudinarian Scottish whig', whose later political writings (and, indeed, political activities) position him firmly as a British imperial Whig Highlander.[130]

The rest of the introduction continues to establish Macpherson as a reputable historian. Although Carte's transcription of James II's journal was 'large and accurate', Nairne's papers were 'jumbled together in such a mass of confusion, that a great deal of time and industry, and, it may even be said, a very considerable knowledge of the period to which they relate, were absolutely necessary, to give them the importance they deserve'.[131] Because of his diligence and historical expertise, he was not content with merely reprinting Carte's extracts, but instead went to Paris 'to satisfy himself, as well as to authenticate his materials to the public'.[132] Authenticity, we see, was still a burning concern for Macpherson. He is careful to point out that his sources are varied: 'though the correspondences of the house of Stuart are highly important, the Editor is very far from deriving his whole information from that side. He has received original papers from several persons abroad. At home he owes obligations of the same kind to a few.'[133] He admits freely that he was not able to inspect any other private collections, though, he assures the reader, he has nonetheless 'been enabled to give to the public, in this collection, as many particulars, concerning men in office, as the public would wish to know'.[134] Finally, he leaves the reader with an assurance of his impartiality: 'he has religiously adhered, throughout, to Truth; and that it could not be expected he should risk his own reputation, by concealing any facts that came to his knowledge, though they might tend to sully the fame of their ancestors'.[135] The introduction to the *Original Papers* thus situates Macpherson in contemporary debates about impartiality, echoing the emphasis placed upon this in the work of Hume and Blair.[136]

The *Original Papers* were also intended to whet the public's appetite for *The History of Great Britain*. Macpherson is sure that 'the papers contained in the following collection will [...] convince the public, that he has very much to say, that is both striking and new'.[137] He emphasises this again in the preface to *The History of Great Britain*: 'the new light thrown upon public transactions [...] will, he hopes, atone for his defects as a writer, and recommend his work to the public'.[138] As with the *Original Papers*, authenticity was ever-present in Macpherson's mind, and in the opening paragraph of the preface he assures the reader of the veracity of *The History of Great Britain*. Whether this stems from an Ossian-related need to justify his sources, or from a desire to increase interest in the *Original Papers* is unclear, but Macpherson very consciously presents himself as an historian concerned with authenticity.[139]

THE HISTORY OF GREAT BRITAIN (1775)

The two-volume *History of Great Britain, from the Restoration, to the Accession of the House of Hannover* was published in 1775. It is the high point of Macpherson's career as an historian, signalling a mature, confident Macpherson. This Macpherson is a scholar who undertook archival work to present a balanced picture of a fairly recent past that aims to be objective, focuses on the detail of primary source evidence, and is footnoted in a modern fashion. As we shall see below, Macpherson's self-conscious historical methodology was outlined in the preface to *The History of Great Britain*, in ways that bear comparison to similar work in the 1770s and 1780s by William Robertson and Edward Gibbon. Macpherson structures his history of the late Stuarts and the Williamite revolution around a narrative that focuses on the history of 'politics, statecraft and war'.[140] Within this narrative, however, Macpherson weaves elements of contemporary Enlightenment historiographical practice, reflecting on both characters and events, the nature and purpose of history writing, the use of sources and the nature of historical truth. These elements of Macpherson's methodology and historiography have largely eluded scholars. While Jones has recently analysed how reflections on the characters of the various monarchs 'borrow from the sentimental literature of Richardson and Sterne' as a form of mimetic sentimentalism, Macpherson also reflects on broader political and constitutional issues, demonstrating how he was becoming an avid proponent of Whig constitutionalism.[141]

The preface to *The History of Great Britain* is Macpherson's most detailed historiographical work. Here, he discusses a number of different points of historiographical theory: what makes a good historian (truth, impartiality); sources (new material, comparisons, distinctions between different kinds of sources, when to cite or quote); and the justifications for this particular narrative of British history (it focuses on an under-researched period). In his approach, here, he is modern, and his emphasis on truth and impartiality is in line with Enlightenment historiographical theory developed by Blair, Hume and others.[142] However, his emphasis on and detailed engagement with sources is different and demonstrates that Macpherson shared the same 'historiographical universe' as the two giants of later Enlightenment history writing – Robertson and Gibbon.[143]

The preface details Macpherson's approach to history writing. His object, he says, is truth, and he presents himself as an empiricist who is objective and impartial, without 'predilection for any party'.[144] For Macpherson, objectivity is tied to evidence, and this is the heart of Enlightenment cultural theory: the application of a scientific methodology to history, philosophy and literature. Like Blair and Smith in their *Lectures on Rhetoric and Belles Lettres*, like Hume's *Treatise of Human Nature* and *Enquiry Concerning Human Understanding*, like Hutcheson's 'common sense' philosophy, like Ferguson's anthropology and like Smith's economics, Macpherson placed central importance on the concept of evidence.[145] Evidence leads to impartiality: he is 'not conscious of having once departed from the obvious line of evidence', and the need for this evidence lies at the heart of his detailed engagement with sources.[146] It has been suggested that Macpherson published the *Original Papers* – the 'secret' sources of his *History* – as a response to the authenticity debate, and to forestall any criticism of his *History of Great Britain*, but this is naïve. Macpherson's emphasis on sources – both the discussion in the preface and indeed the separate publication of the *Original Papers* – speaks to his deep-rooted Enlightenment belief in the value and necessity of empirical evidence. Without evidence there can be no impartiality or objectivity, and this explains the detail of the preface about how, why and when Macpherson uses sources. This concern with sources speaks to empiricism, rather than to Ossian and the authenticity debate, and this situates Macpherson in the heart of the Enlightenment.

'Enlightenment' and 'empiricism' are contextual necessities for understanding Macpherson's preface. His opening remark that the papers of the families of Brunswick-Lunenburgh (that is, Hanover) and Stuart were 'placed into the author's hands' is an example of this: here we see Macpherson ready to conduct his scholarly investigation of these papers.[147] This, then, sets him up as impartial from the start: Macpherson has access to both Hanover and Stuart family papers and, as we will see, he uses these equally frequently and critically in his *History of Great Britain*. But he does more here than to set up a framework of impartiality: the papers are not publicly accessible records (at least not until he publishes them as the *Original Papers*), and Macpherson sees his role as that of a philosopher, analysing evidence and presenting facts. As such, he consciously adopts the methodology of empirical research: analysing documented experience, and writing a history based on evidence.

Macpherson is careful to assure his readers that his *History of Great Britain* is balanced, and evidence-based; it is 'truth'. He argues that his *History* throws 'new light [...] upon public transactions': through his examination of hitherto publicly unavailable documents he reshapes our understanding of politics in the late seventeenth and early eighteenth centuries.[148] Indeed, the focus of his history is on *public* affairs, not private ones; this relates to Macpherson's methodology regarding truth and impartiality because he is facilitating a clearer way for the public to understand its own past, and pre-empts his approach to political history writing in his later work on the East India Company (see Chapter 4). Prior to *The History of Great Britain* and the *Original Papers* the public had not had access to important documents for this period of upheaval, but through Macpherson's publication *and* analysis of these papers these 'public transactions' become accessible. Because the public could read both the *Original Papers* and Macpherson's narrative of them, impartiality and, for want of a better word, historical 'truth' became publicly accessible: it was easy for the public to compare the sources with the interpretation (unlike, say, in the case of the Ossianic Collections). This process of publishing both materials and historical narrative helps to authenticate Macpherson's history and confirms his methodological comments on truth and impartiality.

When discussing his aims Macpherson uses the language of the scientific method, which had become commonplace in the discourse of the Scottish Enlightenment.[149] He argues, for example, that there is 'certainty established with regard to the real characters of particular persons'; in other words, that his empirical method allows him to narrate people as they really were.[150] 'Certainty' about the characters of people is a big claim, and a difficult one to prove, but it isn't just empty rhetoric: because his sources are published with *The History of Great Britain*, and because of the nature of the sources, Macpherson's role as narrator of facts – as establisher of certainty – differs from earlier pre-Enlightenment histories. His historiographical method is grounded in sources not witnesses; traceable written evidence rather than hearsay. This is why Macpherson can claim 'certainty' – it resides not only in his confidence of having treated his characters fairly, or his Enlightenment belief in the necessity of evidence, but in the fact that the certainty is, indeed, verifiable given the accessibility of the sources.

Macpherson states his political impartiality in the preface to *The History of Great Britain*, claiming 'undeviating justice' in the rendering of 'all' persons.[151] This is a necessary claim for methodological and personal reasons. In terms of methodology, Enlightenment empiricism places crucial importance on objectivity, and weighing up evidence; Macpherson's approach of consulting many sources, and especially private personal sources from both the Hanovers and Stuarts, fulfils this need. On a personal level Macpherson also had to claim impartiality: as a government spin-doctor, embroiled in government affairs and with high-ranking patrons, as a Highlander from a Jacobite clan in London, it was imperative that he attempted to relate an impartial history. The chronology of *The History of Great Britain*, ending with Queen Anne's death, allows Macpherson to avoid discussing Hanoverian rule, but the book nonetheless contains a great deal of characterisation of both Whigs and Tories, of Stuarts and Hanoverians, and of Jacobites. Macpherson's claim in the preface that he will render 'undeviating justice' to all makes him a judge of character – but then, as the sources are published, so are his readers. Whether or not we believe Macpherson's claims to justness, the fact remains that these claims set the tone for *The History of Great Britain* – once made in writing any hint of partiality can be fuelled by such claims. As such, making this claim works doubly in Macpherson's favour: firstly, because it signals to the public that he is writing as a scholarly historian, not a party-political hack; secondly, because it forces him to be objective. Having experienced the debate, confusion and damage caused by unguarded claims about the Ossianic sources, and having learnt from this experience, Macpherson is careful to only make promises that he can keep. He is keenly aware of the need to forestall any arguments about authenticity and 'Caledonian bias', and he delivers this from the outset. This is why he opens the preface in this way, and why he explicitly discusses his methodology here. Macpherson writes that he has been 'unwilling to advance any matter of fact, without proof', and that this proof is the *Original Papers*, which he calls 'his materials'. Indeed, he 'refers the reader to the papers themselves' to ascertain 'their authenticity' – the authenticity of his narrative, that is. Authenticity is, then, a key historiographical concept for Macpherson. Authenticity and impartiality confer truth, which – in this Enlightenment mode – is created through evidence.[152]

This line of argument about authenticity and impartiality is picked up at the end of the preface with a focus on objectivity. Macpherson states that 'he is not conscious of having once departed from the obvious line of evidence'; another instance of the scientific language that we noted earlier.[153] His empirical historiographical method, deriving results from a line of evidence, is clear. This serves to assure his readers that his history is impartial and unbiased, without (as he says) 'predilection for any party'.[154] But it does more than that: it sets Macpherson up as a serious, modern historian. In his *History of Great Britain* Macpherson is no Celtic antiquary – no amateur historian like Walter Scott's Oldbuck in *The Antiquary* (1816). Macpherson is a professional – a man of science, who uses empiricist methods in his analysis of historical sources in order to write a modern analytical history.

The bulk of the preface of *The History of Great Britain* is devoted to evidence: the sources it is drawn from and methodological thoughts on comparing sources; a discussion about when to quote or cite sources; and distinctions between different kinds of sources. Like the methodology itself – evidence-based empiricism – this emphasis on sources adds to the modernity of Macpherson's process: like a modern historian he shares where his information comes from, has clear rules about what does and does not need a citation, and he evaluates these sources. The narrative he constructs in the body of *The History of Great Britain* is thus informed by contemporary historiographical methods, and it serves as a key example to demonstrate how the Enlightenment was the tipping point for modernity in so many ways. Of course, history writing is usually seen as becoming modern in the nineteenth century, but Macpherson's preface shows that the discipline was well on the way before Ranke. 'Historical Science', as Ranke calls it, is an Enlightenment product, and Macpherson's methodology is a key example of this.[155]

Macpherson begins his methodological discussion by highlighting the different kinds of evidence he has used in compiling his history. He has consulted, he says, records and journals of Parliament; military writers; print primary sources of authors who wrote in the times; manuscripts (which he terms 'original papers'); and foreign writers. Macpherson is clear as to the purpose that each kind of source serves. He has consulted parliamentary records and journals for dates; publicly discussed facts; decisions of importance; and the state of debts, taxes, grants and supplies. The details of battles have come from military writers. Print primary sources composed during the period that *The History of Great Britain* covers have been used to narrate well-known events. The focus of the book and its new contribution to knowledge comes from the 'original papers', and they largely concern secret political intrigues, private political negotiations, ministerial intrigues and royal motives. Foreign writers are used to provide context; throughout *The History of Great Britain*, Macpherson discusses Britain within the wider context of European affairs. These different kinds of sources, each with their own purpose, allow him to offer what he terms a 'comprehensive view'.[156] Now, we can question the extent to which he achieved that completeness and balance – as did, indeed, his contemporaries. However, it is Macpherson's objectives – his methodology – which make his *History of Great Britain* significant: it is Macpherson's self-conscious historiographical approach and the fact that he explicitly discusses this in the preface which situates his thought in broader Enlightenment discourses about history writing.

One of Macpherson's key methodological points is the distinction between new and well-known facts. This is tied to his historiographical practice: new facts warrant a quotation or citation, well-known facts do not. This approach with its clearly defined distinction between old and new is another aspect of Macpherson's Enlightenment historiography.[157] Here, his citation rules are part of his scientific method of history writing; his empirical historiography mirrors scientific experiments in this distinction between old and new knowledge. Macpherson also shows an understanding of the differences between quoting and paraphrasing; instead of an amateur laissez-faire attitude to quotations he distinguishes between the careful quoting of authorities for important and little-known facts and paraphrasing for established ones that are 'universally admitted'.[158] In addition, Macpherson talks about his wider reading: his *History of Great Britain*, he says, is the result of consulting far more works than he references. This means that his narrative 'is the general result of an intense inquiry into what has been advanced on all sides' but unlike today's academic historians, Macpherson does not see referencing as a way of acknowledging previous scholarship.[159] For him – and this is typical of some Enlightenment historiography – referencing is about highlighting what is new about his history, so that readers can trace his narrative back to its sources. Its purpose is not to engage with other historians' narratives. Indeed, Macpherson contends that sidenotes and references are only useful to impress 'the superficial', but not 'the judicious'.[160] As a professional historian it is his job to evaluate sources, and to narrate the past for a non-scholarly audience. For Macpherson, the historian is a trustworthy expert who does not need to prove their credentials by leaving a trail of historiographical evidence; instead, they highlight sources only when they are adding new material to the discussion. This is how Macpherson operates in *The History of Great Britain* and it contrasts to his use of footnotes in his later political works (see Chapter 4) and, indeed, to how Gibbon was beginning to develop a discursive and reflective use of footnotes. However, Macpherson's approach to footnotes compares to Robertson's use of such scholarly scaffolding in his work, where he 'identifies the historians, or more rarely the archives, which authorise his statements, [but] there are no further exercises in the discourse of erudition'.[161] Indeed, Macpherson argues that to 'crowd a margin with the names of different writers' – to provide a trail of references – is 'an easy [...] imposture' that serves to impress only amateurs, but not those 'judicious' professionals – historians, men of letters, politicians – for whom he is writing.[162] Furthermore, it demonstrates Macpherson's continuing fidelity to Hugh Blair's historiographical preference for a historical narrative uncluttered by overbearing references and how Macpherson employed this neoclassical Enlightenment approach to history writing in his own work.[163]

One other aspect of Enlightenment historiographical theory is evident from the preface to *The History of Great Britain*: the idea, advanced by Hume, that historians should contextualise events in their narrative.[164] Enlightenment historians are not chroniclers; they explain facts and events and draw comparisons between the specific subject matter they are writing about and the wider history of the period, topic or region. This allows these historians to not only list events, but to establish causality, and to discuss how and why things came to be. Macpherson does this in *The History of Great Britain*, and explicitly talks about this process in the preface. He has endeavoured to 'carefully connect' events with 'the great line of history', delineating 'effects' and circumstances. In doing so he has 'traced [affairs] through their whole progress', rather than depicting them in isolation.[165] This is another way in which Macpherson operates as an Enlightenment historian: through this causational way of writing history, echoing an approach outlined most clearly in Hume's *Enquiry Concerning Human Understanding* (1748).[166] For Macpherson, history writing necessitates exploring causes and effect, and placing events and facts into context.

The thoroughness of Macpherson's preface to *The History of Great Britain* can be usefully contrasted to two of his contemporary Enlightenment historians – Robertson and Gibbon – and how they used prefaces to outline their methodological and historiographical approaches. In the work of these historians' illustrious predecessor, David Hume, most of his reflection on his practice as an historian occurred in the privacy of letters to friends and publishers.[167] Phillips argues that the changing nature of the eighteenth-century book market and the development of new and larger audiences for this commercial product led to an increasing awareness of the need to communicate with the reader and to establish their authorial intent: 'Hence the recurring apologies for venturing into publication, the convention of anonymous publication, the continued importance of dedications, though with new meaning, and the recurrent invocations of readers through various forms of addresses in advertisements, prefaces, and textual interpretations.'[168] This context helps us to understand the increasing impetus given to prefaces by historians such as Robertson.

In the three texts that are most closely related to the topics of Macpherson's history writings (*The History of Scotland* (1759); *The History of America* (1777); *An Historical Disquisition Concerning the Knowledge which the Ancients Had of India* (1791)), Robertson outlines his approach and method in clear and precise prefaces. In *The History of Scotland*, Robertson uses the preface to emphasise his reliance on extensive primary source material and how his interpretation differs from other historians. Robertson notes that his narrative of the past 'departed, in many instances, from former Historians, as I have placed facts in a different light, and have drawn characters with new colours'.[169] Robertson goes on to engage in explicit historiographical debate – just as we have seen in Macpherson's preface to *The History of Great Britain* – in which he criticises older historians of this period, especially in connection to the key Enlightenment notion of truth: 'Truth was not the sole object of these Authors. Blinded by prejudices, and heated by the part which they themselves had acted in the scenes they described, they wrote an apology for a faction, rather than the history of their country.'[170] Like Macpherson, Robertson's history writing sought to overcome the division of faction, which could be done through the historian's archival research method: 'Records have therefore been searched, original papers have been produced, and public archives, as well as the repositories of private men, have been ransacked.'[171] Consulting these primary sources then allowed Robertson to 'correct the inaccuracies of former Historians, to avoid their mistakes, and to detect their misrepresentations'.[172] Historical truth, for both Robertson and Macpherson, lay in the evidence of the sources. At the end of this preface, Robertson tells the reader that some of this source material was included in the book, as part of an appendix. The effect of this, again, was to underline the authenticity of Robertson's interpretation: 'I have satisfied myself with publishing a few of the most curious among them, to which I found it necessary to appeal as vouchers for my own veracity.'[173] In the preface to the *History of America*, Robertson builds on these arguments. In detailing the extensive list of archives and sources that have informed his account of Spanish colonisation of America, Robertson once more claims that his interpretation is different to previous historians and, like Macpherson, emphasises the novelty of his evidence:

> I have departed in many instances from the accounts of preceding historians, and often related facts which seem to have been unknown to them. It is a duty I owe the Public, to mention the sources from which I have derived such intelligence, as justifies me either in placing transactions in a new light, or in forming any new opinion with respect to causes and effects.[174]

While Robertson fills the rest of this preface with details of his impressive archive-grubbing across Europe, he concludes by once more emphasising that it is these sources that create an authentic analysis:

> All those books and manuscripts I have consulted with that attention, which the respect due from an Author to the Public required; and by minute references to them, I have endeavoured to authenticate whatever I relate. The longer I reflect on the nature of historical composition, the more I am convinced that this scrupulous accuracy is necessary. The historian who records the events of his own time, is credited in proportion to the opinion which the Public entertains with respect to his means of information and his veracity. He who delineates the transactions of a remote period, has no title to claim assent, unless he produces evidence in proof of his assertions. Without this, he may write an amusing tale, but cannot be said to have composed an authentic history.[175]

Much like Macpherson, Robertson emphasises not only the importance of primary sources from the period, but also the need to use footnotes – the 'minute references' which authenticate his account of the past. Here, Robertson explicitly acknowledges his debt to Gibbon and, in particular, his influence on Robertson's decision to publish a separate 'catalogue of the Spanish books I have consulted', rather than 'encumbering the page with an insertion of their full titles', in a nod to the kind of Enlightenment concerns about avoiding interrupting the narrative flow of history writing that we saw above.[176] This narrative purity was once again emphasised by Robertson in the preface to his final publication, on the history of India, where he stated that 'I have kept historical narrative as much separate as possible from scientific and critical discussions, by reserving the latter for Notes and Illustrations.'[177] Once more, like Macpherson, Robertson stressed the reliability of his historical method, 'having referred, with scrupulous accuracy, to the authors from whom I have derived information'.[178] Robertson also balances this attention to authenticity with earlier Enlightenment notions about the purpose of history writing, arguing that 'I imagined that the result of my researches might prove amusing and instructive to others.'[179] Finally, it is useful to reflect on Gibbon's rather briefer account of his historical methodology. It was not until the fourth volume of *The Decline and Fall of the Roman Empire* that Gibbon was moved to include a preface, and his brevity stands in contrast to the rather more fulsome accounts of their research practice given by Macpherson and Robertson. In this preface, Gibbon refers explicitly to Robertson's practice of publishing a separate list of the works he had consulted in his *History of America* – on the advice of Gibbon, who then declines to follow his own suggestion![180] Instead, Gibbon outlines an approach to using evidence similar to Macpherson and Robertson, where he draws his material 'from the fountain-head'.[181] While Gibbon states his fidelity to the source material, his methodology lacks the detail and precision of both Robertson and Macpherson, with their more thorough analysis of sources, evidence, footnotes and the all-important concepts of historical truth and authenticity.

In the main body text of *The History of Great Britain* Macpherson explores a number of historiographical concerns. Yet both his contemporaries and modern scholars have not taken note of where Macpherson was self-consciously historiographical in this historical narrative of seventeenth- and early eighteenth-century Britain. *The History of Great Britain* sold well, but those with public voices (such as Hume and Walpole, as we have seen above) were upset by the book but not specifically at Macpherson's methodology.[182] They disliked his style, and the evidence he presented; indeed, the *Original Papers* were far more controversial than *The History of Great Britain* itself. It was hard to believe that someone like Macpherson – poetic dabbler, hack writer, from the fringes of the British imperial state – would write a history that sold well. They did not believe his methodological claims in the preface, and dismissed the *History* as partial, un-historical and badly written. Our book, however, is not concerned with the reception of Macpherson's work, or with judging the quality of his histories; instead, its purpose is to demonstrate *how* Macpherson approached history writing. Here, then, we are looking to see if the historiographical ideas set up in the preface are then used to frame the main body of *The History of Great Britain*. In particular, we will explore how Macpherson writes history and how he deals with sources. We argue that Macpherson was a modern Enlightenment historian who practised what he preached; whose writing about the seventeenth and early eighteenth centuries matched the theoretical framework established in the preface. We make this point by showcasing a variety of approaches in the main text of *The History of Great Britain* where Macpherson is explicitly historiographic: where he discusses sources and other historians; where he speaks of 'truth'; and where he evaluates knowledge and compares sources. This is not to say that his book is comparable to today's works of academic history, footnoted to show a trail of research but, instead, that Macpherson was writing history using similar techniques and approaches as those of his Enlightenment historian colleagues. Here, William Robertson stands out as a particular analogue of Macpherson's practice in the *History*, especially in terms of its focus on the 'narrative actions of the state', supported by occasional reflection and digression to explain the evolution of the British state and underpinned by footnotes to primary sources and other historians' work.[183]

Macpherson frames his practice throughout *The History of Great Britain* with self-consciously historiographical remarks, along the lines of 'as far as was then known' or 'as is usually done'. He uses such statements to contextualise his research, but not to disagree with their historical judgement. For example, when discussing the character of Charles II, Macpherson writes that 'the disposition and character of Charles, as far as they were THEN known, were well suited to the times'.[184] There is a hint of disagreement – the bold emphasis on 'THEN' leads us to expect that more is known about Charles now. But here Macpherson is not concerned with proving other historians wrong: he is commenting on the fact that what was known of Charles fitted the period, which means that any new knowledge gained from archival research might help us, the modern reader, understand Charles and the times, but might not be as relevant to his own time. Later, he takes a slightly different approach: when discussing Titus Oates, the fabricator of a Catholic plot to assassinate Charles, Macpherson emphasises facts that have emerged since the events happened, and he argues that 'a brief detail of the circumstances, as they have since appeared, will throw more light on the subject, than a narration of the facts as they gradually rose to view'.[185] Here, Macpherson justifies his decision not to stick to chronology because of his desire to illuminate his subject; because he is concerned with explaining the past, rather than commenting on how things were perceived *in* the past, he allows himself to overwrite chronology with later knowledge, echoing Hume's emphasis on 'the importance of the retrospective view that is adopted by the historian'.[186] What is significant about this, however, is not the process, but the fact that he is explicit about this: he justifies his decision and invites the reader to share his historiographical motivation. Macpherson's approach to narrative, here, resembles Hume's, in that they both wrestle with the key point of Enlightenment historiographical debate: that 'exemplary narrative' needed to be combined with 'more systematic arguments of philosophical history'.[187] What is different in Macpherson's work is his explicit reflection in the body of the text in such issues, whereas most of Hume's historiographical remarks can be found outwith *The History of England* and, instead, either in his philosophical and historical essays or in the private realm of letters.

Throughout the *History* Macpherson openly refers to sources, scholars and other evidence in both his text and footnotes. Early on, for example, he discusses James II's opinion of Clarendon, the English statesman and historian. Instead of simply footnoting his source Macpherson tells us that James's views may be found 'in his Memoirs' and this is the first in-text reference to any source in *The History of Great Britain*.[188] The source is significant here: James's *Memoirs* is one of Macpherson's principal primary sources, alongside James's journals. In the same section of *The History of Great Britain* he quotes from James's journals, as he does, indeed, later in the book. This is an important historiographical technique: like a scholarly historian of today, Macpherson supports his idea in the text with evidence. Significantly he does so when he discusses individuals' opinions – James II, in this case – and primary sources, and it lends credibility to his account, *showing* the reader where his information comes from. That is, instances like this do not tell the reader information, but allow the reader to see the evidence for themselves, and this makes Macpherson's argument not only more believable or sustainable, but it also empowers his reader. Here, then, is an example of what makes Macpherson a modern historian: instead of setting himself up as an authority on his subject he shares his research journey – and his material – with his reader, which in turn makes the reader accept his argument more easily. This way of presenting evidence is used by Macpherson throughout his *History of Great Britain*, and particularly with regard to manuscript primary sources. In volume I, chapter 8, for example, Macpherson evaluates 'the design of seizing the King'. This, he argues, 'is ascertained from various quarters' – a fact well-known enough not to require more specific references. The detail of the attack, however, is uncertain, and in particular Macpherson discusses rumoured intentions to 'stab or pistol' the king. It is in this detail that he refers to specific manuscript evidence – a primary source he has unearthed in his research: 'The only evidence of the fact is in the death-bed confession of Sir George Hewitt.'[189] Like the reference to James II's *Memoirs* earlier, the explicit in-text reference here shows Macpherson as a careful and considered Enlightenment historian, who is open with his evidence. The variety of evidence thus explicitly integrated into his argument adds to Macpherson's desired effect of portraying himself as an impartial historian, who has weighed up sources, tracked down manuscripts, and who openly shares his sources with his readers. His evaluative comments on his sources confirm this. A letter of the Princess of Denmark, for example, 'bears all the marks of compunction and affection', a comment supported by a lengthy quotation from the hitherto unpublished letter.[190] In this, then, Macpherson is seen to be evaluative, and takes care to represent his selection of sources as unbiased.

Macpherson's direct acknowledgement of engagement with sources is also echoed in his attribution of ideas. This is a more oblique approach and follows on from the earlier detailed in-text engagement with his sources. Once a source has been established, and Macpherson has set himself up as impartial and trustworthy, he can be less specific in his references while retaining the same level of conviction in his argument. It is then enough to reference facts as 'according to' a source – for example, once he has established James II's *Memoirs* as his manuscript primary source, he can then add new detail as 'according to James the II' a page later.[191] This is a fruitful use of referencing when used in the context of in-text citations but used on its own, outwith in-text citations, its effect is less persuasive. Then, instead of emphasising the reliability of the historian's argument, it sets them up as a know-it-all storyteller rather than a modern, impartial, Enlightenment historian – again, a reflection of some of the tensions that still persisted in Macpherson's writing.

Macpherson often engages with ideas that are thought to be true in *The History of Great Britain* in order to refute them with his manuscript primary sources. Macpherson here acknowledges popular opinion, but specifically to disprove it, or to add new information from his manuscript primary sources. He engages with what is widely thought to strengthen his argument, and to make it obvious when he is adding new information to the wider historiographical discussion on a given topic. This allows Macpherson to add to the stock of existing knowledge and at the same time to contextualise his sources, showing the reader why manuscript study is useful, and how this new way of writing history – through the critical and philosophical analysis of manuscript primary sources, rather than from established secondary sources – is beneficial and efficient, in an Enlightenment way. This new way of writing history perpetuates Enlightenment concerns with impartiality, truth and chronology; it is the history equivalent of scientific experiments in its evidence-based approach. We see this in *The History of Great Britain* when Macpherson uses his research to correct assumptions and other historians' interpretations. For example, he confirms that James, when Duke of York, was not actually at the wedding of Charles II and Catherine of Braganza in 1662: 'the Duke of York, who is said to have been present, was not then arrived from Plymouth'.[192] Here, Macpherson counters public opinion with the facts he gained from his manuscript research. A little later he uses a similar approach to evaluate the English selling of Dunkirk in the same year: 'the sale of Dunkirk, though stigmatized as one of the worst measures of the reign of Charles, was less excusable, as a mark of meanness in the King, than for its detriment to the nation', for which he then gives evidence.[193] As in the earlier example, Macpherson engages with public and perceived opinion, and uses evidence to argue against this – much like an historian would today. At other times in *The History of Great Britain* he explicitly corrects earlier assumptions. When discussing the restoration of fellows at the University of Oxford in 1688, for example, he first outlines what historians and the public have generally assumed: 'this delay has always been produced as an irrefragable proof of James's want of sincerity in his concessions'. But, he argues, 'there is no truth in the assertion'. Macpherson has evidence for this and shares it with his readers: 'the letter which accidentally recalled the Bishop of Winchester was written on the nineteenth of October; and the Prince of Orange was not driven back by the tempest till the twenty-first of the same month'.[194] Indeed, here we can see Macpherson refuting assumptions with manuscript evidence, which he references in a footnote. As with all of these aspects of his historiographical practice, these are just some examples of the different ways in which his historiographical methodology – clearing up facts, in this case – forms the underlying basis for his approach to history writing.

Macpherson's historiographical practice can also be seen in his direct engagement with ideas of the public and public opinion. This is different from simply disagreeing with perceived opinions; here, Macpherson sets up 'the public' as an entity in its own right, and one that historians can engage with just like they engage with other historians' arguments. And while he does not often discuss public opinion in this way, when he does it is significant. For example, when narrating the Great Fire of London of 1666, Macpherson argues that 'Distrust, jealousy, and suspicion, as is usual, were joined to consternation and terror in the minds of the people, who are ever ready to ascribe public misfortune to private design.'[195] Here, the focus is on 'the people'. It is their opinion that Macpherson explores, rather than what actually happened, echoing some of Hume's accounts of public 'experience and perception' in the *History of England*.[196] This is significant because it shows that Macpherson is not only concerned with narrating the story of the past – of telling his readers what happened. Instead, he is interested in opinions and reasons for why things occurred, balancing his historical narrative with philosophical reflection and interpretation.

Throughout *The History of Great Britain* Macpherson's approach is evaluative. He assesses sources, opinions and events, and when there is no direct evidence circumstantial evaluation forms the basis of his analysis. This is particularly the case when Macpherson makes grand, overarching statements, rather than engaging with specific evidence. For example, he argues that 'the national happiness, which began with the Restoration, seems to have terminated with the Dutch war'.[197] 'Seems' is key here: it indicates that while Macpherson is not absolutely certain that this is the case, and while he does not have any direct manuscript evidence that confirms this, his careful analysis of sources makes this explanation most likely. Another version of this approach consists in Macpherson's evaluative language, such as 'the fact is improbable', or 'and it is not likely'.[198] He employs this when he has analysed facts and sources, and then presents his considered professional assessment. Similarly, Macpherson uses the phrase 'there is reason to conclude' in this way.[199] It indicates to the reader that what follows is not fact, but evaluation, but that this evaluation is considered and trustworthy, rather than mere speculation. This is why Macpherson's judgements, when he makes them, are a considered part of his historiographical methodology.

Like other Enlightenment historians, Macpherson realises the importance of cause and effect, and of detailing the consequences of actions to build a sustained and convincing argument.[200] It is a key principle that underscores much of his *History of Great Britain*, and there are some examples where he explicitly engages with causation in the text. For example, when giving a character sketch of James II, Macpherson argues that 'had the Duke of York continued a Protestant, the monarchy would have become absolute through his perseverance and obstinacy, qualities which supplied in him the place of great abilities and firmness of mind'.[201] Here, Macpherson is concerned with consequences, not with what actually happened; he outlines this alternative future with a focus on what would have been the significance of James II's continuing Protestantism. In a similar vein, he traces public fears to James II's Catholic beliefs: 'though the bigoted adherence of the Duke of York to the Romish faith was the obvious cause of the uncommon fears which had seized the nation, there were secret springs, which greatly contributed to set the whole machine of opposition in motion'.[202] Here, Macpherson's focus on the 'obvious cause' is indicative of his Enlightenment attitude to history writing: it is not what happened, but being able to show why things happened that is the key to good history writing. Similarly, Macpherson explicitly engages with the idea of causation at another point in *The History of Great Britain*: '... these, co-operating together, produced events in the present year, which require a prior detail of facts to be understood'.[203] In this case his emphasis is not on the events in the present year, or what these prior facts are, but the fact that the reader needs to have knowledge of them in order to understand their effect on the present. Macpherson does not simply offer the causes here – the prior facts – but explicitly discusses the reasons for engaging with causation as part of his historiographical practice. At other points he takes care to explain the process of causation

– the chain of events that links one event with another. Again, like in the example of prior facts, Macpherson's explicit engagement with historiographical theory allows him to build a convincing argument that actively involves his reader. Here, he argues that 'such were the beginnings of a connection which afterwards actually brought Monmouth to the block, and paved the way to the throne for the Prince of Orange'.[204] As in the earlier examples, Macpherson does not only explain what happens, but emphasises why he is presenting information in a certain way.

Macpherson incorporates two further Enlightenment historiographical principles into his historiographical practice. These are, on the one hand, the classical idea that history writing should be both instructive and entertaining, and, on the other hand, an insistence on historical truth. These concepts are not part of the methodology expressed in the preface, but they are part of his practice in the main text, and can be traced to other Enlightenment historiographers such as Hume and Blair.[205] The example of history as amusement and instruction – Horatian *delectare et prodesse* – is a negative example; Macpherson comments on the absence of instruction and entertainment: 'the affairs of Scotland, during five years, furnish little of importance, and nothing of amusement'.[206] While this might seem unnecessarily dismissive, it is in fact a key example of Macpherson's Enlightenment methodology. Scotland is unremarkable, he argues, not because its affairs do not have any bearing on the parliamentary history with which he is first and foremost concerned, but because he can pick out nothing that is instructive or amusing. Either would be appropriate, but the fact that Macpherson places both concepts together in his dismissal of Scottish affairs during this period is indicative of his wider Enlightenment concerns. He does not dismiss Scotland because it does not matter, but because its history in this period does not lend itself to instruction and amusement. In such a way, Macpherson was following the north British tendencies of much of the Scottish Enlightenment, seeing pre-Union, seventeenth-century Scotland as outwith history itself, an idea we shall see Macpherson developing in his later works on the crisis of empire.[207] There is nothing, he argues, for his reader to learn from Scottish history in this period, and nothing entertaining either. In other words, Scottish history in this five-year period is *un*-Enlightening.

In the main text of *The History of Great Britain* Macpherson reflects on the process of history writing and its instructional, didactic qualities. His guiding principle here is the idea that 'men formed their judgment of the future from the events of past times', that is, that we can learn from the past.[208] History writing, for Macpherson, is instructional, and the writing and reading of history has a direct bearing on the future.

He explores this idea at length in a paragraph in the first volume of *The History of Great Britain*, alongside a discussion of the difference that distance makes to events and how we perceive individuals and their actions:

> To live in times and to read of their transactions, suggest different and sometimes opposite ideas to the human mind. Measures pass without reprehension in common life, that would offend in narration; and those who are deemed bad members of society in history, are often treated, by their contemporaries, with a degree of applause. The cause of this is as obvious as the fact itself is true. Public transactions are slow in their succession, and the motives which produced them are unknown. The impression made by one evil is obliterated before another arrives. Mankind are deceived by the speciousness which is generally given to the worst measures. They see but a part of the great machine of government, as it moves before them; and that partiality, which people naturally entertain for their country, justifies to them its most exceptionable conduct toward foreign powers. Time, by unveiling the secret springs of action, opens a field either for censure or applause. But both are frequently ill applied. To judge of the measures of the last age by the feelings of the present, may be as unjust, as it would be unreasonable to expect the same strict adherence to virtue in states which we commend in individuals.[209]

Here, Macpherson emphasises the difference between *experiencing* and *reading about* a period and its events, and – by extension – the role of the historian in connecting one with the other. The historian is here seen as narrator who helps the readers understand the past, and who facilitates judgement not based on current prejudices and tastes, but in relation to the 'feelings' of the period in question. Macpherson emphasises the great advantage that the historian has over those living through the events; that distance allows for the 'secret springs of actions' – motives and causes – to be unveiled by the historian. This is in line with his discussions, elsewhere in *The History of Great Britain*, concerning the importance of cause and effect. It also demonstrates that Macpherson was beginning to think about one of the most pressing issues of history writing during this period – that the past could offer a guide to morality. As Priya Satia argues, history emerged as a 'system of ethical accountability' during the second half of the eighteenth century in the work of Adam Smith and others, and Macpherson echoes this in his claim that 'Time ... opens a field either for censure or applause.'[210] In the next sentence, 'To judge of the measures of the last age by the feelings of the present, may be as unjust ...', Macpherson argues that history writing then defers that moral judgement. Here, Macpherson pre-empts an argument that later became familiar in defence of empire and colonialism – that 'no one can be held personally accountable for the sly unfolding of history'.[211]

This paragraph, then, is central to understanding Macpherson's practice as an historian, where we see his direct engagement with the idea of history, and why history writing matters, and it is the only such explicitly historiographical paragraph in *The History of Great Britain*.

The History of Great Britain begins and ends with case studies – of King Charles II and Queen Anne respectively – which illustrate how Macpherson's history writing both built upon and differed from the approach of his illustrious predecessor, David Hume. The subject of the first is the Restoration of the monarchy in 1660. This is where Hume's and Macpherson's histories overlap, and where we can see that their understandings of narrative and character differ. Let us consider, first, the actual Restoration itself – Charles II's physical return to Britain. It is found in volume VI, chapter LXII of Hume's *History* and forms the opening chapter of the first volume of Macpherson's *History of Great Britain*. Though the sentiment is similar – Charles returned after a period of upheaval, welcomed by friend and foe alike – the execution and emphasis in the two texts differ considerably. Hume's depiction of Charles's entry into London is short: 'the two houses attended; while the King was proclaimed with great solemnity, in Palace-Yard, at White-hall, and at Temple-Bar'.[212] Macpherson, on the other hand, launches into a much fuller account:

> Charles the Second was proclaimed, at London, on the eighth of May, in the year one thousand six hundred and sixty. He entered that city, on the twenty-ninth of the month, amid the acclamations of an infinite concourse of spectators. The two houses of Parliament attended the King, at Whitehall; and, by their speakers, congratulated him, in terms full of submission and loyalty. The populace, with their usual extravagance, expressed their satisfaction in riot and intemperance.[213]

Macpherson's version is far more narrative: it tells the story, adding particulars and descriptions. His example is extensive, while Hume is merely concerned with objective facts: facts that are measurable, quantifiable, and lend themselves to interpretation. 'The commons', Hume explains,

> voted 500 pounds to buy a jewel for Granville, who had brought them the king's gracious messages: A present of 50,000 pounds was conferred to the king, 10,000 pounds on the duke of York, 5000 pounds on the duke of Gloucester [...] The rapidity, with which all these events were conducted, was marvellous, and discovered the passionate zeal and entire unanimity of the nation.[214]

His admiration for the swiftness of proceedings, as well as his delineation of the exact cost, clashes with Macpherson's vivid insistence on unity and patriotism in the face of earlier 'anarchy and confusion' that, under the new king, 'yielded to the hopes of a regular steadiness in government'. Indeed, 'the pomp of royalty pleased the bulk of mankind; its novelty all'.[215] For Macpherson, Charles brought cohesion to his countries long before the Union of 1707 did. In his account of the Restoration Macpherson embraces Bolingbroke's philosophical insistence on examples to illustrate and, perhaps, encourage his readers to emulate the past.[216]

Hume and Macpherson, for all their Enlightenment philosophical modernity, continued to rely on neoclassical reflections on the character of prominent individuals in their respective historical narratives, emphasising history's mimetic qualities as 'largely the story of the revelation of character in action'.[217] Like Hume, Macpherson includes a number of character sketches in his *History of Great Britain*, 'where formal enumerations of virtues or vices serve, as they always had done, to bring closure to prominent lives'.[218] However, Macpherson's analysis of character in his historical practice owes much to his poetics: he narrates the deeds of heroes, and to do this he needs to describe his characters. This is why Macpherson treats his readers to a character sketch of the king. Hume does not, in marked contrast to his earlier representation of his predecessor, Charles I, as 'a sentimental hero'.[219] What interests Macpherson here and elsewhere are the deeds and characters of individuals, and they explain why events have unfolded in a certain way and allow the historian to think about the progress of society. With Macpherson, history is centred in his characters — in his fiction as well as in his histories. Of Charles II, he says that

> the disposition and character of Charles, as far as they were Then known, were well suited to the times. Attached to no system of religion, he seemed favourable to all. In appearance destitute of political ambition, his sudden elevation was more an object of admiration, than of jealousy. Accommodating in his possessions and easy in his manner, he pleased even those whom he could not gratify. Men, from principle, enemies to monarchy, were prejudiced in favour of the person of the Prince. Those in whom fear might excite aversion, lost their hatred, in his apparent forgetfulness of past injuries [...] Insinuating, dissembling, but frequently judicious, he came upon mankind, through the channel of their ruling passions.[220]

Charles is at the centre of this part of Macpherson's *History of Great Britain*. He is both the starting point and the focus; without knowledge of his character there can be no true history for an Enlightenment historian such as Macpherson. Similarly, Macpherson ends his *History of*

Great Britain with a decidedly more critical character sketch of Queen Anne, which follows after the description of her death:

> She was always generous, sometimes liberal, but never profuse. Like the rest of her family, she was good-natured, to a degree of weakness. Indolent in her disposition, timid by nature, devoted to the company of her favourites, easily led. She possessed all the virtues of her father, except political courage. She was subject to all his weaknesses, except enthusiasm in religion. She was jealous of her authority, and sullenly irreconcilable toward those who treated either herself or her prerogative with disrespect. But, like him also, she was much better qualified to discharge the duties of a private life, than to act the part of a sovereign. As a friend, a mother, a wife, she deserved every praise. Her conduct, as a daughter, could scarcely be excused by a virtue much superior to all these. Upon the whole, though her reign was crowded with great events, she cannot, with any justice, be called a great Princess. Subject to terror, beyond the constitutional timidity of her sex, she was altogether incapable of decisive councils; and nothing, but her irresistible popularity could have supported her authority, amidst the ferment of those distracted times.[221]

This, then, again emphasises the idea that Macpherson was an Enlightenment historian. Finishing *The History of Great Britain* with this biographical sketch of Anne does not mark a return to earlier historiographical ideas but instead demonstrates Macpherson's Enlightenment credentials; for him, these character sketches are necessary to contextualise the chains of cause and effect that his *History of Great Britain* delineates.

Macpherson's status as an Enlightenment historian is further demonstrated by the emphasis in *The History of Great Britain* on Whig constitutionalism. As we have seen in his application of stadial theory to the early Celtic history of Britain and Ireland, Macpherson had long engaged with such ideas that placed notions of the 'ancient constitution' and the liberties of 'freeborn Englishmen' (or, indeed, freeborn Celts, in Macpherson's view) at the heart of a history of progress. In *The History of Great Britain*, we see Macpherson's belief in notions of the ancient constitution come into sharper focus, especially around the idea of a balanced constitutional settlement that cuts through the instability of faction. The absence of that balance helped Macpherson to explain the demise of Charles II and revolution of 1688, while William III's greater success at navigating faction was testimony to the constitutional changes that had led to his accession to the English throne. In *The History of Great Britain*, Macpherson also began to link his belief in Whig constitutionalism to a critique of the corruption of the East India Company, foreshadowing his later history writing and its focus on the crisis of empire during the late 1770s. Finally, in one last comparison with Hume, we briefly dwell on Macpherson's representation of war. Here, Macpherson's narrative is reminiscent of his poetics, reminding the reader of the Ossianic Collections and *The Highlander* in its depictions of conflict and the valiant deeds of heroes. More than this, Macpherson's emphasis on war as a driver of British history during the seventeenth century marks his historiographical modernity, demonstrating how 'Enlightenment faith in the progressive nature of war helped normalize the violence of imperial conquest and industrial capitalism'.[222]

Given the focus of *The History of Great Britain* on the second half of the seventeenth century, it is perhaps no surprise that constitutional issues loom large in Macpherson's historical narrative. From the beginning of the book, though, Macpherson frames this narrative in terms of Whig notions of the evolution of the British state. In discussing the restoration of the monarchy in 1660, Macpherson describes the general support for the return of Charles II to the throne and that 'The eagerness of the body of the people, to return to the ancient constitution, had formed the firmest foundation for its support'.[223] Macpherson labels the restoration as a return to the purities of the ancient constitution, but his narrative of Charles II's reign soon begins to focus on how those constitutional rights were once more eroded. In a key passage, Macpherson analyses how Parliament resisted the increasingly absolutist tendencies of the King through successfully enacting legislation to uphold one of the key tenets of the ancient constitution: habeas corpus. The Habeas Corpus Act of 1679 was described by Macpherson as 'a law which peculiarly distinguishes the freedom of the constitution of England'.[224] This idea of freedom could be traced back to that great Whig shibboleth – Magna Carta, which had established that 'The personal liberty of individuals is a property of human nature, which nothing but the certainty of a crime committed ought ever to abridge or refrain.'[225] However, the power of the monarch continued to impinge on these notions of freedom and liberty, leading to the kind of constitutional imbalance in which, according to Macpherson, faction could thrive. By the end of Charles II's reign, the emergence of the Whigs and the Tories (terminologies dismissed by Macpherson as the products of 'Scottish covenanters' and 'the wild Irish') had led to the conduct of government becoming shrouded by faction.[226] Macpherson's reflection on Charles II concludes that 'The nation being long divided into two parties, history became an engine of faction, more than the vehicle of truth.'[227] Here, Macpherson criticises 'the supporters of the Revolution' for their 'misrepresentations and factions of party'. Instead, Macpherson emphasises his balance as an historian, steering a line 'between the two extremes' as 'the path to truth, in the character of this Prince and the history of his reign'.[228]

However, it was this lack of constitutional balance in the restoration of the monarchy that then led to the crisis of James II's reign. James used his first address to the Privy Council on becoming king in February 1685 to proclaim his adherence to constitutional principles – 'that as he was resolved not to depart from the just rights and prerogatives of the crown, he was determined never to invade the property of the subject'. Despite such constitutional assurances to preserve 'all their just rights and liberties', James soon erred.[229] In continuing his enthusiastic Catholicism, James 'encroach[ed] upon the constitution', leading to the fear that 'the King's measures' were 'nothing less than a settled system to introduce his own religion and an unlimited power in the crown'.[230] In accounting for the fall of James and the rise of William, Macpherson adopts a version of Whig constitutionalism that sees Parliament as supreme: 'The whole authority of the crown was now vested in William, by the opinion of the people.'[231] Macpherson, though, is no Williamite apologist. Once more pausing his narrative at William's death in 1702 to offer broader philosophical reflection, Macpherson comments on William's character and conduct as king. Macpherson notes the tension between the constitutional principles upon which William became king and his actual conduct when in office: 'He was raised to the throne of Great Britain under the name of her deliverance from civil tyranny and religious persecution', yet once king 'he scarce adhered, in any thing, to the moderate declaration which paved his way to the throne'.[232] While Macpherson does acknowledge William's relative success in navigating faction, parties and opinions continued to cause tension: 'this Prince must have been too much praised by the one side, and by the other as extravagantly condemned'.[233] In outlining the faction-riven nature of Williamite politics, Macpherson takes the opportunity to comment on the value of historiographical balance:

> The nearest path to truth, must certainly lie between these two extremes. But that path, though obvious, has not, hitherto been trod by historians; who have uniformly yielded to the prejudices of others, or have been swayed by their own. Their proximity to the period concerning which they wrote, may form, for many, a complete excuse.[234]

Here, Macpherson argues that an historian's sense of balance and impartiality comes from a certain historical distance from events. In this assessment, despite dismissing other historians' approaches, Macpherson was, once more, closer to Hume's historiographical practice than he might care to admit. As Phillips argues, Hume's *History of England* discussed the 'faction-ridden historiography that had preceded him' in order to emphasise the historical distance between now and then and to 'declare that the English revolution was over'.[235] Macpherson's approach is similar, emphasising how his impartiality as an historian arises from the greater distance between the writer and the events being described. Ironically, as Macpherson's history writing develops in the late 1770s, that sense of historical distance begins to collapse, as we shall see in Chapter 4, when he writes history in order to defend particular political positions in the present within the British imperial state.

Macpherson's approach to Whig constitutionalism in *The History of Great Britain* also begins to take on an imperial dimension, foreshadowing his later political writing on empire. Here, Macpherson links his narrative of political developments in the last decade of the seventeenth century to a critique of East India Company corruption. While never being a prominent theme, British imperialism runs throughout *The History of Great Britain*, from his account of Charles II's founding of the Royal African Company 'under the auspices of the duke of York, to supply the West-India islands with slaves' to his later description of British interests in the East Indies.[236] Here, Macpherson was not afraid to criticise William, demonstrating once again his argument that the constitution was more important than the character of the king in determining the course of history. Early 1694 had seen Parliament spend increasing amounts of time on the 'affairs of the East-India company' and the 'train of corruption ... [that] had already been laid'.[237] These 'corrupt practices' continued into 1695, where Macpherson implicates King William as involved 'in the same scene of corruption with his servants'.[238] This was the context in which a new charter for the EIC 'exclusive of the interlopers on their trade' was granted in September 1694 'by bribing the King and corrupting his servants'.[239] Macpherson's concern with EIC corruption was then taken up with gusto in his *History and Management of the East-India Company* (1779), where he attacks the company in defence of his own interests with the Nawab of Arcot and to promote a greater role for the British government in the affairs of their Indian empire.

Macpherson's focus on issues of empire finds clearest expression in *The History of Great Britain* through his account of warfare and descriptions of battles. For much of the second half of the seventeenth century, the Dutch Republic had been the most significant threat to the nascent English (soon to be British) empire.[240] This contest for imperial supremacy occupies much of Macpherson's narrative in *The History of Great Britain* and offers another point of comparison with Hume's account of the same period in volume 6 of his *History of England*. Macpherson's description of the famous Four Days' Battle in June 1666 during the second Anglo-Dutch war covers the same events as Hume, but with a greater emphasis on the drama of the conflict. As he declares in introducing his account of the battle, Hume's focus was on the 'chief events of each day's engagement' rather than delving 'minutely into particulars'.[241] A comparison of Hume's account of the second day reveals Macpherson's flair for poetic drama, echoing some of the battle scenes in the Ossianic Collections. Hume provides a precise and distanced narrative of the beginning of the second day's battle: 'the wind was somewhat fallen and the combat became more steady and terrible. The English now found, that the greatest valour cannot compensate the superiority of numbers, against an enemy who is well conducted, and who is not defective in courage.' Macpherson, in contrast, set the scene with more dramatic language: 'Though night interrupted the fight, the ardour of neither side was abated. The Dutch were animated with hopes of conquest; the English were fired with indignation at their not being victorious.'[242] Macpherson's language is lively and poetic; Hume's more straightforwardly descriptive. When battle begins in earnest, Hume describes the arrival of Dutch reinforcements with similar matter-of-factness:

> Sixteen fresh ships joined the Dutch fleet during the action: And the English were so shattered, that their fighting ships were reduced to twenty-eight, and they found themselves obliged to retreat towards their own coast. The Dutch followed them, and were on the point of renewing the combat; when a calm, which came a little before night, prevented the engagement.[243]

Macpherson, on the other hand, channels the language of Ossianic warfare:

> At six of the clock the battle began with redoubled fierceness; but when the Dutch were upon the point of flying, they were reinforced with sixteen capital ships. They renewed the fury of combat. Many were slain on the side of the English; many of their ships were disabled; Albermarle, however, would yield to nothing but the night. Though the Dutch lost a vice-admiral, though many of their ships were disabled, and Van Tromp himself obliged to repeatedly change his flag, the enemy had greatly the disadvantage in the action of the second day. The English had lost no ship, but many were shattered and in no condition to face the enemy with any prospect of success. Darkness had scarce given them a respite from battle.[244]

Macpherson's account is full of drama, tension and poetic language (the 'fury' and 'darkness' of battle), in contrast to Hume's more pedestrian narrative.

The depiction of warfare was another barometer of how Macpherson's writing reflected the historiographical trends of the 1770s. Hume's account was written in the 1750s and focuses on the role of warfare in developing the functions of government and the state. As Schmidt argues, Hume believed that 'monarchy, as the earliest type of government, is modelled on military leadership rather than patriarchal authority'.[245] Macpherson's greater emphasis on warfare and more fulsome and exciting descriptions of battles indicate his engagement with emerging Enlightenment thought about 'war as a historical force'.[246] Adam Smith's account of empire in *The Wealth of Nations* (1776) emphasised the necessity of war in resolving the clash between Britain and the American colonists, echoing Macpherson's similar argument in *The Rights of Great Britain* (1775/6). In Macpherson's *History of Great Britain*, battles push British history forward, providing not only the kind of dramatic set pieces that we have seen above, but also indicating the inevitability of force, its use in defending or attacking the interests of the state and how, in turn, war became a driver of history.

CONCLUSION

The three texts examined in this chapter, *An Introduction to the History of Great Britain and Ireland*, the *Original Papers* and *The History of Great Britain*, demonstrate Macpherson's evolution as an Enlightenment historian. *An Introduction* can be seen as a hinge point between Macpherson's earlier poetic works (examined in Chapter 2) and his development as a writer of prose history. Stadial ideas about the progress of history that Macpherson had used to frame the Ossianic Collections (inspired by his friend, Adam Ferguson) were then applied to the history of the Celtic peoples in *An Introduction*. Here, Macpherson used stadial theories to account for the civilisation of the Celts and to make an argument about the Celtic origins of Whig constitutional notions of British history. Macpherson's historiographical practice was also strongly influenced by his more illustrious Enlightenment colleagues. David Hume's injunction that history should 'amuse and instruct' was coupled with Hugh Blair's notions about the 'Truth, Impartiality, Fidelity, and Accuracy' of history writing in Macpherson's *Introduction*. These key Enlightenment notions about the purpose of history were then taken further by Macpherson in his later works, the *Original Papers* and *The History of Great Britain*. Here, Macpherson discusses at length the importance of sources, evidence and footnotes in creating an argument that aligns with Hume and Blair's ideas. In 1775, Macpherson was writing in a mode that demonstrated his interest in the latest historiographical ideas, building on the earlier work of William Robertson and foreshadowing both Robertson's and Edward Gibbon's history writing of the second half of the 1770s. Like all of these historians, Macpherson grappled with the best way to combine the erudition of one's source materials, with the neoclassical necessity to narrate events, while balancing this with philosophical reflection on causes and connections. In the *Original Papers* and *The History of Great Britain*, Macpherson demonstrates that he is thoroughly appraised of this 'new, advanced type of historiography', as Nathaniel Wolloch labels it.[247] What makes Macpherson stand out in this distinguished company is the explicitness with which he discusses his methodology, going beyond even the scholarly Robertson and the rather more whimsical Gibbon, especially in his prefaces. In *The History of Great Britain*, Macpherson further develops his engagement with ideas of Whig constitutionalism, shifting his focus firmly on to the political issues that led to the Williamite revolution. This then leads to further innovation in his final works of history about the 1770s crisis of empire. In the following chapter, we turn our attention to Macpherson's writing about contemporary political events in America and India, and how he uses these advanced techniques of Enlightenment history writing, honed in *An Introduction*, the *Original Papers* and *The History of Great Britain*, to defend the politics of the British imperial state.

Notes

1. For an overview of the centrality of stadial history to Enlightenment thought, see O'Brien, *Narratives of Enlightenment*, pp. 11–12, 132–4.
2. Smith, *Lectures on Rhetoric and Belles Lettres*, p. 104.
3. For a recent account of Dr Johnson's tour of the Highlands and Islands as a response to Ossian, see Nigel Leask, 'Fingalian Topographies: Ossian and the Highland Tour, 1760–1805', *Journal for Eighteenth-Century Studies* 39:2 (2016), pp. 188–9.
4. See Colin Kidd's astute analysis, discussed further below, in *Subverting Scotland's Past*, pp. 223–4.
5. Moore, 'James Macpherson and "Celtic Whiggism"', p. 19.
6. *Scots Magazine*, 33, April 1771, p. 206.
7. Eliot Warburton (ed.), *Memoirs of Horace Walpole and his Contemporaries; Including Numerous Original Letters, Chiefly from Strawberry Hill* (London: H. Colburn, 1851), p. 352.
8. 'Obituary of Remarkable Persons; with Biographical Anecdotes', *The Gentleman's Magazine*, 66:3 (March 1776), p. 256.

9 Letter of David Hume to Col. Alexander Dow [1772], in Greig (ed.), *The Letters of David Hume*, Vol. II, p. 267.
10 Gibbon, *The History of the Decline and Fall of the Roman Empire*, Vol. IV, p. 292. For the later antiquarian backlash to Macpherson's Celtic history, see Ian B. Stewart, 'The Mother Tongue: Historical Study of the Celts and their Language(s) in Eighteenth-Century Britain and Ireland', *Past and Present*, 243 (2019), pp. 71–107; and Ian B. Stewart, 'Celticism and the Four Nations in the Long Nineteenth Century', in Naomi Lloyd-Jones and Maggie Scull (eds), *Four Nations Approaches to Modern 'British' History* (London: Palgrave Macmillan, 2018), pp. 135–59.
11 deGategno, *James Macpherson*, p. 7. See also Kenneth McNeil, *Scotland, Britain, Empire: Writing the Highlands, 1760–1860* (Columbus: Ohio State University Press, 2007), p. 35.
12 Kidd, *Subverting Scotland's Past*, pp. 230, 234.
13 Moore, 'James Macpherson and "Celtic Whiggism"', p. 2.
14 Ibid., p. 3.
15 Macpherson, 'Preface', *Introduction*, n.p.
16 Hume, 'Of the Study of History', p. 565.
17 Hugh Blair, 'Lecture XXXVI: Historical Writing', in Hugh Blair, *Lectures in Rhetoric and Belles Lettres* (London, 1839), p. 482.
18 Phillips, *Society and Sentiment*, pp. 40–5.
19 Pocock, *Barbarism and Religion, Vol. II. Narratives of Civil Government*, p. 207.
20 Phillips, *Society and Sentiment*, p. 41. For the distinction, made by Gibbon and others, between 'facts' (as erudition) and 'conjectures' as philosophy, see Nathaniel Wolloch, '"Facts, or Conjectures": Antoine-Yves Goguet's Historiography', *Journal of the History of Ideas*, 68:3 (2007), p. 449.
21 See, for example, Pocock's analysis of classical history writing as relating 'exemplary deeds … of ruling individuals'. Pocock, *Barbarism and Religion. Vol. II. Narratives of Civil Government*, p. 8.
22 Kidd, *Subverting Scotland's Past*, p. 101.
23 Phillips, *Sentiment and Society*, p. 60.
24 Pocock, *Barbarism and Religion. Vol. II. Narratives of Civil Government*, p. 278; Pocock, *Barbarism and Religion. Vol. IV. Barbarians, Savages and Empires*, pp. 183–4.
25 John Macpherson, *Critical Dissertations on the Origin, Antiquities, Language, Government, Manners, Religion of the Ancient Caledonians, their Posterity, the Picts, and the British and Irish Scots* (Dublin: Boulton Grierson, 1768). For the connection between James and John (which begins during James's collecting tour of Gaelic manuscripts and stories during the early 1760s and leads to the great friendship between him and Rev. Dr John's son, John (later Sir John, and Governor-General of Bengal)), see Kidd, *Subverting Scotland's Past*, p. 227.

26 Kidd, *Subverting Scotland's Past*, p. 236.
27 Macpherson, *An Introduction*, p. 92.
28 Ibid.
29 Horace, 'Ars Poetica', in Rudd, *Horace*, line 333, p. 69.
30 Phillips, *Society and Sentiment*, pp. 41, 21–4.
31 Macpherson, *An Introduction*, p. 37.
32 Ibid., p. 38.
33 Ibid., p. 151.
34 Ibid., p. 3.
35 For the importance of genealogy as a way of understanding the past in late medieval and early modern Gaelic Scotland, see Ulrike Hogg and Martin MacGregor, 'Historiography in Highlands and Lowlands', in Nicola Royan (ed.), *The International Companion to Scottish Literature 1400–1650* (Glasgow: Scottish Literature International, 2018), p. 115. For more on how the 'genealogical network' functioned as a way of structuring the world in the *Gàidhealtachd*, see Domhnall Uilleam Stiùbhart, 'A Global Gàidhealtachd?', p. 7. My thanks to John Macdonald for this reference.
36 Macpherson, *An Introduction*, pp. 3–4.
37 Ibid., pp. 4–5.
38 Ibid., p. 5.
39 Phillips, *Society and Sentiment*, pp. 48–52; Schmidt, *David Hume*, pp. 400–8.
40 Macpherson, *An Introduction*, pp. 1, 43.
41 Ibid., p. 2.
42 Ibid., pp. 2, 37.
43 Ibid., p. 2.
44 Ibid., p. 41.
45 Ibid., p. 6.
46 Letter from David Hume to Gilbert Eliot of Minto, 12 March 1763, in Raymond Klibansky and Ernest Campbell Mossner (eds), *New Letters of David Hume* (Oxford: Clarendon Press, 1954), pp. 69–70, quoted in Schmidt, *David Hume*, pp. 394–5.
47 Pocock, *Barbarism and Religion. Vol. II. Narratives of Civil Government*, p. 278.
48 Phillips, *Society and Sentiment*, p. 43.
49 Pocock, *Barbarism and Religion. Vol. II. Narratives of Civil Government*, p. 186.
50 Macpherson, *An Introduction*, p. 12.
51 Schmidt, *David Hume*, p. 379.
52 Macpherson, *An Introduction*, p. 18.
53 Ibid., p. 22.
54 Ibid.
55 Zachs, *Without Regard to Good Manners*, pp. 11–12.

56 Macpherson, *An Introduction*, pp. 24–5.
57 Ibid., p. 28.
58 Ibid., pp. 52–3.
59 Ibid.
60 Ibid., p. 60.
61 Ibid., p. 61.
62 Ibid., p. 72.
63 Ibid., p. 61.
64 Ibid., p. 79.
65 Ibid.
66 Ibid., p. 80.
67 Hume also explicitly engages with other historians, but largely in his private letters. See Schmidt, *David Hume*, p. 395. Other contemporaries of Macpherson, such as Gilbert Stuart, were more forthcoming in their published criticism of fellow historians. See the discussion of Stuart's challenge to Hume in Zachs, *Without Regard to Good Manners*, pp. 19–20.
68 Macpherson, *An Introduction*, p. 44.
69 Ibid., p. 70.
70 Clare O'Halloran, 'Irish Re-Creations of the Gaelic Past: The Challenge of Macpherson's Ossian', *Past and Present*, 124 (1989), p. 74.
71 Macpherson, *An Introduction*, p. 74.
72 Ibid., p. 75.
73 Ibid., pp. 75–6.
74 Ibid., p. 76.
75 Ibid., p. 139.
76 Ibid., pp. 143–4.
77 Ibid., pp. 44–5.
78 Ibid., p. 45.
79 Ibid.
80 Ibid., p. 49.
81 Ibid.
82 Here, Macpherson's emphasis on source material and historiographical engagement counters Silvia Sebastiani's recent characterisation of his work in *An Introduction* as that of an 'antiquarian historian'. See Sebastiani, *The Scottish Enlightenment*, p. 156.
83 Macpherson, *An Introduction*, pp. 19–20.
84 Stewart, 'The Mother Tongue', p. 100.
85 Macpherson, *An Introduction*, p. 20.
86 Ibid., pp. 26–7.
87 This view was most recently upheld by Thomas Curley, who argues that Macpherson was only 'somewhat familiar with Gaelic'. See *Samuel Johnson, the Ossian Fraud, and the Celtic Revival*, p. 27.
88 Macpherson, *An Introduction*, p. 45.

89 Ibid., pp. 45–6.
90 See, for example, John Macpherson's emphasis on using ancient historians as source material and the importance of the written record in determining a nation's history, in John Macpherson, *Critical Dissertations*, pp. 1–8.
91 For Ferguson's influence on Macpherson, see Moore, 'Adam Ferguson, *The Poems of Ossian* and the imaginative life of the Scottish Enlightenment', pp. 277–88.
92 Macpherson, *An Introduction*, p. 59.
93 Ibid., p. 58.
94 Ibid., pp. 72–3.
95 Guha, *History at the Limit of World-History*, p. 9.
96 Moore, 'James Macpherson and "Celtic Whiggism"', p. 19.
97 Ibid., p. 16; Macpherson, *An Introduction*, pp. 232–3.
98 Macpherson, *An Introduction*, p. 233.
99 Zachs, *Without Regard to Good Manners*, p. 18.
100 Moore, 'James Macpherson and "Celtic Whiggism"', p. 14; see also Mackillop, *Human Capital and Empire*, pp. 119–56.
101 Kidd, *Subverting Scotland's Past*, p. 234.
102 Moore, 'James Macpherson and "Celtic Whiggism"', p. 17; Macpherson, *An Introduction*, p. 290.
103 Matthew McCormack, 'Citizenship, Nationhood, and Masculinity in the Affair of the Hanoverian Soldier, 1756', *Historical Journal*, 49:4 (2006), pp. 981–2.
104 deGategno, *James Macpherson*, p. 137.
105 William Strahan to Hume, 25 January 1773, *The Letters of David Hume*, Vol. II, p. 269.
106 Hume to Strahan, 30 January 1773, *The Letters of David Hume*, Vol. II, p. 269. Of Dalrymple he says that he 'has Spirit, but no Style, and still less Judgement than the other'.
107 'Advertisements and Notices', *St. James's Chronicle*, 14 March 1775, p. 1. Saunders assumes that Macpherson published the *Original Papers* 'to forestall criticism' of *The History of Great Britain* (*Life and Letters of James Macpherson*, p. 228).
108 For the publication history of Hume's *History of England*, see Pocock, *Barbarism and Religion. Vol. II. Narratives of Civil Government*, pp. 199–200.
109 deGategno, *James Macpherson*, p. 137.
110 Pocock, *Barbarism and Religion. Vol. II. Narratives of Civil Government*, p. 255. As we shall see below and in Chapter 4, Macpherson did not hold to Hume's scruples and was an enthusiastic contributor to debate in the 1770s about the nature of the British constitution.
111 deGategno, *James Macpherson*, pp. 138–9.

112 Quoted in G. Birkbeck Hill (ed.), *Letters of David Hume to William Strahan* (Oxford: Clarendon Press, 1888), p. 309; deGategno, *James Macpherson*, p. 138.
113 *London Chronicle*, 21 January 1775, p. 71.
114 Moore, 'Introduction', in Moore, *The International Companion to James Macpherson*, p. 5.
115 Jones, 'Principles, Prejudices, and the Politics of James Macpherson's Historical Writing', pp. 119–20.
116 Ibid., p. 120; deGategno, *James Macpherson*, p. 138.
117 Saunders, *Life and Letters of James Macpherson*, p. 227. The Nairne papers form part of Carte's archives in the Bodleian Library at the University of Oxford (GB 1061 MSS Carte 1–290) and were deposited in the 1750s. For a sceptical view of the value of the papers, based on a Jacobite reading of Macpherson's character and politics, see Parnell, 'James Macpherson and the Nairne Papers'.
118 James Macpherson, 'Advertisement' to the *Original Papers; Containing the Secret History of Great Britain, from the Restoration, to the Accession of the House of Hannover. To which are Prefixed, Extracts from the Life of James II, As Written by Himself,* 2 vols (London: W. Strahan and T. Cadell, 1775), Vol. I, n.p.; O'Brien, *Narratives of Enlightenment*, p. 68.
119 Macpherson, 'Advertisement' to the *Original Papers*. Exhibiting originals is something also claimed to have been done for the Ossianic Collections. See Howard Gaskill, 'What Did James Macpherson Really Leave on Display at his Publisher's Shop in 1762?', *Scottish Gaelic Studies*, 16 (1990), pp. 67–89.
120 Horn, 'Some Scottish Writers of History in the Eighteenth Century', p. 15. Unlike other historians, Macpherson 'wrote a narrative of events based on much more complete sources than had hitherto been available' (ibid., p. 11). Horn also grants this to Dalrymple's work. Indeed, Horn assures us, 'their works are still frequently used and referred to by present-day historians, largely because their works was so well done that no one has found it necessary to republish most of the documents they contributed to the store of knowledge' (ibid., p. 15.).
121 Alastair J. Mann, 'James VII as Unionist and Nationalist: A Monarch's View of the Scottish Parliament as Revealed Through his Writings', *Parliaments, Estates and Representation*, 33:2 (2013), p. 105.
122 See, for example, Georg G. Iggers, 'The Image of Ranke in American and German Historical Thought', *History and Theory*, 2:1 (1962), pp. 17–40. For a critical analysis of the notion that Ranke is the progenitor of the modern academic discipline of history, see Anthony Grafton, *The Footnote: A Curious History* (Cambridge, MA: Harvard University Press, 1999), pp. 34–61.

123 Leopold von Ranke, *A History of England, Principally in the Seventeenth Century. Vol. VI* (Oxford: Oxford University Press, 1875), p. 35. Ironically, Ranke himself doesn't use footnotes to reference Macpherson's work, and is rather sparse in his footnoting throughout the book.
124 Ranke's famous instruction to historians – 'nur sagen, wie es eigentlich gewesen / only to say how it essentially was', was, of course, taken from Thucydides. See Grafton, *The Footnote*, p. 69. For the resurgence of European interest in Macpherson and Ossian during the late nineteenth century, see Kristin Lindfield-Ott, 'Jules Verne's Ossianic Adventures: *Le Rayon Vert*, Scotland and Macpherson's Ossianic Legacy', in Camille Manfredi and Michel Byrne (eds), *Bretagne-Ecosse: Contacts, Transferts et Dissonances/Brittany-Scotland: Contacts, Transfers and Dissonances* (Brest: Université de Bretagne Occidentale, 2017), pp. 251–72.
125 Nicholas Phillipson, *David Hume: The Philosopher as Historian* (London: Penguin,1989), p. 133; Pocock, *Barbarism and Religion. Vol. II. Narratives of Civil Government*, p. 201.
126 James Macpherson, 'Introduction' to the *Original Papers*, p. 3.
127 Macpherson, *Original Papers*, p. 3; Schmidt, *David Hume*, pp. 277–80; 406–7.
128 Macpherson, *Original Papers*, p. 3.
129 Saunders, *Life and Letters of James Macpherson*, pp. 228–31. For a recent example, see Paul Baines, Julian Ferraro and Pat Rogers (eds), *The Wiley-Blackwell Encyclopedia of Eighteenth-Century Writers and Writing 1660–1789* (Chichester: Wiley-Blackwell, 2011).
130 Kidd, *Subverting Scotland's Past*, p. 223. For similar assessments of Hume's politics, see Phillips, *Society and Sentiment*, p. 37; O'Brien, *Narratives of Enlightenment*, p. 59; and Pocock, *Barbarism and Religion. Vol. II. Narratives of Civil Government*, p. 245, where Pocock argues that 'Hume could whig it with the best'. The same description could apply, perhaps even more so, to Macpherson.
131 Macpherson, *Original Papers*, pp. 5–6. Later in the Introduction Macpherson emphasises his knowledge: 'the Editor, expecting little that was new, especially to HIM, on the period he has chosen' (pp. 8–9), and assures us that his 'reading, on the period of his history, has been pretty extensive' (p. 10).
132 Macpherson, *Original Papers*, p. 6.
133 Ibid., p. 7. He names a number of British people whose papers he accessed: Thomas Astle, archivist and book collector, Matthew Duane, lawyer and art patron, and John Price, Keeper of the Bodleian.
134 Ibid., p. 8.
135 Ibid., p. 12.
136 Phillips, *Society and Sentiment*, pp. 40–7; O'Brien, *Narratives of Enlightenment*, pp. 59–60.
137 Macpherson, *Original Papers*, p. 12.

138 James Macpherson, 'Preface' to *The History of Great Britain*, Vol. I, p. iii.
139 He has availed himself of 'the records and journals of the houses of parliament', of 'the best military writers', of 'the authors who wrote in the times', following 'unerring guides, original papers', and having 'consulted, with the utmost attention, the best writers of foreign nations', all to 'give a comprehensive view of the state of other countries, in order to throw a more complete light on our own' (Macpherson, 'Preface' to *The History of Great Britain*, pp. iii–iv).
140 Jones, 'Principles, Prejudices, and the Politics of James Macpherson's Historical Writing', p. 121.
141 Ibid., pp. 128–9. Phillips writes in a similar fashion about Adam Smith's 'sentimental history', in Phillips, *Society and Sentiment*, pp. 82–7.
142 Phillips, *Society and Sentiment*, p. 40.
143 Pocock, *Barbarism and Religion. Vol. II. Narratives of Civil Government*, p. 364.
144 Macpherson, *The History of Great Britain*, Vol. I, p. vii.
145 See, for example, Schmidt, *David Hume*, p. 379.
146 Macpherson, *The History of Great Britain*, Vol. I, p. vii.
147 Ibid., p. iii.
148 Ibid.
149 For an overview of the relationship between the Scottish Enlightenment and the scientific method, see Richard B. Sher, 'Science and Medicine in the Scottish Enlightenment: The Lessons in Book History', in Paul Wood (ed.), *The Scottish Enlightenment: Essays in Reinterpretation* (Rochester, NY: University of Rochester Press, 2001), pp. 99–156; Paul Wood, 'Science in the Scottish Enlightenment', in Alexander Brodie (ed.), *The Cambridge Companion to the Scottish Enlightenment* (Cambridge: Cambridge University Press, 2003), pp. 94–116.
150 Macpherson, *The History of Great Britain*, Vol. I, p. iii.
151 Ibid.
152 Ibid.
153 Ibid., p. vii.
154 Ibid., p. iii.
155 For the Enlightenment roots of Ranke's historiography, see Grafton, *The Footnote*.
156 Macpherson, *The History of Great Britain*, Vol. I, p. iv.
157 See, for example, Wolloch, '"Facts, or Conjectures": Antoine-Yves Goguet's Historiography', p. 433.
158 Macpherson, *The History of Great Britain*, Vol. I, p. iv.
159 Ibid.
160 Ibid.
161 Pocock, *Barbarism and Religion. Vol. II. Narratives of Civil Government*, p. 278.
162 Macpherson, *The History of Great Britain*, Vol. I, p. iv.

163 We are grateful to our wonderful students at the University of the Highlands and Islands for their discussion of this point in our module 'Historians and History'.
164 Schmidt, *David Hume*, p. 385.
165 Macpherson, *The History of Great Britain*, Vol. I, pp. v–vi.
166 Schmidt, *David Hume*, p. 385. See also Faria, 'David Hume, the Académie des Inscriptions and the Nature of Historical Evidence in the Early Eighteenth Century'.
167 See, for example, Phillipson, *David Hume*, p. 100; Schmidt, *David Hume*, pp. 394–5.
168 Phillips, *Society and Sentiment*, p. 11.
169 Robertson, *The History of Scotland*, p. iii.
170 Ibid., pp. iii–iv.
171 Ibid., p. iv.
172 Ibid., p. v.
173 Ibid., p. viii.
174 Robertson, *The History of America. Vol. I*, pp. vi–vii.
175 Ibid. p. xv; Pocock, *Barbarism and Religion. Vol. IV. Barbarians, Savages and Empires*, p. 184.
176 Robertson, *The History of America. Vol. I*, pp. xv–xvi; Phillips, *Society and Sentiment*, p. 43.
177 William Robertson, *An Historical Disquisition Concerning the Knowledge Which the Ancients Had of India; and the Progress of Trade with that Country Prior to the Discovery of the Passage to it by the Cape of Good Hope*, 2nd edition (London: A. Strahan and T. Cadell, 1794), p. vi.
178 Ibid.
179 Ibid., p. iii.
180 Gibbon, *The History of the Decline and Fall of the Roman Empire. Vol. IV*, p. ii.
181 Ibid., p. iii.
182 Saunders, *Life and Letters of James Macpherson*, pp. 228–32.
183 Pocock, *Barbarism and Religion. Vol. II. Narratives of Civil Government*, p. 278.
184 Macpherson, *The History of Great Britain*, Vol. I, p. 3.
185 Ibid., p. 246.
186 Schmidt, *David Hume*, p. 387.
187 Phillips, *Society and Sentiment*, p. 47.
188 Macpherson, *The History of Great Britain*, Vol. I, p. 8.
189 Ibid., p. 530.
190 Ibid., pp. 681–2.
191 Ibid., pp. 8, 9.
192 Ibid., p. 46.
193 Ibid., p. 51.
194 Ibid., p. 518.

195 Ibid., p. 88.
196 Phillips, *Society and Sentiment*, p. 51. Macpherson's conception of 'the public' and 'the people' does not indicate any kind of proto-democratic sentiment. Instead, Macpherson's notion of who 'the people' were is probably closer to his friend Adam Ferguson's analysis, where 'the public' was a broad group of gentleman military citizens, committed to 'stabilising and preserving an expanding commercial nation'. See Smith, *Adam Ferguson and the Idea of Civil Society*, pp. 142–3.
197 Macpherson, *The History of Great Britain*, Vol. I, p. 97.
198 Ibid., p. 361.
199 Ibid., p. 612.
200 Schmidt, *David Hume*, p. 385.
201 Macpherson, *The History of Great Britain*, Vol. I, p. 124.
202 Ibid., p. 261.
203 Ibid., p. 291.
204 Ibid., p. 306.
205 Phillips, *Society and Sentiment*, p. 41; Pocock, *Barbarism and Religion. Vol. II. Narratives of Civil Government*, pp. 180–2.
206 Macpherson, *The History of Great Britain*, Vol. I, p. 163.
207 Kidd, 'North Britishness and the Nature of Eighteenth-Century British Patriotisms', p. 367.
208 Macpherson, *The History of Great Britain*, Vol. I, p. 299.
209 Ibid., p. 171.
210 Satia, *Time's Monster*, p. 15.
211 Ibid., p. 50.
212 David Hume, *The History of England from the Invasion of Julius Caesar to the Revolution in 1688*, 6 vols (Indianapolis, IN: Liberty Fund, 1983), Vol. VI, p. 139.
213 Macpherson, *The History of Great Britain*, Vol. I, pp. 1–2.
214 Hume, *History of England*, Vol. VI, p. 139.
215 Macpherson, *The History of Great Britain*, Vol. I, p. 2.
216 Phillips, *Society and Sentiment*, p. 22.
217 Ibid., p. 65; Jones, 'Principles, Prejudices, and the Politics of James Macpherson's Historical Writing', p. 125.
218 Phillips, *Society and Sentiment*, p. 65.
219 O'Brien, *Narratives of Enlightenment*, p. 64.
220 Macpherson, *The History of Great Britain*, Vol. I, p. 3.
221 Ibid., pp. 587–8.
222 Satia, *Time's Monster*, p. 28.
223 Macpherson, *The History of Great Britain*, Vol. I, p. 2.
224 Ibid., p. 287.
225 Ibid.
226 Ibid., p. 315.
227 Ibid., p. 422.

228 Ibid., p. 423.
229 Ibid., p. 427.
230 Ibid., p. 496.
231 Ibid., p. 576.
232 Macpherson, *The History of Great Britain*, Vol. II, pp. 225, 226.
233 Ibid., p. 223.
234 Ibid.
235 Phillips, *Society and Sentiment*, p. 61.
236 Macpherson, *The History of Great Britain*, Vol. I, p. 69.
237 Macpherson, *The History of Great Britain*, Vol. II, p. 57.
238 Ibid., pp. 79, 81.
239 Ibid., p. 146.
240 For a succinct overview of the seventeenth-century Anglo-Dutch wars and their fundamentally imperial character, see Peter Linebaugh and Marcus Rediker, *The Many-Headed Hydra: Sailors, Slaves, Commoners, and the Hidden History of the Revolutionary Atlantic* (Boston: Beacon Press, 2000), pp. 145–9.
241 Hume, *History of England*, Vol. VI, p. 202.
242 Macpherson, *The History of Great Britain*, Vol. I, p. 84.
243 Hume, *History of England*, Vol. VI, p. 202.
244 Macpherson, *The History of Great Britain*, Vol. I, p. 84.
245 Schmidt, *David Hume*, p. 264; see also Bruce Buchan, 'Enlightened Histories: Civilization, War and the Scottish Enlightenment', *The European Legacy*, 10:2 (2005), pp. 177–92.
246 Satia, *Time's Monster*, p. 38.
247 Wolloch, '"Facts or Conjectures": Antoine-Yves Goguet's Historiography', p. 431.

4

Politics and Empire: James Macpherson's Political Writings and the Crisis of Empire in the Late 1770s

> The destruction of the East-India Company's tea, at Boston, is well known to have been the deliberate act of a very great majority of the inhabitants.[1]

The British Empire was in crisis during the second half of the 1770s. From the American colonists' uprising against British rule, to increasing controversy over the corrupting influence of the East India Company (EIC) on the imperial state, debate about empire was everywhere in British politics during this period. In the Thirteen Colonies, long-standing tension between the Americans and the British bubbled over into outright conflict in 1775. Rumbling disputes over the right of the British Parliament to tax the colonists led to the beginnings of armed rebellion against the state following the battles of Lexington and Concord in April 1775.[2] As the East India Company became ever more powerful following its significant territorial expansion of the 1750s and 1760s, generating 'a new tide of corruption', in Edmund Burke's resonant phrase, EIC affairs became increasingly the concern of the British government and Parliament.[3] Into this political tumult stepped James Macpherson.

As we have seen, Macpherson had been involved in political affairs ever since the publication of *The Highlander* (1758) at the height of the Scottish militia crisis and his subsequently attracting the patronage of the Earl of Bute in support of the publication of *Fingal* (1761/2) and *Temora* (1763).[4] Such Prime Ministerial backing was then instrumental in Macpherson acquiring the post of Secretary to the Governor of West Florida, George Johnstone, in 1763.[5] However, Macpherson's political ambitions and writing career intersected most clearly during the second half of the 1770s, when he combined the techniques of history writing, carefully honed earlier in the decade, with political polemic. Macpherson had begun his political writing career in 1766 soon after his short-lived sojourn in Florida as a colonial administrator. Writing first for Lord Shelburne, then Lord North, Macpherson was soon considered a key government political writer for the Earl of Chatham's administration. When Lord North became Prime Minister in 1770, Macpherson's responsibilities increased.[6] As North wrote to George III, Macpherson was 'a most laborious and able writer' and was kept busy by the growing crises of empire during the 1770s.[7]

This chapter argues that Macpherson used the techniques of an historian in defending the government's position against the American colonists and, in India, against what John Dickinson, an American Patriot, described as the 'rapine, oppression and cruelty' of the EIC.[8] Macpherson wrote as an historian in his two key pamphlets in response to the American revolution: *The Rights of Great Britain Asserted Against the Claims of America* (1775/6) and *A Short History of the Opposition During the Last Session* (1779). *The Rights of Great Britain* is a straightforward defence of the British imperial state's sovereignty in the Thirteen Colonies – what Macpherson termed the 'uncontroulable authority' of Parliament over the Americans.[9] His second pamphlet on the American war, *A Short History*, is a little different. While ostensibly an account of domestic political affairs during the parliamentary session of 1778–9, Macpherson's pamphlet focuses on attacking the Whig opposition's criticism of the government's conduct in America, where France and Spain had just entered the war in support of the colonists and the conflict was beginning to turn in the Americans' favour.[10] Macpherson's intent was to blame this ongoing crisis of empire not on Lord North's administration but, instead, on the parliamentary opposition's fomenting of anti-colonial resistance in America. Macpherson's credentials as an Enlightenment historian are even more to the fore in his book-length defence of his and Sir John Macpherson's interests in India, *The History and Management of the East-India Company* (1779). Macpherson's aim in this book was to justify the position of his patron, Muhammad Ali Khan Wallajah, the Nawab of Arcot, against the increasing political ambitions of the East India Company. At first, this might seem a little contradictory: in his writings on America, Macpherson writes firmly against the interests of a local colonial elite, whereas in the *History and Management of the EIC*, his book mounts a robust defence of the Nawab of Arcot, a leading member of India's political ruling class. While Macpherson's account of Indian history is certainly sympathetic to local culture and politics (like William Robertson in his work on India), his main aim was to ensure that the interests of the British government (along with his own private concerns) were defended against the colonial ambitions of the EIC.[11]

Macpherson's defence of British imperial policy during the second half of the eighteenth century is made using the techniques of Enlightenment history writing that he had so successfully honed in *An Introduction to the History of Great Britain and Ireland* (1771) and *The History of Great Britain* (1775). This chapter is structured around Macpherson's three texts on the politics of empire – *The Rights of Great Britain* (1775/6), *A Short History of the Opposition During the Last Session* (1779), and *The History and Management of the East-India Company* (1779). In sections on each of these texts, we examine how Macpherson writes as an historian, establishing his use of the methodological tools of Enlightenment history writing. As in our earlier chapters, we look, in turn, at how Macpherson deals with concepts of truth and impartiality, what sources he uses, how he deploys footnotes, and how he juggles the great Enlightenment balancing act between narrating the past and explaining it. Furthermore, a key focus of our analysis of each of these texts is on how Macpherson uses a narrative of the past to make a political argument in the present. Macpherson places a different emphasis on these component parts of history writing in each of these texts. The first book examined in this chapter, *The History and Management of the EIC*, is more obviously a work of history, where Macpherson creates a historical narrative spanning almost 200 years and constructs this using an impressive range of primary sources, copiously footnoted, in almost 300 pages of text. Macpherson's aim, however, was firmly of the political moment in which he was writing: to make an argument against the EIC's efforts to challenge the local authority of his patron, the Nawab of Arcot, and, by extension, the colonial authority of the British imperial state. The chapter then considers Macpherson's two pamphlets on the American Revolution: *The Rights of Great Britain* (1775/6) and *A Short History* (1779). Here, the priorities of Macpherson's argument and methodology are reversed: his aim in both these texts is to defend the British government's decision to wage war against the Americans and to justify the subsequent conduct of the war. But Macpherson's methodology in making this argument is firmly that of an historian, drawing on primary sources, supporting his text with the scholarly scaffolding of footnotes and creating a balance between narrative and explanation that is rooted in concepts of truth and impartiality. The key difference between Macpherson's book on India and his political pamphlets about America is the emphasis he places on a narrative of the British constitutional past. In *The Rights of Great Britain* and *A Short History*, Macpherson argues that the sovereignty of the British state was imperial in scope and, crucially, that this was a consequence of Britain's constitutional evolution during the seventeenth and eighteenth centuries, following the 'Glorious Revolution' of 1688. Such a Whig approach to history writing in these pamphlets about the American Revolution was, however, rather different to the 'Celtic Whiggism' identified by Colin Kidd and Dafydd Moore in the Ossianic Collections and *An Introduction to the History of Great Britain and Ireland*, examined in the previous two chapters.[12] Rather than inserting the Celtic past into a narrative of English ancient constitutionalism (and, thereby, subverting 'English Whig shibboleths'), Macpherson created a Whig narrative of the constitutional nature of British imperial rule in which the Gael was noticeably absent.[13] Instead, the Gael – Macpherson himself – was responsible for writing a defence of British imperial rule during this great moment of existential crisis in the late 1770s. As Priya Satia has argued, the emergence of the discipline of history during the eighteenth century was crucial to the work of empire building and Macpherson's defence of the British imperial state in America and India was accomplished by creating a narrative of the past.[14] This chapter begins with arguably Macpherson's clearest articulation of both his defence of the British imperial state and the principles of Enlightenment history writing – *The History and Management of the East-India Company*.

THE HISTORY AND MANAGEMENT OF THE EAST-INDIA COMPANY (1779)

Macpherson's most sustained engagement with the Empire comes in the form of *The History and Management of the East-India Company, from its Origin in 1600 to the Present Times* (1779). This work has not received much critical attention, and those who have written about it have largely done so in the context of the Ossian controversy. Older scholarship views *The History and Management* through debates about authenticity, such as George McElroy's dismissive focus on the text's 'imagination and prevarication'.[15] More recent research on the development of the British Empire and the East India Company has recognised Macpherson's book as part of a response to imperial crisis through history writing. As Joanna de Groot argues, the work of scholars such as Alexander Dow, Robert Orme and James Macpherson were part of a broader trend from the 1760s onwards, in which 'contemporary controversy over the East India Company was framed in "historical" accounts of the subcontinent'.[16] Indeed, Macpherson's *History and Management* is most frequently discussed by historians of the EIC during the 1770s and 1780s, where it is recognised as part of the broader critique of the

Company that led to Warren Hastings's demise as Governor-General in 1785.[17] Here, Macpherson's status as an historian is acknowledged in a way that is often overlooked in the broader Ossian scholarship. Jack P. Greene outlines Macpherson's contribution to the 'growing crescendo of criticism' of the EIC in the late 1770s and describes him, correctly, as 'a Government pamphleteer and historian'.[18] Likewise, other work on the EIC recognises the connections between Macpherson and Enlightenment history writing. Identifying *The History and Management* as a key text in establishing the Nawab of Arcot's claims to sovereignty in the Carnatic, Nicholas B. Dirks argues that Macpherson's work 'was deliberately modelled on Edward Gibbon's *Decline and Fall*, beginning with deliberate references to the decline of Rome'.[19] Dirks situates Macpherson as a contemporary of Gibbon whose approach to history writing was similar. However, Dirks's analysis focuses on examining how Macpherson's book pours scorn on the EIC and contributes to the debate about its corrupt practices, rather than establishing how Gibbon and Macpherson shared the methodologies and techniques of Enlightenment history writing.[20] Most recently, Leith Davis has written about *The History and Management* as evidence for Macpherson's status as an imperial Gael. Davis's focus, however, is on how Macpherson represents India, rather than how he writes as an historian in defence of the British imperial state and the Nawab of Arcot.[21]

Like Macpherson's other works, however, *The History and Management* is, first and foremost, a history, and as such displays similar markers of his nuanced understanding of history writing as his books on British history. In reading *The History and Management* in this way – with a focus on the *how*, not the *why* or *what* – we can see, yet again, an approach to history writing that is decidedly modern. Here as elsewhere, Macpherson's history is one that is compiled from a myriad of sources, which is made explicit both in the text and through his extensive footnoting. Spanning some 180 years, *The History and Management* connects past to present through 'authentic records', as the title page advertises. Macpherson explores this particular political crisis of empire through history writing. The book makes the case for the Nawab of Arcot (and, by extension, the British government) against the perceived corruption of the EIC using techniques of history writing that Macpherson had developed in his earlier histories, examined in the previous chapter. In this section we explore the specific elements of history writing in *The History and Management* that make Macpherson an Enlightenment historian, from his sources and use of footnotes, through to his efforts at balancing a narrative of the past against an explanation of events – the classic dynamic of more 'philosophical' modes of history writing that were emerging in the second half of the eighteenth century.

The History and Management of the East-India Company emerged out of Macpherson's growing interest and involvement in Indian affairs and his political journalism in support of these. James was brought into the world of Indian politics by his friend and kinsman, John Macpherson, who was later knighted and, briefly, became Governor-General of Bengal following Hastings's demise in 1785. James had met John during the early 1760s, when he had embarked on a tour of the Highlands and Islands to collect Ossianic material that would form the basis of *Fingal* and *Temora*. In Skye, James had visited the great Gaelic scholar, the Rev. Dr John Macpherson and had been introduced to his son, also John.[22] Through this connection, a lifelong friendship developed and formed the foundation of their respective later political and financial success.[23] James and John began working together on Indian affairs in the early 1770s, following John's first encounter with the Nawab of Arcot in 1767 and his appointment as an EIC writer in 1771. James ensured that John was hired as paymaster to the EIC's army in 1773 and encouraged his continuing (and secretive) relationship with the Nawab.[24] Following his dismissal from EIC service in 1776 for continuing to work covertly for the Nawab, John returned to England in 1777 and he and James began 'a press campaign in the ministry paper, *The Public Advertiser*, to support the nawab and Hastings'.[25] This journalism and James's pamphlet *A Letter from Mohammed Ali Chan, Nabob of Arcot to the Court of Directors* (1777) formed the basis for the writing and publication of *The History and Management of the East-India Company* in 1779. While Paul deGategno argues that Macpherson's book 'served no other purpose than objecting to the Company's mistreatment of the Indian prince' and Leith Davis emphasises how the text can be read as 'an important connection between "eighteenth-century colonial space" and the "internal complexity" of the British nation', this section argues that *The History and Management* is a key example of how Macpherson wrote as an historian and how his work can be better understood if we place him in the context of Enlightenment history writing.[26] Macpherson's work on India was no outlier, but reflects his lifelong concern with both empire and Enlightenment.

Macpherson's history of the East India Company is divided into eight chapters, covering the period from 1600 to his present day in 1779. The first three chapters are framed by Macpherson as explicit histories: Chapter 1 is entitled 'A Short History of the Company, from its Origin in 1600 to the year 1744'; Chapter 2 discusses the 'Origin of the three Presidencies – The Conquests of the Mahomedans in the Decan deduced from the earliest Times'; and the third chapter is 'A Summary of the History of the Carnatic and its Dependencies, from 1686 to 1756'. The next four chapters cover the crux of Macpherson's argument against the East India Company: that in the dispute between Macpherson's patron, the Nawab of Arcot, and his rival in the Carnatic, the Rajah of Tanjore, the Company acted unjustly and illegally. These chapters cover, respectively, events on the coast of the Carnatic, from 1756 to the treaty between the Nawab and the Rajah in 1762; events in the region up until the treaty with Hyder Ali, an ally of the Rajah, in 1769; the Nawab's campaign against Tanjore in 1771; and the Nawab's occupation of Tanjore in 1773, with the full support of the Company. It is this narrative, chronological chapter structure which Macpherson uses to lead the reader to his ultimate argument: that 'The Nabob of Arcot possesses the acknowledged and lawful sovereignty of the whole Carnatic' and that any claims by the EIC to political power in the region were therefore without substance.[27] As before, we begin our analysis of *The History and Management* by first examining Macpherson's 'Preface' to the book, where he outlines his methodology as an historian. It is here that Macpherson establishes his approach to history writing, rooted in more philosophically inclined Enlightenment notions of truth, impartiality and explanation. What really stands out in the preface is Macpherson's adherence to sources and footnotes, and by beginning with this methodological exegesis we can then analyse the extent to which Macpherson then reflects historiographically in his narrative of the Indian past.

Right from the first line of the preface to *The History and Management*, Macpherson outlines his use of sources, the process through which he deploys these sources as evidence, and how both demonstrate his credibility as an historian. In response to the 'obscurity' of the 'Court of the East-India Directors', Macpherson marshals his case against them through the process of history writing. By 'deduc[ing] his accounts from an early period of time', Macpherson establishes the past and its interpretation at the heart of his efforts to explain 'the Rights of the NABOB' and to prove 'the INJUSTICE of the COMPANY'.[28] The preface introduces the reader to Macpherson's methodology as an historian: it identifies the types of sources he uses; how he uses these sources as evidence in making his argument against the EIC; and how this credible and verifiable use of the past demonstrates the validity of his case. In both his methodology and approach, then, Macpherson writes about the past in a similar way to that established in his earlier two-volume *History of Great Britain*, published just four years earlier. Macpherson's approach in *The History and Management*, though, lays different emphasis on the elements of historiographical theory which he outlined in *The History of Great Britain*. As we saw in Chapter 3, the preface to Macpherson's *History of Great Britain* argued that an historian is objective and impartial; that these notions of truth and impartiality were demonstrated by the evidence of primary sources; and that history writing served a broader purpose by filling in gaps in knowledge. In the preface to *The History and Management*, Macpherson reiterates all of these justifications for history writing, but with important differences in emphasis. Here, Macpherson pays greater attention to the nature and quality of the source material and less on the truth and impartiality of the historian. Following the example of Hume, Macpherson argues that the past is instructional and, therefore, that history writing can be used as the basis for moral judgement in the present, as we explored in the previous chapter. This is a crucial function of history writing in Macpherson's *History and Management*: writing about the history of India and the Company from 1600 to the present day in the late 1770s enables Macpherson to defend his own interests in the 'affairs of the Carnatic', most notably through his and Sir John Macpherson's representation of the Nawab of Arcot. Having established his credentials as a thoroughly scientific man of the Enlightenment in *The History of Great Britain*, Macpherson puts this historiographical methodology to work in the present: it is precisely because history writing is impartial and truthful, according to Macpherson, that his case against the EIC is so strong. For Macpherson, it is the truth of historical evidence and the interpretation of that evidence through history writing which makes the past so crucial to the defence of his Indian interests in the 1770s.

Macpherson pays less attention to notions of truth and impartiality in the preface to *The History and Management* than he does in *The History of Great Britain*, largely because his key contention here is that the evidence of the source material from the past demonstrates his argument about India in the present. Macpherson's credentials as an historian had already been firmly established by *The History of Great Britain*, so in *The History and Management* Macpherson was able to focus on proving his case about contemporary India. Instead, Macpherson's focus is firmly on the process of historical research and writing, upon which the truth of his argument rests:

> His arguments and reasonings are only such, as naturally result from his facts; and his facts are founded upon the most incontrovertible evidence, to which the Reader is referred, at the bottom of every page.[29]

For Macpherson, an historian's arguments were derived from facts, which came from the evidence of the past. Crucially, though, it was the footnotes which then demonstrated the nature of this 'incontrovertible evidence'. Here, then, Macpherson is using footnotes as a means of demonstrating how we have knowledge about the past. Footnotes are not simply a means of citing 'authorities' who can then be used to support an argument; they are used by Macpherson, instead, as the basis of the knowledge from which his argument about the EIC proceeds. This epistemological use of footnotes once again marks Macpherson as a thoroughly modern historian, whose approach and methodology place him firmly in the company of other Enlightenment historians, and especially his contemporaries of the 1770s, Gibbon and Robertson.

Macpherson's sources, then, are the raw materials from which his interpretation stems. In the preface to *The History and Management*, Macpherson goes to great lengths to demonstrate that these sources are 'authentic'. Just as he did in *The History of Great Britain*, Macpherson highlights the authenticity of his material, yet here the provenance of these sources and the way in which they are used underpins this claim. Here, it is the EIC Directors, not Macpherson himself, who provide the 'volumes of Original Papers, published under their inspection' upon which Macpherson bases his interpretation. Macpherson notes that the EIC produced these 'authentic materials' in order to mount a 'voluminous Defence' to the charges of corruption and mismanagement laid against them, 'sufficient to overset entirely the system, which they wished to defend'.[30] Thus, the authenticity of Macpherson's material is demonstrated by the fact that these sources came from the EIC themselves.

Hoisted by their own petard, Macpherson proceeds to reiterate that his interpretation is derived entirely from the public record. In addition to the Directors' 'Original Papers', Macpherson makes use of sources of 'EQUAL AUTHORITY', which he appeared to have acquired through the eighteenth-century equivalent of a Whitehall leak: these papers came from 'a Gentleman employed by the Crown, for some years, in a public capacity on the Coast, was pleased to place in his hands'. Macpherson explicitly eschews the kinds of private archival material that were the backbone of *The History of Great Britain*. Despite 'private papers and documents, together with written evidences of a PRIVATE nature' coming into 'his possession', Macpherson omits these sources from his interpretation. Instead, Macpherson's sources are publicly available documents, and it is this very availability which further lends impartiality and authenticity to his interpretation, using public documents 'to expose PUBLIC injustice'.[31]

Here, Macpherson's choice of source material then shapes how he interprets the EIC. Not only does Macpherson explicitly select only material available in the public domain, but he also uses this source material to examine just the *public* conduct of the EIC. In this approach, Macpherson stands in contrast to the work of Gibbon, who had published the first volume of his *The History of the Decline and Fall of the Roman Empire* in 1776, just three years before Macpherson's *History and Management*.[32] Gibbon's account of the fall of Rome was not only a work of serious historical scholarship – it was also cut through with withering judgements on the character of individuals and garnished thoroughly with salacious details of their private lives, especially in Gibbon's voluminous footnotes.[33] While Macpherson was just as thorough and scholarly in his use of footnotes, as we shall see below, neither the text nor notes in *The History and Management* focus on such details. Instead, for Macpherson, the corruption of the EIC was a matter of public conduct, not the private behaviour of individuals. Therefore, in making his case that the EIC was corrupt, his evidence had to be both about public conduct and from sources that were publicly available – Macpherson's point was not to drag up dirt and spread gossip, but instead to prove his case against the EIC using the evidence of the public record.

Macpherson's decision, then, to focus on public sources about public activities reveals a methodological choice which had significant interpretative implications. In deciding to expose 'public injustice' instead of 'trac[ing] the delinquency of individuals', Macpherson revealed a broader, philosophical approach to history writing. Macpherson's concern in *The History and Management* was to uncover the wider, more structural issues which underpinned the conduct of British interests in the eastern stretches of the Empire. This explains why Macpherson focused on the EIC's Directors as the creators of public policy in India rather than examining the conduct of the Company's writers as administrators of that policy. In setting out his historical practice and methodology in this volume, Macpherson argued that 'The writers, who have espoused the cause of the Directors, are seldom alluded to.' Of course, Macpherson's research strategy may well have been more than simply an adherence to the principles of Enlightenment historiography. His great collaborator in Indian affairs, Sir John Macpherson, had been appointed a writer in the East India Company in 1771, and it is from this bridgehead that both John's and James's interest in (and profit from) India had arisen.[34] James duly acknowledges the work of John and his fellow EIC writers, stating that his neglect of sources derived from them 'processed neither from any disrespect for their genius, nor any want of attention to their labours'. Yet Macpherson's selection of source material was not simply a strategy to get his friend, Sir John, off the hook. In deciding to prioritise the Directors and their policy in India and allowing the EIC's writers to 'escape from censure', Macpherson was emphasising his philosophical approach to history writing.[35] Here, Macpherson was adhering to the historiographical practices that had been established by Hume in writing his six-volume *History of England*, completed in the 1760s. As J. G. A. Pocock argues, Hume was the first historian to 'produce a historiography "philosophical" in the eighteenth-century sense'.[36] This 'philosophical' approach to history writing involved reconciling and interpreting the deeds of individuals (usually men) within the broader societal contexts in which they operated. In his *History of England*, Hume became 'the first of British historians to master the writing of history in the double key of political narrative and sociological generalisation', one that accounted for 'social and cultural' change and reconciled a narrative of the actions of great men with this kind of philosophical reflection.[37] Macpherson's emphasis on using the sources of the EIC's Directors and not their employees – the writers – was, then, a philosophical choice, demonstrating his fidelity to the precepts of Enlightenment historiography: as he writes in the preface to *The History and Management*: 'To pursue phantoms [the writers], through the foggy regions of romance, was no part of the labour, which the Author imposed on himself. Truth, and only truth was his object.'[38] Here, Macpherson's approach resembles that of Adam Smith, who emphasised such broader structural issues in his accounts of both history writing and his critiques of the British Empire.[39] And, in adopting this approach in making his argument against the EIC, Macpherson once more establishes his credentials as an Enlightenment historian, whose historiographical methodology is comparable with those of his more acclaimed contemporaries, such as Smith, Gibbon and others.

The preface to *The History and Management* further emphasises Macpherson's scholarly (and, therefore, plausible and 'authentic') approach to history writing in his account of how he processes these public sources. Macpherson is eager to highlight the craft and graft involved in compiling his case against the EIC: 'The labour and toil, which attended the selection of the materials, upon which this Volume is founded, employed a considerable portion of time.' In emphasising the sheer hard work involved in the process of research and history writing, Macpherson was once more establishing his scholarly credentials. In such a way, Macpherson was pre-empting some of the practices which became associated with the emergence of history writing as an 'accredited profession' that was institutionalised as a discipline within the structures of the university.[40] Macpherson's pleasure in the hard work of research echoed that of Leopold von Ranke – as we have seen, the nineteenth-century German historian who is often characterised as the founder of the modern academic discipline of history.[41] Once more, Macpherson's approach to history writing places him firmly within the intellectual tradition of his more illustrious Enlightenment peers, while also demonstrating how, in seeing history as a craft which required hard work, he looked forward to nineteenth-century historiographical innovations.

Macpherson's attention to issues of evidence, truth and sources in the preface to *The History and Management* is further demonstrated by his emphasis on footnotes.[42] As we have seen, the epistemological and practical functioning of footnotes lay at the heart of debates in Enlightenment historiography. Footnotes became the mechanism linking the two great precepts of history writing during the second half of the eighteenth-century: narrative and philosophy. While Gibbon has been rightly identified as one of the leading exponents of this technical and philosophical use of footnotes, this approach had already been explored and established by two other leading figures of Scottish history writing – Hume and Robertson – who, as Grafton argues, 'combined elegance and erudition, sharp philosophical narrative, and (more or less) erudite reflection on sources'.[43] Having outlined his belief that hard work lay at the heart of the historian's craft, Macpherson uses the preface to *The History and Management* to establish footnoting as a key part of his practice as an historian. Footnotes, for Macpherson, were key to demonstrating his case against the EIC because they contained details of what he termed 'the authorities'. As Macpherson's case was based upon the Directors of the EIC's own evidence, it was their work which Macpherson highlights as appearing 'at the bottoms of the pages'.[44] Macpherson's use of the term 'authorities' is revealing, indicating how he, just like Hume, Robertson and Gibbon, was writing history in such a way that reconciled 'erudite or antiquarian scholarship' with the more 'philosophical' desire of Enlightenment historiography to explain social structures and change over time.[45] Macpherson, though, places this long-standing use of footnotes as an appeal to 'authorities' in a thoroughly contemporary context. Macpherson describes the evidence contained within these footnotes using the highly charged phrase 'cloud of witnesses'.[46] Here, his choice of the word 'witnesses' reveals his pivotal place in a broader shift in eighteenth-century intellectual cultures of evidence, experience and testimony. As Matthew Wickman argues, Macpherson's Ossianic works demonstrate how the evidentiary power of witness testimony was gradually compromised by a more legalistic definition of 'truth' based on the balance of probabilities.[47]

Here, Macpherson reiterates his Enlightenment credentials by defending the credibility and reliability of the evidence of witnesses. Moreover, Macpherson's use of the phrase 'cloud of witnesses' is a deliberate echo of one of his key allies in the controversy over the Ossianic Collections during the 1760s and 1770s, Dr Thomas Pringle.[48] In describing the defence of the Ossianic Collections, Pringle used the exact same phrase, 'a cloud of witnesses'. By echoing the controversy surrounding his greatest (and most problematic) success, Macpherson was using the defence of his past poetical works to underpin his approach to history writing in the late 1770s. This underlines how much of Macpherson's later work was, at least partly, a post-ad hoc justification of his youthful Ossianic Collections – as an ardent proponent of Enlightenment principles of truth, fidelity, authenticity and impartiality in history writing such as *The History and Management*, Macpherson was making the argument that this had been his approach all along.

Macpherson's preface to *The History and Management* established his approach to history writing, based on an adherence to the principles of Enlightenment historiography. The remainder of this section seeks to examine how Macpherson writes in a self-consciously historiographical way in the main body of the text, looking at the types of sources Macpherson actually uses in making his case against the Directors of the EIC, how he uses these sources, and how he employs scholarly apparatus such as footnotes in outlining his history of the EIC. This section focuses on where Macpherson explicitly refers to his methodology in the text, analysing his discussion of sources and philosophical digressions, and how he uses sources and footnotes. It is not an attempt to evaluate how successful Macpherson is in these endeavours or to measure how 'reliable' he is as an historian – there are no 'gotcha!' moments here. Instead, what matters is that Macpherson frames his analysis of the EIC with these methodological and philosophical considerations, and this is what makes him an Enlightenment historian.

The structure of *The History and Management*, then, reveals Macpherson's preoccupation with history writing. It is not simply in the preface and the first three chapters that he writes in an historical mode, but throughout the book, with Macpherson justifying action in the present (and by extension, defending his and Sir John's interests and their partnership with the Nawab of Arcot) by making an argument based upon understanding of the past. Throughout the book's main chapters, Macpherson follows this approach that he had established in the preface. In Chapter 2 of *The History and Management*, Macpherson begins his analysis by deferring to the past as a necessary tool in explaining events in the here and now: 'To throw complete light on the subject of this disquisition, it may not be improper to return to events, which, as they are placed far back in antiquity, are perhaps overlooked, though they deserve to be known.' Indeed, as he established in the preface, Macpherson is ever eager to condemn the EIC by its own words, and justifies this use of the past precisely because it is how the EIC has justified its conduct: 'Writers [in this context, of the EIC], who, by defending the conduct of the Company, admit that it stands in need of defence, have recurred to the ancient history of India, for arguments of exculpation.'[49] Macpherson repeats this appeal to the past throughout *The History and Management*. In Chapter 2, Macpherson unpicks the early modern period in the Carnatic by situating his analysis even further back in time, arguing that 'To explain this subject, it is necessary to recur to a period of more remote antiquity.'[50] Having dealt with the medieval Carnatic, Macpherson then applies the same use of the past in his analysis of more recent times. Examining the 1760s in Chapter 5, Macpherson uses a familiar formulation, once again arguing that 'To explain this subject, we must recur to former times.'[51] Macpherson's virtual repetition of the same phrase indicates how central the past was to his interpretation of the present. As we have seen in other chapters, Macpherson consistently uses the past in this way, collapsing the 'historical distance', to borrow Mark Salber Phillips's phrase between historical times and the present day. Indeed, it is this willingness to view the contemporary world through a historical lens which, at least partly, differentiates Macpherson from other Enlightenment historians. Because the likes of Hume and Blair and Robertson were all writing history for a more overtly intellectual purpose, as men of letters or holders of university posts, the idea of historical distance becomes of greater importance. As Phillips argues, placing distance between the historian and their subject was a key part of establishing the author's impartiality and fidelity to notions of 'truth', especially in the work of David Hume.[52] Macpherson's approach, though, was different, especially here in *The History and Management* because he was using the past for a very specific purpose – to defend his interests in the Carnatic. Here, Macpherson's use of present-minded ideas of history becomes more like later nineteenth- and twentieth-century historians, including the likes of R. G. Collingwood who criticised Hume for the very lack of immediacy in his insistence on the virtue of distance between an historian and their topic.[53] Collingwood's emphasis on how the 'historical imagination' can 'recapture the immediacy of the past' would also have been a familiar notion to Macpherson.[54] However, at least in his methodology, this eagerness to see the historical in the present did not in any way dilute Macpherson's commitment to ideals of both classical and Enlightenment history writing.

Both Macpherson's chronological narrative and his emphasis on an historical present demonstrate his concern for and engagement with Enlightenment debates about history writing. Throughout *The History and Management*, Macpherson moves between narrative and philosophy, between telling us what happened and explaining why it did and how the specificities of the past fitted into a broader 'history of social and cultural change'.[55] From the very outset of the book, Macpherson places himself at the heart of these discussions. In concluding Chapter 1, his 'Short History of the Company, from its Origins in 1600 to the Year 1744', Macpherson establishes his historiographical aims: as the war between Britain and France spread 'its flame ... to Asia', 'New scenes were opened; and events arose, which became the foundation of that state of things, to explain which is the principal object of this work.'[56] So, for Macpherson, it is not sufficient simply to narrate the past – explanation is key to history writing. He begins this chapter by deploying one of the central concepts of Enlightenment historiography: stadial history. As we have seen, this was most closely associated with the work of Adam Ferguson, William Robertson and Adam Smith, and was a way of explaining structural change over time in society by subdividing the past into different 'stages' of development.[57] Macpherson's approach to this stadial view of history bore close resemblance to the ideas of Adam Ferguson, his friend and fellow Highlander. Published in 1767, Ferguson's *Essay on the History of Civil Society* outlined a theory of societal progress that was different to the likes of Robertson, in that he largely eschewed 'the issue of subsistence', instead focusing on how changes in relations of property determine the evolution of society.[58] As previous chapters have explored, Macpherson made use of such property-based stadial history writing in his introduction to *Temora* (1763), describing how relations in 'human society' moved from being determined by family, to property and, finally, by the 'laws and subordinations of government'.[59] Macpherson follows suit in *The History and Management*, describing in the first few pages of Chapter 1 how society evolves to the point at which, in early modern Europe at least, 'Government, relaxing its habitual severity, and laying aside its former pride, gave security to property, and some protection to industry.'[60] Macpherson's starting point for this particular stadial view of history begins in *The History and Management* with a self-conscious and deliberate historiographical point of departure. The very first sentence places the evolution of Europe and Asia in the context of 'the decline and after the fall of the Roman Empire'. Just three years before Macpherson wrote *The History and Management*, Gibbon had published the first volume of his *History of the Decline and Fall of the Roman Empire* (1776). Here, Macpherson deliberately echoes Gibbon, not only placing the content of his book in relation to Gibbon's wider analysis, but also to demonstrate that he, too, is an Enlightenment historian, engaging with key ideas about history writing, philosophy and the stadial evolution of society.[61] Macpherson also does this in order to explain that his subject – the history and management of the East India Company – can only be understood by placing British involvement in Asia in this broader context of the evolution of Western society, as outlined in Gibbon's historical narrative. As such, Macpherson's use of stadial history in introducing his analysis of the East India Company is a clear argument for using the past in order to understand the present. It was only through appreciating the broader evolution of human society that one could then make sense of the tyranny, oppression and corruption of which Macpherson accuses the EIC, under the protection of the English, then British, state.

Macpherson's use of a stadial model of the past to frame the beginning of *The History and Management* then sets the tone for his engagement with another key element in Enlightenment historiography: drawing broad observations about society from the specificities of the past. Throughout the book, Macpherson makes generalisations derived from historical knowledge, which he then applies to his analysis of the EIC. In establishing the early history of EIC control of the Carnatic and Bengal during the seventeenth century, Macpherson breaks off from his narrative of the past to reflect on this wider process of colonisation. Here, Macpherson's specific focus is on the role of plunder in conquest, where he invokes the classical authority of Aristotle's *Republic* to justify his belief that when war 'ends in conquest, it invests the victor with all the property of the vanquished'.[62] Macpherson then makes quite the philosophical leap, arguing that previous historians have not questioned the role of monarchs and the state in this process:

> The best writers on the laws of nature and of nations terminate, at this point, their enquiries into the rights, by which monarchs sit on thrones, or nations possess dominions. To push their examination further, might justly invalidate every claim of a prince and right of a people. Almost every period of antiquity, in every country, owes perhaps its being remembered at all to revolutions accomplished by resentment, ambition, or rapacity. Mankind therefore, being either guilty themselves of this species of injustice, or deriving benefits from it, have uniformly acquiesced in the absolute right, which every man, in a solemn war, acquires in the property which he takes from the enemy, and that without rule of measure.[63]

Here, Macpherson establishes that historians should write on the 'laws of nature and of nations', but that they should be critical of how these laws operate, especially when it comes to plunder, theft and conquest. While such a critique may seem strange coming from the pen of the author of the British government's response to the American's Declaration of the General Congress in 1776, here it serves a useful purpose, justifying an inquiry into the EIC's corruption in order that Macpherson can make his key argument about his and Sir John's interests in the dealings of the Nawab of Arcot. Macpherson's use of broad reflection is further linked to his defence of the Nawab in Chapter 7, where he explores the specific affairs of the Carnatic between 1769 and 1771 by making sweeping statements about 'the injustice and oppression committed by the servants of the Company in India'. Macpherson argues that 'These general observations are not intended, as a general censure; for in the conduct of the Court, we sometimes meet with some commendable deviations, from the lines we have above described and stigmatised.'[64] What matters here for Macpherson and his approach to history writing is that the connection between the general and the specific must always be proved, and that this is done by using primary sources as evidence – by writing, in short, as an historian.

Like other Enlightenment historians, Macpherson combined these kinds of broader reflections with an explicitly narrative approach to the past. For Macpherson, history was a succession of facts, which were then put together by the historian as a narrative. Yet, as Phillips argues in the context of Hume's history writing, this emphasis on narrative was, itself, philosophical.[65] In his discussion of the early modern Carnatic in Chapter 2, Macpherson pauses to reflect on the importance of arranging facts in a narrative structure: 'Where the great line of facts is ascertained by domestic history, we may safely rely on their fidelity relative to circumstances.' Here, Macpherson stresses the importance of linear narrative in history writing, but with a caveat. The 'circumstances' in which an historian finds these facts is key, but if 'we find them without a guide, we are in danger of being led into a region of clouds and darkness'.[66] The notion that history writing is a narration of 'facts' is further emphasised in the following chapter, where Macpherson explores early eighteenth-century developments in the Carnatic. Again, Macpherson argues that the causes of broader societal change can only be understood through historical narrative: 'To explain the causes of those revolutions, which formed the foundation of the power and influence of the British nation in Hindostan, we must recur to facts, further back in point of time, than some of those already related.'[67] Such a narrative relies, fundamentally, on the skill of the historian in selecting evidence and using it as the basis for an interpretation of the past. As Macpherson argues in his introduction to Chapter 6's discussion of the period 1769 to 1771, his 'preceding narrative' has been 'succinct', but through such a selective narration of facts, he has 'comprehended the most material transactions, on the Coast ...'[68]

Macpherson summarises his historiographical approach in the book's final chapter, where he once more reflects on the interrelationship between evidence, narrative and interpretation:

> The chain of facts, with the arguments, which naturally arose from those facts, contained in the preceding pages, and founded chiefly on the authority of the papers published by the Directors in their own *defence*, may be thought sufficient to decide the judgement of the public.[69]

Through this process, Macpherson created 'a concise narrative of transactions', but one based upon the evidence of source material (in this case, the EIC's own papers), which are then used by Macpherson to generate broader arguments about the nature of the British state and its empire. Such an approach demonstrates how Macpherson's mode of history writing was both narrative and philosophical, engaging with ideas and methodologies that were similar to other Enlightenment historians.

Throughout *The History and Management*, Macpherson's combination of narrative and philosophical approaches is further demonstrated by his juxtaposition of cause and effect. In Chapter 3, Macpherson argues that understanding the causes of early modern conflict in the Carnatic and their subsequent effects on both the EIC and local rulers is important to understanding the present: 'The preceding chain of facts has, it is hoped, rendered more clear a subject hitherto very imperfectly understood.'[70] Yet Macpherson switches immediately in this passage to a more interpretative mode of narration, introducing each point of argument with the word 'that'. This technique is used frequently by Macpherson in *The History and Management*, and echoes a similar mode of history writing deployed by Hume where, according to Phillips, 'The effect is to emphasize the argumentative structure of a given position while checking its rhetorical flow.'[71] While Hume uses 'that' in the context of his imitation of the classical tradition of inventing speeches for key characters, Macpherson's use is distinctly more functional and, as we have seen, linked firmly to the 'preceding chain of facts'. For Macpherson, the strength of his argument was based not only on how well he narrated these facts, but also on the evidence what underpinned his interpretation.

Having established Macpherson's broader approach to narrative, philosophy and history writing, the next section of this chapter considers how Macpherson applies this to his source material. Here, we examine Macpherson's methodology: what sources he draws upon for this history of the EIC and how he uses them in an argument against the corrupt practices of the Company. This helps us to measure one of Macpherson's key criteria which we saw outlined in the preface to *The History and Management*: the extent to which the case against the Company can be made from its own papers. Unlike in some of his other pieces of history writing which we have examined in previous chapters, Macpherson is predominantly reliant here on published material – but which very often contains printed versions of archival and manuscript sources.

Macpherson's *History and Management* is based on a wide range of material, the majority of which follow his key precepts for source selection: that they should be the printed material produced by the EIC and those individuals serving it and close to it. In more than 1,000 footnotes, referring to more than fifty different published and unpublished sources, Macpherson is most reliant throughout the book on the work of three key authors – George Rous, Robert Orme and Alexander Dow – all of whom worked for the EIC in a variety of different capacities. As Philip J. Stern argued recently, historians have long been reliant on the work of 'Company or India Office employees' in writing about the British Empire in this part of the world, and Macpherson was no different.[72]

George Rous's work features most heavily in Macpherson's *History and Management*, being referred to almost 400 times in the book's capacious footnotes. George Rous (1744?–1802) was the son of Thomas Rous, a Director of the EIC, and he himself served as legal counsel to the Company from 1781 until his death.[73] Rous was also a prolific author, writing over a dozen books about legal affairs and the EIC. In *The History and Management*, Macpherson refers in his footnotes to many different volumes of what he terms 'Rous's Appendix'. Of course, bibliographic conventions were a long way from emerging, and Macpherson's footnotes are light on such detail; as Anthony Grafton argues in the context of Gibbon, eighteenth-century footnotes can often be 'tantalizingly precise and yet frustratingly uninformative to the modern reader'.[74] However, one of Rous's key works on India – *The Restoration of the King of Tanjore Considered* (1777) – contains many appendices, so we can be fairly certain that this was the text consulted by Macpherson in writing his history of the EIC.[75] Given Rous's defence of the Rajah of Tanjore, the nemesis of Macpherson's client, the Nawab of Arcot, his reasons for relying on this book become obvious. The extensive appendices to Rous's work contain printed copies of Company papers and letters, an approach designed to open up EIC policy to public scrutiny and to demonstrate that the Director's support of the Rajah was correct: 'The original papers now given to the public are more voluminous than the occasion might seem to require. This has arisen from delicacy on the part of the Court of Directors, who, in vindicating themselves, were anxious not to with-hold what might possibly tend to the exculpation of others.'[76] Given this approach in the key text used by Macpherson, it is no surprise that, in making his counter-argument in support of the Nawab, he insisted on using the very same evidence and the very same technique of analysing 'original papers' – the primary sources.

Macpherson's second most-used source in *The History and Management* is, again, the work of a key figure in the EIC – Nicholas Orme. Employed as a writer by the EIC from 1744, Orme rapidly turned his attention to studying Indian history and society, publishing *A General Idea of the Government and People of Indostan* in 1752.[77] Orme's fame as an historian grew during the 1760s, with the publication of the *History of the Military Transactions of the British Nation in Indostan* (1763) leading to his appointment as the first official historiographer of the EIC in 1769.[78] While Macpherson's reference to Orme's work is again sparse in its bibliographic detail, we can deduce from his footnotes that he uses both volumes of Orme's *History of the Military Transactions*, published in 1763 and 1778.[79] Once more, we see Macpherson engaging with one of the leading British scholars of India, who had a significant influence on the emergence of Orientalist approaches to empire, especially in his close connections with major Orientalist scholars, such as William Robertson and Sir William Jones.[80] Such an engagement with leading intellectual figures again demonstrates the seriousness of Macpherson's scholarship.

The final author to whom Macpherson refers consistently throughout *The History and Management* is another author who had strong Company connections and was also a highly respected scholar of India – Alexander Dow. A fellow Highlander, Dow was born in Perthshire in 1735, and he left behind a dangerous and dubious career as a smuggler to become an officer in the EIC army.[81] Dow rose rapidly in the ranks during the 1760s to become a lieutenant colonel, learning Persian along the way and becoming a translator and historian.[82] Dow was one of the first writers in English about India, publishing two volumes of his *History of Hindostan* in 1768 and the third in 1772.[83] It is this work which Macpherson uses in his *History and Management*, in a rare moment of bibliographic clarity, referring to Dow's work by its title and to the different volumes which comprised it.[84] Dow's book proved useful to Macpherson in *The History and Management*, not just for his condemnation of the likes of Lord Clive for their actions in India, but for his defence of property rights – as we have seen, a key concern of Macpherson in his version of stadial history.[85] During this period at the end of the 1760s when he began to publish his histories, Dow, rather extraordinarily, was a flatmate in London of another Highland Scot who had both literary talent and an interest in India – our very own James Macpherson. Dismissed in an analysis of Dow's career as 'the perpetrator of the Ossian hoax', Macpherson was, in fact, the vital bridge between Dow's EIC service, his Orientalist scholarship, fellow Enlightenment figures and the literary world of London.[86] While it may be coincidence that Dow and Macpherson shared a publisher (Becket and de Hondt in the Strand) when they lived together during 1768 and 1769, they were also frequent visitors to and correspondents with one of the Enlightenment's leading lights – the great David Hume.[87] Indeed, it was Dow who passed on a 'kindly message' from Hume to Macpherson on the publication of Macpherson's *Introduction to the History of Great Britain and Ireland* in 1771.[88] As Jessica Patterson argues, Dow's interpretation of Hindu religion was most likely influenced by Macpherson's analysis of Celtic religiosity and its decline into superstition, as explored in Macpherson's *Fragments of Ancient Poetry* (1760) and in the Celtic history.[89] Dow also worked closely with Macpherson's great collaborator on Indian affairs, Sir John Macpherson, who contributed a section to the *History of Hindostan*.[90] Given this close, personal connection it is no surprise that Macpherson made great use of Dow's work in his *History and Management*, especially considering Dow's defence of the Nawab of Arcot in the *History of Hindostan*.[91] For instance, when dealing with a dispute in the evidence regarding the political succession of Indian leaders in the Carnatic, Macpherson sides with his friend, because of his expertise: 'on the internal state of India, we chuse [sic] to follow the authority of Mr. Dow'.[92] Indeed, it was perhaps Dow's example of an historian who had a practical impact and influence on contemporary political affairs in India that persuaded Macpherson to write a history in defence of his and Sir John's interest in the Carnatic. Dow, then, was a leading Orientalist, whose work had a profound influence on his friend and fellow Gael and demonstrates Macpherson's serious engagement with the broader intellectual concerns with India during the second half of the eighteenth century.

The remainder of Macpherson's sources in *The History and Management* follow this focus on using printed material produced by those who were part of, or close to, the Company. In Chapter 3, Macpherson deals with the conflict between the British and French during the late 1740s and early 1750s for control of the area of the Carnatic around Pondicherry. In writing about this extension of the Seven Years War into India, Macpherson drew heavily upon the account of this period written by one of its chief actors: Major-General Stringer Lawrence.[93] 'Major Lawrence's Narrative', as it is referred to in Macpherson's text, provides an account of how the EIC defeated the French in the battle for control of Trichinopoly, in which conflict the Nawab of Arcot was an ally of the Company.[94] Macpherson uses Lawrence's 'Narrative' to remind his readers that, over twenty years previously, there was a strong alliance between the Nawab and the EIC, indicating a loyalty to the Company and the Empire more broadly which, Macpherson argues, had been forgotten by the late 1770s. Such contemporary ignorance was, according to Macpherson, largely linked to critics' failure to read sources such as Lawrence's narrative:

> Fortunately for the memory of the late General Lawrence, they seem to have known nothing of his narrative of his own campaigns; otherwise that gallant officer might have been raised from the dead to support falsehoods, which his honest heart abhorred, when alive.[95]

Once more, we see Macpherson reflecting in a self-consciously historiographical way, following the principles of the preface to *The History and Management*, and committing to his claims that the Company could be condemned in the late 1770s using its very own documents and materials.

While Macpherson's other sources remain close to this model, there are, however, a handful of exceptions in Macpherson's source material that fall outwith the EIC's printed material. In dealing with the EIC's increasingly threatening behaviour towards the Nawab of Arcot in the late 1760s, Macpherson draws upon the narrative of Sir John Lindsay, a Highlander of the Lindsays of Evelix, near Dornoch in Sutherland, who rose to prominence as a naval commodore and commander-in-chief in the East Indies.[96] Macpherson's analysis of the EIC's conduct during the 1770s uses the account of one of the Company's key figures during this period, Josias Du Pré, who was Governor of Madras from 1770 to 1773.[97] Likewise, Macpherson once more demonstrates his scholarly credentials by referring to the work of one of the leading British orientalists, Richard Owen Cambridge, whose 1761 *An Account of the War in India*, provided Macpherson not only with 'Lawrence's Narrative', but also Cambridge's own 'Transactions on the Coast of Coromandel in the Year 1755'.[98] While Macpherson uses a range of other EIC and related printed material (such as the vaguely referenced 'papers published by the Company'), he also draws upon private and manuscript sources that are outwith the strictures of the methodology outlined in the preface to *The History and Management*.[99] Given his extensive use of archival and manuscript sources in *The History of Great Britain*, it is perhaps no surprise that Macpherson cannot resist making use of such material in *The History and Management*. Throughout the text, there are a handful of references to a variety of manuscript sources. In writing about dramatic changes in the Carnatic, '[t]his revolution, in the government of Tanjore', at the end of the seventeenth century, Macpherson footnotes his narrative with reference to an 'Authentic MS Account of Tanjore, taken on the spot, and now in the hands of the Author of this Disquisition' (i.e. Macpherson himself).[100] Here, Macpherson emphasises the crucial importance of eye-witness accounts in establishing the veracity of historical evidence.[101] In describing the interrelationship between local rulers in the Carnatic during the 1760s, Macpherson refers to specific manuscript sources of the Nawab. Letters written by the Nawab to Mahommed Nazab Chan and to Lord Clive in 1765 indicate the close working relationship of Macpherson with the Nawab, who was most likely passing on material useful to Macpherson in making the Nawab's case against the EIC.[102] Macpherson also indicates 'Private Information' as the source of his material in a number of footnotes, probably arising from similar connections Macpherson had with India and the EIC.[103] Macpherson's reliance on material collected from his allies in Indian affairs also explains his use of a range of printed material published by the Nawab and his agents. In summarising his case against the EIC, Macpherson makes reference to 'Original Papers', here, most likely, the *Original Papers, Transmitted by the Nabob of Arcot, to his Agent in Great Britain*, published in 1777. As John Maclean's research has made clear, the Nawab's agent in London at this time, from 1775–1778, was Lauchlin Macleane.[104] However, by this stage Macpherson was already assisting Macleane in serving the Nawab and, in 1778, James and John Macpherson took turns functioning as the agent in London.[105]

Macpherson's sources, then, reveal that, as an historian, he was largely true to his methodology. Having established a devotion to using the EIC's own material (and work published by its servants) in the preface, Macpherson fills his footnotes with references to papers published by the company and its agents. In doing so, Macpherson reveals his engagement with the most cutting-edge Orientalist scholarship of the day, from Alexander Dow to Richard Cambridge, and demonstrates how he was personally embroiled in Enlightenment intellectual circles. While in his continuing use of manuscript sources Macpherson reveals his scholarly concern for using the kinds of 'original papers' that were central to his earlier history writings, the argument of *The History and Management* was built predominantly upon the published material of the Company itself. Macpherson was determined to prove his case against the EIC using its own words, and the sheer weight of footnotes in this book demonstrates his commitment to this principle.

Having established the kind of evidence to which Macpherson refers in *The History and Management*'s footnotes, it is also important to consider the precise ways in which he deploys these references. Clearly, Macpherson uses these footnotes as scholarly apparatus, demonstrating the sources upon which his argument is based and developing his use of them in ways that go beyond his citation practice in earlier publications. However, Macpherson also indulges in explanation and digression – as his historiographical practice develops, so too does his use of footnotes. Anthony Grafton has identified Hume, Gibbon and Robertson as the founders of the modern footnote, who fused together newer ideas about narrative and philosophy with more classical notions of erudition.[106] The footnote was, of course, not an invention of eighteenth-century history writing and, as Grafton demonstrates, it was a staple of writing about the past during the Renaissance and even before.[107] By the middle of the eighteenth century, the idea that an historian should cite their sources in some kind of note was entirely commonplace.[108] What the likes of Gibbon and others do differently is to repurpose the footnote as part of their broader interest in the philosophical power of history writing. As we have seen throughout our book, one of the central problems of eighteenth-century historiography was the issue of reconciling the desire to tell a story about the past, with the need to both explain and evidence it: 'There remained the literary as well as scientific problem of reconciling narrative, philosophy, and erudition. The first concerned the deeds of individuals; the second generated reflections and digressions; and the third footnotes.'[109] Of course, an historian such as Gibbon managed to combine narrative, philosophy and erudition just in the footnotes to *The Decline and Fall*, investing 'bibliographical citation with the grave symmetry of Ciceronian peroration'.[110] However, as we have seen above, Macpherson's combination of storytelling, explanation and scholarly robustness was not dissimilar to the likes of Gibbon and Robertson, and in his use of footnotes in *The History and Management*, Macpherson reminds us once more of his credentials as an Enlightenment historian.[111]

While the majority of the footnotes in *The History and Management* are straightforward records of bibliographic detail, there are a number of examples in this text where Macpherson demonstrates his ability to use footnotes in a more discursive fashion. Throughout the book, Macpherson deploys footnotes to add an additional level of explanation, making clear to the reader the meaning of certain terms. Indian terminology and currency are frequently glossed in the footnotes, defining key words and emphasising the sheer amount of money at stake in these Carnatic disputes, while also reinforcing Macpherson's scholarly credibility. For example, in his account of competing claims to power in the early eighteenth-century Carnatic, Macpherson provides us with a footnote explaining differences in how the term 'Rajah' was used, and how this sowed the seeds of later confusion about the legitimacy of certain rulers: 'In all the countries and provinces of India, it is a fixed custom among the great Rajahs, to put the title of Rajah on their chops, but neither Iseko-jî nor the other Maratta Naigs of Tanjore ever put that title on their chops.'[112] Macpherson also constantly translates Indian currency into pounds sterling in his footnotes, a crucial part in demonstrating his argument about the value of EIC corruption.[113] In his final reference to money in *The History and Management*, Macpherson both translates the amount of Indian currency into pounds ('17,984,916 pagodas, a sum exceeding SEVEN MILLIONS STERLING'), and also uses the footnote to provide direct quotation from a primary source – another key device used by Macpherson to demonstrate his credentials as an historian.[114] For Macpherson, the footnote was not just a reference, it was also additional space in the text where the reader's attention could be drawn towards the evidence of the primary sources. At a number of points, Macpherson quotes extensively from this source material in the footnotes. In making his argument about EIC corruption during the 1770s, Macpherson follows his own rules of evidence, providing an extract from an EIC primary source (a letter from Sir Robert Harland to the Secretary of State in January 1773) to make his case.[115] In explaining the troubled relationship between the Nawab and the EIC in Tanjore during the early 1760s, Macpherson provides what he terms an 'abstract' of one of his key sources, 'Mr Du Pré's Vindication'. In a footnote extending over four pages, Macpherson provides an abridged version of Du Pré's text, which Macpherson uses to underpin (quite literally) his argument that 'the risque and expence of the war were to fall on the Nabob; and that, therefore, by the law of nations, he was entitled to the reward of victory'.[116] Macpherson prefaces this extensive abridged use of Du Pré's work with an explanatory note, within the footnote, which touches upon a number of the underlying principles of argument, evidence, truth and impartiality that guided his history writing:

> In addition to the facts and arguments, in the preceding pages, it is thought proper to throw into a note the SUBSTANCE of Mr Du Pre's Vindication of the Expedition of 1771. Though that gentleman's reasonings are not so forcibly expressed, in the following abstract, as in his own work, some advantage may be derived from them being compendiously collected into one point of view. Whoever will be at the trouble of reading the ENORMOUS volumes published by the Court of Directors, in their own defence, will readily allow, that Mr Du Pre is, at least, and IMPARTIAL authority, in whatever regards the interests of the Nabob of Arcot.[117]

Here, Macpherson establishes that evidence is derived from facts and arguments and that, as critical readers, his audience should be minded to return to the source of this evidence: in this case, the work of a key authority on India, drawing upon the source material of the EIC itself.

Just as Gibbon enjoyed scattering 'cheerfully sarcastic comments' into his footnotes, Macpherson also reserves some of his more cutting remarks about the EIC for the footnotes.[118] The very first extended note in the book provides Macpherson with a chance to stick the boot into the EIC and its dubious practices. In Chapter 1, Macpherson establishes some of the broad arguments of the book, chiefly his claims that EIC corruption in the 1770s was there in the very bones of the organisation from its foundation at the beginning of the previous century, which he had hinted at in *The History of Great Britain*. Macpherson shifts from a general observation about the corrupting influence of avarice in commerce to a specific attack on the EIC's practices. As we have seen, such a dynamic between the general and the specific lay at the heart of Enlightenment history writing practices and, as a close adherent of these principles, Macpherson uses his footnotes to apply withering, Gibbon-esque judgement on the EIC. In explaining why the Company became so corrupt in its 'wanton and uncontrolled exercise of power', Macpherson's note concludes in caustic fashion, leaving the reader in no doubt as to his opinion of the EIC:

> Hence it happened that private refinements and selfish views were too frequently the only rules of their conduct, and that their administration had scarce any other principle of union, than a mutual permission to commit injustice. Even the exclusive privilege, which was thought necessary for the prosperity of their commerce, became an engine of tyranny against all those whom they considered as interlopers, and such instances of their barbarity might be produced, supported by facts, as would excite horror.[119]

Even in such fervent attack on the Company, Macpherson reminds his readers of the aim of the book – to make this impassioned argument against the EIC, but drawing upon the evidence of the sources, a key tool in his history-writing methodology. A couple of pages later, Macpherson once again resorts to footnotes for his most cutting commentary on the EIC, excusing himself from listing all the Company's corrupt practices and crimes precisely because he is an historian, and should, by the emerging conventions of history-writing practice, be above moral judgements. Perhaps making a sly dig at Gibbon and his fondness for using footnotes for irony and rhetorical flourishes, Macpherson states that 'The instances of rapacity, oppression and injustice, committed by the superior servants of the Company, are too mean for the pen of an historian, at least they are too numerous to be comprehended in a disquisition, where brevity is to be studied.'[120] While Gibbon indulges his penchant for using footnotes as a forum for personal insults, Macpherson claims, as a serious historian, to be above all this. Here, Macpherson argues that he is not listing all the abuses of the EIC precisely because he is an historian – while simultaneously passing moral judgement on the Company *and* throwing shade at Gibbon.

Macpherson develops a nice line in sarcastic footnotes through *The History and Management*, using them as barbs in making his case against the Company. In describing the retreat of the Maratha Empire from the Carnatic in 1771, Macpherson's footnote casts doubt on the significance of Sir Robert Harland's military intervention, arguing that while he (Harland) 'takes the merit of having reduced the Marattas to retreat ... it is probable, that the money and jewels of the Nabob added some weight to this interposition'.[121] It is not only the EIC and other historians upon whom Macpherson casts aspersions in his footnotes. Referring in Chapter 3 to how other commentators have 'misrepresented' the 'great, and decisive services rendered, by the Nabob, to the Company', Macpherson uses the supporting footnote to pull the reader from his account of the 1740s back into the present day. Explaining the Nabob's critics' choice of the word 'INIMICAL' to describe his relationship to the 'British nation', Macpherson makes a sarcastic reference to the American revolutionaries whom he had attacked with such gusto in his 1775/6 publication, *The Rights of Great Britain Asserted Against the Claims of America*: 'This awkward, unanalogical word seems to have been purloined from those respectable bodies of men, the American Committees of Safety.'[122] Macpherson concludes the entire book with a beast of a footnote, stretching over three whole pages. Here, Macpherson provides further evidence to support his argument ('it is necessary to state a few facts, relative to the respective situations of the Nabob and the Rajah'), sets out the consistency of the Nabob's support for the EIC, in the face of, according to Macpherson, equally consistent treachery on the part of the Company, and makes a closing argument in support of 'the hope that justice will be effectually rendered to the Nabob'.[123] Macpherson once again establishes his credentials as an Enlightenment historian, demonstrating his commitment to the historian's technique of using footnotes as both a citation device and a space in which to continue one's argument, often with a more sarcastic and personal tone than the main body of the text, following the example set by Gibbon himself just a few years earlier in *The Decline and Fall of the Roman Empire*.

Having established that Macpherson followed the methodology outlined in the preface to *The History and Management* in his use of material, evidence and footnotes, we conclude this section with a brief discussion of one of the key issues of Enlightenment historiography: the extent to which history writing could be an impartial representation of the 'truth' of the past. As we have seen, Macpherson set out to write an 'authentic and impartial narrative', where 'Truth, and only truth, was his object'.[124] Once again, Macpherson uses the main body of the text to deploy these concepts and reflect on their meaning, both for history writing and in his argument against the corrupt practices of the EIC.

Ideas of truth and impartiality were central to Enlightenment debates about history writing. Commenting in 1754 on his *History of England*, David Hume argued that 'The first Quality of an Historian is to be true and impartial; the next to be interesting.'[125] Macpherson's great mentor, Hugh Blair, elaborated at length on these topics in his lectures at the University of Edinburgh in the late 1750s and early 1760s. Here, Blair outlined his belief in the 'mimetic and didactic' purpose of history writing.[126] Blair's influence on Macpherson was significant and, as his history of the EIC demonstrates, not just limited to Macpherson's earlier Ossianic Collections. In making his argument against the Company, Macpherson was eager throughout the main body of the book to stress his impartiality. In outlining the internecine power struggles in the Carnatic during the 1740s, Macpherson states that his account represents 'the real state of Tanjore in 1744', while other writers lacked Macpherson's impartiality: 'some late writers, blinded by zeal, misled by faction, or swayed by interest, have erected that province into a kingdom'.[127] The Nawab's actions were, according to Macpherson, 'misrepresented by the prejudices of individuals and the malice of party'.[128] As we know, Macpherson was anything but impartial in his dealings with the EIC, at every turn being a robust advocate of his client, the Nawab. Yet, that is beside the point: Macpherson, in order for his argument to be taken seriously, was eager to stress his unimpeachable credentials as an Enlightenment historian, one who followed the precepts of Hume, Blair and others in his devotion to the importance of impartiality in history writing. For Macpherson, this kind of scholarly detachment was linked to use of source material, where one's credentials as an impartial historian were established by a fidelity to the sources, which were then used to support one's arguments. In his account of the EIC, there was nothing worse than other historians of the Company making arguments that were disproved by the very evidence they sought to deploy in their support:

> Some late writers, who call fiction to the support of their party, where truth fails, have, from one of the authorities so often quoted, framed a tale very different, from the facts we have stated above. Contempt is too slight a punishment, for men, who wilfully deceive. Had the intelligent historian, on whom they father their falsehoods, written ambiguously on the character and conduct of Pretaupa Sing, the world might be induced to ascribe their errors to zeal, and their misrepresentations to prejudice. But what judgment are we to form of their candour, what opinion of their morality when we find that the very pages, which they cite, present irrefragable proofs of their perversion of truth?[129]

Macpherson's chutzpah in railing against those who 'wilfully deceive' is quite something, given the controversies surrounding the Ossianic Collections, but the fact that someone like Macpherson, so embroiled in this *cause célèbre* of the eighteenth-century literary world, should place such an emphasis on truth and impartiality (as he does, with differing emphasis, throughout his literary output) demonstrates his commitment to being taken seriously as an Enlightenment history writer. Finally, in the concluding passages to the book, where Macpherson revisits his argument against the EIC, he once more contrasts his fidelity to truth in history writing with its stark absence (according to his analysis) in the work of his opponents. Macpherson blames these other historians of the EIC for having the intention of restoring 'the transactions of the Company to their original obscurity and uncertainty'. On the contrary, Macpherson's approach in this book had been to 'develop [sic] truth, and to present her, in her native simplicity, before the eye of the public'.[130] Once more, the fact that Macpherson engages seriously with these ideas of truth, alongside his extensive use of scholarly methodologies and mechanisms, demonstrates his sustained engagement with Enlightenment thought and that it is important, therefore, to recognise Macpherson, himself, as an Enlightenment historian.

THE RIGHTS OF GREAT BRITAIN ASSERTED AGAINST THE CLAIMS OF AMERICA (1775/6)

Macpherson's appointment as both agent for the Nawab of Arcot and government pamphleteer for Lord North's ministry produced two seemingly contradictory responses to the crisis of empire experienced by Britain in the 1770s. As we have seen, Macpherson reacted to the Empire's troubles in the Carnatic during the second half of the eighteenth century by writing a robust defence of the interests of a specific portion local Indian elite (especially his patron, Muhammad Ali Khan Wallajah) against those of the East India Company (but, as we have seen, also in support of the British government's position in its struggle against the EIC's increasing power). However, in the mid-1770s, as the Empire was facing its greatest existential threat (at least since the conclusion of the Seven Years War with France), Macpherson wrote against the claims of local elites in the Thirteen Colonies. As the leading writer for Lord North's government, it fell to Macpherson to pen the British response to the increasingly rebellious attitude of the American colonists.[131] Written between August and November 1775, Macpherson's pamphlet is a reply to the Declaration of Congress 'setting forth the causes and necessity of their taking up arms' from the beginning of July that year.[132] Unlike the vacillating and conciliatory response articulated by opposition figures in Parliament, such as Fox and Burke, Macpherson's argument is that the colonists' violence should be met with the violence of the British imperial state. The pamphlet sets out the North government's 'justification of why Britain must go to war'.[133] Passing through thirteen editions, this pamphlet was one of Macpherson's most popular publications and, as James wrote to Sir John Macpherson, one edition in late 1775 sold 'Seven thousand copies ... in three weeks.'[134] However, its status as a piece of history writing remains under-explored. Paul deGategno's detailed analysis of the pamphlet establishes how Macpherson makes his argument against the colonists, paying particular attention to Macpherson's points about taxation, his choice of language, and his use of the poetic metaphor of a 'parent/child' relationship between the imperial metropole and colonial periphery. DeGategno concludes his article by stating that Macpherson deployed 'the methods and discourse of contemporary historiographic practice' in *The Rights of Great Britain* without outlining what exactly these were.[135] In this section, we seek to take up this analysis of Macpherson's history writing where deGategno leaves off, outlining precisely how Macpherson deployed a distinctive historical methodology, following some of the precepts of Enlightenment historiography that we have previously examined. In *The Rights of Great Britain*, Macpherson seeks to establish the 'truth' of his argument through a fidelity to primary sources and by adopting the scholarly scaffolding of Enlightenment history writing in his footnotes. Although not as extensive as in his other publications (after all, this pamphlet was intended to be read by a popular audience in order to most effectively spread word of the North government's American policy), Macpherson once more establishes his credentials as an Enlightenment historian by demonstrating his erudition through judicious use of footnotes. Likewise, Macpherson also uses the nexus of narrative and philosophy – central to Pocock's definition of Enlightenment historiography – to combine narration and analysis of events. In making an argument against the colonists' demands for representation in Parliament, Macpherson further denotes his Enlightened status through his analysis of the constitution and the British imperial state. Crucially, the most significant element of *The Rights of Great Britain* that establishes Macpherson as an historian is his use of the past to make an argument in the present. As we saw in Macpherson's defence of his patron, the Nawab of Arcot, in *The History and Management*, the example of historical precedence was crucial to Macpherson's writing. In *The Rights of Great Britain*, Macpherson dismantles the colonists' case for parliamentary representation by citing examples from the past that demonstrate the nature of British imperial rule, both at home and abroad, from late medieval England to the Stamp Tax of the 1760s. Macpherson, then, as well as being the leading government pamphleteer responding to the immediate concerns of colonial rebellion in America, was thinking and writing as an historian in *The Rights of Great Britain*.

As we have seen in his previous writings, Macpherson outlines his historical methodology in each publication's preliminary material, in the case of *The Rights of Great Britain* presented as an 'Advertisement' instead of a preface.[136] Here, Macpherson informs the reader of the evidence which he has compiled and how he has used it in making his case against America. Macpherson's 'counterrevolutionary text', in Matthew Dziennik's resonant phrase, was based upon 'the best and most incontestible authorities'.[137] Much like in his other writings, these were recognisable as an historian's primary sources, with Macpherson once more attaching evidentiary value to 'original papers', alongside 'accurate estimates, and authentic dispatches'. As deGategno demonstrates, Macpherson was given much of this material by the government itself, eager to lend him the moral authority of access to as much evidence as possible.[138] In keeping with his reliance on printed as well as archival sources, Macpherson also highlights his use of 'the records of both

Houses of Parliament' and 'such printed tracts as might contribute to throw any light on the subject'. Spending 'more labour and time... on this short disquisition, than are general bestowed upon fugitive Publications of the same kind', Macpherson once more establishes his historiographical methodology, using primary sources in constructing an argument and demonstrating that 'he has rigidly adhered to truth throughout'.

To what extent, then, does Macpherson stick to these methodological precepts in *The Rights of Great Britain*? Here, as before, our concern lies not with whether Macpherson's arguments are correct or truthful, but rather in determining the extent to which Macpherson follows his designated method – it's not just how Macpherson writes history, but how he writes *about* writing history which is important. Macpherson's adherence to 'truth' runs through the text from the get-go. Crucially, though, notions of truth in the pamphlet are largely explored through the colonists' alleged lies, rather than by Macpherson positively asserting his own truthfulness. Such a burden of proof comes from Macpherson's key argument, outlined in the first page of the text proper:

> But if Nations, accountable to none for their conduct, deem it necessary to reconcile others to their proceedings, the necessity is still more urgent with regard to those who, breaking through every political duty, draw their swords against the State of which they own themselves Subject. The opinions of mankind are invariably opposed to such men.[139]

Such a negative assessment of truthfulness then places the burden of proof in making an argument for rebellion on the colonists themselves. Because of the colonists' violation of the sovereignty of the state, 'their assertions are heard with distrust, their arguments weighed with caution; and, therefore, it is as necessary for THEM to adhere to truth, in the former, as it is prudent to avoid sophistry in the latter'.[140] Macpherson attacks Congress and its 'Declaration of the United Colonies of North America' because, in this text, they misrepresent evidence, therefore making their arguments false: 'The facts are either wilfully or ignorantly misrepresented; and the arguments deduced from premises that have no foundation in truth.'[141] Throughout the pamphlet, Macpherson moves from one argument of the colonists to another, decrying 'the fictitious grievances of America since the same period' following the end of the Seven Years War.[142] In a paragraph-by-paragraph analysis of the Declaration and grievances against British conduct in suppressing the initial stages of the American's armed rebellion, Macpherson dismisses them as 'not supported by truth' and that the colonists rely on making an emotional appeal to their fellow citizens of empire: 'THEIR business is to engage the passions, where they can make no impression with their arguments.'⁴³

Having established the colonists' 'want of impartiality and fairness' and their 'same disregard to truth', Macpherson's own fidelity to the principle of truth is attested to, in his estimation, by deploying primary sources and the scaffolding of erudite scholarship – footnotes.¹⁴⁴ Throughout the text, Macpherson quotes liberally from primary sources. Given Macpherson's reliance on making his argument based on historical precedence, it is no surprise to see him using primary source documents from the past. In demonstrating the beneficence of the state in granting representation to English counties, Macpherson quotes directly from the statutes of Henry VIII and Charles II and argues that the colonists should have followed the example of Chester and Durham in their respective petitions: 'Had the Americans, instead of flying to arms, submitted the same supposed grievance, in a peaceable and dutiful manner, to the Legislature, I can perceive no reason why their request should be refused.'¹⁴⁵ Macpherson makes greater use of primary source evidence in countering the American's key claim – that there could be no taxation of the colonists by the British state unless they had representation in the UK Parliament. Here, Macpherson justifies his extensive use of evidence about colonial expenditure in making an 'argument in favour of the right of Taxation' by once again suggesting that the Americans' Declaration was based on the absence of such evidence: 'The Americans themselves have deserted that ground.'¹⁴⁶ The evidence Macpherson then provides, largely in the footnotes to this section of the pamphlet, comes from the government's 'Account of what Sums have been granted to the different Provinces in North America' and is used to demonstrate that such expenditure has been 'so enormous ... that without the authority of incontestible vouchers, they could scarcely obtain credit'.¹⁴⁷ The evidence of such primary sources then proves Macpherson's argument. In demonstrating how Parliament has always and consistently applied the principle of its 'uncontroulable authority over the Colonies', Macpherson provides more primary source evidence. Here, House of Commons resolutions from 1740 about the issuing of currency in the colonies are quoted extensively by Macpherson to 'carry the proof of this position beyond the power of reply' – the sovereignty of the UK parliament was unchallengeable.¹⁴⁸ Macpherson does, on occasion, admit the inconclusive nature of the evidence of the past, such as in his discussion of the Jamaican Assembly's refusal to 'raise levies for the support of Government' in 1680, where he concedes that the source material does not reveal the outcome of the dispute.¹⁴⁹ Yet, for much of the pamphlet, Macpherson is bold in asserting the power of his, and therefore the British government's, argument precisely because of its basis in the evidence of primary sources: 'It appears from this detail of facts, that the right of Parliament to bind the Colonies, in all cases whatsoever, is not a claim founded on mere theory: on the contrary, that the controuling power of the Legislature is warranted by constant usage, and uninterrupted practice.'[150]

Macpherson's reliance on primary source material in making a case against the colonists is further demonstrated by his use of footnotes. Although not as extensive as in *The History and Management*, Macpherson still employs these scholarly tools in a way befitting an Enlightenment historian. Macpherson frequently footnotes simply to refer to the sources he has used in making his argument, demonstrating his erudite engagement with primary source material such as the statutes of Henry VIII or Charles II discussed above.[151] As in *The History and Management*, Macpherson also uses footnotes to quote extensively from such primary sources. For example, early in the text, Macpherson reflects on how the Seven Years War ('the last expensive war') was fought partly to 'defend the Americans' and involved extensive British state expenditure:

> Did not Great-Britain [sic], like a Guardian Angel, stretch forth her hand to their aid; and, be expelling their enemies from the Continent of America, rescue them, not only from danger, but the very fear of danger? Did she not, over and above the many millions she expended upon the fleets and armies employed in defence of the Colonies, advance more than ONE MILLION to pay THEIR own native forces, employed in THEIR own Cause?

In substantiating this point, Macpherson then provides extensive evidence in a footnote stretching across three pages to demonstrate precisely how much financial support was given to the Americans, from 'Grants in Parliament for Rewards, Encouragement, and Indemnification to the Provinces in North America for their Service and Expences [sic] during the last War' to 'An Account of Bounties on American Commodities'.[152] Like his Enlightenment historian contemporaries, Macpherson also uses footnotes to provide further commentary on the text and to extend his argument. In criticising the parliamentary opposition's support of the American cause (to which Macpherson returns in *A Short History of the Opposition* in 1779), Macpherson uses a footnote to provide factual clarification about the Whig position on America, stating that 'Lord Rockingham and others in Opposition came into office July 10, 1765', just shortly after the passing of the Stamp Act, which they had vehemently opposed.[153] Macpherson also uses footnotes to reinforce his argument, such as in the later section of the text where he deconstructs the claims of the colonists in the Declaration of Congress. In countering the Americans' characterisation of General Gage's response to the initial stages of armed rebellion in Massachusetts Bay, Macpherson uses a footnote to point out that Gage's actions were supported by historical precedence. In declaring martial law, Macpherson argues that Gage 'was authorised to do, as Civil Governor, by a Law passed in the Province, many years ago'.[154] Demonstrating that the precedence of past laws and actions is key to Macpherson's argument against the colonists (see below), footnotes are deployed here in an analytical fashion. As established by Anthony Grafton, Enlightenment historians often used footnotes as a space for asides to the main body of the text. Like Gibbon, Macpherson also uses footnotes in this way to add sarcastic commentary to his argument.[155] In the section on the Rockingham and Pitt administrations' actions in Quebec during the 1760s, Macpherson points out that these were far more arbitrary and tyrannical than the measures being opposed a decade later by the very same Whigs who had 'approved this POPISH, ARBITRARY, TYRANNICAL system of Government'. In the footnote to this section, Macpherson reserves the full ire of his disapproval for the leader of the Whig opposition, Lord Rockingham, who appointed John Oliver Bernard as the Catholic Bishop of Quebec in 1766: 'Lord Rockingham had the *merit* of sending a *Popish* Bishop to Quebec'.[156] Macpherson's sarcastic use of emphasis here points out the political irony of the Whig party, emerging in the late 1670s as a bulwark of the Protestant succession against perceived threats of a Catholic monarchy, then pragmatically appointing a Catholic bishop in Canada.[157] Once more, we see Macpherson's political argument framed historiographically, with the erudition of sources and footnotes being deployed in making his case against the Americans.

Macpherson's use of footnotes in *The Rights of Great Britain* once more mark him as a writer of history in the Enlightenment mode. While these footnotes demonstrated his erudition (basing his argument on primary sources), further sections of Macpherson's attack on the Declaration of Congress indicate how he deployed those other components of Enlightenment history writing identified by Pocock: narrative and philosophy.

Throughout *The Rights of Great Britain*, Macpherson explicitly narrates the past in order to explain it, demonstrating his fidelity to the Enlightenment principle of analysis through narration. Macpherson proves one of his key arguments – that Parliament was always sovereign and supreme 'over all the Colonies' – by providing readers with a careful narration of the past. This account is framed as a deliberate narrative: 'A brief recital of some of those instances may throw light on a subject, rendered obscure and perplexed by the prejudices of the ignorant, and the arts of designing men.'[158] It was by creating a narrative sequence of events that Macpherson would then create an argument against the Americans – at this precise point, to demonstrate that the most recent 'coercive regulations' imposed on the colonists were the product of Whig governments, not the atavistic 'principles of Toryism' that they feared.[159] Macpherson's narrative strategy, then, is to arrange events sequentially in order to analyse the past. Shifting his attention to specific arguments in the Declaration of the General Congress, Macpherson counters the Americans' claim that Parliamentary efforts to negotiate a settlement in February 1775 were 'an insidious manoeuvre'. To do this, Macpherson recites events in the House of Commons and the Lords, arguing that 'some previous facts must be explained'.[160] For Macpherson, it is through the narration of 'facts' that meaning is derived. And the key to countering the arguments of the Americans was to create a particular narrative of the past which, for Macpherson, also was a narrative of truth. A central passage in Congress's Declaration focuses on one of the earliest military engagements of the revolutionary war, the Battle of Concord in April 1775. Here, there are two competing narratives at play about the conduct of General Thomas Gage, the leader of the British forces who escalated the conflict by sending Redcoats to seize the Patriots' store of arms in Concord. According to the Americans, it was Gage who was responsible for an 'unprovoked assault' on the towns of Lexington and Concord, where the British troops 'murdered' several of the inhabitants. 'Hostilities thus commenced', concluded Congress, laying the blame firmly on the actions of the British under Gage.[161] Macpherson's narrative is, of course, rather different, seeking to exculpate the actions of Gage and demonstrate that his troops were ordered to 'observe the most strict discipline' and that there was 'not one LOADED MUSQUET in the whole detachment'. Whether correct or not, what matters here is the way in which Macpherson frames this particular narrative. For Macpherson, the truth is established by a narration of events: 'The audacity of the Congress, in asserting FALSEHOODS, demands a brief detail of the TRUTH.'[162] Thus, for Macpherson, the Americans, through their actions at Lexington and Concord, display that they are outwith history. In Macpherson's narrative, the colonists thereby become savages and barbarians. It was the Americans who displayed 'BARBAROUS CRUELTY to the wounded soldiers' (the British), two of whom, according to Macpherson, 'had been scalped by the savage Provincials'.[163] Here,

Macpherson follows the conventions of Enlightenment history writing, that, in the works of Robertson, Gibbon and others, made firm distinctions between the peoples of Western Europe and elsewhere.[164] As Ranjit Guha argues, notions of what constituted history were firmly codified by Hegel's idea of 'world-history' at the beginning of the nineteenth century, where having a history (a past) and being able to write about this were tethered to the possession of statehood.[165] Those without a state, therefore, had neither history nor history writing, thereby rendering them outwith the bounds of Western civilisation.

Macpherson's analysis of the Americans differed to William Robertson's account in his *History of America* in 1777. Robertson's book focused on the earlier history of European colonisation and the competition between the emerging Spanish and Portuguese empires. Robertson's description of the indigenous American population as 'savages' aligned with the developing Enlightenment belief that this 'savagery' lay outwith the bounds of history because they lacked the stadial development of European culture. Macpherson, however, describes the European population of America as 'savage' precisely because they have rejected the model of progress offered to them by British constitutional history and, in Macpherson's argument, returned to a 'barbarous' state.[166] In this passage on General Gage and Concord, we see Macpherson establishing a dichotomy between his faithful narration of the past and the colonists' 'falsehoods', which is immediately juxtaposed with their 'barbarous' conduct. According to Macpherson, the American's narrative of the past did not demonstrate a fidelity to truth, which then explained their status as 'savages'. As Guha argues, labelling one's enemies as 'barbarians' was an important strategy in treating them as less than equal subjects, which then underpinned Macpherson's justification of British colonial violence.[167]

Macpherson's use of history in *The Rights of Great Britain* is also determined by a certain narrative of the development of the constitution and the rise of the state in Britain and its empire. Of course, this was a commonplace notion in Enlightenment history writing, where the likes of Gibbon saw the emergence of the state during the early modern period as a counterpoint to the 'barbarism and religion' of previous periods.[168] Throughout his response to the Declaration of Congress, Macpherson makes the key argument about the inviolability of a British state that was global in reach and unbounded by the geographical constraints of the British Isles' archipelago. In doing so, Macpherson once more pre-empts Hegel's later ideas about history writing and the rise of the Western state, and Macpherson's response to the Americans made it perfectly clear that his mode of writing about the past, in this particular context, was firmly connected with support for the British state, as a constitutional institution.

Macpherson emphasises the centrality of the state from the outset of *The Rights of Great Britain*. His key point is that the American cause is unjust because they themselves are British subjects: 'those who, breaking through every political duty, draw their swords against the State of which they own themselves Subject. The opinions of mankind are invariably opposed to such men.'[169] Having established the illegitimacy of American claims on this basis, Macpherson then proceeds to briefly outline his own theory of the state. For Macpherson, the state is defined by power. Contrary to Congress's argument that no one could exert 'an unbounded authority over others', Macpherson argues 'that a supreme and uncountroulable power must exist somewhere in every State'.[170] Macpherson's idea of the state was tied to his understanding of the constitution. The constitutional triumvirate of 'King, Lords, and Commons', established following the revolution of the late seventeenth century, was the state, and therefore the source of incontrovertible power: 'In the British Empire it [power] is vested, where it is most safe, in King, Lords and Commons, under the collective appellation of the Legislature. The Legislature is another name for the Constitution of the State; and, in fact, the State itself.' This emphasis on the mutually constitutive relationship of the constitution was a direct response to the Americans' emphasis on their loyalty to the King, rather than to Parliament.[171] For Macpherson, then, this constitutional settlement meant that the state extended across the whole of the Empire – for him, there was no difference, in terms of the constitution or the distribution and reach of the state's power, between London and Pennsylvania or, indeed, Putney and Pensacola.[172] This model of the British constitution underpinned Macpherson's riposte to the American's key argument of 'no taxation without representation'. Macpherson's understanding of the constitution meant that 'the authority of the British Legislature' was 'uncontroulable' and, therefore, its 'right to tax all the Subjects of the British Empire can never be denied'.[173] Towards the end of his argument, Macpherson makes this point with yet more force: 'The general supremacy of the Legislature, which by pervading the whole British Empire renders it ONE state', meant that the colonists were ruled by the authority of the same British state.[174] Thus, a certain reading of recent British constitutional history framed Macpherson's argument against Congress, one which emphasised the emergence of the state as the undisputed source of power across the

British Empire. In doing so, Macpherson was following some of the conventions established by other historians of the Scottish Enlightenment, in particular the notion of conjectural history based on a stadial theory of the past in which human societies move through various stages of development. For the likes of Ferguson and Smith, the liberty of English constitutionalism reached its apogee in the constitutional settlement that Macpherson outlines here – the 'balanced' constitution of King, Lords and Commons.[175] Macpherson was careful, however, to emphasise the constitutional (and, indeed, British) nature of this power – this was not the absolutism of the Stuarts that radical critics of the American war, such as John Wilkes, maintained, but was, instead, rooted in the 'Glorious Revolution' of 1689.[176] And, crucially, Macpherson made this historical argument in a contemporary political pamphlet – once more demonstrating his commitment to writing as an historian, but in his role as political propagandist for Lord North's ministry. As such, we can see Macpherson writing in this mode of 'Celtic neo-Whiggism', but going beyond the Ossianic Collections in which Colin Kidd identifies this approach, or the early history writing where Dafydd Moore also observes this phenomenon.[177] As Kidd argues, 'Macpherson ... valued the glories of English constitutional history, and was keen to explain them by the sophisticated methods of Scottish sociology' – but applied them across his writing, including the political work of his later years.[178]

This use of the past to make an argument in the present emerges as a key strategy in Macpherson's case against the Americans in the 1770s. Ranging from the Romans, to the evolution of the state in medieval England and the changing nature of the relationship between Britain and the Thirteen Colonies since the end of the seventeenth century, Macpherson builds his argument using certain narratives of the past. This is the most distinctive feature of *The Rights of Great Britain*, where Macpherson's analysis in 1775 is rooted in Enlightenment historiography, narrating the past in order to explain the present.

At the outset of *The Rights of Great Britain*, Macpherson situates his response to Congress in an ancient classical and distant English past. Having established the constitutional supremacy of the 'British Legislature' in the opening pages of the pamphlet, Macpherson's first historical reference is to Rome. Macpherson outlines his argument against the American's position on tax by stating that 'The truth is, Representation never accompanied Taxation in any State.'[179] This is immediately placed in a narrative of the past in which the classical age is used as a point of comparison: 'The Romans were a free nation; yet the

Senate, that is, the great body of the Nobility, possessed the sole right of taxing the people.'[180] Here, Macpherson's use of an ancient past, at the very beginning of the text, establishes his credentials as an Enlightenment historian – as Pocock argues, much history writing of this period was neoclassical in its adherence to ancient historians' focus on narrating the past through the 'exemplary deeds' of great men but, here, Macpherson uses this Roman historical allusion to explain and justify the politics of the present.[181] Macpherson builds his argument about the powers of the state to raise taxation by translating this narrative of the past into an account of the medieval evolution of the English state. The position of parts of Northern England are compared to the Thirteen Colonies: 'The Counties Palatine of Chester, Durham, and Lancaster, were anciently in the same predicament with the Americans, on the article of Taxation.'[182] These areas of Northern England had considerable authority and agency over matters of law and justice:

> 'though, in short, they possessed exclusively the whole internal Government of their several Counties, their SUBJECTS (if the expression may be used were "always bound by the Acts and Statutes" of an Assembly, in which they had no Representation. They were also "liable to all payments, rates and subsidies, granted by the Parliament of England."'[183]

Macpherson argues that the Americans should have followed the historical example of those in the north of England who then sought to gain parliamentary representation, presenting their grievances through petition. Macpherson refers specifically to the examples of Chester during the reign of Henry VIII and Durham during the reign of Charles II, both of whom gained representation through this mode of peaceful petition. This, Macpherson maintained, should have been the approach of Congress.[184] In his use of historical precedent from a medieval and early modern past, Macpherson makes reference to a startlingly modern claim – that the constitutional modernity of the British state, stemming from the revolution of 1688, was, in fact, rooted in the older idea of the 'ancient constitution', stretching back to Magna Carta, and a key tenet of radical English political claims during the eighteenth century.[185]

Macpherson's use of narratives of the past continues into his account of recent history and how that demonstrated the invalidity of the American cause. The Seven Years War against the French (1756–1763) had been an extraordinarily complex and expensive global conflict. While ultimately resulting in British victory, the extent of British imperial gains and new responsibilities was interpreted by many as a turn towards authoritarianism and absolutism. As Linda Colley astutely observes, the British were 'perplexed by the problem of having acquired too much power too quickly over too many people'.[186] Macpherson argues against the prevailing wisdom, echoed by Congress, that, having defeated the French, the Americans were now compelled to pay for their own defence. Detailing the extensive reimbursements paid to the Americans, Macpherson demonstrates the flow of money to the colonies during the conflict in a lengthy footnote, stretching over three pages.[187] Macpherson's narrative of the recent past is then applied to his analysis of how American hostility to Britain grew as a result of victory in the Seven Years War: 'But their habitual fears from France were, it seems, removed only to give room to their ingratitude to Great Britain.'[188] In making a case against the Americans in 1775, Macpherson is writing as an historian, focusing on the Seven Years War in the early sections of his pamphlet in creating a narrative of the past to underpin his argument in the present.

Macpherson further uses his skills as an historian to undermine American support for William Pitt and his pro-American parliamentary opposition in the 1770s. Drawing on a narrative of Pitt's actions during the 1760s, Macpherson demonstrates that the Americans' current great champion had in fact acted against their interests until very recently. Macpherson accuses the Americans of historical amnesia, forgetting that Pitt had been a supporter of the Declaratory Act of 1766, which made the colonies '"subordinate to and dependent upon the Imperial Crown and PARLIAMENT OF GREAT BRITAIN"'.[189] Yet the Americans, a decade later, now saw Pitt as the great supporter of their political claims. Macpherson the historian has no patience for this: 'THAT Party and THAT MAN [Pitt], being now in opposition to Government, the Americans endeavour to secure their support, by flattering their vanity at the expense of truth.' For Macpherson, the Americans' argument falls down because they present a narrative which fails to take the past into account.

In turn, Macpherson counters their claims by calling upon the example and narrative of the past to demonstrate the long-standing precedent of parliamentary intervention in America: 'Instances of this interposition, in both cases, present themselves, in almost every volume of the Statutes, from the Restoration down to the present reign.'[190] Macpherson presents this as a self-consciously historical narration, arguing that 'A brief recital of some of those instances may throw light on a subject, rendered obscure and perplexed by the prejudices of the ignorant, and the arts of designing men.'[191] This narrative revealed, for Macpherson, that the Whigs, the party which the Americans now supported in the 1770s had, in fact, been the architects of many of their political complaints in the past:

> To gain the ears of the Populace, by awakening their ancient jealousies, the Americans affect to ascribe the present system of measures to principles of Toryism, which, they pretend, prevail in our Councils. But, unfortunately for this part of their plan of deception, it will appear, that most of the Acts, which bind America in coercive regulations, were passed soon after the Revolution; in the reign of the very Prince, who brought about that great event. The WHIG Ministers of King William (perceiving that the Colonies, even then, had entertained views of placing themselves on a ground of independence on Parliament) advised their Sovereign, and their advice now stands on record, to pursue measures, which, in their consequence, should effectually secure their thorough dependent on the Legislature of this Kingdom.[192]

Macpherson's narrative of the past is clear: it is not just that there was a long-standing convention of parliamentary intervention in the colonies, but that this had been pursued eagerly by the very party which now claimed to support the cause of the Americans in the 1770s.

Macpherson then extends this narrative into the eighteenth century in sections exploring parliamentary control of the colonies through trade, fisheries and justice. The authority of Parliament 'was never disputed' at that time, only becoming a grievance for the Americans later in the century, long after, according to Macpherson, 'The same principles, and the same policy, were carried down by Parliament through the three succeeding reigns of Queen Anne, and of George I. and George II.'[193] For Macpherson, the Americans' argument that Parliament had overstepped its authority in the colonies collapsed precisely because the evidence of the past demonstrated that Parliament had always acted in this way. Macpherson's historical narrative drives his analysis – as he moves through an account of the eighteenth century, he builds his argument against the Americans: 'In the reign of George II. the instances of the controuling authority of Parliament over the Colonies, are numerous and striking.'[194]

The key complaint of the Americans – taxation without representation – is also placed in the context of Macpherson's historical narrative. Once again, Macpherson constructs his argument against the Americans from the evidence of the past to demonstrate 'that the controlling power of Parliament had been perpetually exerted, and never disputed'.[195] Macpherson establishes that, from the seventeenth century onwards, taxation had been raised in the colonies. The first example he provides is from the reign of Charles II, the Act of Tonnage and Poundage in 1660, which explicitly included the colonies: 'the duties abovementioned "shall be payable upon commodities not only imported into the realm of England, but also into the DOMINIONS THEREUNTO BELONGING."'[196] It was the power of historical precedent, narrated here by Macpherson, which gave Parliament authority over the Thirteen Colonies in 1775:

> It appears from this detail of facts, that the right of Parliament to bind the Colonies, in all cases whatsoever, is not a claim founded on mere theory: on the contrary, that the controlling power of the Legislature is warranted by constant usage, and uninterrupted practice. That the Declaratory Act, of which the Americans complain, contains no new, no assumed powers over the Plantations; and that there is scarce any channel of Legislation, through which the British Parliament has NOT exerted its supremacy, in as full and ample a manner as it has been exerted over the inhabitants of Great-Britain; and all this prior to the present reign, in which the Congress place the commencement of 'Public Ruin'.[197]

Macpherson's use of the past to argue against the Americans in the present reaches into his conclusion, where he compares the colonists to the authoritarian monarchs of the Stuart dynasty: 'the haughty Monarch who dreamt of universal monarch in the last century, could scarcely have expressed himself in more insolent terms to the petty Princes surrounding his dominions, than the Congress have done to the powerful Empire to which they owe the allegiance of subjects'.[198] While this is not quite the zinger which Macpherson thought it was, given some Americans' admiration for Stuart absolutism, the use of historical analogy and the creation of an historical narrative, in which the British state is seen to follow Whig constitutional principles established following the overthrow of the Stuart dynasty, demonstrates Macpherson's commitment to writing as an historian, even when discussing the machinations of contemporary politics.[199]

A SHORT HISTORY OF THE OPPOSITION DURING THE LAST SESSION OF PARLIAMENT (1779)

James Macpherson's final attributable publication was also his shortest. Amounting to a mere fifty-eight pages (fewer pages, even, than *The Fragments* of 1760), *A Short History of the Opposition During the Last Session of Parliament* was published anonymously at the beginning of July 1779.[200] Running to four editions by the end of the following month, the pamphlet was 'well received' and was attributed by some to Gibbon, Macpherson's fellow historian-cum-politician.[201] However, when this rumour reached Gibbon himself, he dismissed the text as 'the little foundling which so many friends or enemies chose to lay at my door' and that '*all* the faults or merits of the History of the Opposition must, as I am informed, be imputed to Macpherson, the Author or translator of Fingal'.[202] Like *The Rights of Great Britain* four years earlier, Macpherson's pamphlet was no piece of ephemeral political fluff. As with his full-length history of the East India Company from the same year, *A Short History* marked the culmination of the final phase of Macpherson's career as an historian. Intended primarily as a piece of political propaganda, Macpherson used the techniques of Enlightenment history writing that he had honed in *An Introduction to the History of Great Britain and Ireland* (1771) and *The History of Great Britain* (1775) and applied them to make claims in the present. As he does in *The Rights of Great Britain* and *The History and Management*, Macpherson writes as an historian about the crisis of empire during the 1770s, using key Enlightenment techniques to make an argument about the need to defend Britain's hold on the Thirteen Colonies. As such, *A Short History* is very much a companion piece to *The Rights of Great Britain*, especially in Macpherson's use of a narrative of the past to demonstrate his case against the opposition in Parliament.[203] Just like the Americans, the opposition were cast by Macpherson as being outwith history and that the only true narrators of the past – who, therefore, had a history to write about – were the British imperial state and its supporters. Once again, in his argument about who can write history and who has *a* history, we see Macpherson engaging with ideas similar to William Robertson's on America (also written in the late 1770s) and pre-empting the colonial framing of Hegel and others, identified by Ranajit Guha.[204] History writing itself becomes political, in this context, where Macpherson uses it to mark the boundaries of belonging to the nation and empire.[205] In this section, we see Macpherson using familiar approaches to history writing – engaging with concepts of 'truth' and 'facts', using primary sources as evidence and as a means of creating a narrative of the past that is analytical, reflecting on the recent constitutional history of the British imperial state, and using the past to make political points in the present – but, in *A Short History*, he uses them to narrate and historicise the (very) immediate past of the imperial crisis of the late 1770s. The title of the pamphlet is important: *A Short History* carries different connotations than, say, *Report of the Opposition During the Last Session of Parliament*, or

Account, or *Narration*. As examined above, 'history' was resonant of authenticity, truth, causation and sources to an Enlightenment audience. This is a conscious rhetorical tool, but it also emphasises the fact that Macpherson's mind is never far from the past, and that – particularly post-*The History of Great Britain* – he thinks, acts and writes explicitly as an historian, no matter the subject.

Macpherson's *Short History* provides an account of the Whig opposition during the 1778–9 parliamentary session. It focuses on Whig criticism of the government's conduct of the revolutionary war in America, at a time when the war was beginning to turn in the colonists' favour and France and Spain had entered the conflict on the side of the Americans.[206] Macpherson's purpose in writing this pamphlet was to deflect criticism from Lord North – his employer – and blame the disasters of the war on the opposition's encouragement of dissent in the colonies and at home, in Parliament. Lord North was appreciative of Macpherson's efforts, writing to George III in 1782 that *A Short History* was 'the best defence of the American war, and almost all the pamphlets on the side of the Administration were the productions of his pen'.[207] *A Short History* has received little critical attention as a text, and has so far been examined as an example of opposition politics in the period (by historians) and to further illustrate Macpherson's politics and explain Ossian (by literary scholars).[208] While Robert W. Jones's recent chapter on Macpherson's historical writing includes a brief assessment of this pamphlet, it does so in terms of Macpherson's approach to the 'history of opposition' and its threat to Great Britain: according to Jones, in *A Short History*, 'opposition to the Crown appears dangerous and, moreover, inimical to the fabric of the nation' and the crisis of empire is presented in terms of Ossianic defeat.[209] However, as this section demonstrates, it is more fruitful to place Macpherson's final publication in the context of his recent career as an historian and to see *A Short History* as part of Macpherson's continuing process of applying the principles of Enlightenment history writing to the intrigues of contemporary Georgian imperial politics.

From the very outset of *A Short History*, Macpherson emphasises the centrality of 'truth' and 'facts' to his argument against the opposition. Like the *Original Papers*, the *Short History* begins with an 'Advertisement', which functions similarly to the preface in *The History of Great Britain*. However, while the preface outlines Macpherson's historiographical procedure – his sources, what he is doing with them, and his intentions – the advertisement that precedes the text of the *Short History* is all about the author's reasons for writing the pamphlet. While we might not want to take these at face value and any discussion of

Macpherson's intentions would necessarily need to engage with the extent to which such a publication is mere political opportunism, it is worth taking this advertisement seriously as a piece of history writing: in it, we see Macpherson tapping into the same historiographical mode as in other, less political publications. The advertisement consists of three paragraphs that explore, respectively, the notion that writing a pamphlet such as this is a 'public service', patriotic, and a matter of 'public safety'. This does not seem particularly historiographical, but its implication is that the pamphlet is designed to 'contribute to throw light' by 'advanc[ing] facts' like all Enlightenment history writing. While we can question the extent to which the pamphlet achieves that, or dismiss it as biased political hackwork, the way it is framed is historiographical. And, in addition, Macpherson sets out the purpose of the pamphlet as contributing to the effort to 'extricate us, from our present situation' – that is, to use knowledge to change the future.[210] This is one of the key Enlightenment purposes of history writing: to learn from the past, and in the advertisement, we see Macpherson use the same rhetoric effectively. While the *Short History* may well be considered contrary to Enlightenment historiographical theory – especially in its one-sided and politically biased nature – its argument is, essentially, historiographical. Whether or not it is a convincing pamphlet is another matter, but the methodology of the advertisement is consistent with the pamphlet's titular claim of being a history.

In the advertisement for the pamphlet, Macpherson makes clear that the greatest threat to Britain was an 'enemy within' – 'That the most formidable foes of Great Britain were nursed in her own bosom.'[211] Here, Macpherson outlines two objectives necessary for continuing British prosperity: 'These are, the knowledge of our friends from our enemies; and that spirited exertion, which alone can extricate us from our present situation.' For Macpherson, the way to do this was to use a key historians' technique – appealing to evidence. Macpherson argued 'If the facts advanced, and encouragements exhibited, in the following Essay, shall contribute to throw light on the one, or to add vigour to the other, the Writer has attained his purpose.'[212] The truth of Macpherson's case, as we have seen in his other history and political writing, would be established by the strength of the evidence. Macpherson's case against the opposition hinged on the argument that they did not use evidence in the same way. In explaining the opposition's political factionalism, Macpherson argues that they were prone to this because they were incapable of basing their arguments in facts: 'But what the party could not effect by facts and arguments, they endeavoured to accomplish by address and intrigue.'[213] According to Macpherson's logic, the 'assertions' of these 'Lazy Whigs' were invalid because they were not based on evidence.[214] In examining the debate about Admiral Augustus Keppel's encounter with the French fleet near Brest in 1778, Macpherson dismissed the opposition's claim that the Navy were inadequately supplied with ships: 'That, therefore, as the premises, endeavoured to be established by Opposition, were not founded in fact, their conclusions must of course fall to the ground.'[215] Referring to the British Army's withdrawal from Philadelphia in 1778, Macpherson argued that the opposition stuck to their previous account based on an overestimation of the Americans' military prowess:

> Though these facts came forward with a force which commanded conviction, the faction adhere, with invincible obstinacy, to the line of their former conduct. With their usual insult upon the common feelings and common sense of mankind, they established false premises; and deduced, from these premises, arguments for the total dereliction, and consequently for the independence, of America.[216]

The oppositions' 'assertions' were then, according to Macpherson, believed by the people: that 'The grim tyrant, Arbitrary Power, had taken up arms against that innocent little child, American Liberty.'[217] Such arguments, ignoring Macpherson's narrative of the 'facts', were the basis of the opposition's 'unmanly oratory', demonstrating how Macpherson's conception of the past (and, therefore, of history writing and historians) was framed by certain notions of British patriotic masculinity, linked to the kinds of ideas Macpherson and others promoted about the liberty and freedom of the Williamite constitution.[218]

For Macpherson, the 'truth' was established by one of the central techniques of Enlightenment history writing – narrating the events of the past. As Macpherson moves towards the conclusion of his examination of the opposition's 'political assassination' of the loyal government, he argues that 'The stamp of truth has been affixed to the representation contained in this Essay, by the most incontrovertible of all arguments, the events of the times: events unparalleled in the history of any other age or country.'[219] Truth was established by a narrative of events, a key writing strategy that Macpherson returns to time and again throughout *A Short History*. One of the principal narratives that Macpherson emphasises in this pamphlet was an account of the rise of the idea of opposition. This Macpherson dates to the end of the previous century. In accounting for the emergence of party and faction, Macpherson provides us with an historical narrative that begins with 'The Revolution, which happened about ninety years ago.'[220] For Macpherson, the 'balance of influence between the Crown and the People' meant that faction was absent for much of the eighteenth century: 'No distinction was made, in this respect, between *Whig* and *Tory*.'[221] From the 'present reign' of George III, faction developed through the growth of royal preferment. Macpherson's narrative concludes that this led to the emergence of party and faction: 'but through this liberal conduct might have pleased the unprejudiced, it was incapable of extinguishing party among the interested. These, though of different principles and characters, by imposing on the weak and credulous, formed new factions on the shadows of departed political tenets.'[222] Here, Macpherson uses a narrative of the past to explain the present political situation. This strategy continues in Macpherson's analysis of the opposition during the 'last session' of parliament – the principle aim of the pamphlet. Macpherson sought to establish the 'strange positions' of faction 'on incontestable authorities, by a plain narrative of the conduct of Opposition since the commencement of the present parliament'.[223] For Macpherson, narrative led to explanation, echoing the approach to history writing taken by his great mentor, Hugh Blair. For Blair, narrating the past could take on instructional and philosophical virtues and here we see Macpherson adopting a similar historiographical technique, providing a narrative of events in order to make his argument against the opposition.[224]

Macpherson's analytical narrative continues into the heart of the pamphlet, where he delves into the inquiry instigated to investigate some of the opposition's allegations about the misconduct of the American war. Here, Macpherson provides evidence against these claims in a narrative of events. Instead of following the opposition's critique of government conduct, Macpherson focuses on demonstrating the skill of the British soldiers – 'That, upon all occasions, the British troops executed their duty, with energy, bravery, and effect.'[225] This narrative of evidence allows Macpherson to build his argument: 'The inferences deducible from these facts, were, that the British army were either unskilfully or languidly led.'[226] By placing evidence in a narrative sequence, Macpherson was then able to explain why the American war was going so badly, in five pages establishing the conclusion that bad management in America had led to revolution: 'In the course of the evidence taken at home, and more especially by the most authentic information from abroad, it has appeared, that the injudicious and inactive management of the war has been the sole obstacle to the restoration of peace.'[27] In so doing, we see Macpherson at the top of his Enlightenment historiographical game, skilfully using narrative itself as a philosophical tool of explanation.

The nature of the evidence which Macpherson uses for this narrative explanation of the past once more demonstrates his operation as an

Enlightenment historian. Macpherson deploys a range of primary source material, from speeches in Parliament to the Earl of Clarendon's autobiographical writings, using footnotes to demonstrate (and authenticate) the provenance of his sources.[228]

While not as liberally sprinkled with quotation from sources or footnotes as some of his other history writing, *A Short History* still relies on this scholarly apparatus to make a case against the opposition. Macpherson's evidence comprises both published and unpublished material. The pamphlet's final footnote demonstrates this, mixing archival letters from Lord Torrington with official printed documents such as the *Journal of the House of Commons*.[229] As in *The History and Management*, however, Macpherson builds much of his argument from the weight of evidence contained in the 'official' record. In establishing that Admiral Keppel had been well supplied by the British government in his battles against the French during 1777–8, Macpherson explicitly counters the claims of Keppel's Whig supporters with an appeal to this kind of evidence: 'In opposition to these assertions, it was proved, from official documents, That, in November 1777, there were actually thirty-five ships of the line ready for service.'[230]

Much of Macpherson's evidence, then, comes from material like this, with an emphasis on speeches and proceedings of Parliament – unsurprising, given that this pamphlet is an examination of recent political events that focus on parliamentary opposition. Macpherson begins his account of 'the last session' with a quotation from the King's opening of parliament.[231] The argument against the opposition is then built from the evidence of these 'orators in the Lower House', where Macpherson quotes the speeches of leading Whigs, such as Charles Fox, at length.[232] The footnotes referencing these speeches are often quite precise, referring to 'Speech of C. F-x, Nov. 26. 1778.' or 'Governor J-st-ne's Speech, Nov. 26. 1778.' but sometimes evidence is vaguely footnoted as 'Speeches of all the Opposition'.[233] At the heart of Macpherson's case against the opposition lay the evidence of Major General James Robertson, the British commandant in New York, given to a Parliamentary inquiry in 1779 into the causes of the American war. In making his argument that it was poor British leadership in America that led to colonial disaster, Macpherson uses extensive quotation from Robertson's evidence and references the House of Commons proceedings in his footnotes.[234]

Macpherson also demonstrates his engagement with the cutting edge of Enlightenment historiography by again using one of Gibbon's techniques – the use of the caustic and sarcastic footnote. Focusing once more on the trial of Admiral Keppel, Macpherson includes two footnotes that demonstrate this kind of rhetorical flourish. Referring to General Burgoyne's defence of Keppel and their shared position that the military command of the British forces was not to blame for the conduct of the war, Macpherson comments on the lack of Whig support for the pair during their public trials, remarking that 'all the attention scarce amounted to one "dolorous anhelation" from the feeling bosom of Mr E—d B–ke'.[235] The footnote reveals the rather startling source of this quotation – Macpherson's very own nemesis, Samuel Johnson.[236] In an ironic deployment of his old enemy's words, Macpherson criticises Edmund Burke (himself an ally of Johnson who, as we've seen above, clashed with Macpherson on India) for the lack of support for his fellow Whigs. At the end of the section dealing with Whig support for Admiral Keppel, Macpherson again resorts to a sarcastic aside in a footnote. Macpherson comments that the Admiral's trial had deflated the Whig's position, leading to some of the opposition retreating from public life: 'A few orators are said to have actually retired, to vent the tropes of unfinished speeches to the "echo of trees and murmur of rills" on some friend's estate.'[237] Macpherson provides a mocking footnote for such poetic political rehearsals, commenting that 'A certain Baronet, who in a fit if despair relative to the good *Old Cause* has lately become a zealous *Whig*, is much given to such solitary *rehearsals* of the speech which he intends to *fire off* upon the House.'[38] Just like Gibbon, Macpherson makes use of the footnote aside to score points against his political opponents.

At the very heart of Macpherson's case against the opposition was his conceptualisation of the imperial nature of the British constitution. This was framed in *A Short History* by a distinctive narrative of constitutional history which emphasised the 'balance' of a 'mixed' constitution, where power was split between monarch, Lords and Commons, just as we have seen above in *The Rights of Great Britain*.[239] On the very first page of the pamphlet, Macpherson establishes this as his historical and constitutional frame of reference:

> In despotic monarchies, the favour of the Prince, who is the fountain of all preferment, is generally procured by intrigue or address. In republics, influence and authority are acquired, by gaining the confidence, or by seducing the principles, of the People; and, in mixed governments, like that of Great Britain, the nearest road to power lies between those two extremes.[240]

Macpherson immediately places this in the context of history. Here, he provides a clear narrative of constitutional progress that sprang from the Williamite revolution of 1688: 'The Revolution, which happened about ninety years ago, though it made but few changes in the forms of authority, established a balance of influence between the Crown and the People.'[241] While the 'Glorious Revolution' was key to Macpherson's understanding of British constitutional evolution, what is interesting in this passage is his argument about the longer-standing nature of this political position and structure. Macpherson appears to be articulating a form of 'ancient constitutionalism' – the argument that the constitutional settlement of the late seventeenth century was simply the restatement of older forms of political rights, the 'freeborn Englishman' that could be found at the heart of much eighteenth-century political thought. Here, there is no suggestion of the 'Celtic Whiggism' identified by Kidd and Moore in some of Macpherson's earlier work. Instead, these Whig ideas are framed by a decidedly imperial context.[242] Just as we saw in *The Rights of Great Britain*, Macpherson argues that the British constitution is an imperial one, where the opposition's 'intemperate joy of faction' renders it (and their American friends) unpatriotic.[243] Such actions and ideas were disloyal to the British state precisely because they were unconstitutional: 'It was perceived, that they meant to sacrifice Great Britain, her rights, her interests, and even honour, to the demagogues of America by rendering her independent of the parent from whom she sprung'.[244] As we have seen in *The Rights of Great Britain*, the very idea of American independence was constitutionally impossible, given the imperial nature of the British state and, here, at the end of the 1770s, Macpherson reiterates this key political point. For Macpherson, any support for the American cause undermined the entire constitutional settlement of the British imperial state, 'perhaps kindling a rebellion in Ireland' and feeding the kind of 'emulative patriotisms' that Kidd identifies as underpinning American and Irish threats to empire during this period.[245]

The *Short History* also makes an interesting contribution to our discussion of British identity. As we have seen in *The Highlander*, Macpherson always had his eye on union; the hermit's prophecy culminates in the Unionist prediction that sees 'Scot and Saxon coalesc'd in one', supporting one crown, and one empire, sovereign 'o'er the trembling nations'. Twenty years later, in the *Short History*, we can see a sophisticated confirmation of Macpherson's earlier assured Britishness; where union was a prediction for the future in the tenth-century present of *The Highlander*, in the *Short History* it is the British imperial state, and British patriotism in the face of American revolt, that underscores Macpherson's argument. Here, Great Britain is at once the wronged motherland and a signifier of patriotism: a place and an identity. 'Great Britain' is the entity against which the colonies are rebelling, and 'British' is the mindset that will conquer this. Macpherson argues that the 'perfidy of France' and the 'obstinacy of America' threaten Britain's 'very existence' and, in expected government manner, Britain is described as the 'parent and benefactress' of America.[246] Just as the union between 'Scot and Saxon' was the foundation for British success in *The Highlander*, the *Short History* requires British union – at home, and in the empire. Without America Britain is incomplete; its primary identity of victorious naval power cannot abide separation.[247] Indeed, naval successes and losses occupy much of the middle section of the *Short History*, linked to another staple of British identity, 'commerce'.[248] This is joined, in the concluding remarks of the *Short History*, with an appeal to the patriotic 'spirit becoming Britons' – unanimity, vigour, and exertion' – evident throughout the 'whole kingdom'; a spirit that, nurtured in the mother-and, will soon 'diffuse itself through both the British isles', and into the empire beyond.[249]

Running through Macpherson's defence of the imperial constitution lies an understanding of the past. It is not just constitutional history that Macpherson draws upon here. In making his argument against the opposition and the Americans, Macpherson appeals to the example of the past. By the end of this short pamphlet, Macpherson creates a narrative of the past, referring to his own history writing in *The History of Great Britain* to make the argument that the British state had survived turmoil in the past and would, he was certain, overcome the current crisis of empire in the Thirteen Colonies. Macpherson's use of the past becomes almost an exercise in imperial nostalgia. Macpherson does not quite summon the 'Blitz spirit' of twenty-first-century crises such as Brexit, and neither does he echo Jim Callaghan's 'Crisis? What crisis?' response to the so-called 'winter of discontent' of the late 1970s. Rather, we see here an example of an early form of history writing as consolation – that the example of the past provides an indicator of how the current imperial catastrophe of the 1770s could be overcome. As Peter Mitchell argues in his recent book *Imperial Nostalgia: How the British Conquered Themselves* (2021), 'We escape the trauma of the history we happen to be living through be entering the mythic time of the history we didn't' and Macpherson's historical narrative of the seventeenth century fulfils that role at the end of the eighteenth.[250]

Macphers's takes the reader of *A Short History* on a trip down memory lane from the very outset of the pamphlet, establishing his history writing as an act of patriotism that contrasts with the ahistorical nature of the opposition's argument against the American war. The work's advertisement establishes this on the very first page, where Macpherson outlines the severity of this particular imperial crisis: 'Every individual possesses a power which can aid and support his country. He can draw his sword in her defence; contribute to her resources; or combat with argument, and expose to just indignation, those who have proved themselves her internal, and consequently her unnatural enemies.'[251] While flinging his opposition enemies into the unconstitutional outer darkness, Macpherson justifies his position as a patriot, using his role as government spin doctor to serve the nation. Of course, as we have argued throughout this book, by this stage in his career, Macpherson was writing as an historian, regardless of genre or purpose. Related to the ideas of Hume and Kant, Macpherson saw history writing as key to nation building and, here, Macpherson believed it to be his patriotic duty to use the past to defend Britain's position in the American war.[252] As Priya Satia argues, writing about the past became a key technique of defending the present, especially in the context of late eighteenth-century colonialism: 'The historical imagination became essential to the modernity of the modern period.'[253] Throughout *A Short History*, Macpherson compares the last session in parliament to the past, using the idea of 'history' to distinguish the present and make sense of it. Here, Macpherson emphasises the exceptional nature of the current crisis, using comparison with the past to demonstrate how the circumstances of the American war were unprecedented. From the beginning of his narrative of the 'present parliament', Macpherson claims the peculiarity of the present. Remarking on how the King's speech at the opening urged 'unanimity' in British political culture, Macpherson argues that 'surely no period in history more required the unanimous exertion of the whole nation'.[254] Towards the pamphlet's conclusion, Macpherson makes a similar claim. The case against the opposition had been made using 'the most uncontrovertible of all arguments, the events of the times: events unparalleled in the history of any other age or country'.[255] Here, Macpherson uses the past to claim the uniqueness of the present – that there weren't any historical parallels to the situation currently experienced by Britain and its empire.

Being outwith history then becomes a key argument made against the claims of the opposition. Macpherson outlines the arguments made by the opposition about the American war at the outset of the pamphlet, which 'traced the cause of that war to the pretended tyranny of Great Britain'.[256] In suggesting that the American revolutionaries were 'peaceable fellow-subjects' the opposition were making an argument 'unknown in any other times' – without the evidence of historical precedent, their defence of the Americans was invalid.[257] The very fact that Macpherson is unable to find historical examples of similar political conduct damns the opposition. In his account of the trial of Admiral Keppel, Macpherson briefly narrates the opposition's conduct and condemns their 'unjustifiable tricks of faction, as can scarcely be paralleled by any example in history'.[258] The opposition were, therefore, outwith history and therefore without political justification in the present – just as Macpherson deemed the Americans in *The Rights of Great Britain*.

Of course, Macpherson identified the state itself (and therefore its conduct in the American war) with his celebration of a glorious British past. The final six pages of the pamphlet focus on narrating the past in order to demonstrate the resilience of Britain in the present. Having established the 'unprecedented' nature of the crisis (or, rather, the Americans' and their opposition friends' reaction to it), Macpherson then claims that Britain had been through far worse and survived: 'This country, with much smaller resources, and much less unanimity, has repeatedly weathered more dreadful storms than that which only seems to threaten it at present.'[259] In particular, Macpherson finds nostalgic consolation in the second half of the seventeenth century, with a focus on the Second Anglo-Dutch War of 1665–7 and the Great Fire of London and plague of the same period. This is no surprise, given that this era was the subject of Macpherson's substantial *History of Great Britain*, written just four years earlier than *A Short History*. Indeed, there is a strong element of intertextuality at play here, where Macpherson borrows the historical narrative and the phrasing from his earlier work. In *A Short History*, Macpherson describes the fire and the plague as 'two of the most dreadful calamities that can afflict a people', in which 'Near eighty thousand persons had been carried off by the first, in London alone.' 'The city had become a kind of desert; and grass was observed to grow in the middle of Cheapside.' Virtually the same description of these events appears in the earlier *History of Great Britain* – as Macpherson reached for the concluding rhetorical flourish of his case against the opposition, he reached for his own history writing.[260] Similarly, when describing the fire of 1666, Macpherson copies his own narrative of events: the fire 'consumed fifteen out of the twenty-six wards of the city, consisting of four hundred streets and lanes, thirteen thousand houses, and eighty-nine parish-churches'.[261] However, in footnoting this passage in his later publication, Macpherson changes the source that is referenced – from 'James II. 1666' in the 1775 *History of Great Britain*, to '*Vide* Clarendon, Heath, Burnet' in 1779. This is most likely a slip of the pen – when referring to 'James II. 1666' (probably the James II papers which Macpherson consults at the Scots College in Paris), this is on a page where all the other references are to the works by Clarendon, Heath and Burnet.[262] The effect of all this reflection on earlier catastrophes is to make clear that things are not so bad now – that the imperial crisis of the 1770s was certainly a challenge, but not insurmountable. Macpherson rightly points out that the power and wealth of the British imperial state had grown significantly in the last century or so: 'In the present times, our resources are much greater, our spirit equal, and our danger less, than at either of those periods. We have an ample revenue, an untainted credit, a great and a growing navy.'[263] This is then once more explicitly linked to ideas about the peculiarly British constitutional notions that lay at the heart of this imperial crisis: 'Our nobility and gentry, with a spirit becoming Britons, either serve in our constitutional defence, the militia, or with their influence and purses exert themselves in raising new corps.'[264] The idea of a commercial society defending itself through a citizen militia lay at the heart of debates about 'English' liberty and the 'ancient constitution' during this period – and had, of course, inspired Macpherson's own early forays into history writing in *The Highlander* and the Ossianic Collections.[265] It is no surprise, then, to see Macpherson linking this more positive assessment of the British imperial state's fortunes to two final examples of 'pluck' in the face of adversity. On the pamphlet's penultimate page, Macpherson advocates the need to 'reflect on the glory of former times'. The example he refers to is Agincourt – a particularly English myth of defeating a foreign enemy against the odds and predicated on the liberties and freedoms of the yeoman archers. The historical precedent of beating the French in battle served to stiffen the sinews of the British state in their current war with French-supported Americans: 'The posterity of those who conquered at Poitiers, Cressy, and Agincourt, and annexed France itself to the English crown, cannot form to themselves any fear from a French invasion.'[266]

Macpherson's final historical allusion and analogy borrows a technique familiar to Enlightenment historians. Here, on the final page of *A Short History*, he compares the imperial crisis of the present to the challenges faced by the Roman empire: 'The Romans themselves were not always invincible. They frequently lost provinces and armies; yet they rose superior to all nations.'[267] Here, Macpherson is making a deliberate reference to the key work of history writing from the second half of the 1770s: Edward Gibbon's six-volume *The History of the Decline and Fall of the Roman Empire*, the first volume of which appeared in 1776. Gibbon's work, like Macpherson's, was all about the revival of empire and securing it for the future. As Priya Satia argues, Gibbon 'strove to moralize for the present through an account of the past'. By analysing the example of the Roman past, the British Empire could avoid the 'pitfalls in their own imperial story' and 'the British Empire might succeed where Rome failed'.[268] In echoing Gibbon's ideas Macpherson was also demonstrating his mastery of the techniques of Enlightenment history writing and, also like Gibbon, using his approach to writing about the past to make arguments about the imperial crisis of the 1770s. As we remember from *The Highlander*, the British Empire would not befall the same fate as Rome but would 'shall shake no more with native storms, / But o'er the trembling nations lift her arms'.[269]

CONCLUSION

A Short History of the Opposition was Macpherson's final publication, in which he ended his literary career as he began it – writing as an historian. While the political motivations of the three texts examined in this chapter were paramount, the method by which Macpherson wrote about these crises of empire was firmly that of an Enlightenment man of letters. The content and purpose of Macpherson's writing may well have been to advocate for his patrons at home and abroad (Lord North and the Nawab of Arcot, respectively) in the colonial contexts of America and India, but the form taken by these books and pamphlets was history writing. Subsequently, the politics of empire in America and, increasingly, India came to dominate Macpherson's working life. In 1780, Macpherson was elected as Member of Parliament for Camelford, in Cornwall, becoming the 'senior member' of that constituency for the rest of his life following William Pitt's victory in the general election of 1784.[270] Macpherson continued to function as the Nawab of Arcot's agent, during a period in which India remained central to British politics, with Pitt's India Act of 1784 introducing significant reform and greater government control of the East India Company.[271] While not directly involved in public debate, James kept busy orchestrating the government's relationship with and response to the press. Macpherson had put down his own pen and was now behind the scenes, pulling the strings – the proverbial poacher turned gamekeeper.[272] When his great friend and collaborator, Sir John Macpherson, became the Governor-General of Bengal in 1785, it marked the culmination of a career dedicated to the political advancement of himself and Sir John.[273] A minister's son from Skye (John) and a tacksman's son from Badenoch (James) had risen to the top of the British imperial state.

While the politics of empire occupied most of Macpherson's time during the 1780s, there was one final twist to Macpherson's literary career in 1782 and 1783. As debate about reforming the EIC heated up, James decided to publish a new edition of *History and Management* in 1782.[274] Macpherson was then approached in 1783 by a number of Highland gentlemen to produce 'the original Gaelic manuscripts that he had collected for *The Poems of Ossian*.[275] Despite the sweetener of a thousand pounds, raised by Highlanders serving in the EIC, and the efforts of John Mackenzie, friend and secretary of the Highland Society of London, Macpherson struggled to find the time or inclination to return to his literary origins.[276] While Macpherson had physically moved to the Highlands during the 1780s, living during the winter months at his Badenoch estate of Belleville (now Balavil), his efforts to revisit the poetry of Gaeldom were unsuccessful.[277] There is a certain irony that, in becoming fully an Enlightenment historian in his later works, Macpherson found it hard to go back to where his history writing started – in the poetry of *The Highlander* and Ossian. Perhaps this tells us more about how history writing and empire had changed since the 1760s than it does about Macpherson himself. By the 1780s, Macpherson's conception of the past and how to write about it had evolved, in tune with the broader development of Enlightenment history writing at the hands of Hume, Gibbon and others. To unpick that mode of thought, that method of writing about the past was perhaps too much to ask of the man Macpherson had become – the MP, political string-puller and oiler of the wheels of the imperial machine.

Macpherson's history writing was at the heart of the crisis of empire during the 1770s. Given how writing about the past evolved at this time, perhaps it is no surprise that Macpherson becomes a highly developed Enlightenment historian in his work on imperial politics. Here, as we have seen above, Macpherson's approach followed that of both Gibbon and Robertson, whose major works of history in the second half of this decade defined an Enlightenment state of the art. It is important to acknowledge that Macpherson was part of this broader intellectual movement, not just in his use of history writing to promote the project of colonialism, but also in his methodology. Just as Robertson did in his *History of America* and Gibbon in the *Decline and Fall of the Roman Empire*, Macpherson made use of original sources, both print and manuscript, in making his argument about the position of the British imperial state in America and India.[278] Likewise, Macpherson's deployment of scholarly scaffolding such as footnotes bears comparison with the methodology of Gibbon and Robertson.[279] Beyond these methodological concerns, Macpherson was adept at following the emerging 'philosophy' of the new Enlightenment history writing. Building on a way of thinking about the past that he had developed in his history writing from the first half of the 1770s (examined in Chapter 3), Macpherson also demonstrated his ability to combine narrative of the past with an explanation of events, all supported by the erudition of sources and footnotes. But, most importantly, it was through a narrative of British constitutional history in his work on America that Macpherson demonstrated his engagement with the key Enlightenment notion of stadial theory.[280] In this thoroughly imperial narrative, Macpherson used examples from the past to argue that the current British imperial state had evolved through this particular narrative of political freedom and liberty. Anyone defying or not acknowledging this narrative was outwith history. As Pocock argues, 'The history of modern empire thus became that of encounter between European civil society and those excluded from its history.'[281] Macpherson's later political history writing, therefore, marked the culmination of two decades of writing and thinking about the past. And it is important to see this work as a continuation (if a highly evolved one) from his earlier work, rooted in the Highlands. Macpherson, as a Gael, saw himself and his fellow Highlanders as part of the broader political project of the British imperial state, and history writing was key to demonstrating this.

Notes

1. James Macpherson, *The Rights of Great Britain Asserted against the Claims of America: Being an Answer to the Declaration of the General Congress*, 2nd edition (London: T. Cadell, 1775/6), p. 42.
2. See Jack P. Greene, *The Constitutional Origins of the American Revolution* (Cambridge: Cambridge University Press, 2011), pp. 149–86; P. J. Marshall, *The Making and Unmaking of Empires: Britain, India, and America c.1750–1783* (Oxford: Oxford University Press, 2007), pp. 1–2.
3. Richard Connors and Ben Gilding, '"Hereditary Guardians of the Nation": The House of Lords and the East India Company in the Age of the American Revolution', *Parliamentary History*, 39:1 (2020), pp. 159–89; Marshall, *The Making and Unmaking of Empires*, pp. 207–29; Philip J. Stern, 'Seeing (and Not Seeing) Like a Company State: Hybridity, Heterotopia, Historiography', *Journal of Early Modern Cultural Studies*, 17:3 (2017), pp. 105–20.
4. Stafford, *The Sublime Savage*, p. 134.
5. Ibid., p. 181; Rothschild, *The Inner Life of Empires*, p. 39.
6. deGategno, *James Macpherson*, pp. 6–7.
7. Ibid., p. 139. See also Maclean, 'The Early Political Careers'.
8. Quoted in William Dalrymple, *The Anarchy: The Relentless Rise of the East India Company* (London: Bloomsbury, 2019), p. 258.
9. Macpherson, *The Rights of Great Britain*, pp. 33, 34.
10. deGategno, *James Macpherson*, p. 139; Frank O'Gorman, 'The Parliamentary Opposition to the Government's American Policy 1760–1782', in H. T. Dickinson (ed.), *Britain and the American Revolution* (London: Longman, 1998), pp. 97–124; Paul Langford, 'Old Whigs, Old Tories, and the American

Revolution', *Journal of Imperial and Commonwealth History*, 8:2 (1980), pp. 106–30; Solomon Lutnick, *The American Revolution and the British Press 1775–1783* (Columbia: University of Missouri Press, 1967), p. 18.

11 Macpherson's sympathy for Indian culture is similar to that of William Robertson, one of Macpherson's early supporters and part of the shared intellectual milieu of the Scottish Enlightenment. For Robertson's writings on India, see Robertson, *An Historical Disquisition concerning the Knowledge which the Ancients had of India* and Stewart J. Brown, 'William Robertson, Early Orientalism and the *Historical Disquisition* on India of 1791', *Scottish Historical Review*, 88:2 (2009), pp. 289–312.

12 Kidd, *Subverting Scotland's Past*, pp. 219–24; Moore, 'James Macpherson and "Celtic Whiggism"'.

13 Kidd, *Subverting Scotland's Past*, p. 223.

14 Satia, *Time's Monster*, p. 6.

15 George McElroy, 'Ossianic Imagination and the History of India: James and John Macpherson as Propagandists and Intriguers', in Jennifer J. Carter and Joan H. Pittock (eds), *Aberdeen and the Enlightenment* (Aberdeen: Aberdeen University Press, 1987), p. 363.

16 Joanna de Groot, *Empire and History Writing in Britain c. 1750–2012* (Manchester: Manchester University Press, 2013), pp. 65, 69, n.68, p. 95.

17 See, for example, Richard Bourke, *Empire and Revolution: The Political Life of Edmund Burke* (Princeton, NJ: Princeton University Press, 2017), p. 355; and Jack P. Greene, *Evaluating Empire and Confronting Colonialism in Eighteenth-Century Britain* (Cambridge: Cambridge University Press, 2013), pp. 149–50.

18 Greene, *Evaluating Empire*, p. 149.

19 Nicholas B. Dirks, *The Scandal of Empire: India and the Creation of Imperial Britain* (Cambridge, MA: Harvard University Press, 2009), p. 264. See also Phiroze Vasunia, *The Classics and Colonial India* (Oxford: Oxford University Press, 2013), p. 257.

20 Dirks, *The Scandal of Empire*, pp. 264–8. Macpherson's book was directly rebutted by Edmund and William Burke in their pamphlet *An Enquiry into the Policy of Making Conquests for the Mahometans in India, by the British Arms* (London: J. Dodsley, 1779). William Burke was the agent of the Rajah of Tanjore, the sworn enemy of the Nawab of Arcot. See Dirks, *The Scandal of Empire*, p. 269.

21 Davis, 'Transnational Articulations'.

22 Stafford, *The Sublime Savage*, pp. 117, 120; Derick S. Thomson, 'Macpherson, James (1736–1796)', *Oxford Dictionary of National Biography* (Oxford: Oxford University Press, 2004), available at: https://doi.org/10.1093/ref:odnb/17728 (accessed 24 November 2021).

23 For the significant amount of money repatriated by Sir John Macpherson from India to Britain from his time in the EIC, see Mackillop, *Human Capital and Empire*, p. 244.

24 See also Maclean, 'The Early Political Careers'. James used his Indian connections to place many kinsmen and locals from Badenoch in the service of the EIC, including Colonel Allan Macpherson. See Foster, *A Private Empire*, pp. 66–102; and Taylor, *The Wild Black Region*, pp. 205–7.
25 Paul J. deGategno, 'Macpherson, Sir John, First Baronet (*c.* 1745–1821)', *Oxford Dictionary of National Biography* (Oxford: Oxford University Press, 2004), available at: https://doi.org/10.1093/ref:odnb/17730 (accessed 25 November 2021); Davis, 'Transnational Articulations', p. 448.
26 deGategno, *James Macpherson*, p. 9; Davis, 'Transnational Articulations', p. 449.
27 Macpherson, *The History and Management of the East-India Company*, p. 248. For an overview of the political machinations of the Carnatic during the second half of the eighteenth century, see Jim Phillips, 'A Successor to the Moguls: The Nawab of the Carnatic and the East India Company, 1763–1785', *International History Review*, 7:3 (1985), pp. 364–89. For a recent analysis of James Macpherson's work in Indian affairs, see Thomas Archambaud, 'Un clan dans l'Empire: James Macpherson, des Lumières écossaises à l'Inde britannique', *Dix-huitième siècle*, 50 (2018), pp. 561–77.
28 Macpherson, *History and Management*, title page. See Maclean, 'The Early Political Careers'.
29 Macpherson, 'Preface', *History and Management*, n.p.
30 Ibid.
31 Ibid.
32 Gibbon, *The History of the Decline and Fall of the Roman Empire*, Vol. I.
33 Anthony Grafton, 'The Footnote from De Thou to Ranke', *History and Theory*, 33:4 (1994), p. 54.
34 deGategno, 'Macpherson, Sir John, First Baronet'.
35 Macpherson, 'Preface', *History and Management*, n.p.
36 Pocock, *Barbarism and Religion, Volume II: Narratives of Civil Government*, p. 208.
37 Ibid., pp. 207, 208.
38 Macpherson, 'Preface', *History and Management*, n.p.
39 Lisa Hill, 'Adam Smith and the Theme of Corruption', *The Review of Politics*, 68 (2006), pp. 636–62.
40 Pocock, *Barbarism and Religion, Volume II. Narratives of Civil Government*, p. 7.
41 Grafton, *The Footnote*, pp. 35–6.
42 Yola Schmitz, 'Faked Translations: James Macpherson's Ossianic Poetry', in Daniel Becker, Annalisa Fischer and Yola Schmitz (eds), *Faking, Forging, Counterfeiting: Discredited Practices at the Margins of Mimesis* (Bielefeld: Transcript Verlag, 2018), pp. 167–80.
43 Grafton, 'The Footnote from De Thou to Ranke', p. 62. For Gibbon's refinement of this approach to footnotes, and the debt that this owed to

Hume, see Pocock, *Barbarism and Religion, Vol. II. Narratives of Civil Government*, pp. 207–8.
44 Macpherson, 'Preface', *History and Management*, n.p.
45 Pocock, *Barbarism and Religion, Vol. II. Narratives of Civil Government*, p. 5.
46 Macpherson, 'Preface', *History and Management*, n.p.
47 Wickman, *The Ruins of Experience*, pp. 8, 116.
48 Ibid., p. 117; David Raynor, 'Ossian and Hume', in Gaskill, *Ossian Revisited*.
49 Macpherson, *History and Management*, p. 26.
50 Ibid., p. 42.
51 Ibid., p. 143.
52 Phillips, *Society and Sentiment*, pp. 60–78.
53 Ibid., pp. 78, 347.
54 Ibid., p. 78.
55 Pocock, *Barbarism and Religion. Vol II. Narratives of Civil Government*, p. 208.
56 Macpherson, *History and Management*, p. 23.
57 O'Brien, *Narratives of Enlightenment*, p. 133.
58 Stafford, *The Sublime Savage*, p. 158; O'Brien, *Narratives of Enlightenment*, p. 134. For a recent analysis of how Macpherson engages with Ferguson's ideas in the Ossianic Collections, see Moore, 'Adam Ferguson, *The Poems of Ossian* and the Imaginative Life of the Scottish Enlightenment'.
59 Macpherson, *Temora*, p. xii; Stafford, *The Sublime Savage*, p. 158.
60 Macpherson, *History and Management*, p. 2.
61 For Gibbon's engagement with stadial history, see O'Brien, *Narratives of Enlightenment*, p. 201. See also Dirks, *The Scandal of Empire*, p. 264.
62 Macpherson, *History and Management*, p. 27.
63 Ibid.
64 Ibid., p. 161.
65 Phillips, *Society and Sentiment*, pp. 45–59.
66 Macpherson, *History and Management*, pp. 35–6.
67 Ibid., p. 50.
68 Ibid., p. 160.
69 Ibid., pp. 249–50.
70 Ibid., p. 60.
71 Phillips, *Society and Sentiment*, p. 63.
72 Philip J. Stern, 'History and Historiography of the English East India Company: Past, Present, and Future!', *History Compass*, 7:4 (2009), pp. 1148–9.
73 L. Namier and J. Brooke (eds), *The History of Parliament: The House of Commons 1754–1790* (Woodbridge: Boydell & Brewer, 1964), available at: https://www.historyofparliamentonline.org/volume/1754-1790/member/rous-george-1744-1802 (accessed 9 April 2020).

74 Grafton, *The Footnote*, p. 98. Macpherson's footnotes are analysed briefly in George McElroy's work but lacking Grafton's awareness broader conventions in history writing of this period. See McElroy, 'Ossianic Imagination', p. 369.
75 Rous, *The Restoration of the King of Tanjore Considered*.
76 Ibid., p. iv.
77 SinhaRaja Tammita-Delgoda, 'Orme, Robert (1728–1801)', *Oxford Dictionary of National Biography* (Oxford: Oxford University Press, 2004), available at: https://doi.org/10.1093/ref:odnb/20833 (accessed 10 April 2020).
78 Ibid.
79 Robert Orme, *A History of the Military Transactions of the British Nation in Indostan* (London: John Nourse, 1773); Robert Orme, *A History of the Military Transactions of the British Nation in Indostan*, Vol. II (London: John Nourse, 1778). For example, Macpherson refers to volume 1 of Orme's work on p. 65 of *The History and Management* and volume 2 on p. 70.
80 Tammita-Delgoda, 'Orme, Robert'.
81 John M. MacKenzie, 'Scottish Orientalists, Administrators and Missions: A Distinctive Scots Approach to Asia?', in T. M. Devine and Angela McCarthy (eds), *The Scottish Experience in Asia, c. 1700 to the Present: Settlers and Sojourners* (Basingstoke: Palgrave Macmillan, 2017), p. 53.
82 Other ambitious Highlanders also demonstrated an aptitude for Indian languages, perhaps a product of a bilingual Gaelic and English-language upbringing. See, for example, the experience of Colonel Allan Macpherson in the East India Company army, in Foster, *A Private Empire*, pp. 30–2.
83 MacKenzie, 'Scottish Orientalists, Administrators and Missions', p. 53; Willem G. J. Kuiters, 'Dow, Alexander (1735/6–1779)', *Oxford Dictionary of National Biography* (Oxford: Oxford University Press, 2004), available at: https://doi.org/10.1093/ref:odnb/7957 (accessed 10 April 2020). Alexander Dow, *The History of Hindostan from the Earliest Account of Time to the Death of Akbar. Vol. I and II* (London: T. Becket and D. A. de Hondt, 1768); Alexander Dow, *The History of Hindostan from the Death of Akbar to the Complete Settlement of the Empire under Aurungzebe. Vol. III* (London: T. Becket and D. A. de Hondt, 1772).
84 Macpherson, *History and Management*, pp. 29, 44, 45. While Macpherson does make extensive use of Dow's work in this book, it is not quite as reliant as some scholars suggest. See Davis, 'Transnational Articulations', p. 448.
85 Kuiters, 'Dow, Alexander'. See also Davis, 'Transnational Articulations', p. 448.
86 Kuiters, 'Dow, Alexander'.
87 Patterson, 'Enlightenment and Empire: Mughals and Marathas', p. 974.
88 Saunders, *The Life and Letters of James Macpherson*, p. 218. Hume's relationship with Macpherson indicates how closely connected Macpherson

was to such intellectual circles during the 1770s. For another example, see Macpherson's friendship with Adam Smith, described by Macpherson as 'Dr Adam Smith, one of my best friends' in a letter sent in March 1776 to Madras, soliciting support for one of Smith's friends' sons to be placed with the EIC. See Rothschild, 'Adam Smith in the British Empire', p. 192.

89 Patterson, 'Enlightenment and Empire', p. 976. Jessica Patterson, *Religion, Enlightenment and Empire* (Cambridge: Cambridge University Press, 2021), pp. 113–15.
90 Maclean, 'The Early Political Careers', pp. xxxii, 175.
91 Macpherson MSS/1, 39/6, John to James Macpherson, 29 September 1773, quoted in Ibid., p. 297. Macpherson also shared a mistress, Mrs Elizabeth Draper, with Alexander Dow. See Ibid., p. 188.
92 Macpherson, *History and Management*, p. 71.
93 'Colonel Lawrence's Narrative of the War, on the Coast of the Coromandel, From the Beginning of the Troubles to the Year 1754', in Richard Owen Cambridge, *An Account of the War in India between the English and French, on the Coast of Coromandel, From the Year 1750 to the Year 1761* (London: Jeffreys, 1762), pp. 1–100.
94 G. J. Bryant, 'Lawrence, Stringer (1697–1775)', *Oxford Dictionary of National Biography* (Oxford: Oxford University Press, 2004), available at: https://doi.org/10.1093/ref:odnb/16187 (accessed 1 May 2020); G. J. Bryant, *The Emergence of British Power in India, 1600–1784: A Grand Strategic Interpretation* (Woodbridge: Boydell & Brewer, 2013).
95 Macpherson, *History and Management*, p. 91.
96 Ibid., pp. 136–59; J. K. Laughton, revised by Clive Wilkinson, 'Lindsay, Sir John (1737–1788)', *Oxford Dictionary of National Biography* (Oxford: Oxford University Press, 2004), available at: https://doi.org/10.1093/ref:odnb/16710 (accessed 1 May 2020).
97 Henry Davidson Love, *Indian Records Series Vestiges of Old Madras*, Volume 3 (London: Murray, 1913), pp. 1–5.
98 Macpherson, *History and Management*, pp. 93–111; James Watt, *British Orientalisms, 1759–1835* (Cambridge: Cambridge University Press, 2019), p. 1; Cambridge, *An Account of the War in India*, pp. 101–19.
99 Macpherson, *History and Management*, p. 220. The first footnote on this page refers to 'Papers published by the Company, relative to the restoration of Tanjore, vol. 1, p. 4.' This is most likely a reference to Anon., *Copies of Papers Relative to the Restoration of the King of Tanjore* (London: n.p., 1777).
100 Macpherson, *History and Management*, p. 57.
101 Charles W. J. Withers, *Placing the Enlightenment: Thinking Geographically About the Age of Reason* (Chicago: Chicago University Press, 2008), p. 44.
102 Macpherson, *History and Management*, pp. 149–50.
103 Ibid. p. 84.
104 Maclean, 'The Early Political Careers', p. xxiv.
105 Ibid., pp. 317–61.

106 Grafton, *The Footnote*, pp. 97–8.
107 Ibid., pp. 122–47.
108 Ibid., p. 101.
109 Pocock, *Barbarism and Religion. Volume II. Narratives of Civil Government*, p. 185.
110 Grafton, *The Footnote*, p. 3.
111 For Robertson's use of footnotes, see Pocock, *Barbarism and Religion. Vol. IV Barbarians, Savages and Empires*, pp. 184–5.
112 Macpherson, *History and Management*, p. 58. 'Chops' is a Hindi term, meaning 'a seal, or the impression of a seal'. See *Oxford English Dictionary* (Oxford, 1889).
113 For examples of this, see Macpherson, *History and Management*, pp. 60, 97, 98, 101, 104, 136, 137, 165, 191, 223.
114 Ibid., p. 249.
115 Ibid., p. 206.
116 Ibid., pp.191–4.
117 Ibid., p. 191.
118 Grafton, *The Footnote*, p. 2.
119 Macpherson, *History and Management*, p. 13.
120 Ibid., p. 21. For the differences between Gibbon's and Robertson's approach to footnote writing, see Pocock, *Barbarism and Religion. Volume IV. Barbarians, Savages and Empires*, p. 192.
121 Macpherson, *History and Management*, p. 210. G. J. Bryant, 'British Logistics and the Conduct of the Carnatic Wars', *War in History*, 11:3 (2004), pp. 278–306.
122 Macpherson, *History and Management*, p. 65.
123 Ibid., pp. 266–9.
124 Ibid., 'Preface', n.p.
125 Hume to William Mure, October 1754, in Greig, *Letters of David Hume. Vol. I*, p. 210, quoted in Phillips, *Society and Sentiment*, p. 60.
126 Phillips, *Society and Sentiment*, p. 40.
127 Macpherson, *History and Management*, p. 62.
128 Ibid., p. 65.
129 Ibid., pp. 90–1.
130 Ibid., p. 237.
131 For Gibbon's writing in support of Lord North's policy against the French during the American War, see Pocock, *Barbarism and Religion. Vol. IV. Barbarians, Savages and Empires*, p. 5; Edward Gibbon, *Mémoire Justificatif pour Servir de Réponse à L'exposé des Motifs de la Conduite du Roi de France Relativement à l'Angleterre* (London, 1778), in Lord Sheffield (ed.), *The Miscellaneous Works of Edward Gibbon, Esq., with Memoirs of His Life and Writings, Composed by Himself; Illustrated from His Letters, with Occasional Notes and Narrative. A New Edition, with Considerable Additions* (London: John Murray, 1814), pp. 1–34.

132 Anon., *A Declaration by the Representatives of the United Colonies of North-America, now met in Congress at Philadelphia, setting forth the Causes and Necessity of their taking up Arms* (Philadelphia, PA: W. & T. Bradford, and Devizes, 1775).
133 deGategno, 'Replying to a Crisis: James Macpherson's *The Rights of Great Britain Asserted against the Claims of America*', p. 198.
134 Ibid., p. 201. Matthew Dziennik details how the pamphlet was also distributed by post, at the government's expense, giving the example of William Tod, the Duke of Gordon's factor, finding a copy waiting for him on his arrival in Ruthven in March 1776. See Matthew P. Dziennik, *The Fatal Land: War, Empire, and the Highland Soldier in British America* (New Haven, CT: Yale University Press, 2015), p. 193.
135 deGategno, 'Replying to a Crisis: James Macpherson's *The Rights of Great Britain Asserted against the Claims of America*', p. 211.
136 The 'Advertisement' appears from at least the fourth edition of the pamphlet. See James Macpherson, *The Rights of Great Britain Asserted Against the Claims of America: Being an Answer to the Declaration of the General Congress*, 4th edition (London: T. Cadell, 1775/6), n.p.
137 Dziennik, *The Fatal Land*, p. 192. Macpherson, *The Rights of Great Britain*, 9th edition, n.p.
138 deGategno, 'Replying to a Crisis', p. 208.
139 Macpherson, *The Rights of Great Britain*, 2nd edition, p. 1.
140 Ibid., p. 2.
141 Ibid.
142 Ibid., p. 17.
143 Ibid., pp. 62, 63.
144 Ibid., pp. 63, 65.
145 Ibid., p. 8.
146 Ibid., p. 10.
147 Ibid., p. 11.
148 Ibid., pp. 33, 34.
149 Ibid., p. 38.
150 Ibid., p. 40.
151 Ibid., pp. 7, 8.
152 Ibid., pp. 12–14.
153 Ibid., p. 19.
154 Ibid., p. 63.
155 Although it is important to point out that Gibbon, in his pamphlet in support of Lord North's government against the French in their participation in the American War, does not use any footnotes at all. See Gibbon, *Mémoire Justificative* (1778), in Sheffield, *The Miscellaneous Works of Edward Gibbon*, pp. 1–34.
156 Macpherson, *The Rights of Great Britain*, p. 46. On Rockingham's policy in Quebec during this period, see Phillip Lawson, *The Imperial Challenge:*

Quebec and Britain in the Age of the American Revolution (Montreal and Kingston: McGill-Queen's University Press, 1994), pp. 74–6.

157 On the emergence of the Whigs in the late 1670s, see Melinda S. Zook, *Radical Whigs and Conspiratorial Politics in Late Stuart England* (University Park, PA: Pennsylvania State University Press, 1999).
158 Macpherson, *The Rights of Great Britain*, p. 26.
159 See also Ibid., p. 31.
160 Ibid., p. 50.
161 Ibid., p. 90.
162 Ibid., p. 58.
163 Ibid., p. 59.
164 Pocock, *Barbarism and Religion. Vol. IV. Barbarians, Savages and Empires*, p. 6.
165 Guha, *History at the Limit of World-History*, p. 9.
166 Pocock, *Barbarism and Religion. Vol. IV. Barbarians, Savages and Empires*, pp. 2–5, 186–90.
167 Guha, *History at the Limit of World-History*, p. 42.
168 Pocock, *Barbarism and Religion. Vol. II. Narratives of Civil Government*, p. 2.
169 Macpherson, *The Rights of Great Britain*, p. 1.
170 Ibid., p. 3.
171 Linda Colley, *Britons: Forging the Nation 1707–1837* (London: Vintage, 1996), p. 143.
172 Macpherson kept a house in Putney during his time in London during the 1780s and spent a couple of years in Pensacola during the 1760s as secretary to the Governor of West Florida, George Johnstone. Rothschild, *The Inner Life of Empires*, p. 39; Saunders, *The Life and Letters of James Macpherson*, p. 275.
173 Macpherson, *The Rights of Great Britain*, p. 4.
174 Ibid., p. 69.
175 Kidd, 'North Britishness and the Nature of Eighteenth-Century British Patriotisms', pp. 374–6.
176 Colley, *Britons*, pp. 137–9. See also Eric Nelson, 'Patriot Royalism: The Stuart Monarchy in American Political Thought, 1769–75', *William and Mary Quarterly*, 68:4 (2011), pp. 533–72.
177 Moore, 'James Macpherson and "Celtic Whiggism"'.
178 Kidd, *Subverting Scotland's Past*, pp. 227, 234.
179 Macpherson, *The Rights of Great Britain*, p. 4.
180 Ibid.
181 Pocock, *Barbarism and Religion. Vol. II. Narratives of Civil Government*, pp. 8–9.
182 Macpherson, *The Rights of Great Britain*, p. 6.
183 Ibid., p. 7.

184 Ibid., p. 8.
185 J. G. A. Pocock, 'Hume and the American Revolution: The Dying Thoughts of a North Briton', in *idem.*, *Virtue, Commerce, and History: Essays On Political Thought and History, Chiefly In the Eighteenth Century* (Cambridge: Cambridge University Press, 1985), pp. 134–5; Hugh Cunningham, 'The Language of Patriotism', *History Workshop Journal*, 12 (1981), pp. 8–33.
186 Colley, *Britons*, pp. 110–11. See also Jack P. Greene, 'The Seven Years' War and the American Revolution: The Causal Relationship Reconsidered', *Journal of Imperial and Commonwealth History*, 8:2 (1980), pp. 85–105; Justin du Rivage, *Revolution Against Empire: Taxes, Politics, and the Origins of American Independence* (New Haven, CT: Yale University Press, 2017).
187 Macpherson, *The Rights of Great Britain*, pp. 12–14. Here, Macpherson's analysis has been confirmed by Justin du Rivage's recent research. See du Rivage, *Revolution against Empire*, p. 78.
188 Macpherson, *The Rights of Great Britain*, p. 16.
189 Ibid., p. 21.
190 Ibid., p. 25.
191 Ibid., p. 26.
192 Ibid.
193 Ibid., pp. 29–30.
194 Ibid., p. 31.
195 Ibid., p. 37.
196 Ibid.
197 Ibid., p. 40.
198 Ibid., p. 70.
199 Nelson, 'Patriot Royalism'.
200 *The London Chronicle*, 8–10 July 1779, p. 28.
201 *The Gazetteer and New Daily Advertiser*, 24 August 1779, p. 1; Saunders, *The Life and Letters of James Macpherson*, p. 265.
202 Edward Gibbon, 'Letter to his Stepmother', 17 September 1779, in Rowland E. Prothero (ed.), *Private Letters of Edward Gibbon (1753–1794)*, Vol. I (London: John Murray, 1897), p. 369; emphasis in the original.
203 Saunders describes *A Short History* as 'a counterpart' to *The Rights of Great Britain*. See Saunders, *Life and Letters*, p. 264.
204 Pocock, *Barbarism and Religion. Vol. IV. Barbarians, Savages and Empires*, p. 6.
205 Satia, *Time's Monster*, p. 16.
206 deGategno, *James Macpherson*, p. 139; O'Gorman, 'The Parliamentary Opposition to the Government's American Policy 1760–1782'; Langford, 'Old Whigs, Old Tories, and the American Revolution'; Solomon Lutnick, *The American Revolution and the British Press*, p. 18.

207 Sir John W. Fortescue (ed.), *The Correspondence of King George III: 1760–83*, vol. 5 (London: Macmillan, 1927–8), p. 414, quoted in deGategno, *James Macpherson*, p. 139.

208 For example, Nevil Johnson, 'Opposition in the British Political System', *Government and Opposition*, 32:04 (1997), pp. 487–510; Dror Wahrman, 'The English Problem of Identity in the American Revolution', *The American Historical Review*, 106:4 (2001), pp. 1236–62; Sebastian Mitchell, 'James Macpherson's *Ossian* and the Empire of Sentiment', *Journal for Eighteenth-Century Studies*, 22:2 (1999), pp. 155–72; Leith Davis, '"Origins of the Specious": James Macpherson's Ossian and the Forging of the British Empire, *The Eighteenth Century: Theory and Interpretation*, 34:2 (1993), pp. 132–50.

209 Jones, 'Principles, Prejudices, and the Politics of James Macpherson's Historical Writing', pp. 131–3. See also Robert W. Jones, *Literature, Gender and Politics in Britain During the War for America 1770–1785* (Cambridge: Cambridge University Press, 2011), pp. 13, 43.

210 James Macpherson, *A Short History*, p. iii.

211 Ibid.

212 Ibid., p. iv.

213 Ibid., p. 14. For the focus of much history writing from this period on the issue of political factionalism, see de Groot, *Empire and History Writing in Britain*, p. 45.

214 Macpherson, *A Short History*, p. 26.

215 Ibid., p. 25. For Admiral Keppel's conduct during the American War, see Nicholas Rogers, 'The Dynamic of News in Britain During the American War: The Case of Admiral Keppel', *Parliamentary History*, 25:1 (2006), pp. 49–67. See also Jones, *Literature, Gender and Politics in Britain*, pp. 119–21.

216 Macpherson, *A Short History*, pp. 40–1.

217 Ibid., p. 42.

218 For discussions of 'manliness' and the constitution, see McCormack, 'Citizenship, Nationhood, and Masculinity in the Affair of the Hanoverian Soldier'; Kathleen Wilson, *The Sense of the People: Politics, Culture and Imperialism in England, 1715–1785* (Cambridge: Cambridge University Press, 1995).

219 Macpherson, *A Short History*, p. 49.

220 Ibid., p. 6.

221 Ibid., p. 7.

222 Ibid.

223 Ibid., p. 8.

224 Phillips, *Society and Sentiment*, p. 57.

225 Macpherson, *A Short History*, pp. 34–5.

226 Ibid., p. 35.

227 Ibid., p. 38.

228 Ibid., p. 54. Footnote to 'Life of Clarendon'. Edward Hyde Clarendon, *Life of Edward Earl of Clarendon* (Dublin: P. Wilson & J. Hoey, 1759).
229 Macpherson, *A Short History*, p. 56.
230 Ibid., p. 25.
231 Ibid., p. 9.
232 Ibid., p. 11.
233 Ibid., p. 12. Governor George Johnstone was, of course, Macpherson's former boss during their time together in West Florida in 1764–5, where Johnstone was Governor of the new colony. See Rothschild, *The Inner Life of Empires*, pp. 39–43.
234 Ibid., pp. 34–40; Milton M. Klein, 'Robertson, James (1717–1788)', *Oxford Dictionary of National Biography* (Oxford: Oxford University Press, 2004), available at: https://doi.org/10.1093/ref:odnb/23796 (accessed 12 October 2021).
235 Macpherson, *A Short History*, pp. 20–1. For Burgoyne, see John Brooke, 'Burgoyne, John, 1723–92', in Namier and Brooke, *The History of Parliament: The House of Commons 1754–1790*, available at: http://www.historyofparliamentonline.org/volume/1754-1790/member/burgoyne-john-1723-92 (accessed 12 October 2021).
236 'Dr Johnson on the Irish Howl, p. 13', in Macpherson, *A Short History*, p. 21.
237 Ibid., p. 29.
238 Ibid., pp. 28–9; emphasis in the original.
239 de Groot, *Empire and History Writing in Britain*, p. 62.
240 Macpherson, *A Short History*, pp. 5–6.
241 Ibid., p. 6.
242 See Kidd, *Subverting Scotland's Past*, p. 234; Moore, 'James Macpherson and "Celtic Whiggism"'.
243 Macpherson, *A Short History*, p. 20.
244 Ibid., p. 27.
245 Ibid., p. 30. Kidd, 'North Britishness and the Nature of Eighteenth-Century British Patriotisms'.
246 Macpherson, *A Short History*, pp. 5, 4, 8.
247 Ibid., p. 14.
248 Ibid., p. 27.
249 Ibid., p. 56.
250 Peter Mitchell, *Imperial Nostalgia: How the British Conquered Themselves* (Manchester: Manchester University Press, 2021), p. 23.
251 Macpherson, *A Short History*, p. iii.
252 Satia, *Time's Monster*, pp. 15–16.
253 Ibid., p. 51.
254 Macpherson, *A Short History*, p. 9.
255 Ibid., p. 49.
256 Ibid., p. 11.

257 Ibid., p. 12.
258 Ibid., p. 21.
259 Ibid., p. 54.
260 Macpherson, *The History of Great Britain*, pp. 80–1.
261 Macpherson, *A Short History*, p. 55.
262 Macpherson, *The History of Great Britain*, p. 66.
263 Macpherson, *A Short History*, p. 57.
264 Ibid., p. 57.
265 For these debates, see Matthew McCormack, 'The New Militia: War, Politics and Gender in 1750s Britain', *Gender & History*, 19:3 (2007), pp. 483–500.
266 Macpherson, *A Short History*, p. 57. For eighteenth-century uses of Agincourt in the context of contemporary conflict with France, see Anne Curry, 'Agincourt, 1415–2015', *Historical Association*, 1 October 2015, available at: https://www.history.org.uk/publications/resource/8648/agincourt-1415-2015 (accessed 13 October 2021).
267 Macpherson, *A Short History*, p. 58.
268 Satia, *Time's Monster*, p. 39. See also Solomon Lutnick, 'Edward Gibbon and the Decline of the First British Empire: The Historian as Politician', *Studies in Burke and his Time*, 10:2 (1968).
269 Macpherson, *The Highlander*, p. 64.
270 Saunders, *The Life and Letters of James Macpherson*, pp. 273–4. For Pitt's triumph in 1784, see Michael J. Turner, *Pitt the Younger: A Life* (London: Hambledon, 2003), p. 57.
271 Ben J. Golding, 'British Politics, Imperial Ideology, and East India Company Reform, 1773–1784', unpublished PhD thesis (University of Cambridge, 2020); Mackillop, *Human Capital and Empire*, p. 66; Dirks, *The Scandal of Empire*, p. 21.
272 Saunders, *The Life and Letters of James Macpherson*, p. 274.
273 deGategno, 'Macpherson, Sir John, First Baronet'.
274 James Macpherson, *The History and Management of the East India Company from its Origin in 1600 to the Present Times. Volume the First. Containing the Affairs of the Carnatic; in which the Rights of the Nabob are explained, and the Injustice of the Company proved. The Whole Compiled from Authentic Records. A New Edition* (London: T. Cadell, 1782).
275 Davis, 'Transnational Articulations', p. 454.
276 Saunders, *The Life and Letters of James Macpherson*, pp. 278–80, 288–96.
277 deGategno, *James Macpherson*, p. 10.
278 Pocock, *Barbarism and Religion. Vol. IV. Barbarians, Savages and Empires*, pp. 183–4.
279 Ibid., p. 185.
280 Ibid., p. 2.
281 Ibid., p. 6.

Conclusion: James Macpherson – Enlightenment Historian and Imperial Gael

Ged a gheibhinn e sgrìobhta,	Should I even find it written,
Na mìorbhailean rinn e	The wonders he wrought
'S na chost e dhe nì	And all the wealth he expended
Cur malailì air an oighreachd	In decorating the estate
De na h-àilleagain phrìseil	With precious things of beauty
Nach robh dìomhain gun fhoinn daibh,	Not vain or void of substance,
S dubh a' bhoile dhomh innseadh	It is mad for me to tell it
'S nì dìomhain duibh fhaighneachd.	And in vain for you to ask it.

Donnchadh MacAoidh, 'Cumha Sheumais Bhàin'
Duncan MacKay, 'James Macpherson's Lament' (1796)[1]

This book ends where it began – at Macpherson's Badenoch estate at Belleville (now Balavil, just outside the town of Kingussie). In his elegy for *Seumas Bàn*, Duncan MacKay reflects on the grandeur of Macpherson's Highland home and the impossibility of capturing 'The wonders he wrought' through his long and varied literary and political career. As MacKay suggests, there is a certain 'madness' in trying to make sense of how a young, Gaelic-speaking Highlander like Macpherson could rise from relatively modest beginnings as the son of an impecunious tacksman, and on the fringes of the Clan social elite, to become a writer of world renown and a politician of power and wealth, spending his final years in the late Palladian mansion designed by Robert Adam.[2] But all this and more can be said about James Macpherson, and this book, we hope, has added a further dimension to this story: that in addition to the literary achievement and subsequent controversy of Ossian, we need to also consider Macpherson as an Enlightenment historian and intellectual.

Macpherson's return to the Highlands in the 1780s as a successful writer, politician and man of empire indicates how important it is to understand him as a proud Gael. For several years before he built Belleville, Macpherson had campaigned for the return of the forfeited Clan Macpherson estates to the current Chief, Duncan of the Kiln. Apparently declining the lands himself, Macpherson's powers of political persuasion at Westminster were decisive in restoring the Cluny estate to Colonel Duncan in 1784. While the clan estates were in government hands and when the Chief, Colonel Duncan, was off fighting for the British Army in the American revolutionary war, James was manoeuvring and cajoling, making the case for the Macphersons as if he were de facto clan Chief.[3] At the end of his life, then, it is perhaps no surprise that the Highlands once more became Macpherson's geographical focal point. We can only understand Macpherson's life and writing if we appreciate the centrality of the *Gàidhealtachd* to his vision of the world – a world that was also, crucially, shaped by history writing. These two factors – that Macpherson was an historian whose identity was profoundly shaped by the Highlands – help us to understand why he wrote about the past in the way that he did.

Understanding Macpherson as an historian also helps us to see the Highlands afresh, in terms of intellectual and geopolitical position. Macpherson's early writings (*The Highlander* and the Ossianic Collections) sought to use the ancient Celtic and medieval Highland past to make a political claim in the present – that Scots and Highlanders were commercially and militarily important to the British imperial state during the late 1750s and early 1760s in the context of the Seven Years War with the French. Macpherson adopted a stadial view of the past (borrowed, in part, from his friend and fellow Gael, Adam Ferguson) and retrofitted it to a modern 'Celtic Whig' account of British constitutional history. Macpherson's later history writing of the 1770s developed the techniques and methodologies of Enlightenment historiography. In such books as *The History of Great Britain*, Macpherson combined historical narrative with philosophical reflection and scholarly erudition, demonstrating that history writing of cutting-edge modernity could be produced by someone from the Highlands.

Macpherson, then, is an example of a Highland Enlightenment, articulated through history writing.[4] Just as Enlightenment history writing was not fixed so, too, we find that Macpherson's approach to writing about the past developed and changed over time.[5] From *The Highlander* onwards, we see Macpherson concerned with the nature of historical sources. In these earlier, poetic works, Macpherson uses evidence from the past as source material in constructing historical narratives in verse. This interest in sources and evidence soon becomes rather more philosophical in Macpherson's prose writing about the past. From the paratextual material to the Ossianic Collections onwards, we see Macpherson functioning in an explicit and self-consciously historiographical way, not just writing about the past, but thinking about *how* to do this. In doing so, Macpherson positions his approach firmly in the context of contemporary debates about historiography, in which the work of Hume, Blair and Smith are central. In particular, we can understand the prefaces and dissertations to *Fingal* and *Temora* as an extended conversation and dialogue with Blair's and Smith's respective *Lectures on Rhetoric and Belles Lettres*. Ideas about an historian's fidelity to the source material abound in Macpherson's prefatory writing to the Ossianic Collections, where his debt to Blair is most apparent. In *Fingal*, we see Macpherson using the ancient Celtic past to make claims about the place of the Highlands in the commercial modernity of the British imperial state – but, in the process, Macpherson reveals the tension between the evidence of oral tradition and emerging Enlightenment methodologies of source criticism. This paradox is then reflected in *Temora*, where Macpherson acknowledges Adam Smith's reverence for classical historical narratives but then challenges their authenticity as source material and their usefulness as a guide for historiographical method, especially given the increasing emphasis in Macpherson's and others' history writing on philosophical explanation.

During the 1770s, Macpherson turned to book-length prose history, where erudition and philosophy became increasingly important components of how he wrote about the past. Once again, we can see this as Macpherson's response to the latest debates about the nature of history writing. Building on Hume's desire to philosophically explain the past, we find Robertson, Gibbon and other Enlightenment historians placing a greater emphasis on scholarly erudition. In *An Introduction to the History of Great Britain and Ireland* (1771) and in *The History of Great Britain* and the *Original Papers* (both 1775), Macpherson situates the evidence of primary sources at the heart of his analysis of the past and increasingly uses scholarly apparatus such as footnotes to demonstrate the epistemological underpinnings of his history writing. Finally, the second half of the 1770s sees a further shift in Macpherson's approach to the past. The crisis of empire in America and India mobilises Macpherson to write about contemporary imperial politics in his role both as propagandist for Lord North's administration and agent for the Nawab of Arcot. Macpherson explains the perilous condition of the Empire and defends imperial policy by writing about the past. In supporting British policy in America and the conduct of the Nawab of Arcot, and in criticising the rebellious American colonists and the corruption of the East India Company, Macpherson frames his political propaganda with extensive historical narratives. In turn, Macpherson narrates the past using the techniques and methodologies of Enlightenment history writing. *The History and Management of the East-India Company* is a clear example of Macpherson's development as an historian, where he combines a Blairite concern for sources and truth with the erudition of historical research, the evidence of primary sources, and the scholarly scaffolding of footnotes. Just as we find in the work of Hume and in the writings of Robertson and Gibbon in the 1770s, Macpherson frames his historical narratives in these later political writings with extensive explanation and reflection. By 1779, Macpherson had firmly established himself as an historian who was part of the same historiographical universe as his more illustrious Enlightenment colleagues. Pocock's assessment of Gibbon can equally be applied to Macpherson: 'Here is the mental world of historians who were his equals, whom he recognised as such, and with whom he aspired to equality.'[6]

Why did Macpherson stop writing history (and writing altogether) in the 1780s? Given that Macpherson was writing in such a confident way about the past, combining his own and the government's political ambitions with a refined Enlightenment historiography, it seems strange that he would put his talents to one side at the height of his literary powers. As we have seen, Macpherson had become an MP by this stage, and the work of parliament took up increasing time and energy. This was especially so given that his own interests in India came to dominate the political stage at Westminster. The crisis of East India Company corruption and its power struggle with the British state permeated political discourse. It consistently intersected with his personal and political connections with the Nawab of Arcot, especially when his great friend, Sir John Macpherson, became the interim Governor-General of Bengal following the demise of Warren Hastings in 1785. Like Hume, Macpherson was also increasingly in ill-health.[7]

In addition to these personal and political concerns, the world around Macpherson was also changing. Given the turn towards erudition in the later works of Robertson and Gibbon, it must have been difficult for Macpherson to find the time and energy to keep up with the latest historiographical methodologies.[8] The kind of lengthy research trips across the archives of Europe that Macpherson had conducted during the 1770s must have been more difficult a decade later, when his political career and less robust health would have made it hard to return to the archive grubbing favoured by Robertson and others. As well as the nature of history writing changing, so too had the British imperial state's relationship with the Highlands which had framed Macpherson's engagement with the past since the late 1750s. The loss of the American colonies in 1783 coincided with the government's return of the Forfeited and Annexed Estates in 1784 to create a different wave of 'improvement' in the Highlands. The commercial opportunities afforded by military recruitment in the Highlands became less lucrative, while new schemes for 'internal colonization and urbanization' such as the British Fisheries Society (founded in 1786) and the Highland Society of Scotland (1784) sought to develop the *Gàidhealtachd* in new ways.[9] The changing nature of the Highlands' relationship with the commercial modernity of the British imperial state was also reflected in Macpherson's paradoxical attitude towards his newly-acquired Badenoch estate, Belleville. On the one hand, the benevolent and generous laird of MacKay's 'Lament', Macpherson was also a commercially minded 'improver', intent on maximising profits from his estate and not shy about using the methods of clearance that he himself had promoted in the region during the late 1760s.[10]

In a world that had changed, from the Highlands to empire and to history writing, James Macpherson saw out his final years at Belleville with no further publications about the past. But the very fact of returning to this Highland location helps us to understand the nature of Macpherson's history writing, bookended at the beginning and end of his career by Badenoch. It helps us to recognise the role played by Gaels such as Macpherson in the Enlightenment – and that this was an Enlightenment, in Scotland and the Highlands, where history writing was important. Acknowledging Macpherson as an historian opens up the intellectual world of the second half of the eighteenth century, where Gaels had presence and agency. The fact that Macpherson then uses Enlightenment history writing to support the British imperial state is no surprise, given the increasing role of writing about the past in the contemporary political project of empire building. But Macpherson also uses the techniques and methodologies of eighteenth-century historiography to promote his vision of an imperial Gaelic Highlands. Much recent scholarship on the Highlands and empire has recognised the duality of Highlanders' position within empire, both as victims and perpetrators of colonialism.[11] Using history writing, Macpherson firmly rejected the notion of Highland victimhood. He was an imperial Gael and, in reckoning with legacies of empire in the Highlands, Macpherson helps us to understand the connections between slavery in the West Indies, the East India Company, and the emergence of history writing as a tool of Enlightenment thought that underpinned this colonial domination and violence.

This is part of Macpherson's complex legacy. While he was only tangentially connected with slavery, Macpherson was fully immersed in the realm of the East Indies and his history writing – with its Enlightenment concerns with narrative, philosophy and erudition – created a worldview that rationalised and promoted Highland participation in empire. This is related to the complex legacy of empire in the Highlands, where we need to acknowledge the role Highlanders played in the violence of empire. In the end, then, Macpherson's history writing – as with so much Enlightenment writing about the past – should be seen as part of the technologies of colonial domination.[12] Writing about the past was Macpherson's way of thinking about the present – especially the intricate and developing relationship between the Highlands and the British imperial state – and he wrote about all this, from his earliest poetry to his final political pamphlets, as an historian.

Notes

1   Black, *An Lasair*, p. 333.
2   For Macpherson's family background, see Maclean, 'The Early Political Careers of James "Fingal" Macpherson and Sir John Macpherson', pp. 14–15. See also Alan G. Macpherson, 'James "Ossian" Macpherson's Ancestry', *Creag Dhubh*, 16 (1964), pp. 20–2.
3   Taylor, *The Wild Black Region*, pp. 196–7.
4   For the idea of a Highland Enlightenment, see Donald E. Meek, 'Evangelicalism, Ossianism and the Enlightenment: The Many Masks of Dugald Buchanan', in Christopher MacLachlan (ed.), *Crossing the Highland Line: Cross-Currents in Eighteenth-Century Scottish Writing* (Glasgow: Association for Scottish Literary Studies, 2009), pp. 97–112.
5   For the protean and multiple nature of 'Enlightenment', see, for example, J. G. A. Pocock, 'Historiography and Enlightenment: A View of Their History', *Modern Intellectual History*, 5:1 (2008), 83–96.
6   Pocock, *Barbarism and Religion. Vol. II. Narratives of Civil Government*, p. 369.
7   deGategno, *James Macpherson*, p. 10.
8   Pocock, 'Response and Commentary', pp. 159, 161.
9   Jonsson, *Enlightenment's Frontier*, pp. 2, 104. Macpherson was a member of the Highland Society of London, the earlier, sister association to the Highland Society of Scotland. See Katie McCullough, 'Building the Highland Empire: The Highland Society of London and the Formation of Charitable Networks in Great Britain and Canada, 1778–1857', unpublished PhD thesis (University of Guelph, 2014), pp. 70, 131.
10 Taylor, *The Wild Black Region*, pp. 127–31, 196, 221–2, 251.

11 See, for example, Kehoe, 'Jacobites, Jamaica and the Establishment of a Highland Catholic Community in the Canadian Maritimes'; Iain MacKinnon and Andrew Mackillop, 'Plantation Slavery and Landownership in the West Highlands and Islands: Legacies and Lessons', *Community Land Scotland*, November 2020, available at: https://www.communitylandscotland.org.uk/wp-content/uploads/2020/11/Plantation-slavery-and-landownership-in-the-west-Highlands-and-Islands-legacies-and-lessons.pdf (accessed 18 January 2022); Alston, *Slaves and Highlanders*.
12 As Priya Satia argues, 'the discourse of history shaped the unfolding of imperial history'; Satia, *Time's Monster*, p. 287.

Bibliography

PRIMARY SOURCES: JAMES MACPHERSON

Fingal, an Ancient Epic Poem, in Six Books: Together with Several Other Poems, Composed by Ossian the Son of Fingal. Translated from the Galic Language, by James Macpherson (London: T. Becket and A. de Hondt, 1762).

Fragments of Ancient Poetry, Collected in the Highlands of Scotland, and Translated from the Galic or Erse Language by James Macpherson (Edinburgh: G. Hamilton and J. Balfour, 1760).

The Highlander: A Poem in Six Cantos (Edinburgh: W. Ruddiman Jr, 1758).

The History of Great Britain, from the Restoration, to the Accession of the House of Hannover, 2 vols (London: W. Strahan and T. Cadell, 1775).

The History and Management of the East-India Company, from Its Origin in 1600 to the Present Times (London: T. Cadell, 1779).

The History and Management of the East India Company from its Origin in 1600 to the Present Times. Volume the First. Containing the Affairs of the Carnatic; in which the Rights of the Nabob are explained, and the Injustice of the Company proved. The Whole Compiled from Authentic Records. A New Edition (London: T. Cadell, 1782).

The Iliad of Homer, 3 vols (London: T. Becket and P. A. de Hondt, 1773).

An Introduction to the History of Great Britain and Ireland (London: T. Becket and A. de Hondt, 1771).

Original Papers; Containing the Secret History of Great Britain, from the Restoration, to the Accession of the House of Hannover. To Which Are Prefixed, Extracts from the Life of James II, As Written by Himself, 2 vols (London: W. Strahan and T. Cadell, 1775).

Poems of Ossian, edited by George E. Todd (London: Sir Walter Scott, 1888).

The Poems of Ossian &c. Containing the Poetical Works of James Macpherson, Esq. in Prose and Rhyme, edited by Malcolm Laing (Edinburgh: T. Cadell Jr and W. Davies, 1805).

The Poems of Ossian and Related Works, edited by Howard Gaskill and Fiona Stafford (Edinburgh: Edinburgh University Press, 1996).

The Poems of Ossian. Translated by James Macpherson, Esq, 2 vols (London: W. Strahan and T. Becket, 1773).

The Poetical Works of James Macpherson (Edinburgh: P. Hill, 1802).

The Rights of Great Britain Asserted against the Claims of America: Being an Answer to the Declaration of the General Congress, 2nd edition (London: T. Cadell, 1775/6).

A Short History of the Opposition During the Last Session of Parliament (London: T. Cadell, 1779).

Temora, an Ancient Epic Poem, in Eight Books: Together with Several Other Poems, Composed by Ossian, the Son of Fingal. Translated from the Galic Language, by James Macpherson (London: T. Becket and P. A. de Hondt, 1763).

The Works of Ossian, the Son of Fingal: In Two Volumes. Translated from the Galic Language by James Macpherson (London: T. Becket and P. A. de Hondt, 1765).

MANUSCRIPTS

Aberdeen University Library, Aberdeen
  MS K 14 Album D.
  MS M 2 Album 2.
Bodleian Library, University of Oxford
  GB 1061 MSS Carte 1–290.
National Library of Scotland, Edinburgh
  MS ADV 73.2.13.
  MS ADV 34.7.3.
The National Archives, London
  Prob 11/1272.

OTHER PRINTED PRIMARY SOURCES

Anon., *Accounts of the Rise, Constitution and Management of the Society in Scotland for Propagating Christian Knowledge* (Edinburgh: William Bowen, 1820).

Anon., *Advice to the Writers in Defence of Douglas* (Edinburgh: no publisher, 1757).

Anon., *Copies of Papers Relative to the Restoration of the King of Tanjore* (London: no publisher, 1777).

Anon., *A Declaration by the Representatives of the United Colonies of North-America, now met in Congress at Philadelphia, setting forth the Causes and Necessity of their taking up Arms* (Philadelphia, PA: W. & T. Bradford, and Devizes, 1775).

Anon., 'Ossian Redivivus', *The Times*, 14 October 1869.

Aristotle, 'Poetics', *Classical Literary Criticism*, edited by T. S. Dorsch and Penelope Murray (London: Penguin, 2000), pp. 57–97.

Blackwell, Thomas, *An Enquiry into the Life and Writings of Homer* (London: no publisher, 1735).
Blair, Hugh, *A Critical Dissertation on the Poems of Ossian, the Son of Fingal* (London: T. Becket and P. A. De Hondt, 1763).
Blair, Hugh, *Lectures on Rhetoric and Belles Lettres* (Carbondale: Southern Illinois University Press, 2005).
Bolingbroke, Henry St John, 1st Viscount, *Letters on the Study and Use of History* (London: A. Millar, 1752).
Boswell, James. *Boswell's Edinburgh Journals 1767–1786*, edited by Hugh M. Milne (Edinburgh: Mercat Press, 2003).
Boswell, James, *The Journal of a Tour to the Hebrides with Samuel Johnson*, in *Journey to the Hebrides*, edited by Ian McGowan (Edinburgh: Canongate, 1996).
Bower, Walter, *Scotichronicon in Latin and English*, edited by John and Winifred MacQueen, 2 vols (Aberdeen: Aberdeen University Press, 1989).
Buchanan, George, *Buchanan's History of Scotland. In Twenty Books. The Second Edition, Revised and Corrected from the Latin Original, by Mr. Bond* (London: J. Bettenham, 1722).
Burke, Edmund and William Burke, *An Enquiry into the Policy of Making Conquests for the Mahometans in India, by the British Arms* (London: J. Dodsley, 1779).
Cambridge, Richard Owen, *An Account of the War in India between the English and French, on the Coast of Coromandel, From the Year 1750 to the Year 1761* (London: Jeffreys, 1762).
Campbell, Alexander, *An Introduction to the History of Poetry in Scotland, from the Beginning of the Thirteenth Century to the Present Time* (Edinburgh: Andrew Foulis, 1798).
Carlyle, Alexander, *The Autobiography of Dr Alexander Carlyle of Inveresk 1722–1805*, edited by John H. Burton (Bristol: Thoemmes, 1990).
Clarendon, Edward Hyde, *Life of Edward Earl of Clarendon* (Dublin: P. Wilson & J. Hoey, 1759).
Dow, Alexander, *The History of Hindostan from the Earliest Account of Time to the Death of Akbar. Vol. I and II* (London: T. Becket and P. A. de Hondt, 1768).
Dow, Alexander, *The History of Hindostan from the Death of Akbar to the Complete Settlement of the Empire under Aurungzebe. Vol. III* (London: T. Becket and P. A. de Hondt, 1772).
Fordun, John, *John of Fordun's Chronicle of the Scottish Nation*, edited by William F. Skene, translated by Felix J. H. Skene, 2 vols (Edinburgh: Edmonston and Douglas, 1872).
Fortescue, Sir John W. (ed.), *The Correspondence of King George III: 1760–83*, vol. 5 (London: Macmillan, 1927–8).
Gerard, Alexander, *An Essay on Taste*, 1st edition (London: A. Millar, 1759).
Gerard, Alexander, *An Essay on Taste*, 3rd edition (Edinburgh: J. Bell, W. Creech, 1780).

Gibbon, Edward, *The History of the Decline and Fall of the Roman Empire*, *Vol. I* (London: Strahan and Cadell, 1776).
Gibbon, Edward, *The History of the Decline and Fall of the Roman Empire*. *Vol. IV* (London: W. Strahan and T. Cadell, 1788).
Gibbon, Edward, *Mémoire Justificatif pour Servir de Réponse à L'exposé des Motifs de la Conduite du Roi de France Relativement à l'Angleterre* (London, 1778), in Lord Sheffield (ed.), *The Miscellaneous Works of Edward Gibbon, Esq., with Memoirs of His Life and Writings, Composed by Himself; Illustrated from His Letters, with Occasional Notes and Narrative. A New Edition, with Considerable Additions* (London: John Murray, 1814), pp. 1–34.
Grant, Anne, *Letters from the Mountains; Being the Correspondence with Her Friends, Between the Years 1773 and 1803, of Mrs Grant of Laggan. Vol. II*, edited by J. P. Grant (London: Longman, Brown, Green, and Longmans, 1845).
Henry, Robert, *History of Great Britain from the Invasion of it by the Romans under Julius Caesar* (London: T. Cadell, 1771).
Hill, G. Birkbeck (ed.), *Letters of David Hume to William Strahan* (Oxford: Clarendon Press, 1888).
Home, John, *Douglas*, edited by Gerald Parker (Edinburgh: Oliver & Boyd, 1972).
Home, John, *Douglas; A Tragedy* (Edinburgh: John Beugo, 1792).
Horace, 'Ars Poetica', in Niall Rudd (ed.), *Horace: Epistles Book II and Epistle to the Pisones ('Ars Poetica')* (Cambridge: Cambridge University Press, 1989).
Hume, David, *Essays: Moral, Political, and Literary* (Indianapolis, IN: Liberty Fund, 1987).
Hume, David, *Four Dissertations*, edited by John Immerwahr (Bristol: Thoemmes, 1995).
Hume, David, *The History of England from the Invasion of Julius Caesar to the Revolution in 1688*, 6 vols (Indianapolis, IN: Liberty Fund, 1983).
Hume, David, *The Letters of David Hume*, edited by John Y. T. Greig, 2 vols (Oxford: Clarendon Press, 1932).
Hume, David, *New Letters of David Hume*, edited by Raymond Klibansky and Ernest C. Mossner (Oxford: Clarendon Press, 1954).
Hurd, Richard, *The Works of Richard Hurd*, 8 vols (London: T. Cadell, W. Davies, 1811).
Johnson, Samuel, *A Dictionary of the English Language: in which The Words are deduced from their Originals, and Illustrated in their Different Significations by Examples from the best Writers*, 2 vols (London: W. Strahan, 1755).
Johnson, Samuel, *A Journey to the Western Islands of Scotland*, in *Journey to the Hebrides*, edited by Ian McGowan (Edinburgh: Canongate, 1996).
Johnson, Samuel, *The Lives of the Most Eminent English Poets; with critical observations on their works*, 4 vols (London: C. Bathurst and others, 1783).
Laing, Malcolm, *The History of Scotland, from the Union of the Crowns on the Accession of James VI to the Throne of England, to the Union of the Kingdoms in the Reign of Queen Anne, with 'An Historical and Critical Dissertation on*

the *Supposed Authenticity of Ossian's Poems'*, 4 vols (London: T. Cadell Jr and W. Davies, 1800).

Mackenzie, Henry, *An Account of the Life and Writings of John Home*, edited by Susan Manning (Bristol: Thoemmes, 1997).

Mackenzie, Henry, *Report of the Committee of the Highland Society of Scotland Appointed to Inquire in the Nature and Authenticity of the Poems of Ossian* (Edinburgh: Constable and others, 1805).

Macpherson, John, *Critical Dissertations on the Origin, Antiquities, Language, Government, Manners, Religion of the Ancient Caledonians, their Posterity, the Picts, and the British and Irish Scots* (Dublin: Boulton Grierson, 1768).

MacQueen, Daniel, *Letters on Hume's History of Great Britain*, edited by John V. Price (Bristol: Thoemmes, 1990).

Mallett, David, *Britannia: A Masque. Acted at the Theatre-Royal in Drury Lane* (London: A. Millar, 1755).

Malmesbury, William of, *The History of the English Kings*, edited by Roger A. B. Mynors, Rodney M. Thomson and Michael Winterbottom (Oxford: Clarendon Press, 1998–9).

Milton, John, *Paradise Lost*, edited by Jonathan Goldberg and Stephen Orgel (Oxford: Oxford University Press, 2004).

Monmouth, Geoffrey of, *The History of the Kings of Britain*, translated by Lewis Thorpe (Harmondsworth: Penguin 1966).

Orme, Robert, *A History of the Military Transactions of the British Nation in Indostan* (London: John Nourse, 1773).

Orme, Robert, *A History of the Military Transactions of the British Nation in Indostan. Vol. II* (London: John Nourse, 1778).

Percy, Thomas, *Reliques of Ancient English Poetry: Consisting of Old Heroic Ballads, Songs, and Other Pieces of Our Earlier Poets, Together With Some Few of Later Date*, 3 vols (London: R. and J. Dodsley, 1765).

Pope, Alexander, *The Iliad of Homer*, edited by Steven Shankman (London: Penguin, 1996).

Prothero, Rowland E. (ed.), *Private Letters of Edward Gibbon (1753–1794)*, vol. I (London: John Murray, 1897).

Ramsay, Allan, *The Ever Green, Being a Collection of Scots Poems, Wrote by the Ingenius Before 1600*, 2 vols (Edinburgh: T. Ruddiman, 1724).

Ramsay, Allan, *Tea-Table Miscellany* (Edinburgh: T. Ruddiman, 1724–32).

von Ranke, Leopold, *A History of England, Principally in the Seventeenth Century. Vol. VI* (Oxford: Oxford University Press, 1875).

Robertson, William, *An Historical Disquisition Concerning the Knowledge Which the Ancients Had of India; and the Progress of Trade with that Country Prior to the Discovery of the Passage to it by the Cape of Good Hope*, 2nd edition (London: A. Strahan and T. Cadell, 1794).

Robertson, William, *The History of America. Vol. I* (Dublin: Whitestone, 1777).

Robertson, William, *The History of Scotland, During the Reigns of Queen Mary and King James VI. Till the Accession to the Crown of England. With a Review of the Scotch History previous to that Period, And an Appendix containing Original Papers*, 2 vols (London: A. Millar, 1759).

Rous, George, *The Restoration of the King of Tanjore Considered* (London: no publisher, 1777).

Scott, Walter, *The Antiquary*, edited by Nicola J. Watson (Oxford: Oxford University Press, 2002).

Smith, Adam, *Lectures on Jurisprudence*, edited by R. Meek, D. Raphael and P. Stein (Oxford: Clarendon Press, 1978).

Smith, Adam, *Lectures on Rhetoric and Belles Lettres*, edited by J. G. Bryce (Indianapolis, IN: Liberty Fund, 1985).

Smollett, Tobias, *The Expedition of Humphry Clinker*, edited by Lewis M. Knapp (Oxford: Oxford University Press, 1998).

Sterne, Laurence, *The Life and Opinions of Tristram Shandy, Gentleman*, edited by Melvyn New (London: Penguin, 1997).

Stewart, Dugald, 'Account of the Life and Writings of Adam Smith, LL.D.', in W. P. D. Wightman and J. C. Bryce, *Essays on Philosophical Subjects* (Oxford: Clarendon Press, 1980), pp. 269–352.

Stoddart, John, *Remarks on Local Scenery and Manners in Scotland During the Years 1799 and 1800*, 2 vols (London: W. Miller, 1801).

Stuart, Gilbert, *Critical Observations Concerning the Scottish Historians Hume, Stuart, and Robertson* (London: Evans, 1782).

Tacitus, Cornelius, *Agricola; and Germany*, translated by Anthony R. Birley (Oxford: Oxford University Press, 1999).

Thomson, James, *The Seasons*, edited by James Sambrook (Oxford: Clarendon Press, 1981).

Verne, Jules, *The Green Ray*, translated by Karen Loukes (Edinburgh: Luath Press, 2009).

Voltaire, *An Essay upon the Civil Wars of France, Extracted from curious Manuscripts, And also upon the Epick Poetry of the European Nations from Homer down to Milton* (London: S. Jallason, 1727).

Warburton, Eliot (ed.), *Memoirs of Horace Walpole and his Contemporaries; Including Numerous Original Letters, Chiefly from Strawberry Hill* (London: H. Colburn, 1851).

Watson, James, *Choice Collection of Comic and Serios Scots Poems both Ancient and Modern* (Edinburgh: J. Watson, 1706–11).

Wilkie, William, *The Epigoniad* (Edinburgh: Hamilton, Balfour and Neill, 1757).

Wordsworth, Dorothy, *Recollections of a Tour Made in Scotland*, edited by Carol K. Walker (New Haven, CT: Yale University Press, 1997).

Young, Edward, *Conjectures on Original Composition. In a Letter to the Author of Sir Charles Grandison* (Dublin: P. Wilson, 1759).

NEWSPAPER TITLES

Scots Magazine, 33, April 1771, p. 206.
St. James's Chronicle, 27 January 1763, p. 2.
The Gazeteer and New Daily Advertiser, 24 August 1779, p. 1.
The Gentleman's Magazine: 'Obituary of Remarkable Persons; with Biographical Anecdotes', 66:3 (March 1776), p. 256.
The London Chronicle, 8–10 July 1779, p. 28.
The Weekly Magazine, or Edinburgh Amusement: Anon., 'Literary Anecdotes of James Macpherson, Esq', 18 January 1776, p. 97.

SECONDARY SOURCES

Allan, David, *Making British Culture: English Readers and the Scottish Enlightenment, 1740–1830* (London: Routledge, 2008).

Allan, David, *Scotland in the Eighteenth Century: Union and Enlightenment* (Harlow: Longman, 2002).

Allan, David, 'Scottish Historical Writing of the Enlightenment', in José Rabasa, Masayuki Sato, Edoardo Tortarolo and Daniel Woolf (eds), *The Oxford History of Historical Writing: Volume 3: 1400–1800* (Oxford: Oxford University Press, 2012), pp. 497–517.

Allen, Paul M. and Joan deRis, *Fingal's Cave, the Poems of Ossian, and Celtic Christianity* (New York: Continuum, 1999).

Alston, David, *Slaves and Highlanders: Silenced Histories of Scotland and the Caribbean* (Edinburgh: Edinburgh University Press, 2021).

Anderson, Alan O., *Early Sources of Scottish History, A.D. 500 to 1286*, edited by Marjorie Anderson (Stamford, CA: Paul Watkins, 1990).

Anderson, Marjorie O., *Kings and Kingship in Early Scotland* (Edinburgh: Scottish Academic Press, 1973).

Anderson, Peter J., *List of Officers: University and King's College, Aberdeen, 1495–1860* (Aberdeen: no publisher, 1893).

Anderson, Peter J., *Officers of the Marischal College and University of Aberdeen, 1593–1860* (Aberdeen: Aberdeen University Press, 1897).

Anderson, William, *The Scottish Nation; or the Surnames, Families, Literature, Honours, and Biographical History of the People of Scotland*, 3 vols (Edinburgh: Fullarton, 1863).

Andrews, Corey, *Literary Nationalism in Eighteenth-Century Scottish Club Poetry* (Lewiston, NY: Edwin Mellen Press, 2004).

Archambaud, Thomas, 'Un clan dans l'Empire: James Macpherson, des Lumières écossaises à l'Inde britannique', *Dix-huitième siècle*, 50 (2018), pp. 561–77.

Argyll, George Douglas Campbell, Duke of, *Scotland As It Was and As It Is* (Edinburgh: D. Douglas, 1887).

Aristotle, 'Poetics', *Classical Literary Criticism*, edited by T. S. Dorsch and Penelope Murray (London: Penguin, 2000), pp. 57–97.

Armitage, David (ed.), *British Political Thought in History, Literature and Theory, 1500–1800* (Cambridge: Cambridge University Press, 2006).

Arnold, Martin and Tom Shippey (eds), *Appropriating the Middle Ages: Scholarship, Politics, Fraud* (Cambridge: D. S. Brewer, 2001).

Aspinall-Oglander, Cecil F., *Freshly Remembered: The Story of Thomas Graham, Lord Lynedoch* (London: Hogarth Press, 1956).

Bagnani, Gilbert, 'On Fakes and Forgeries', *Phoenix*, 14:4 (1960), pp. 228–44.

Bain, Alexander, *The Life and Time of the Schoolmaster in Central Scotland in the 17th and 18th Centuries* (Callendar Park College of Education: Department of Educational Studies, 1977).

Baines, Paul, *The House of Forgery in Eighteenth-Century Britain* (Aldershot: Ashgate, 1999).

Baines, Paul, 'Ossianic Geographies: Fingalian Figures on the Scottish Tour, 1760–1830', *Scotlands*, 4:1 (1997), pp. 44–61.

Baines, Paul, Julian Ferraro and Pat Rogers (eds), *The Wiley-Blackwell Encyclopedia of Eighteenth-Century Writers and Writing 1660–1789* (Chichester: Wiley-Blackwell, 2011).

Bär, Gerard and Howard Gaskill (eds), *Ossian and National Epic* (Frankfurt: Peter Lang, 2012).

Barclay, William, *The Schools and Schoolmasters of Banffshire* (Banff: no publisher, 1925).

Barrell, John, 'Putting Down the Rising', in Leith Davis, Ian Duncan and Janet Sorensen (eds), *Scotland and the Borders of Romanticism* (Cambridge: Cambridge University Press, 2004), pp. 130–8.

Basker, James G., 'Scotticisms and the Problem of Cultural Identity in Eighteenth-Century Britain', in John Dwyer and Richard B. Sher (eds), *Sociability and Society in Eighteenth-Century Scotland* (Edinburgh: Mercat, 1993), pp. 81–95.

Bhambra, Gurminder K., 'Relations of Extraction, Relations of Redistribution: Empire, Nation, and the Construction of the British Welfare State', *British Journal of Sociology*, 73:1 (2022), pp. 4–15.

Biddle, Sheila, *Bolingbroke and Harley* (London: Allen and Unwin, 1975).

Black, Ronald, *An Lasair: Anthology of 18th Century Scottish Gaelic Verse* (Edinburgh: Birlinn, 2001).

Blanning, Tim, *The Romantic Revolution* (London: Weidenfeld & Nicolson, 2010).

Bode, Christopher and Jacqueline Labbe (eds), *Romantic Localities: Europe Writes Place* (London: Pickering & Chatto, 2010).

Bold, Valentina, '"Rude Bard of the North': James Macpherson and the Folklore of Democracy', *Journal of American Folklore*, 114:454 (2001), pp. 464–77.

Bourke, Richard, *Empire and Revolution: The Political Life of Edmund Burke* (Princeton, NJ: Princeton University Press, 2017).

Bourke, Richard, 'J. G. A. Pocock and the Presuppositions of the New British History', *Historical Journal*, 53:3 (2010), pp. 747–70.

Braudy, Leo, *Narrative Form in History and Fiction: Hume, Fielding & Gibbon* (Princeton, NJ: Princeton University Press, 1970).
Brett-James, Anthony, *General Graham, Lord Lynedoch* (London: Macmillan, 1959).
Brewer, John D., 'Conjectural History, Sociology and Social Change in Eighteenth-Century Scotland', in Stephen Kendrick, David McCrone and Pat Straw, *The Making of Scotland: Nation, Culture and Social Change* (Edinburgh: Edinburgh University Press, 1989), pp. 13–30.
Brewer, John D., *The Pleasures of the Imagination: English Culture in the Eighteenth Century* (London: HarperCollins, 1997).
Broadie, Alexander, *The Scottish Enlightenment: The Historical Age of the Historical Nation* (Edinburgh: Birlinn, 2001).
Brown, Peter H., *Early Travellers in Scotland* (Edinburgh: D. Douglas, 1891).
Brown, Stewart J., 'William Robertson, Early Orientalism and the *Historical Disquisition* on India of 1791', *Scottish Historical Review*, 88:2 (2009), pp. 289–312.
Brown, Terence (ed.), *Celticism* (Amsterdam: Rodopi, 1996).
Bryant, G. J., 'British Logistics and the Conduct of the Carnatic Wars', *War in History*, 11:3 (2004), pp. 278–306.
Bryant, G. J., *The Emergence of British Power in India, 1600–1784: A Grand Strategic Interpretation* (Woodbridge: Boydell & Brewer, 2013).
Buchan, Bruce, 'Enlightened Histories: Civilization, War and the Scottish Enlightenment', *The European Legacy*, 10:2 (2005), pp. 177–92.
Buchan, Bruce and Silvia Sebastiani, '"No Distinction of Black or Fair": The Natural History of Race in Adam Ferguson's Lectures on Moral Philosophy', *Journal of the History of Ideas*, 82:2 (2021), pp. 207–29.
Buchan, James, *Capital of the Mind: How Edinburgh Changed the World* (Edinburgh: Birlinn, 2007).
Bulloch, John M., *A History of the University of Aberdeen: 1495–1895* (London: Hodder and Stoughton, 1895).
Butler, Marilyn, 'Romanticism in England', in Roy Porter and Mikulas Teich (eds), *Romanticism in National Context* (Cambridge: Cambridge University Press, 1988), pp. 37–67.
Butterfield, Herbert, *The Whig Interpretation of History* (London: W. W. Norton & Co., 1965).
Byrne, Michel and Sheila Kidd (eds), *Lìontan Lìonmhor: Local, National and Global Gaelic Networks from the 18th to the 20th Century* (Glasgow: Roinn na Ceiltis & na Gàidhlig, Oilthigh Ghlaschu, 2019).
Bysveen, Josef, *Epic Tradition and Innovation in James Macpherson's 'Fingal'* (Uppsala: University of Uppsala, 1982).
Caldwell, David H. (ed.), *Scottish Weapons and Fortifications 1100–1800* (Edinburgh: John Donald, 1981).
Campbell, John L., *Gaelic in Scottish Education and Life: Past, Present and Future* (Edinburgh: Saltire Society, 1945).

Carboni, Pierre, 'Ossian and Belles Lettres: Scottish Influence on J.-B.-A. Suard and Late-Eighteenth-Century French Taste and Criticism', in Deidre Dawson and Pierre Morère (eds), *Scotland and France in the Enlightenment* (Lewisburg, PA: Bucknell University Press, 2004), pp. 74–89.

Carr, David, 'Narrative Explanation and its Malcontents', *History and Theory*, 47:1 (2008), pp. 19–30.

Carter, Jennifer J. and Colin A. Maclaren, *Crown and Gown 1495–1995: An Illustrated History of the University of Aberdeen* (Aberdeen: Aberdeen University Press, 1994).

Carter, Jennifer J. and Joan Pittock (eds), *Aberdeen and the Enlightenment: Proceedings of a Conference Held at the University of Aberdeen* (Aberdeen: Aberdeen University Press, 1987).

Cartlidge, Neil (ed.), *Boundaries in Medieval Romance* (Woodbridge: Boydell & Brewer, 2008).

Chance, J. F., 'Corrections to James Macpherson's "Original Papers"', *The English Historical Review*, 13:51 (1898), pp. 533–49.

Chapman, Malcolm, *The Gaelic Vision in Scottish Culture* (London: Croom Helm, 1978).

Chapman, R. W., 'Blair on Ossian', *The Review of English Studies*, 7:25 (1931), pp. 80–3.

Cheape, Hugh, *Bagpipes: A National Collection of a National Instrument* (Edinburgh: National Museums Scotland, 2008).

Cheape, Hugh, 'The Culture and Material Culture of Ossian', *Scotlands*, 4:1 (1997), pp. 1–24.

Cheape, Hugh, '"A Mind Restless Seeking": Sorley MacLean's Historical Research and the Poet as Historian', in Ronald W. Renton and Ian MacDonald (eds), *Ainmeil thar Cheudan: Presentations to the 2011 Sorley MacLean Conference* (Sabhal Mòr Ostaig, An t-Eilean Sgitheanach: Clò Ostaig, 2016), pp. 121–34.

Christiansen, Reidar T., *The Vikings and the Viking Wars in Irish and Gaelic Tradition* (Oslo: no publisher, 1931).

Clyde, Robert, *From Rebel to Hero: The Image of the Highlander, 1745–1830* (East Linton: Tuckwell Press, 1995).

Coleridge, Samuel T., *Breaking Away: Coleridge in Scotland*, edited by Carol K. Walker (New Haven, CT: Yale University Press, 2002).

Colley, Linda, *Britons: Forging the Nation, 1707–1837* (London: Vintage, 1996).

Connell, Philip, 'British Identities and the Politics of Ancient Poetry in Later Eighteenth-Century England', *The Historical Journal*, 49:1 (2006), pp. 161–92.

Connors, Richard and Ben Gilding, '"Hereditary Guardians of the Nation": The House of Lords and the East India Company in the Age of the American Revolution', *Parliamentary History*, 39:1 (2020), pp. 159–89.

Cowan, Edward J., *Folk in Print: Scotland's Chapbook Heritage, 1750–1850* (Edinburgh: John Donald, 2007).

Cowper, A. S., *SSPCK Schoolmasters 1709–1872* (Edinburgh: Scottish Record Society, 1997).
Craig, Cairns, 'Coleridge, Hume, and the Chains of Romantic Imagination', in Leith Davis, Ian Duncan and Janet Sorensen (eds), *Scotland and the Borders of Romanticism* (Cambridge: Cambridge University Press, 2004), pp. 20–37.
Craig, Cairns, *Intending Scotland: Explorations in Scottish Culture Since the Enlightenment* (Edinburgh: Edinburgh University Press, 2009).
Craig, Mary E., *Scottish Periodical Press 1750–1789* (Edinburgh: Oliver & Boyd, 1931).
Crawford, Robert, *Devolving English Literature* (Edinburgh: Edinburgh University Press, 2000).
Crawford, Robert, *The Modern Poet: Poetry, Academia and Knowledge since the 1750s* (Oxford: Oxford University Press, 2001).
Crawford, Robert, *Scotland's Books: The Penguin History of Scottish Literature* (London: Penguin, 2007).
Creed, Robert P., 'The Singer Looks at His Sources', *Comparative Literature*, 14:1 (1962), pp. 44–52.
Croce, Benedetto, *History, as the Story of Liberty* (London: Allan and Unwin, 1941).
Cunningham, Hugh, 'The Language of Patriotism', *History Workshop Journal*, 12 (1981), pp. 8–33.
Curley, Thomas M., *Samuel Johnson, The* Ossian *Fraud, and the Celtic Revival in Great Britain and Ireland* (Cambridge: Cambridge University Press, 2009).
Curran, Stuart, *Poetic Form and British Romanticism* (Oxford: Oxford University Press, 1986).
Daiches, David, *The Paradox of Scottish Culture: The Eighteenth-Century Experience* (London: Oxford University Press, 1964).
Dalrymple, William, *The Anarchy: The Relentless Rise of the East India Company* (London: Bloomsbury, 2019).
Davies, G., 'Macpherson and the Nairne Papers', *The English Historical Review*, 35:139 (1920), pp. 367–76.
Davis, Leith, *Acts of Union: Scotland and the Literary Negotiation of the British Nation, 1707–1830* (Stanford, CA: Stanford University Press, 1998).
Davis, Leith, '"Origins of the Specious": James Macpherson's Ossian and the Forging of the British Empire', *The Eighteenth Century: Theory and Interpretation*, 34:2 (1993), pp. 132–50.
Davis, Leith, 'Transnational Articulations in James Macpherson's *Poems of Ossian* and *The History and Management of the East-India Company*', *The Eighteenth Century*, 60:4 (2019), pp. 441–60.
Davis, Leith, Ian Duncan and Janet Sorensen (eds), *Scotland and the Borders of Romanticism* (Cambridge: Cambridge University Press, 2004).
Dawson, Deirdre and Pierre Morère (eds), *Scotland and France in the Enlightenment* (Lewisburg, PA: Bucknell University Press, 2003).

Dean, Carolyn J., '*Metahistory: The Historical Imagination in Nineteenth-Century Europe*, by Hayden White', *American Historical Review*, 124:4 (2019), pp. 1337–50.
DeBolla, Peter, *The Discourse of the Sublime: Readings in History, Aesthetics and the Subject* (Oxford: Blackwell, 1989).
DeBolla, Peter, Nigel Leask and David Simpson (eds), *Land, Nation and Culture, 1740–1840: Thinking the Republic of Taste* (Basingstoke: Palgrave Macmillan, 2005).
deGategno, Paul J., *James Macpherson* (Boston, MA: Twayne, 1989).
deGategno, Paul J., 'Replying to a Crisis: James Macpherson's *The Rights of Great Britain Asserted against the Claims of America*', *Britain and the World*, 11:2 (2018), pp. 195–211.
de Groot, Joanna, *Empire and History Writing in Britain c. 1750–2012* (Manchester: Manchester University Press, 2013).
DeLuca, JoEllen, *A Feminine Enlightenment* (Edinburgh: Edinburgh University Press, 2015).
Dentith, Simon, *Epic and Empire in Nineteenth-Century Britain* (Cambridge: Cambridge University Press, 2006).
Devine, Thomas M., *Exploring the Scottish Past: Themes in the History of Scottish Society* (Phantassie: Tuckwell Press, 1995).
Devine, Thomas M., *The Transformation of Rural Scotland: Social Change and the Agrarian Economy 1660–1815* (Edinburgh: John Donald, 1999).
Dingwall, Christopher, 'Ossian and Dunkeld', *Scotlands*, 4:1 (1997), pp. 62–70.
Dirks, Nicholas B., *The Scandal of Empire: India and the Creation of Imperial Britain* (Cambridge, MA: Harvard University Press, 2009).
Donnachie, Ian and Christopher Whatley (eds), *The Manufacture of Scottish History* (Edinburgh: Polygon, 1992).
Dryden, John, *Virgil's Aeneid*, edited by Frederick Keener (London: Penguin, 1997).
Duff, David and Catherine Jones (eds), *Scotland, Ireland, and the Romantic Aesthetic* (Lewisburg, PA: Bucknell University Press, 2007).
Dunbar, Robert, 'Vernacular Gaelic Tradition', in Sarah Dunnigan and Susan Gilbert (eds), *The Edinburgh Companion to Scottish Traditional Literatures* (Edinburgh: Edinburgh University Press, 2013), pp. 51–62.
Duncan, Archibald, *The Edinburgh History of Scotland. Vol. 1, Scotland: The Making of the Kingdom* (Edinburgh: Mercat Press, 1975).
Duncan, Ian, 'The Pathos of Abstraction: Adam Smith, Ossian, and Samuel Johnson', in Leith Davis, Ian Duncan and Janet Sorensen (eds), *Scotland and the Borders of Romanticism* (Cambridge: Cambridge University Press, 2004), pp. 38–56.
Duncan, Ian (with Leith Davis and Janet Sorensen), 'Introduction', in Leith Davis, Ian Duncan and Janet Sorensen (eds), *Scotland and the Borders of Romanticism* (Cambridge: Cambridge University Press, 2004), pp. 1–20.

Dunn, John J., 'James Macpherson's First Epic', *Studies in Scottish Literature*, 9:1 (1971), pp. 48–54.

Durie, Alastair J., *Scotland for the Holidays: Tourism in Scotland, 1780–1939* (East Linton: Tuckwell, 2003).

Dwyer, John, 'Enlightened Spectators and Classical Moralists: Sympathetic Relations in Eighteenth-Century Scotland', in John Dwyer and Richard B. Sher (eds), *Sociability and Society in Eighteenth-Century Scotland* (Edinburgh: Mercat, 1993), pp. 93–118.

Dwyer, John, 'Introduction – A "Peculiar Blessing": Social Converse in Scotland from Hutcheson to Burns', in John Dwyer and Richard B. Sher (eds), *Sociability and Society in Eighteenth-Century Scotland* (Edinburgh: Mercat, 1993), pp. 1–22.

Dwyer, John, 'The Melancholy Savage: Text and Context in the *Poems of Ossian*', in Howard Gaskill (ed.), *Ossian Revisited* (Edinburgh: Edinburgh University Press, 1991), pp. 164–207.

Dziennik, Matthew P., *The Fatal Land: War, Empire, and the Highland Soldier in British America* (New Haven, CT: Yale University Press, 2015).

Dziennik, Matthew P., '"Under ye Lash of ye Law": The State and the Law in the Post-Culloden Scottish Highlands', *Journal of British Studies*, 60:3 (2021), pp. 609–31.

Dziennik, Matthew P., 'Whig Tartan: Material Culture and its Use in the Scottish Highlands, 1746–1815', *Past and Present*, 217 (2012), pp. 117–47.

Emerson, Roger L., *Academic Patronage in the Scottish Enlightenment: Glasgow, Edinburgh and St Andrews Universities* (Edinburgh: Edinburgh University Press, 2008).

Emerson, Roger L., *Professors, Patronage and Politics: The Aberdeen Universities in the Eighteenth Century* (Aberdeen: Aberdeen University Press, 1992).

Fairer, David, *English Poetry of the Eighteenth Century 1700–1789* (London: Pearson, 2003).

Fairer, David, 'Historical Criticism and the English Canon: A Spenserian Dispute in the 1750s', *Eighteenth-Century Life*, 24 (2000), pp. 43–64.

Faria, Pedro, 'David Hume, the Académie des Inscriptions and the Nature of Historical Evidence in the Early Eighteenth Century', *Modern Intellectual History*, 18:2 (2021), pp. 299–322.

Ferguson, William, *Scotland's Relations with England: A Survey to 1707* (Edinburgh: Saltire Society, 1994).

Ferris, Ina, 'Melancholy, Memory, and the "Narrative Situation" of History in Post-Enlightenment Scotland', in Leith Davis, Ian Duncan and Janet Sorensen (eds), *Scotland and the Borders of Romanticism* (Cambridge: Cambridge University Press, 2004), pp. 77–93.

Fielding, Penny, *Writing and Orality: Nationality, Culture and Nineteenth-Century Scottish Fiction* (Oxford: Clarendon Press, 1996).

Finlay, Richard J., 'Caledonia or North Britain? Scottish Identity in the Eighteenth Century', in Dauvit Broun, R. J. Finlay and Michael Lynch (eds),

Image and Identity: The Making and Re-Making of Scotland Through the Ages (Edinburgh: John Donald, 1998), pp. 143–56.
Forbes, Duncan, *Hume's Philosophical Politics* (Cambridge: Cambridge University Press, 1975).
Force, Pierre, 'The "Exasperating Predecessor": Pocock on Gibbon and Voltaire', *Journal of the History of Ideas*, 77:1 (2016), pp. 129–45.
Force, Pierre, 'Voltaire and the Necessity of Modern History', *Modern Intellectual History*, 6:3 (2009), pp. 457–84.
France, Peter, 'Primitivism and Enlightenment: Rousseau and the Scots', *The Yearbook of English Studies*, 15 (1985), pp. 64–79.
Frenzel, Elisabeth, *Motive Der Weltliteratur. Ein Lexikon Dichtungsgeschichtlicher Längsschnitte* (Stuttgart: Alfred Kröner Verlag, 1980).
Fry, Michael, 'The Whig Interpretation of Scottish History', in Ian Donnachie and Christopher Whatley (eds), *The Manufacture of Scottish History* (Edinburgh: Polygon, 1992), pp. 72–89.
Frye, Northrop, 'Towards Defining an Age of Sensibility', *ELH*, 23 (1956), pp. 144–52.
Fuchs, Barbara, *Romance* (London: Routledge, 2004).
Fugelso, Karl (ed.), *Defining Medievalism(s)* (Cambridge: D. S. Brewer, 2009).
Fulford, Tim, *Landscape, Liberty and Authority: Poetry, Criticism and Politics from Thomson to Wordsworth* (Cambridge: Cambridge University Press, 1996).
Gaskill, Howard (ed.), *Ossian Revisited* (Edinburgh: Edinburgh University Press, 1991).
Gaskill, Howard (ed.), *The Reception of Ossian in Europe* (London: Continuum, 2004).
Gaskill, Howard, 'What Did James Macpherson Really Leave on Display at his Publisher's Shop in 1762?', *Scottish Gaelic Studies*, 16 (1990), pp. 67–89.
Gaskill, Howard and Stafford, Fiona (eds), *From Gaelic to Romantic: Ossianic Translations* (Amsterdam: Rodopi, 1998).
Geddes, Jane (ed.), *King's College Chapel, Aberdeen, 1500–2000* (Leeds: Northern Universities Press, 2000).
Gidal, Eric, *Ossianic Unconformities: Bardic Poetry in the Industrial Age* (Charlottesville: University of Virginia Press, 2015).
Gilroy, Amanda (ed.), *Romantic Geographies: Discourses of Travel, 1775–1844* (Manchester: Manchester University Press, 2000).
Glendening, John, *The High Road: Romantic Tourism, Scotland, and Literature, 1720–1820* (Basingstoke: Macmillan, 1997).
Godwin, William, 'Of History and Romance', *Caleb Williams*, edited by Maurice Hindle (London: Penguin, 2005), pp. 359–74.
Gold, John R. and Margaret M. Gold, *Imagining Scotland: Tradition, Representation, and Promotion in Scottish Tourism Since 1750* (Aldershot: Ashgate, 1995).
Goldie, Mark, 'The Scottish Catholic Enlightenment', *Journal of British Studies*, 30:1 (1991), pp. 20–62.

Goldstein, R. James, *The Matter of Scotland: Historical Narrative in Medieval Scotland* (Lincoln: University of Nebraska Press, 1993).
Grafton, Anthony, *The Footnote: A Curious History* (Cambridge, MA: Harvard University Press, 1999).
Grafton, Anthony, 'The Footnote from De Thou to Ranke', *History and Theory*, 33:4 (1994), pp. 53–76.
Grafton, Anthony, *Forgers and Critics: Creativity and Duplicity in Western Scholarship* (Princeton, NJ: Princeton University Press, 1990).
Graham, Henry G., *Scottish Men of Letters in the Eighteenth Century* (London: Black, 1901).
Greene, Jack P., *The Constitutional Origins of the American Revolution* (Cambridge: Cambridge University Press, 2011).
Greene, Jack P., *Evaluating Empire and Confronting Colonialism in Eighteenth-Century Britain* (Cambridge: Cambridge University Press, 2013).
Greene, Jack P., 'The Seven Years' War and the American Revolution: The Causal Relationship Reconsidered', *Journal of Imperial and Commonwealth History*, 8:2 (1980), pp. 85–105.
Grobman, Neil R., 'David Hume and the Earliest Scientific Methodology for Collecting Balladry', *Western Folklore*, 34:1 (1975), pp. 16–31.
Grobman, Neil R., 'Lord Kames and the Study of Comparative Mythology', *Folklore*, 92:1 (1981), pp. 91–103.
Grobman, Neil R., 'Thomas Blackwell's Commentary on the Oral Nature of Epic', *Western Folklore*, 38:3 (1979), pp. 186–98.
Guha, Ranajit, *History at the Limit of World-History* (New York: Columbia University Press, 2002).
Hägin, Peter, *The Epic Hero and the Decline of Heroic Poetry: A Study of the Neoclassical English Epic with Special Reference to Milton's 'Paradise Lost'* (Bern: Francke, 1964).
Hale, John R., *The Evolution of British Historiography: from Bacon to Namier* (London: Macmillan, 1967).
Hamilton, Douglas J., *Scotland, the Caribbean and the Atlantic World, 1750–1820* (Manchester: Manchester University Press, 2005).
Hamilton, William, of Gilbertfield, *Blind Harry's Wallace*, edited by Elspeth King (Edinburgh: Luath Press, 1998).
Hargreaves, Neil K., 'National History and "Philosophical" History: Character and Narrative in William Robertson's *History of Scotland*', *History of European Ideas*, 26:1 (2000), pp. 19–33.
Hargreaves, Neil K., 'The "Progress of Ambition": Character, Narrative, and Philosophy in the Works of William Robertson', *Journal of the History of Ideas*, 63:2 (2002), pp. 261–82.
Haugen, Kristine L., 'Ossian and the Invention of Textual History', *Journal of the History of Ideas*, 59:2 (1998), pp. 309–27.

Hawes, Clement, 'Johnson's Cosmopolitan Nationalism', in Philip Smallwood (ed.), *Johnson Re-Visioned: Looking Before and After* (Lewisburg, PA: Bucknell University Press, 2001), pp. 37–63.

Haywood, Ian, 'Chatterton's Plans for the Publication of the Forgery', *The Review of English Studies*, 36:141 (1985), pp. 58–68.

Haywood, Ian, *Faking It: Arts and the Politics of Forgery* (Brighton: Harvester Press, 1987).

Haywood, Ian, *The Making of History: A Study of the Literary Forgeries of James Macpherson and Thomas Chatterton in Relation to Eighteenth-Century Idea of History and Fiction* (London: Associated University Presses, 1986).

Heath, Eugene and Vincenzo Merolle, 'Introduction', in E. Heath and V. Merolle (eds), *Adam Ferguson: History, Progress and Human Nature* (London: Pickering & Chatto, 2007).

Henshaw, Victoria, 'James Macpherson and His Contemporaries: The Methods and Networks of Collectors of Gaelic Poetry in Late Eighteenth-Century Scotland', *Journal for Eighteenth-Century Studies*, 39:2 (2016), pp. 197–209.

Herman, Arthur, *The Scottish Enlightenment: The Scots' Invention of the Modern World* (London: Harper Perennial, 2006).

Hewitson, Jim, *Scotching the Myths: An Alternative Route Map to Scottish History* (Edinburgh: Mainstream Publishing, 1995).

Hicks, Dan, 'Event Density', in A. Boyd, J. Meades and D. Hicks (eds), *Isle of Rust* (Edinburgh: Luath Press, 2019), pp. 185–90.

Hicks, Philip, *Neoclassical History and English Culture: From Clarendon to Hume* (Basingstoke: Macmillan, 1996).

Higgins, David M., 'Celebrity, Politics and the Rhetoric of Genius', in Tom Mole (ed.), *Romanticism and Celebrity Culture: 1750–1850* (Cambridge: Cambridge University Press, 2009), pp. 41–59.

Higgins, David M., *Romantic Genius and the Literary Magazine: Biography, Celebrity, Politics* (London: Routledge, 2005).

Hill, Lisa, 'Adam Smith and the Theme of Corruption', *The Review of Politics*, 68 (2006), pp. 636–62.

Hobsbawm, Eric and Terence Ranger (eds), *The Invention of Tradition* (Cambridge: Cambridge University Press, 1992).

Hoffman, Michael J. and Patrick D. Murphy (eds), *Essentials of the Theory of Fiction* (Durham, NC: Duke University Press, 1996).

Hogg, Ulrike and Martin MacGregor, 'Historiography in Highlands and Lowlands', in Nicola Royan (ed.), *The International Companion to Scottish Literature 1400–1650* (Glasgow: Scottish Literature International, 2018), pp. 100–23.

Hook, Andrew (ed.), *The History of Scottish Literature. Vol. 2, 1660–1800* (Aberdeen: Aberdeen University Press, 1987).

Hook, Andrew (ed.), '"Ossian" Macpherson as Image Maker', *The Scottish Review: Arts and Environment*, 36 (1984), pp. 39–44.

Horn, D. B. 'Some Scottish Writers of History in the Eighteenth Century', *The Scottish Historical Review*, 40:129 (1961), pp. 1–18.

Hudson, Benjamin T., *Kings of Celtic Scotland* (Westport, CT: Greenwood Press, 1994).

Hunter, James, *The Making of the Crofting Community* (Edinburgh: John Donald, 1976).

Hunter, James, *On the Other Side of Sorrow: Nature and People in the Scottish Highlands* (Edinburgh: Mainstream, 1995).

Iggers, Georg G., 'The Image of Ranke in American and German Historical Thought', *History and Theory*, 2:1 (1962), pp. 17–40.

Johnson, Nevil, 'Opposition in the British Political System', *Government and Opposition*, 32:04 (1997), pp. 487–510.

Jones, Catherine, *Literary Memory: Scott's Waverley Novels and the Psychology of Narrative* (Lewisburg, PA: Bucknell University Press, 2003).

Jones, Catherine, 'Madame de Staël and Scotland: *Corinne*, Ossian and the Science of Nations', *Romanticism*, 15:3 (2009), pp. 239–53.

Jones, Edwin, *The English Nation: The Great Myth* (Stroud: Sutton, 1998).

Jones, Robert W., *Literature, Gender and Politics in Britain During the War for America 1770–1785* (Cambridge: Cambridge University Press, 2011).

Jones, Robert W., 'Principles, Prejudices, and the Politics of James Macpherson's Historical Writing', in Dafydd Moore (ed.), *The International Companion to James Macpherson and* The Poems of Ossian (Glasgow: Scottish Literature International, 2017), pp. 119–33.

Jones, Tom, 'Pope and the Ends of History: Faction, Atterbury, and Clarendon's *History of the Rebellion*, *Studies in Philology*, 110:4 (2013), pp. 880–902.

Jonsson, Fredrik Albritton, *Enlightenment's Frontier: The Scottish Highlands and the Origins of Environmentalism* (New Haven, CT: Yale University Press, 2013).

Johnston, Arthur, *Enchanted Ground: The Study of Medieval Romance in the Eighteenth Century* (London: Athlone, 1964).

Johnston, George H., *The Ruddimans in Scotland: Their History and Works* (Edinburgh: W. and A. K. Johnston, 1901).

Joynt, Carey B. and Nicholas Rescher, 'The Problem of Uniqueness in History', *History and Theory*, 1:2 (1961), pp. 150–62.

Jung, Sandro, *David Mallett, Anglo-Scot: Poetry, Patronage, and Politics in the Age of Union* (Newark: Delaware University Press, 2008).

Jung, Sandro, *The Fragmentary Poetic: Eighteenth-Century Uses of an Experimental Mode* (Bethlehem, PA: Lehigh University Press, 2009).

Kaul, Suvir, *Poems of Nation, Anthems of Empire: English Verse in the Long Eighteenth Century* (Charlottesville: University Press of Virginia, 2000).

Kehoe, S. Karly, 'Jacobites, Jamaica and the Establishment of a Highland Catholic Community in the Canadian Maritimes', *Scottish Historical Review*, 100:2 (2021), pp. 199–217.
Kelly, Stuart, 'Literary Fake of Epic Proportions', *Scotland on Sunday*, 25 June 2006.
Kenyon, John P., *The History Men: The Historical Profession in England Since the Renaissance* (London: Weidenfeld and Nicholson, 1983).
Kersey, Melvin, 'The Pre-Ossianic Politics of James Macpherson', *British Journal for Eighteenth-Century Studies*, 27 (2004), pp. 51–75.
Kidd, Colin, 'Gaelic Antiquity and National Identity in Enlightenment Ireland and Scotland', *The English Historical Review*, 109:434 (1994), pp. 1197–1214.
Kidd, Colin, 'Macpherson, Burns and the Politics of Sentiment', *Scotlands*, 4:1 (1997), pp. 25–43.
Kidd, Colin, 'North Britishness and the Nature of Eighteenth-Century British Patriotisms', *The Historical Journal*, 39:2 (1996), pp. 361–82.
Kidd, Colin, *Subverting Scotland's Past: Scottish Whig Historians and the Creation of an Anglo-British Identity, 1689–c.1830* (Cambridge: Cambridge University Press, 1993).
Korshin, Paul J., 'Reconfiguring the Past: The Eighteenth Century Confronts Oral Culture', *The Yearbook of English Studies*, 18 (1998), pp. 235–49.
Kozlowski, Lisa, 'Terrible Women and Tender Men: A Study of Gender in Macpherson's *Ossian*', in Howard Gaskill and Fiona Stafford (eds), *From Gaelic to Romantic: Ossianic Translations* (Amsterdam: Rodopi, 1998), pp. 119–35.
Kramnick, Isaac, 'Augustan Politics and English Historiography: The Debate on the English Past', *History and Theory*, 6 (1967), pp. 35–56.
Kramnick, Isaac, *Bolingbroke and his Circle: The Politics of Nostalgia in the Age of Walpole* (Cambridge, MA: Harvard University Press, 1968).
Kristmannsson, Gauti, 'The Subversive Loyalty of Ossian', *Scotlands*, 4:1 (1997), pp. 71–86.
Kumar, Krishan, *The Making of English National Identity* (Cambridge: Cambridge University Press, 2003).
Landry, Donna, *The Invention of the Countryside: Hunting, Walking and Ecology in English Literature, 1671–1831* (Basingstoke: Palgrave, 2001).
Langford, Paul, 'Old Whigs, Old Tories, and the American Revolution', *Journal of Imperial and Commonwealth History*, 8:2 (1980), pp. 106–30.
Laughlin, Corinna, 'The Lawless Language of Macpherson's "Ossian"', *Studies in English Literature 1500–1900*, 40:3 (2000), pp. 511–37.
Lawrence, Eugene, *The Lives of the British Historians*, 2 vols (New York: Scribner, 1855).
Lawson, Phillip, *The Imperial Challenge: Quebec and Britain in the Age of the American Revolution* (Montreal and Kingston: McGill-Queen's University Press, 1994).

Leask, Nigel, *Curiosity and the Aesthetics of Travel Writing 1770–1840* (Oxford: Oxford University Press, 2004).

Leask, Nigel, 'Fingalian Topographies: Ossian and the Highland Tour, 1760–1805', *Journal for Eighteenth-Century Studies* 39:2 (2016), pp. 183–96.

Lee, Yoon S., 'Giants in the North: *Douglas*, the Scottish Enlightenment, and Scott's *Redgauntlet*', *Studies in Romanticism*, 40 (2001), pp. 109–21.

Leerssen, Joep, 'Ossianic Liminality: Between Native Tradition and Preromantic Taste', in Howard Gaskill and Fiona Stafford (eds), *From Gaelic to Romantic: Ossianic Translations* (Amsterdam: Rodopi, 1998), pp. 1–16.

Leisy, Earnest E., 'Thoreau and Ossian', *The New England Quarterly*, 18:1 (1945), pp. 96–8.

Levine, Joseph, *The Battle of the Books: History and Literature in the Augustan Age* (Ithaca, NY: Cornell University Press, 1991).

Levine, Joseph, *Re-enacting the Past: Essays on the Evolution of Modern English Historiography* (Aldershot: Ashgate, 2004).

Lindfield-Ott, Kristin, 'Epic Scotland: Wilkie, Macpherson and Other Homeric Efforts', in Roberts Simms (ed.), *Brill's Companion to Prequels, Sequels, and Retellings of Classical Epic* (Leiden: Brill, 2018), pp. 357–74.

Lindfield-Ott, Kristin, 'Jules Verne's Ossianic Adventures: *Le Rayon Vert*, Scotland and Macpherson's Ossianic Legacy', in Camille Manfredi and Michel Byrne (eds), *Bretagne-Ecosse: Contacts, Transferts et Dissonances/ Brittany-Scotland: Contacts, Transfers and Dissonances* (Brest: Université de Bretagne Occidentale, 2017), pp. 251–72.

Lindfield-Ott, Kristin (as Ott, Kristin), 'Sublime Landscapes and Ancient Traditions: Picturesque Literary Tourism in Scotland', in Christoph Bode and Jacqueline Labbe (eds), *Romantic Localities: Europe Writes Place* (London: Pickering & Chatto, 2010), pp. 39–50.

Lindsay, Maurice, *The Discovery of Scotland: Based on Accounts of Foreign Travellers form the Thirteenth to the Eighteenth Centuries* (London: Robert Hale, 1964).

Linebaugh, Peter and Marcus Rediker, *The Many-Headed Hydra: Sailors, Slaves, Commoners, and the Hidden History of the Revolutionary Atlantic* (Boston, MA: Beacon Press, 2000).

Lock, F. P., 'An Unpublished Letter from Adam Smith to Sir John Macpherson', *Scottish Historical Review*, 85:1 (2006), pp. 135–7.

Love, Henry Davidson, *Indian Records Series Vestiges of Old Madras*, vol. 3 (London: Murray, 1913).

Loyn, Henry R., *The Vikings in Britain* (London: Batsford, 1977).

Lutnick, Solomon, *The American Revolution and the British Press 1775–1783* (Columbia: University of Missouri Press, 1967).

Lutnick, Solomon, 'Edward Gibbon and the Decline of the First British Empire: The Historian as Politician', *Studies in Burke and his Time*, 10:2 (1968).

Lynch, Jack, *Deception and Detection in Eighteenth-Century Britain* (Aldershot: Ashgate, 2008).

Lynch, Michael, *Scotland: A New History* (London: Pimlico, 1992).
Macbain, Alexander, 'Macpherson's Ossian', *The Celtic Magazine*, 137:12 (1887), pp. 145–54, 193–201, 240–54.
McCormack, Matthew, 'Citizenship, Nationhood, and Masculinity in the Affair of the Hanoverian Soldier, 1756', *Historical Journal*, 49:4 (2006), pp. 971–93.
McCormack, Matthew, 'The New Militia: War, Politics and Gender in 1750s Britain', *Gender & History*, 19:3 (2007), pp. 483–500.
McCosh, James, *The Scottish Philosophy: Biographical, Expository, Critical, from Hutcheson to Hamilton* (New York: Carter, 1875).
McCrone, David, 'Representing Scotland: Culture and Nationalism', in Stephen Kendrick, David McCrone and Pat Straw (eds), *The Making of Scotland: Nation, Culture and Social Change* (Edinburgh: Edinburgh University Press, 1989), pp. 161–74.
McElroy, George, 'Ossianic Imagination and the History of India: James and John Macpherson as Propagandists and Intriguers', in Jennifer J. Carter and Joan H. Pittock (eds), *Aberdeen and the Enlightenment: Proceedings of a Conference Held at the University of Aberdeen* (Aberdeen: Aberdeen University Press, 1987), pp. 363–74.
McGann, Jerome J., *The Poetics of Sensibility: A Revolution in Literary Style* (Oxford: Clarendon Press, 1996).
McGann, Jerome J., *The Romantic Ideology: A Critical Investigation* (Chicago: University of Chicago Press, 1983).
Macinnes, Allan I., *Clanship, Commerce, and the House of Stuart, 1603–1788* (East Linton: Tuckwell Press, 1996).
Macinnes, Allan I. and Douglas J. Hamilton (eds), *Jacobitism, Enlightenment and Empire, 1680–1820* (London: Routledge, 2016).
McIntosh, Alastair, 'Foreword', in James Hunter, *On the Other Side of Sorrow: Nature and People in the Scottish Highlands* (Edinburgh: Birlinn, 2014), pp. xv–xxxix.
McKean, Thomas A., 'The Fieldwork Legacy of James Macpherson', *The Journal of American Folklore*, 114:454 (2001), pp. 447–63.
MacKenzie, John M., 'Scottish Orientalists, Administrators and Missions: A Distinctive Scots Approach to Asia?', in T. M. Devine and Angela McCarthy (eds), *The Scottish Experience in Asia, c. 1700 to the Present: Settlers and Sojourners* (Basingstoke: Palgrave Macmillan, 2017), pp. 51–73.
Mackillop, Andrew, 'For King, Country and Regiment? Motive and Identity in Highland Soldiering 1746–1815', in Andrew Mackillop and Steve Murdoch (eds), *Fighting for Identity: Scottish Military Experience c.1550–1900* (Leiden: Brill, 2002), pp. 185–212.
Mackillop, Andrew, *Human Capital and Empire: Scotland, Ireland, Wales and British Imperialism in Asia, c.1690–c.1820* (Manchester: Manchester University Press, 2021).
Mackillop, Andrew, *'More Fruitful than the Soil': Army, Empire and the Scottish Highlands, 1715–1815* (East Linton: Tuckwell Press, 2000).

MacKinnon, Iain, 'Recognising and Reconstituting *Gàidheil* Ethnicity', *Scottish Affairs*, 30:2 (2021), pp. 212–30.

Maclachlan, Christopher (ed.), *Before Burns: Eighteenth-Century Scottish Poetry* (Edinburgh: Canongate, 2002).

McLane, Maureen, *Balladeering, Minstrelsy, and the Making of British Romantic Poetry* (Cambridge: Cambridge University Press, 2008).

McLane, Maureen, 'Ballads and Bards: British Romantic Orality', *Modern Philology*, 98:3 (2001), pp. 423–43.

McLaren, Colin, *Aberdeen Students 1600–1860* (Aberdeen: Aberdeen University Press, 2005).

Macleod, John, *Highlanders: A History of the Gaels* (London: Hodder and Stoughton, 1996).

McLynn, Frank J., *1759: The Year Britain Became Master of the World* (London: Jonathan Cape, 2004).

MacMillan, Dougald, 'David Garrick, Manager: Notes on the Theatre as a Cultural Institution in England in the Eighteenth Century', *Studies in Philology*, 45:4 (1948), pp. 630–64.

MacMillan, Dougald, 'The First Editions of Home's "Douglas"', *Studies in Philology*, 26:3 (1929), pp. 401–9.

McNeil, Kenneth, *Scotland, Britain, Empire: Writing the Highlands, 1760–1860* (Columbus: Ohio State University Press, 2007).

McNeill, Peter G. B. and Hector L. MacQueen, *Atlas of Scottish History to 1707* (Edinburgh: Scottish Medievalists and the Department of Geography, University of Edinburgh, 1996).

MacPhee, Kathleen M., *Somerled: Hammer of the Norse* (Glasgow: Neil Wilson Publishing, 2004).

Macpherson, Alan G., *A Day's March to Ruin: The Badenoch Men in the 'Forty-Fife and Col. Ewan Macpherson of Cluny* (Newtonmore: Clan Macpherson Association, 1996).

Macpherson, Alan G., 'James "Ossian" Macpherson's Ancestry: An Elucidation of a Mystery', *The Scottish Genealogist*, 11:3 (1964), pp. 15–20 (reprinted from *Creagh Dubh*, 16 (1964), pp. 20–4).

Macpherson, Alan G., *The Posterity of the Three Brethren: A Short History of the Clan Macpherson* (Inverness: Clan Macpherson Association, 2004).

Macpherson, Alexander, *Glimpses of Church and Social Life in the Highlands in Olden Times: and Other Papers* (Edinburgh: W. Blackwood, 1893).

MacPherson, Jim, 'History Writing and Agency in the Scottish Highlands: Postcolonial Thought, the Work of James Macpherson (1736–1796) and Researching the Region's Past with Local Communities', *Northern Scotland*, 11:2 (2020), pp. 123–38.

MacQueen, John, *The Enlightenment and Scottish Literature: Volume One: Progress and Poetry* (Edinburgh: Scottish Academic Press, 1982).

MacQueen, John, *The Enlightenment and Scottish Literature: Volume Two: The Rise of the Historical Novel* (Edinburgh: Scottish Academic Press, 1989).

MacQueen, John (ed.), *Poems of Ossian. Vol. II* (Edinburgh: Mercat Press, 1971), pp. 527–83.

Magnusson, Magnus, *Scotland: The Story of a Nation* (New York: Grove Press, 2000).

Mandler, Peter, *The English National Character: The History of an Idea From Edmund Burke to Tony Blair* (New Haven, CT: Yale University Press, 2006).

Mann, Alastair J., 'James VII as Unionist and Nationalist: A Monarch's View of the Scottish Parliament as Revealed Through his Writings', *Parliaments, Estates and Representation*, 33:2 (2013), pp. 101–19.

Manning, Susan, 'Antiquarianism, the Scottish Science of Man, and the Emergence of Modern Disciplinarity', in Leith Davis, Ian Duncan and Janet Sorensen (eds), *Scotland and the Borders of Romanticism* (Cambridge: Cambridge University Press, 2004), pp. 57–76.

Manning, Susan, *Fragments of Union: Making Connections in Scottish and American Writing* (Basingstoke: Palgrave, 2002).

Manning, Susan, 'Henry Mackenzie and Ossian: Or, The Emotional Value of Asterisks', in Howard Gaskill and Fiona Stafford (eds), *From Gaelic to Romantic: Ossianic Translations* (Amsterdam: Rodopi, 1998), pp. 136–52.

Manning, Susan, 'Post-Union Scotland and the Scottish Idiom of Britishness', in Ian Brown (ed.), *The Edinburgh History of Scottish Literature*, 3 vols (Edinburgh: Edinburgh University Press, 2007), II, pp. 45–56.

Marshall, P. J., *The Making and Unmaking of Empires: Britain, India, and America c.1750–1783* (Oxford: Oxford University Press, 2007).

Mason, John, *A History of Scottish Experiments in Rural Education, From the Eighteenth Century to the Present Day* (London: University of London Press, 1935).

Matytsin, Anton M., 'Enlightenment and Erudition: Writing Cultural History at the Académie des Inscriptions', *Modern Intellectual History* (2021), pp. 1–26.

Mazzeo, Tilar, *Plagiarism and Literary Property in the Romantic Period* (Philadelphia: University of Pennsylvania Press, 2007).

Meek, Donald E., 'Evangelicalism, Ossianism and the Enlightenment: The Many Masks of Dugald Buchanan', in Christopher MacLachlan (ed.), *Crossing the Highland Line: Cross-Currents in Eighteenth-Century Scottish Writing* (Glasgow: Association for Scottish Literary Studies, 2009), pp. 97–112.

Meek, Donald E., 'The Sublime Gael: The Impact of Macpherson's *Ossian* on Literary Creativity and Cultural Perception in Gaelic Scotland', in Howard Gaskill (ed.), *The Reception of Ossian in Europe* (London: Continuum, 2004) pp. 40–67.

Meinecke, Friedrich, *Historicism: The Rise of a New Historical Outlook*, translated by G. E. Anderson (London: Routledge and Keegan Paul, 1972).

Mitchell, Peter, *Imperial Nostalgia: How the British Conquered Themselves* (Manchester: Manchester University Press, 2021).

Mitchell, Sebastian, 'James Macpherson's *Ossian* and the Empire of Sentiment', *Journal for Eighteenth-Century Studies*, 22:2 (1999), pp. 155–72.

Mitchell, Sebastian, 'Macpherson, Ossian, and Homer's *Iliad*', in Gerard Bär and Howard Gaskill (eds), *Ossian and National Epic* (Frankfurt: Peter Lang, 2012), pp. 55–72.

Mitchell, Sebastian (ed.) 'Special Issue: Forum on *Ossian in the Twenty-First Century*', *Journal for Eighteenth-Century Studies*, 39:2 (2016), pp. 157–311.

Mitchell, Sebastian, *Visions of Britain, 1730–1830* (Basingstoke, Palgrave Macmillan, 2013).

Mitchison, Rosalind and Nicholas T. Phillipson (eds), *Scotland in the Age of Improvement: Essays in Scottish History in the Eighteenth Century* (Edinburgh: Edinburgh University Press, 1996).

Mole, Tom (ed.), *Romanticism and Celebrity Culture: 1750–1850* (Cambridge: Cambridge University Press, 2009).

Momigliano, Arnaldo, *The Classical Foundations of Modern Historiography* (Berkeley: University of California Press, 1990).

Momigliano, Arnaldo, *Contributo all Storia degli Studi Classici* (Rome: Edizioni di Storia e Letteratura, 1955).

Moore, Dafydd, 'Adam Ferguson, *The Poems of Ossian* and the Imaginative Life of the Scottish Enlightenment', *History of European Ideas*, 31:2 (2005), pp. 277–88.

Moore, Dafydd, '"As Flies the Unconstant Sun": Tradition, Memory and Cultural Transmission in The Poems of Ossian', *Eighteenth-Century Ireland*, 23:1 (2008), pp. 76–93.

Moore, Dafydd, 'The Critical Response to Ossian's Romantic Bequest', in Gerard Carruthers and Alan Rawes (eds), *English Romanticism and the Celtic World* (Cambridge: Cambridge University Press, 2003), pp. 38–53.

Moore, Dafydd, *Enlightenment and Romance in James Macpherson's* The Poems of Ossian: *Myth, Genre and Cultural Change* (Aldershot: Ashgate, 2003).

Moore, Dafydd (ed.), *The International Companion to James Macpherson and* The Poems of Ossian (Glasgow: Scottish Literature International, 2017).

Moore, Dafydd, 'Introduction', in Dafydd Moore (ed.), *The International Companion of James Macpherson and* The Poems of Ossian (Glasgow: Scottish Literature International, 2017), pp. 2–13.

Moore, Dafydd, 'James Macpherson and "Celtic Whiggism"', *Eighteenth-Century Scottish Life*, 30:1 (2005), pp. 1–24.

Moore, Dafydd, 'James Macpherson, *Fingal* and Other Poems', in David Wormsley (ed.), *A Companion to Literature from Milton to Blake* (Oxford: Blackwell, 2001), pp. 380–6.

Moore, Dafydd, 'James Macpherson and William Faulkner: A Sensibility of Defeat', in Howard Gaskill and Fiona Stafford (eds), *From Gaelic to Romantic: Ossianic Translations* (Amsterdam: Rodopi, 1998), pp. 183–215.

Moore, Dafydd, *Ossian and Ossianism*, 4 vols (London: Routledge, 2004).

Moore, John R., 'Wordsworth's Unacknowledged Debt to Macpherson's Ossian', *PMLA* 40:2 (1925), pp. 362–78.

Mossner, Earnest C., *The Forgotten Hume: Le Bon David* (New York: Columbia University Press, 1943).
Mossner, Earnest C., 'Hume and the Scottish Shakespeare', *The Huntington Library Quarterly*, 3:4 (1940), pp. 419–41.
Mulholland, James, 'James Macpherson's Ossian Poems, Oral Traditions, and the Invention of Voice', *Oral Tradition*, 24:2 (2009), pp. 393–414.
Mulholland, James, *Sounding Imperial: Poetic Voice and the Politics of Empire, 1730–1820* (Baltimore, MD: Johns Hopkins University Press, 2012).
Murdoch, Alexander, *British History, 1660–1832: National Identity and Local Culture* (Basingstoke: Macmillan, 1998).
Murphy, Peter T., 'Fool's Gold: The Highland Treasures of MacPherson's Ossian', *ELH*, 53:3 (1986), pp. 567–91.
Nadel, George H., 'Philosophy of History Before Historicism', in George H. Nadel, *Studies in the Philosophy of History: Selected Essays from History and Theory* (New York: Harper & Row, 1965), pp. 49–73.
Namier, L. and J. Brooke (eds), *The History of Parliament: The House of Commons 1754–1790* (Woodbridge: Boydell & Brewer, 1964).
Nelson, Eric, 'Patriot Royalism: The Stuart Monarchy in American Political Thought, 1769–75', *William and Mary Quarterly*, 68:4 (2011), pp. 533–72.
Nelson, William, *Fact or Fiction: The Dilemma of the Renaissance Storyteller* (Cambridge, MA: Harvard University Press, 1973).
Newman, Gerald, *The Rise of English Nationalism* (New York: St. Martin's Press, 1987).
Newton, Michael, *Warriors of the Word: The World of the Scottish Highlanders* (Edinburgh: Birlinn, 2009).
Ní Mhunghaile, Lesa, 'Ossian and the Gaelic World', in Dafydd Moore, *The International Companion to James Macpherson and* The Poems of Ossian (Glasgow: Scottish Literature International 2017), pp. 26–38.
Normand, Tom, *Ossian: Fragments of Ancient Poetry* (Edinburgh: National Galleries of Scotland, 2002).
O'Brien, Karen, 'Between Enlightenment and Stadial History: William Robertson on the History of Europe', *British Journal for Eighteenth-Century Studies*, 16 (1993), pp. 53–63.
O'Brien, Karen, 'English Enlightenment Histories, 1750–c.1815', in José Rabasa, Masayuki Sato, Edoardo Tortarolo and Daniel Woolf (eds), *The Oxford History of Historical Writing: Volume 3: 1400–1800* (Oxford: Oxford University Press, 2012), pp. 518–35.
O'Brien, Karen, 'History as Literature; Literature as Fiction', in John Richetti (ed.), *The Cambridge History of English Literature* (Cambridge: Cambridge University Press, 2005), pp. 363–90.
O'Brien, Karen, 'The History Market in Eighteenth-Century England', in Isabel Rivers (ed.), *Books and their Readers in Eighteenth-Century England* (London: Cassell, 2001), pp. 105–34.

O'Brien, Karen, *Narratives of Enlightenment: Cosmopolitan History from Voltaire to Gibbon* (Cambridge: Cambridge University Press, 1997).
O'Brien, Karen, 'The Return of the Enlightenment', *American Historical Review*, 115:5 (2010), pp. 1426–35.
O'Brien, Karen, 'William Robertson's Place in the Development of Narrative History', in Stewart J. Brown, *William Robertson and the Expansion of Empire* (Cambridge: Cambridge University Press, 1997), pp. 74–91.
O'Brien, Karen and Susan Manning, 'Historiography, Biography and Identity', in Susan Manning (ed.), *The Edinburgh History of Scottish Literature. Vol. II: Enlightenment, Britain and Empire (1707–1918)* (Edinburgh: Edinburgh University Press, 2007), pp. 143–53.
Ochtertyre, John Ramsay of, *Scotland and Scotsmen in the Eighteenth Century* (Edinburgh: Blackwood, 1888).
O'Gorman, Frank, 'The Parliamentary Opposition to the Government's American Policy 1760–1782', in H. T. Dickinson (ed.), *Britain and the American Revolution* (London: Longman, 1998), pp. 97–124.
O'Halloran, Clare, 'Irish Re-creations of the Gaelic Past: The Challenge of Macpherson's Ossian', *Past and Present*, 124 (1989), pp. 69–95.
Okun, Henry, 'Ossian in Painting', *The Journal of the Warburg and Courtauld Institutes*, 30 (1967), pp. 327–56.
Parker, Geoffrey, *The Military Revolution: Military Innovation and the Rise of the West* (Cambridge: Cambridge University Press, 1996).
Parker, Gerald, 'Critical Introduction' to John Home, *Douglas*, edited by Gerald Parker (Edinburgh: Oliver & Boyd, 1972).
Parnell, Arthur, 'James Macpherson and the Nairne Papers', *English Historical Review*, 12:46 (1897), pp. 254–84.
Parry, Milman, *The Making of Homeric Verse: The Collected Papers of Milman Parry* (Oxford: Clarendon Press, 1971).
Passmore, John, 'Explanation in Everyday Life, in Science, and in History', *History and Theory*, 2:2 (1962), pp. 105–23.
Patrick, Derek J. and Christopher Whatley (eds), *The Scots and the Union* (Edinburgh: Edinburgh University Press, 2006).
Patterson, Jessica, 'Enlightenment and Empire, Mughals and Marathas: The Religious History of India in the work of East India Company servant, Alexander Dow', *History of European Ideas*, 45:7 (2019), pp. 972–91.
Patterson, Jessica, *Religion, Enlightenment and Empire* (Cambridge: Cambridge University Press, 2021).
Philip, James, *The Grameid: An Heroic Poem Descriptive of the Campaign of Viscount Dundee in 1689 and Other Pieces*, edited by Alexander D. Murdoch (Edinburgh: T. and A. Constable for the Scottish History Society, 1888).
Phillips, Jim, 'A Successor to the Moguls: The Nawab of the Carnatic and the East India Company, 1763–1785', *International History Review*, 7:3 (1985), pp. 364–89.

Phillips, Mark Salber, *Society and Sentiment: Genres of Historical Writing in Britain, 1740–1820* (Princeton, NJ: Princeton University Press, 2000).
Phillipson, Nicholas, *David Hume: The Philosopher as Historian* (London: Penguin,1989).
Pieters, Jürgen, *Speaking With the Dead: Explorations in Literature and History* (Edinburgh: Edinburgh University Press, 2005).
Pittock, Murray, *Celtic Identity and the British Image* (Manchester: Manchester University Press, 1999).
Pittock, Murray, *Inventing and Resisting Britain: Cultural Identities in Britain and Ireland, 1685–1789* (Basingstoke: Macmillan, 1997).
Pittock, Murray, *The Invention of Scotland: The Stuart Myth and the Scottish Identity, 1638 to the Present* (London: Routledge, 1991).
Pittock, Murray, *The Myth of the Jacobite Clans* (Edinburgh: Edinburgh University Press, 1995).
Pittock, Murray, *Poetry and Jacobite Politics in Eighteenth-Century Britain and Ireland* (Cambridge: Cambridge University Press, 1994).
Pittock, Murray, *Scottish and Irish Romanticism* (Oxford: Oxford University Press, 2008).
Pittock, Murray, *Scottish Nationality* (Basingstoke: Palgrave Macmillan, 2001).
Pocock, J. G. A., *The Ancient Constitution and Feudal Law: A Study of English Historical Thought in the Seventeenth Century* (Cambridge: Cambridge University Press, 1987).
Pocock, J. G. A., *Barbarism and Religion. Vol. II. Narratives of Civil Government* (Cambridge: Cambridge University Press, 1999).
Pocock, J. G. A., *Barbarism and Religion. Vol. IV. Barbarians, Savages and Empire* (Cambridge: Cambridge University Press, 2005).
Pocock, J. G. A., 'British History: A Plea for a New Subject', *Journal of Modern History*, 47:4 (1975), pp. 601–28.
Pocock, J. G. A., 'From *The Ancient Constitution* to *Barbarism and Religion*; *The Machiavellian Moment*, the History of Political Thought and the History of Historiography', *History of European Ideas*, 43:2 (2017), pp. 129–46.
Pocock, J. G. A., 'Gibbon's Second Trilogy: An Introductory Survey', *History of European Ideas*, 43:7 (2017), pp. 701–31.
Pocock, J. G. A., 'Historiography and Enlightenment: A View of Their History', *Modern Intellectual History*, 5:1 (2008), 83–96.
Pocock, J. G. A., 'The Re-description of Enlightenment', *Proceedings of the British Academy*, 125 (2004), pp. 101–17.
Pocock, J. G. A., 'Response and Commentary', *Journal of the History of Ideas*, 77:1 (2016), pp. 157–71.
Pocock, J. G. A., *Virtue, Commerce, and History: Essays on Political Thought and History, Chiefly in the Eighteenth Century* (Cambridge: Cambridge University Press, 1985).

Porter, James, '"Bring Me the Head of James Macpherson": The Execution of Ossian and the Wellsprings of Folkloristic Discourse', *The Journal of American Folklore*, 144:454 (2001), pp. 396–435.

Potkay, Adam, *The Fate of Eloquence in the Age of Hume* (Ithaca, NY: Cornell University Press, 1994).

Potkay, Adam, 'Virtue and Manners in Macpherson's Poems of Ossian', *PMLA*, 107:1 (1992), pp. 120–30.

Prebble, John, *Culloden: The Magnificent Reconstruction of the Highlanders' Tragic Moorland Battle* (London: Penguin, 1988).

Prebble, John, *The Highland Clearances* (London: Penguin, 1988).

Prescott, Sarah, *Eighteenth-Century Writing from Wales: Bards and Britons* (Cardiff: University of Wales Press, 2008).

Price, John V., 'Ossian and the Canon in the Scottish Enlightenment', in Howard Gaskill (ed.), *Ossian Revisited* (Edinburgh: Edinburgh University Press, 1991), pp. 109–28.

Rackwitz, Martin, *Travels to Terra Incognita: The Scottish Highlands and Hebrides in Early Modern Travellers' Accounts c. 1600 to 1800* (New York: Waxmann, 2007).

Radcliffe, David H., 'Ancient Poetry and British Pastoral', in Howard Gaskill and Fiona Stafford (eds), *From Gaelic to Romantic: Ossianic Translations* (Amsterdam: Rodopi, 1998), pp. 27–40.

Rait, Robert S., *The Universities of Aberdeen: A History* (Aberdeen: J. G. Bisset, 1895).

Rancière, Jacques, *The Names of History: On the Poetics of Knowledge*, translated by Hassan Melehy (Minneapolis: University of Minnesota Press, 1994).

Ricoeur, Paul, *Time and Narrative*, translated by Kathleen McLaughlin and David Pellauer, 3 vols (Chicago, IL: Chicago University Press, 1984).

du Rivage, Justin, *Revolution Against Empire: Taxes, Politics, and the Origins of American Independence* (New Haven, CT: Yale University Press, 2017).

Rixson, Denis, *The Hebridean Traveller* (Edinburgh: Birlinn, 2004).

Robel, Gilles, 'David Hume et le Homère des Hautes-Terres', *Écosse des Highlands: Mythes et Réalité*, 8 (2003), pp. 50–65.

Robertson, John, *The Scottish Enlightenment and the Militia Issue* (Edinburgh: John Donald, 1985).

Robertson, John M., *Bolingbroke and Walpole* (London: T. Fisher Unwin, 1919).

Rogers, Nicholas, 'The Dynamic of News in Britain During the American War: The Case of Admiral Keppel', *Parliamentary History*, 25:1 (2006), pp. 49–67.

Rosenblatt, Helen, 'On Context and Meaning in Pocock's *Barbarism and Religion*, and on Gibbon's "Protestantism" in His Chapters on Religion', *Journal of the History of Ideas*, 77:1 (2016), pp. 147–55.

Rothschild, Emma, 'Adam Smith in the British Empire', in Sankar Muthu (ed.), *Empire and Modern Political Thought* (Cambridge: Cambridge University Press, 2012), pp. 184–98.

Rothschild, Emma, *The Inner Life of Empires: An Eighteenth-Century History* (Princeton, NJ: Princeton University Press, 2011).
Rothschild, Emma, 'Values, Classical Political Economy and the Portuguese Empire', *Journal of Economic Methodology*, 19:2 (2012), pp. 109–19.
Royle, Trevor, *The Macmillan Companion to Scottish Literature* (London: Macmillan, 1983).
Samuel, Raphael (ed.), *Patriotism: The Making and Unmaking of British National Identity*, 3 vols (London: Routledge, 1988).
Satia, Priya, *Time's Monster: History, Conscience and Britain's Empire* (London: Allen Lane, 2020).
Saunders, Corinne (ed.), *A Companion to Romance: From Classical to Contemporary* (Oxford: Blackwell, 2004).
Saunders, T. Bailey, *The Life and Letters of James Macpherson: Containing a Particular Account of his famous Quarrel with Dr. Johnson, and a Sketch of the Origin and Influence of the Ossianic Poems* (London: Swan Sonnenschein, 1894).
Schmidt, Claudia M., *David Hume: Reason in History* (University Park: Pennsylvannia University Press, 2003).
Schmidt, Wolfgang G., *"Homer des Nordens" und "Mutter der Romantik": James Macpherson und seine Rezeption in der deutschsprachigen Literatur* (Berlin: W. De Gruyter, 2003).
Schmitz, Robert M., *Hugh Blair* (New York: King's Crown Press, 1948).
Schmitz, Yola, 'Faked Translations: James Macpherson's Ossianic Poetry', in Daniel Becker, Annalisa Fischer and Yola Schmitz (eds), *Faking, Forging, Counterfeiting: Discredited Practices at the Margins of Mimesis* (Bielefeld: Transcript Verlag, 2018), pp. 167–80.
Scott, Paul H., *'The Boasted Advantages': The Consequences of the Union of 1707* (Edinburgh: Saltire Society, 1999).
Scott, Paul H., *Defoe in Edinburgh and Other Papers* (East Linton: Tuckwell Press, 1995).
Scott, Paul H., *Still in Bed With an Elephant* (Edinburgh: Saltire Society, 1998).
Sebastiani, Silvia, *The Scottish Enlightenment: Race, Gender, and the Limits of Progress* (New York: Palgrave Macmillan, 2013).
Shaw, Lachlan, *The History of the Province of Moray: Comprising the counties of Elgin and Nairn, the Greater Part of Inverness and a Portion of the County of Banff*, edited by James F. S. Gordon (London: Hamilton, Adams, 1882).
Sher, Richard B., *Church and University in the Scottish Enlightenment: The Moderate Literati of Edinburgh* (Edinburgh: Edinburgh University Press, 1985).
Sher, Richard B., *The Enlightenment and the Book: Scottish Authors and Their Publishers in Eighteenth-Century Britain, Ireland, and America* (Chicago: Chicago University Press, 2007).
Sher, Richard B., 'Science and Medicine in the Scottish Enlightenment: The Lessons in Book History', in Paul Wood (ed.), *The Scottish Enlightenment:*

Essays in Reinterpretation (Rochester, NY: University of Rochester Press, 2001), pp. 99–156.

Sher, Richard B., '"Those Scotch Imposters and Their Cabal": Ossian and the Scottish Enlightenment', *Man and Nature/L'Homme et La Nature*, 1 (1982), pp. 55–63.

Simonsuuri, Kirsti, *Homer's Original Genius: Eighteenth-Century Notions of the Early Greek Epic (1688–1798)* (Cambridge: Cambridge University Press, 1979).

Simpson, Ian J., *Education in Aberdeenshire Before 1872* (London: University of London Press, 1947).

Simpson, Kenneth, *The Protean Scot: The Crisis of Identity in Eighteenth Century Scottish Literature* (Aberdeen: Aberdeen University Press, 1988).

Sinton, Thomas, *The Poetry of Badenoch* (Inverness: Northern Counties, 1906).

Skene, William F., *Celtic Scotland: A History of Ancient Alban* (Edinburgh: Edmonston & Douglas, 1876–80).

Smart, John S., *James Macpherson: An Episode in Literature* (London: David Nutt, 1905).

Smith, Craig, *Adam Ferguson and the Idea of Civil Society: Moral Science in the Scottish Enlightenment* (Edinburgh: Edinburgh University Press, 2019).

Smitten, Jeffrey, R., *The Life of William Robertson: Minister, Historian, and Principal* (Edinburgh: Edinburgh University Press, 2018).

Smout, Christopher, 'Tours in the Scottish Highlands from the Eighteenth to the Twentieth Centuries', *Northern Scotland*, 5 (1982–83), pp. 99–121.

Snyder, Edward, *The Celtic Revival in English Literature, 1760–1800* (Cambridge, MA: Harvard University Press, 1923).

Snyder, Franklin B., *The Life of Robert Burns* (New York: Macmillan, 1932).

Sowerby, Robin, *The Augustan Art of Poetry: Augustan Translation of the Classics* (Oxford: Oxford University Press, 2006).

Spencer, Mark G., 'Introduction: Hume as Historian', in Mark G. Spencer (ed.), *David Hume: Historical Thinker, Historical Writer* (University Park: Pennsylvania State University Press), pp. 1–12.

Stafford, Fiona J., '"Dangerous Success": Ossian, Wordsworth, and English Romantic Literature', in Howard Gaskill, *Ossian Revisited* (Edinburgh: Edinburgh University Press, 1991), pp. 49–72.

Stafford, Fiona J., *The Last of the Race: The Growth of a Myth from Milton to Darwin* (Oxford: Clarendon Press, 1994).

Stafford, Fiona J., *Local Attachments: The Province of Poetry* (Oxford: Oxford University Press, 2010).

Stafford, Fiona J., 'Romantic Macpherson', in Murray Pittock (ed.), *The Edinburgh Companion to Scottish Romanticism* (Edinburgh: Edinburgh University Press, 2011), pp. 27–38.

Stafford, Fiona J., *Starting Lines in Scottish, Irish, and English Poetry: From Burns to Heaney* (Oxford: Oxford University Press, 2000).

Stafford, Fiona J., *The Sublime Savage: James Macpherson and the Poems of Ossian* (Edinburgh: Edinburgh University Press, 1988).

Stern, Philip J., 'History and Historiography of the English East India Company: Past, Present, and Future!', *History Compass*, 7:4 (2009), pp. 1146–80.

Stern, Philip J., 'Seeing (and Not Seeing) Like a Company State: Hybridity, Heterotopia, Historiography', *Journal of Early Modern Cultural Studies*, 17:3 (2017), pp. 105–20.

Stewart, Ian B., 'Celticism and the Four Nations in the Long Nineteenth Century', in Naomi Lloyd-Jones and Maggie Scull (eds), *Four Nations Approaches to Modern 'British' History* (London: Palgrave Macmillan, 2018), pp. 135–59.

Stewart, Ian B., 'The Mother Tongue: Historical Study of the Celts and their Language(s) in Eighteenth-Century Britain and Ireland', *Past and Present*, 243 (2019), pp. 71–107.

Stewart, Keith, 'Ancient Poetry as History in the 18th Century', *Journal of the History of Ideas*, 19:3 (1958), pp. 335–47.

Stewart, Keith, 'The Ballad and the Genres in the Eighteenth Century', *ELH*, 24:2 (1957), pp. 120–37.

Stiùbhart, Domhnall Uilleam, 'A Global Gàidhealtachd? Historical Gaelic Ethnoscapes', in Michel Byrne and Sheila Kidd (eds), *Lìontan Lìonmhor: Local, National and Global Gaelic Networks from the 18th to the 20th Century* (Glasgow: Roinn na Ceiltis & na Gàidhlig, Oilthigh Ghlaschu, 2019), pp. 1–19.

Taylor, David, *The Wild Black Region: Badenoch 1750–1800* (Edinburgh: Birlinn, 2016).

Taylor, William, *The Military Roads in Scotland* (Newton Abbot: David & Charles, 1976).

Temple, Kathryn, *Scandal Nation: Law and Authorship in Britain, 1750–1832* (Ithaca, NY: Cornell University Press, 2003).

Thomson, Derick S., 'Gaelic Poetry in the Eighteenth Century: The Breaking of the Mould', in Andrew Hook (ed.), *The History of Scottish Literature. Vol. II 1660–1800* (Aberdeen: Aberdeen University Press), pp. 175–90.

Thomson, Derick S., *The Gaelic Sources of Macpherson's 'Ossian'* (Edinburgh: Oliver & Boyd, 1951).

Thomson, Derick S., 'Macpherson's Ossian: Ballads to Epics', in Bo Ahnquist, Séamus O'Catháin and Pádraig O'Héalaí (eds), *The Heroic Process: Form, Function and Fantasy in Folk Epic* (Dun Laoghaire: Glendale Press, 1987), pp. 243–64.

Todd, William B., 'Foreword' to David Hume, *The History of England from the Invasion of Julius Caesar to the Revolution in 1688*, 6 vols (Indianapolis, IN: Liberty Fund, 1983), I, pp. xi–xxiii.

Townsend, Dabney, *Hume's Aesthetic Theory: Taste and Sentiment* (London: Routledge, 2001).

Towsey, Mark R. M., *Reading the Scottish Enlightenment: Books and Their Readers in Provincial Scotland, 1750–1820* (Leiden: Brill, 2010).

Trevor-Roper, Hugh, *History and the Enlightenment* (New Haven, CT: Yale University Press, 2010).

Trevor-Roper, Hugh, *The Invention of Scotland: Myth and History* (New Haven, CT: Yale University Press, 2008).

Trevor-Roper, Hugh, 'The Invention of Tradition: The Highland Tradition of Scotland', in Eric Hobsbawm and Terence Ranger (eds), *The Invention of Tradition* (Cambridge: Cambridge University Press, 1992), pp. 15–42.

Trumpener, Katie, *Bardic Nationalism: The Romantic Novel and the British Empire* (Princeton, NJ: Princeton University Press, 1997).

Tucker, Herbert F., *Britain's Heroic Muse 1790–1910* (Oxford: Oxford University Press, 2008).

Turner, Michael J., *Pitt the Younger: A Life* (London: Hambledon, 2003).

Urry, John, *Consuming Places* (London: Routledge, 1994).

Vasunia, Phiroze, *The Classics and Colonial India* (Oxford: Oxford University Press, 2013).

Vernon, James, 'The History of Britain is Dead; Long Live a Global History of Britain', *History Australia*, 13:1 (2016), pp. 19–34.

Waddell, Peter H., *Ossian and the Clyde. Fingal in Ireland. Oscar in Iceland, or Ossian Historical and Authentic* (Glasgow: J. Maclehose, 1875).

Wahrman, Dror, 'The English Problem of Identity in the American Revolution', *The American Historical Review*, 106:4 (2001), pp. 1236–62.

Walker, Hugh, *Three Centuries of Scottish Literature*, 2 vols (Glasgow: Maclehose and Sons, 1893).

Warner, John M., *Joyce's Grandfathers: Myth and History in Defoe, Smollett, Sterne, and Joyce* (Athens, GA: University of Georgia Press, 1993).

Watson, Nicola J., *The Literary Tourist: Readers and Places in Romantic & Victorian Britain* (Basingstoke: Palgrave Macmillan, 2006).

Watson, Nicola J., 'Readers of Romantic Locality: Tourists, Loch Katrine, and *The Lady of the Lake*', in Christoph Bode and Jacqueline Labbe (eds), *Romantic Localities* (London: Pickering & Chatto, 2010), pp. 67–80.

Watt, James, *British Orientalisms, 1759–1835* (Cambridge: Cambridge University Press, 2019).

Wawn, Andrew, Graham Johnson and John Walter (eds), *Constructing Nations, Reconstructing Myth: Essays in Honour of T. A. Shippey* (Turnhout: Brepols, 2007).

Webb, Timothy, *English Romantic Hellenism: 1700–1824* (Manchester: Manchester University Press, 1982).

Weinbrot, Howard, *Britannia's Issue: The Rise of British Literature from Dryden to Ossian* (Cambridge: Cambridge University Press, 1993).

Wexler, Victor G., *David Hume and the 'History of England'* (Philadelphia, PA: American Philosophical Society, 1979).

Whatley, Christopher A., *Scottish Society, 1707–1830: Beyond Jacobitism, Towards Industrialisation* (Manchester: Manchester University Press, 2000).

Whetter, Kevin S., *Understanding Genre and Medieval Romance* (Aldershot: Ashgate, 2008).
White, Hayden, *The Content of the Form: Narrative Discourse and Historical Representation* (Baltimore, MD: Johns Hopkins University Press, 1987).
White, Hayden, 'The Fictions of Factual Representation', *The Literature of Fact: Selected Papers from the English Institute* (New York: Columbia University Press, 1976).
White, Hayden, *Metahistory: The Historical Imagination in Nineteenth-Century Europe* (Baltimore, MD: Johns Hopkins University Press, 1973).
Whitehead, John, *The Solemn Mockery: The Art of Literary Forgery* (London: Arlington Books, 1973).
Whitney, Lois, 'English Primitivistic Theories of Epic Origins', *Modern Philology*, 21:4 (1924), pp. 337–78.
Wickman, Matthew, 'The Allure of the Improbable: Fingal, Evidence and the Testimony of the "Echoing Heath"', *PMLA*, 15:2 (2000), pp. 181–94.
Wickman, Matthew, 'Imitating Eve Imitating Echo Imitating Originality: The Critical Reverberations of Sentimental Genius in the *Conjectures on Original Composition*', *ELH*, 65:3 (1998), pp. 899–28.
Wickman, Matthew, 'Review of Thomas M. Curley, *Samuel Johnson, the Ossian Fraud, and the Celtic Revival in Great Britain and Ireland*', *Modern Philology*, 110:4 (2013), pp. 277–81.
Wickman, Matthew, *The Ruins of Experience: Scotland's 'Romantick' Highlands and the Birth of the Modern Witness* (Philadelphia: University of Pennsylvania Press, 2007).
Wilkie, Brian, *Romantic Poets and Epic Tradition* (Madison: University of Wisconsin Press, 1965).
Wilson, Kathleen, *The Island Race: Englishness, Empire and Gender in the Eighteenth-Century* (London: Routledge, 2003).
Wilson, Kathleen, *The Sense of the People: Politics, Culture and Imperialism in England, 1715–1785* (Cambridge: Cambridge University Press, 1995).
Withers, Charles W. J., 'Education and Anglicisation: The Policy of the SSPCK toward the Education of the Highlander, 1709–1825', *Scottish Studies*, 26 (1982), pp. 37–56.
Withers, Charles W. J., *Gaelic in Scotland 1698–1981: The Geographical History of a Language* (Edinburgh: John Donald, 1984).
Withers, Charles W. J., 'The Historical Creation of the Scottish Highlands', in Ian Donnachie and Christopher Whatley (eds), *The Manufacture of Scottish History* (Edinburgh: Polygon, 1992).
Withers, Charles W. J., *Placing the Enlightenment: Thinking Geographically About the Age of Reason* (Chicago: Chicago University Press, 2008).
Withers, Charles W. J., *Urban Highlanders: Highland-Lowland Migration and Urban Gaelic Culture, 1700–1900* (East Linton: Tuckwell Press, 1998).
Withrington, Donald J., 'The S.P.C.K. and Highland Schools in the Mid-Eighteenth-Century', *The Scottish Historical Review*, 41:132 (1962), pp. 89–99.

Wittig, Kurt, *The Scottish Tradition in Literature* (Edinburgh: Oliver & Boyd, 1958).
Wolin, Richard, 'Symposium on J. G. A. Pocock's *Barbarism and Religion*', *Journal of the History of Ideas*, 77:1 (2016), pp. 99–106.
Wolloch, Nathaniel, '"Facts, or Conjectures": Antoine-Yves Goguet's Historiography', *Journal of the History of Ideas*, 68:3 (2007), pp. 429–49.
Womack, Peter, *Improvement and Romance: Constructing the Myth of the Highlands* (Basingstoke: Macmillan, 1988).
Womersley, David J, 'Lord Bolingbroke and Eighteenth-Century Historiography', *The Eighteenth Century: Theory and Interpretation*, 28 (1987), pp. 217–34.
Worthington, David, 'The Settlements of the Beauly-Wick Coast and the Historiography of the Moray Firth', *Scottish Historical Review*, 95:2 (2016), pp. 139–63.
Wood, Paul B., *The Aberdeen Enlightenment: The Arts Curriculum in the Eighteenth Century* (Aberdeen: Aberdeen University Press, 1993).
Wood, Paul B., 'Science in the Scottish Enlightenment', in Alexander Brodie (ed.), *The Cambridge Companion to the Scottish Enlightenment* (Cambridge: Cambridge University Press, 2003), pp. 94–116.
Woolf, Alex, *From Pictland to Alba 789–1070* (Edinburgh: Edinburgh University Press, 2007).
Zachs, William, *Without Regard to Good Manners: A Biography of Gilbert Stuart 1743–1786* (Edinburgh: Edinburgh University Press, 1992).
Zimmerman, Everett, *The Boundaries of Fiction: History and the Eighteenth-Century British Novel* (Ithaca, NY: Cornell University Press, 1996).
Zook, Melinda S., *Radical Whigs and Conspiratorial Politics in Late Stuart England* (University Park: Pennsylvania State University Press, 1999).

UNPUBLISHED THESES

Carruthers, Gerard C., 'The Invention of Scottish Literature During the Long Eighteenth Century', unpublished PhD thesis (University of Glasgow, 2001).
Golding, Ben J., 'British Politics, Imperial Ideology, and East India Company Reform, 1773–1784', unpublished PhD thesis (University of Cambridge, 2020).
Higgins, David M., 'The Cult of Genius: Magazines, Readers, and the Creative Artist, 1802–37', unpublished PhD thesis (University of York, 2002).
Kersey, Melvin, '"Where are the originals?" Britishness and Problems of Authenticity in Post-Union Literature from Addison to Macpherson', unpublished PhD thesis (University of Leeds, 2001).
Lindfield-Ott, Kristin, 'See SCOT and SAXON Coalesc'd in One: James Macpherson's *The Highlander* in Its Intellectual and Cultural Contexts, with an Annotated Text of the Poem', unpublished PhD thesis (University of St Andrews, 2011).

McCullough, Katie, 'Building the Highland Empire: The Highland Society of London and the Formation of Charitable Networks in Great Britain and Canada, 1778–1857', unpublished PhD thesis (University of Guelph, 2014).
Maclachlan, Christopher, 'Philosophical Criticism in the Eighteenth Century', unpublished PhD thesis (University of Edinburgh, 1974).
Maclean, John N. M., 'The Early Political Careers of James "Fingal" Macpherson (1736–1796) and Sir John Macpherson, Bart. (1744–1821)', unpublished PhD thesis (University of Edinburgh, 1967).

ONLINE SOURCES

Bhambra, Gurminder K., 'Brexit, Empire, and Decolonization', *History Workshop Online*, 19 December 2018, available at: https://www.historyworkshop.org.uk/brexit-empire-and-decolonization/ (accessed 17 March 2022).
Blaeu, Joan, *Atlas of Scotland*, National Library of Scotland, available at: http://www.nls.uk/maps/early/blaeu/index.html (accessed 15 February 2008).
Bryant, G. J., 'Lawrence, Stringer (1697–1775)', *Oxford Dictionary of National Biography* (Oxford: Oxford University Press, 2004), available at: https://doi.org/10.1093/ref:odnb/16187 (accessed 1 May 2020).
Curry, Anne, 'Agincourt, 1415–2015', *Historical Association*, 1 October 2015, available at: https://www.history.org.uk/publications/resource/8648/agincourt-1415-2015 (accessed 13 October 2021).
deGategno, Paul J., 'Macpherson, Sir John, First Baronet (*c.* 1745–1821)', *Oxford Dictionary of National Biography* (Oxford: Oxford University Press, 2004), available at: https://doi.org/10.1093/ref:odnb/17730 (accessed 25 November 2021).
Klein, Milton M., 'Robertson, James (1717–1788)', *Oxford Dictionary of National Biography* (Oxford: Oxford University Press, 2004), available at: https://doi.org/10.1093/ref:odnb/23796 (accessed 12 October 2021).
Kuiters, Willem G. J., 'Dow, Alexander (1735/6–1779)', *Oxford Dictionary of National Biography* (Oxford: Oxford University Press, 2004), available at: https://doi.org/10.1093/ref:odnb/7957 (accessed 10 April 2020).
Laughton, J. K., revised by Clive Wilkinson, 'Lindsay, Sir John (1737–1788)', *Oxford Dictionary of National Biography* (Oxford: Oxford University Press, 2004), available at: https://doi.org/10.1093/ref:odnb/16710 (accessed 1 May 2020).
Lynch, Jack, 'Authorizing Ossian', delivered at MWASECS, Minneapolis, 5 October 1995, available at: http://andromeda.rutgers.edu/~jlynch/Papers/ossian.html (accessed 12 March 2008).
MacKinnon, Iain and Andrew Mackillop, 'Plantation Slavery and Landownership in the West Highlands and Islands: Legacies and Lessons', *Community Land Scotland*, November 2020, available at: https://www.communitylandscotland.org.uk/wp-content/uploads/2020/11/Plantation-slavery-and-landownership-in-the-west-Highlands-and-Islands-legacies-and-lessons.pdf (accessed 18 January 2022).

Mathison, Hamish, 'Ruddiman, Walter (1719–1781)', *Oxford Dictionary of National Biography* (Oxford: Oxford University Press, 2004), available at: http://www.oxforddnb.com/view/article/64301 (accessed 12 May 2011).

Moore, Dafydd, 'James MacPherson' [sic], in *Oxford Bibliographies Online in British and Irish Literature* (Oxford: Oxford University Press, 2017), available at: https://www.oxfordbibliographies.com/view/document/obo-9780199846719/obo-9780199846719-0066.xml (accessed 11 January 2022).

Ossian Collection, National Library of Scotland, available at: http://digital.nls.uk/pageturner.cfm?id=76750236 (accessed 15 December 2010).

Oz-Salzberger, Fania, 'Ferguson, Adam (1723–1816)', *Oxford Dictionary of National Biography* (Oxford: Oxford University Press, 2004), available at: https://doi-org.eor.uhi.ac.uk/10.1093/ref:odnb/9315 (accessed 23 December 2021).

Sher, Richard B., 'Blair, Hugh (1718–1800)', *Oxford Dictionary of National Biography* (Oxford: Oxford University Press, 2004), available at: https://doi-org.eor.uhi.ac.uk/10.1093/ref:odnb/2563 (accessed 12 January 2022).

Stiùbhart, Domhnall Uilleam, 'Traditionalising Empire: Imperial Commodities in Gaelic Popular Culture', British Studies and Centre for History Seminar, University of the Highlands and Islands, 26 October 2016, available at: https://youtu.be/vUEJmEt1sBI (accessed 28 January 2022).

Tammita-Delgoda, SinhaRaja, 'Orme, Robert (1728–1801)', *Oxford Dictionary of National Biography* (Oxford: Oxford University Press, 2004), available at: https://doi.org/10.1093/ref:odnb/20833 (accessed 10 April 2020).

Thomson, Derick S., 'Macpherson, James (1736–1796)', *Oxford Dictionary of National Biography* (Oxford: Oxford University Press, 2004), available at http://www.oxforddnb.com/view/article/17728 (accessed 13 June 2007).

Index

Aberdeen, 8, 55, 119
Adam, Robert, 1, 241
Agincourt, 225
America, 2, 4, 7, 11, 14, 15, 30, 31, 40, 84, 142, 159, 171–4, 187, 197, 200–28, 243–5
Arcot, Nawab of (Muhammad Ali Khan Wallajah), 4, 8, 15, 157, 172–3, 175–7, 178, 183, 187, 189, 191, 192, 200, 201, 226, 243, 244
Aristotle, 39, 186

Badenoch, 9, 15, 52, 226, 227, 241, 245
Bengal, 176, 186, 226, 244
Blair, Hugh, 2, 4, 5, 8, 12, 13, 15, 23, 24, 25, 28–31, 36–8, 41, 42, 49, 50, 51, 71–4, 79, 82, 85, 90, 91, 92, 94, 105, 106, 107, 111–12, 115, 118, 129, 134, 135, 136, 141,150, 159, 184, 198, 199, 218, 243
  Lectures on Rhetoric and Belles Lettres, 30, 36, 71, 85, 92, 136, 243
Bolingbroke, Lord, 29, 39, 67, 153
Boswell, James, 92
Bower, Walter, 54, 55
British imperial state 2, 3, 4, 5, 8, 10, 11, 12, 13, 15, 24, 28, 29, 30, 40, 42, 49, 50, 51, 52, 61, 63, 64, 70, 77, 80, 84, 92, 94, 106, 127, 128, 130, 144, 157, 160, 171–228, 242–6

crisis of empire in 1770s, 2, 24, 40, 106, 128, 150, 154, 160, 171–228, 243
Buchanan, George, 13, 49, 50, 53–8, 60, 66, 68, 89, 94
Burke, Edmund, 171, 200, 220
Bute, Earl of, 2, 51, 171

Caesar, 80, 119
Carnatic, 175, 177, 178, 184, 186, 187, 188, 191, 192, 193, 195, 197, 198, 200
Carte, Thomas, 132, 133, 134
Church of Scotland, 8, 71
Clarendon, Earl of, 52, 145, 219, 224
Clive, Lord, 191, 193
Colley, Linda, 211
Collingwood, R. G., 184
commercial modernity (18th century), 2, 11, 28, 49, 90, 95, 114, 243, 245
Cullen, 53
Culloden, 2, 84

Dalrymple, John, 129, 132
Davis, Leith, 7, 8, 175, 176
Dean, Carolyn, 5
Declaration of Congress (1775), 200, 205, 206, 207
deGategno, Paul, 7, 9, 64, 110, 176, 200, 201
Dirks, Nicholas B., 175
Dornoch, 192

Dow, Alexander, 9, 105, 109, 174, 189, 190–1, 193
Du Pré, Josias, 192, 195–6
Dziennik, Matthew, 11, 84, 201

East India Company (EIC), 9, 14, 15, 137, 154, 157, 171–99, 200, 214, 226, 227, 244, 245
Edinburgh, 8, 24, 30, 49, 51, 52, 55, 70, 71–2, 74, 91, 94, 105, 198
Enlightenment
 history writing, 3–11, 12, 13, 14, 15, 23–42, 48–52, 60, 62, 70, 72, 73, 74, 77, 79, 80, 85, 86, 89, 90, 91, 92, 94, 107, 108, 109, 111, 114–19, 125, 128, 129, 135, 136, 137, 138, 139, 141–5, 147, 149, 150, 153, 159, 173, 175, 177, 181–8, 198, 201, 205, 207, 209, 210, 215, 216, 217, 225, 227–8, 241–6
 Scottish, 8, 31, 71, 79, 137, 150, 209

Ferguson, Adam, 4, 8, 13, 26, 28, 30, 42, 49, 50, 51, 64–5, 73, 80, 90–2, 95, 127, 136, 159, 185, 209, 242
Fordun, John, 13, 49, 50, 53, 54, 55, 56, 57, 59, 60, 88, 94
Fox, Charles, 200, 219

Gaelosphere, 11
Gage, General Thomas, 205, 206, 207
Gàidhealtachd see Scottish Highlands
Gibbon, 3, 5, 7, 10, 12, 13, 14, 15, 23, 24, 25–8, 31, 32, 33, 36, 38, 39–40, 41, 42, 86, 95, 108, 110, 118, 125, 135, 136, 140, 141, 143–4, 160, 175, 179, 180, 182, 186, 189, 194, 196, 197, 198, 205, 207, 214, 219, 220, 225–6, 227, 243, 244
 The History of the Decline and Fall of the Roman Empire (1776–89), 10, 24, 25–6, 28, 38, 39, 40, 108, 110, 143, 175, 180, 186, 194, 198, 225, 227
Glasgow, 8, 94
Godwin, William, 28, 73, 111
Guha, Ranajit, 51, 79, 88, 207, 214

Harland, Sir Robert, 195, 197
Hastings, Warren, 175, 176, 244
Hegel, G. W. F., 5, 11, 51, 79–80, 207, 214
Henry, Robert, 29, 41
Highland Society of London, 53, 227
Highland Society of Scotland, 245
Home, John, 8, 54, 90
Homer, 48
Horn, D. B., 7, 132
Hume, David, 2, 3, 4, 5, 7, 8, 9, 10, 12–13, 14, 16, 23, 24, 25, 26, 27, 28–36, 41–2, 50, 51, 79, 80, 82, 88, 92, 94, 105, 107, 109, 111, 113, 115, 118, 129, 130–2, 133, 134, 135, 141, 144, 150, 152–5, 158–9, 178, 181, 182, 184, 188, 191, 194, 198, 223, 227, 243, 244
 An Enquiry Concerning Human Understanding (1748), 34, 141
 Essays: Moral, Political, and Literary (1741), 32, 35–6
 History of England (1754–62), 14, 28, 30, 32, 41, 112, 118, 129, 131, 133, 145, 148, 156, 157, 181, 198
 'Of the Study of History' (1741), 32, 115
Hunter, James, 84

India, 2, 4, 8, 9, 14, 15, 143, 157, 171–99, 200, 220, 226, 243–4
Innes, Father Thomas, 113–14, 121, 125, 126

Jamaica, 203
Johnson, Samuel, 6, 92, 106, 131, 220
Johnstone, George (Governor of West Florida), 4, 171
Jones, Robert W., 7–8, 9, 25, 131, 132, 135, 215
Jones, Tom, 52
Jonsson, Fredrik Albritton, 11, 65

Kames, Lord, 9, 91, 92, 94, 95
Kant, Immanuel, 223
Keppel, Admiral Augustus, 217, 219–20, 223
Kersey, Mel, 13, 67–9

Kidd, Colin, 7, 72, 78, 110, 134, 174, 209, 221
King Charles I, 118, 153
King Charles II, 68, 70, 145, 147, 152–5, 157, 203, 204, 210, 213
King George I, 212
King George II, 70, 212
King George III, 172, 215, 218
King Henry VIII, 203, 204, 210
King James II, 132, 133, 134, 145–7, 149, 156, 224
King William III, 69, 154, 156, 157, 212

Laing, Malcolm, 52, 53
Lawrence, Major-General Stringer, 192
Lindsay, Sir John, 192
Logierait, 8, 90
London, 2, 8, 9, 55, 74, 105, 109, 138, 148, 152, 191, 193, 208, 224, 227

McIntosh, Alastair, 84
MacKay, Duncan (Donnchadh MacAoidh), 1–2, 15, 241, 245
Mackintosh, James, 28
Macleane, Lauchlin, 193
Macpherson, Donald, 52, 53
Macpherson, Duncan, 84, 242
Macpherson, James
  and authenticity, 3, 13, 39, 48, 49, 50, 53, 60, 69, 71, 74, 76, 82, 85, 87, 89, 92, 111, 121, 130, 133, 134, 135, 138, 179, 183, 215, 243
  and ancient constitution, 128, 131, 154, 155, 174, 210, 221, 225
  and British Empire, 2, 4, 5, 6, 9, 11, 13, 14, 15, 24, 31, 40, 42, 49, 50, 51, 63, 64, 70, 83, 106, 107, 128, 150, 151, 157, 171–228, 241–6
  and causation, 4, 12, 13, 31, 48, 49, 50, 111, 116, 141, 149, 215
  and Clan Macpherson, 84, 242
  and erudition, 2, 3, 9, 11, 13, 23, 24, 26, 31, 33, 38, 49, 70, 95, 106, 107, 108, 109, 113, 114, 117, 118, 129, 132, 160, 201, 205, 227, 242, 243, 244, 246
  and fiction, 6, 53, 55, 60, 73, 76, 77, 82, 85, 88, 89, 109, 111, 112, 114–16, 121, 122, 124, 127, 199
  and footnotes, 4, 13, 14, 15, 24, 27, 31, 33, 38, 42, 50, 74, 75, 106, 114, 117, 118, 120, 130, 140, 144, 145, 159, 173, 175, 177, 179, 180, 182–3, 189–98, 201, 203–5, 219, 227, 243, 244
  and Gaelic world, 49, 51, 62, 83, 87, 95, 116, 129
  and Jacobites, 64, 66, 69, 84, 106, 107, 120, 134, 138
  and narrative, 2, 3, 9, 10, 11, 13, 14, 15, 24, 26, 27, 32, 35, 40, 42, 48, 51, 52, 55, 62, 70, 71, 77, 86, 91, 93, 94, 95, 106, 107, 108, 109, 113, 114, 118, 120, 129, 130, 132, 141, 145, 148, 173, 175, 181, 182, 185, 187–8, 194, 201, 205, 214, 218, 227, 242, 243, 244, 246
  and oral tradition, 15, 49, 50, 51, 71, 73–7, 79, 80–2, 85, 87–8, 95, 105, 108, 122, 123, 125–7, 129, 243
  and philosophy, 2, 3, 7, 10, 11, 14, 23, 26, 28, 31, 49, 107, 108, 182, 185, 186, 194, 201, 205, 243, 246
  and scientific method, 136–8, 140, 147
  and sources, 3, 4, 7, 13, 14, 24, 27, 32, 33, 34, 39, 41, 42, 48–9, 50, 52–63, 70, 71, 74–7, 80, 81, 86, 87, 88, 89, 94, 105, 106, 107, 108, 109, 111, 112, 113–16, 118–21, 123–4, 126, 129, 130, 132, 134–40, 144–9, 159, 173, 175, 177–81, 183, 187, 189–94, 195, 197, 199, 201–5, 214, 215, 219, 227, 242–4
  and stadial theories, 4, 11, 12, 13, 14, 24, 30, 31, 42, 49, 50, 61, 71, 72, 73, 79, 80, 85, 90–1, 95, 105, 106, 109, 110, 114, 126–9, 154, 159, 185–6, 191, 209, 228, 242
  and truth, 3, 4, 12, 13, 14, 23, 24, 25, 27, 31, 32, 41, 42, 49, 50, 85, 86, 89, 92, 94, 106, 108, 111, 113, 116, 118, 124, 127, 129, 134–7, 138, 142, 148, 150, 156, 173, 177,

178, 181, 182, 183, 196, 198, 199, 201–3, 206, 207, 214, 215–17, 244
and war, 14, 64, 108, 131, 155, 157–9, 186, 215, 218, 224
and Whig constitutionalism, 67, 106, 128, 129, 131, 135, 154, 156, 157, 160, 13, 14, 24, 4
as 'Celtic Whig', 3, 50, 54, 106, 174, 221, 242
as Enlightenment historian, 2, 4, 10, 41, 49, 50, 51, 52, 75, 76, 106, 108, 109, 112, 115, 117, 129, 130, 141, 144, 146, 147, 153, 154, 159, 172, 175, 181, 183, 186, 194, 198, 199, 201, 204, 210, 219, 227, 241–6
as Gael, 2, 3, 8, 75, 77, 174, 175, 191, 228, 241–6
Fingal (1761/2), 13, 31, 32, 42, 49, 50, 51, 52, 65, 74–85, 87, 91, 92, 95, 105, 127, 171, 176, 214, 243
Fragments of Ancient Poetry (1760), 8, 13, 31, 36, 39, 49, 50, 70–4
Highland tours (1760 and 1761), 9, 91
The Highlander (1758) 2, 4, 12, 13, 15, 42, 48–70, 71, 88, 89, 94, 105, 109, 111, 130, 155, 171, 221–2, 225, 226, 227, 242
The History and Management of the East-India Company (1779), 2, 4, 7, 8, 11, 14, 15, 38, 171–99, 201, 204, 214, 219, 244
The History of Great Britain (1775), 2, 4, 5, 7, 14, 24, 36, 38, 42, 92, 106, 107, 129–32, 135–60, 178, 179, 193, 196, 214, 215, 222, 24
The Iliad (1773), 12, 48, 92
An Introduction to the History of Great Britain and Ireland (1771), 5, 14, 24, 39, 78, 85, 92, 106, 107, 108–32, 159, 160, 173, 174, 191, 214, 243
Original Papers (1775), 2, 14, 24, 30, 36, 75, 77, 106, 107, 129–35, 136, 137, 138, 144, 159, 160, 243

Ossianic Collections (1760-73), 2, 3, 4, 6–7, 8, 12, 13–14, 29, 36, 42, 48–52, 54, 60, 63, 65, 68, 70–95, 105, 112, 113, 123, 129, 130, 137, 155, 158, 159, 174, 183, 198, 199, 209, 225, 242, 243; authenticity debate, 6, 25, 72, 74–6, 81–2, 94, 106, 112, 131, 133, 136, 174
The Poems of Ossian (1773), 92–3, 95, 227
poetry, 3, 6, 12, 13, 31, 42, 48–95, 105, 111, 227, 246
political writing, 3, 7, 11, 12, 14, 15, 24, 28, 40, 42, 94, 109, 134, 140, 171–228, 244, 245, 246
politics, 3, 7, 15, 24, 29, 69–70, 94, 133, 135, 137, 156, 171, 172, 176, 210, 213, 215, 226, 243; faction, 30, 133, 134, 142, 154–7, 198, 216–18, 221, 224; opposition, 7, 172, 200, 204, 205, 211, 214–24
The Rights of Great Britain Asserted Against the Claims of America (1775/6), 2, 4, 7, 11, 14, 15, 31, 159, 172–4, 197, 200–13, 214, 220, 221, 224
secretary to George Johnstone (Governor of West Florida), 3–4, 171
A Short History of the Opposition (1779), 4, 7, 11, 12, 14, 15, 172, 173, 204, 213–26
Temora (1763), 13, 31, 32, 34, 42, 49, 50, 51, 55, 85–92, 94, 95, 105, 114, 117, 127, 171, 176, 185, 243
Macpherson, Rev. Dr John, 29, 110, 113, 125–6, 176
Macpherson, Sir John, 4, 176, 180, 191, 193, 200, 226, 244
Madras (Chennai), 9, 192
Mitchell, Peter, 222
Moffat, 8
Momigliano, Alfredo, 10, 12, 26, 41
Montagu, Elizabeth, 94
Montesquieu, 90
Moray Firth, 53

Moore, Dafydd, 6, 7, 9, 13, 52, 60, 72, 82, 91, 110, 128, 129, 131, 174, 209, 221

Nairne, Sir David, 132, 134
North, Lord, 15, 40, 51, 133, 172, 200, 209, 215, 226, 243

O'Brien, Karen, 10, 12, 23, 25, 28–31, 41
Orme, Robert, 174, 189, 190

Parnell, Arthur, 6, 7
Phillips, Mark Salber, 10, 12, 23, 25, 28–31, 34, 37, 41, 72, 141, 156, 184, 187, 188
Pitt, William (Earl of Chatham), 172, 205, 211, 226
Pliny, 80, 86
Pocock, J. G. A., 9–10, 12, 23–8, 31, 33, 36, 40, 41, 112, 118, 131, 181, 201, 205, 210, 228, 244
Pope, Alexander, 52
Pringle, Sir Thomas, 183

Queen Anne, 69, 107, 132, 138, 152, 154, 212

Ramsay, David, 29
Ranke, Leopold von, 5, 133, 139, 182
Robertson, William, 3, 5, 7, 8, 9, 10, 12, 13, 14, 15, 23–31, 32, 33, 36, 38–40, 41, 42, 80, 86, 95, 107, 108, 113, 118, 125, 129, 132, 135, 141–4, 160, 172, 179, 182, 184, 185, 190, 194, 207, 227, 243, 244
  An Historical Disquisition Concerning the Knowledge which the Ancients Had of India (1791), 142
  History of America (1777), 30, 38–40, 90, 108, 142–3, 207, 227
  The History of Scotland (1759), 38, 108, 142
Rockingham, Lord, 204, 205
Rous, George, 189–90
Ruthven, 52

Satia, Priya, 3, 151, 174, 223, 225
Saunders, T. Bailey, 7
Scots College (Paris), 132, 224
Scots Magazine, 52, 108
Scottish Highlands (*Gàidhealtachd*), 1, 2, 5, 6, 11, 13, 14, 15, 28, 50, 51, 61, 74, 78, 80, 83–5, 88, 91, 92, 95, 105, 114, 127, 176, 227–8, 241–6
  agency, 6, 11, 82, 127, 245
  internal colonisation, 51, 84, 91
Scottish militia crisis, 15, 61, 64, 65, 90, 171
Select Society of Edinburgh, 8, 31
Seven Years War (1756–63), 2, 50, 65, 70, 129, 192, 200, 202, 204, 210, 211, 242
Shelburne, Lord, 172
Sher, Richard, 8–9
Siculus, Diodorus, 80, 81, 120
Skye, 176, 226
Smith, Adam, 2, 3, 8, 9, 10, 12, 13, 14, 23–8, 31, 33–5, 36, 37, 41, 42, 50, 73, 77, 86, 88, 90–1, 93, 94–5, 105, 116, 117, 129, 136, 151, 181, 185, 209, 243
  Lectures on Rhetoric and Belles Lettres, 33–4, 93, 136, 243
  and poetry, 32, 34, 77, 79, 105
Strahan, William, 41, 129, 131
Stafford, Fiona, 65, 71, 72, 90, 91
Stone, Jerome, 76
Strabo, 80, 120, 121
Stuart, Charles Edward, 69, 70
Stuart, Gilbert, 119, 128

Tacitus, 9, 27, 80, 81, 86, 109, 117, 120
Tanjore, Rajah of, 177, 189
Taylor, David, 11, 84
Thucydides, 27
Trevor-Roper, Hugh, 11, 32

Vikings, 42, 53
Voltaire, 24, 26, 27, 28, 29

Walker, Rev. John, 91
Walpole, Horace, 131, 144

West Florida, 4, 51, 171
West Indies, 2, 245
White, Hayden, 5, 25

Wickman, Matthew, 82, 182
Wilkes, John, 209
Wilkie, William, 54

EU Authorised Representative:
Easy Access System Europe Mustamäe tee 50, 10621 Tallinn, Estonia
gpsr.requests@easproject.com

Printed and bound by CPI Group (UK) Ltd, Croydon, CR0 4YY
30/12/2025
02026725-0004